A
YEAR
WITH
GOD

MAKE HIS THOUGHTS
YOUR THOUGHTS

A
YEAR
WITH
GOD

DAILY REFLECTIONS AND READINGS ON
GOD'S OWN WORDS

R. P. Nettelhorst

THOMAS NELSON
Since 1798

NASHVILLE   DALLAS   MEXICO CITY   RIO DE JANEIRO

© 2010 by GRQ, Inc.

All rights reserved. No portion of this book may be reproduced, stored in a retrieval system, or transmitted in any form or by any means—electronic, mechanical, photocopy, recording, scanning, or other—except for brief quotations in critical reviews or articles, without the prior written permission of the publisher.

Published in Nashville, Tennessee, by Thomas Nelson. Thomas Nelson is a registered trademark of Thomas Nelson, Inc.

Thomas Nelson, Inc. titles may be purchased in bulk for educational, business, fund-raising, or sales promotional use. For information, please e-mail SpecialMarkets@ThomasNelson. com.

Scripture quotations marked CEV are from the *Contemporary English Version*. ©1991, 1992, 1995 by American Bible Society. Used by permission.

Scripture quotations marked HCSB have been taken from the Holman Christian Standard Bible®, © 1999, 2000, 2002, 2003 by Holman Bible Publishers. Used by permission. Holman Christian Standard Bible®, Holman CSB® and HCSB® are federally registered trademarks of Holman Bible Publishers.

Scripture quotations marked MSG are from *The Message* by Eugene H. Peterson, © 1993, 1994, 1995, 1996, 2000, 2001, 2002. Used by permission of NavPress Publishing Group. All rights reserved.

Scripture quotations marked NASB are from the NEW AMERICAN STANDARD BIBLE®, © The Lockman Foundation 1960, 1962, 1963, 1968, 1971, 1972, 1973, 1975, 1977. Used by permission.

Scripture quotations marked NIV are taken from the *Holy Bible, New International Version*®. NIV®. © 1973, 1978, 1984, by International Bible Society. Used by permission of Zondervan. All rights reserved.

Scripture quotations noted NKJV are from THE NEW KING JAMES VERSION. © 1979, 1980, 1982, Thomas Nelson, Inc., Publishers.

Scripture quotations marked NLT are taken from *The Holy Bible, New Living Translation*, ©1996, 2004. Used by permission of Tyndale House Publishers, Inc., Wheaton, Illinois, 60189. All rights reserved.

Scripture quotations marked NRSV are taken from the NEW REVISED STANDARD VERSION of the Bible. Copyright © 1989 by the Division of Christian Education of the National Council of The Churches of Christ in the U.S.A. All rights reserved.

Library of Congress Control Number: 2010931111

ISBN: 978-0-8499-4698-1

Editor: Lila Empson Wavering

Associate Editor: Jennifer McNeil

Design: Whisner Design Group

Printed in the United States of America

10 11 12 13 14   RRD   9 8 7 6 5 4 3 2 1

The best of all is, God is with us.

John Wesley

Contents

꙳꙳꙳꙳꙳꙳꙳꙳꙳꙳꙳꙳꙳꙳꙳꙳꙳꙳꙳꙳꙳꙳꙳꙳꙳꙳꙳꙳꙳꙳꙳꙳꙳꙳꙳꙳

Contents

Perseverance and Quitting

Contents

Faith and Doubt

Contents

Loyalty and Betrayal

Contents

Contents

Companionship and Isolation

Mercy and Judgment

Contents

꽃꽃꽃꽃꽃꽃꽃꽃꽃꽃꽃꽃꽃꽃꽃꽃꽃꽃꽃꽃꽃꽃꽃꽃꽃꽃꽃꽃꽃꽃꽃꽃꽃

Forgiveness and Anger

Contents

Contents

Joy and Sadness

Contents

Peace and Conflict

❄❄❄❄❄❄❄❄❄❄❄❄❄❄❄❄❄❄❄❄❄❄❄❄❄❄❄❄❄❄❄❄

The best way to get to know people is to spend time listening to them. The same is true for your relationship with God. The best way to get to know him is to pay attention to what he said throughout the Bible. *A Year with God* highlights God's words to his people in the Old Testament. In reading what God actually said, we can discover what really matters to God.

God's words are powerful. God spoke the world into creation and all life into being. God spoke to the first people. He spoke to Noah and Abraham, to Moses, to the kings of Judah and Israel, and to the prophets.

God's words are sometimes shocking, sometimes heartening, and sometimes puzzling. *A Year with God* is a 365-day revelation of God's divine character through his words, with accompanying insight and commentary written in everyday language.

God talked to all sorts of people, ranging from farmers to businesspeople, prophets to kings. God weeps with those who weep and rejoices with those who rejoice. God can become angry and can have his heart broken. Sometimes his words sound harsh, and sometimes they sound gentle. God said some things over and over again because his people failed to listen to him. He kept trying to get his people to stop repeating the same mistakes.

Some of God's words reached beyond their immediate audience. He gave prophecies about Jesus' birth, life, resurrection, and coming kingdom.

In this book you'll discover that

- God considers the freedom to choose worth the chance that people won't make good choices;

- God will discipline his people in order to teach them to make better choices in the future;

- God thinks the best way to destroy his enemies is by turning them into his friends;

- God is willing to resort to violence in order to protect the people he loves;

- God wants us to love him the same way he loves us;

- God wants us to love one another the same way we love ourselves.

Spend a year with God, read his words, and listen to his heart. Love him, and know without a doubt that he loves you.

※

Hope and Fear

Fear is a survival reflex that happens without thought, and sometimes in spite of it. Fear arises from what you experience here and now. Hope, on the other hand, grows from reflection about tomorrow. It leaps from the expectation of what you will experience in the future. Hope springs from fears survived, from troubled waters bridged. It is the fruit of the nightmares past. Fear can keep us alive. But hope makes living worthwhile.

❈

God's eye is on those who respect him, the ones who are looking for his love. He's ready to come to their rescue in bad times; in lean times he keeps body and soul together.
Psalm 33:18–19 MSG

A
YEAR
WITH
GOD

Day 1

He Did It!

The man and his wife heard the sound of the LORD God as he was walking in the garden in the cool of the day, and they hid from the LORD God among the trees of the garden. But the LORD God called to the man, "Where are you?"

He answered, "I heard you in the garden, and I was afraid because I was naked; so I hid."

And he said, "Who told you that you were naked? Have you eaten from the tree that I commanded you not to eat from?"

The man said, "The woman you put here with me—she gave me some fruit from the tree, and I ate it."

Then the LORD God said to the woman, "What is this you have done?"

The woman said, "The serpent deceived me, and I ate."

Genesis 3:8–13 NIV

※

The fear of God is the beginning of wisdom. Ever since Adam and Eve's disobedience, human beings have begun their relationships with God through fear, thanks to their guilty consciences. Adam and Eve didn't really comprehend why God instructed them not to eat the fruit of the Tree of Knowledge of Good and Evil, so they followed their own reasoning. One of the notions that came to Eve was that the fruit was supposed to make her wise. Sure enough.

Where before eating the fruit Adam and Eve stood naked before God without fear, they now hid from him in terror. When God confronted them, remarkably they did not lie. Not so remarkably, they shifted the blame. The man blamed the woman, and the woman blamed the serpent.

When God issued his punishments, he started with the serpent and worked back to the man.

Adam and Eve ate from the Tree of Knowledge of Good and Evil because they began to doubt that God loved them. They began to think—to fear—that God was trying to hold something back from them, something good. And so they doubted God's goodness, and they doubted his love. They soon acted according to their fear—first in eating, then in hiding, and finally in passing the blame. Fear has dominated the hearts of human beings ever since.

We fear God, and we fear that God does not love us. But God has always been dominated by love. When we love God, we want to obey him even when we don't understand. God wants us to overcome our fears. He wants us to move beyond them to love him and to love one another.

Pretty Rainbows

God said to Noah and his sons:

I am going to make a solemn promise to you and to everyone who will live after you. This includes the birds and the animals that came out of the boat. I promise every living creature that the earth and those living on it will never again be destroyed by a flood.

The rainbow that I have put in the sky will be my sign to you and to every living creature on earth. It will remind you that I will keep this promise forever. When I send clouds over the earth, and a rainbow appears in the sky, I will remember my promise to you and to all other living creatures. Never again will I let floodwaters destroy all life. When I see the rainbow in the sky, I will always remember the promise that I have made to every living creature.

Genesis 9:8–16 CEV

The need for punishment was long past. On the surface, the story of the post-Flood rainbow resembles stories like "How Did the Bear Lose Its Tail?" But the story of Noah and the ark was not devised simply to explain where rainbows come from. In fact, rainbows predated the Flood, just as circumcision predated Abraham. God simply imbued the rainbow, and later circumcision, with a new significance. They became signs or symbols of a promise. Flood tales appear in other cultures around the world, for instance among the ancient Sumerians and Babylonians. Although those stories were very similar to the story in the Bible, they all lack the promise signified by the rainbow.

The rainbow was the equivalent of what would happen later when patriarchs such as Jacob set up a stone or a pile of stones to serve as a kind of marker for an agreement, promise, or significant incident. The rainbow served as an everlasting reminder to the human race and to every other creature living on earth that God would never again allow all life to be destroyed by a great flood. It also served as a reminder to God. The rainbow was an everlasting promise that God would always keep and never break, despite the sad reality that human behavior had not changed at all. Since Noah, bad behavior has continued with wars and rumors of wars, murder, and violence of every kind.

Whenever we see a rainbow today, we are reminded that God is faithful and his promises are binding. The reasons for the Flood have not gone away, but we can know God will never again punish us like that.

God Is Always There for You

Jacob left Beer-sheba and went toward Haran. He came to a certain place and stayed there for the night, because the sun had set. Taking one of the stones of the place, he put it under his head and lay down in that place. And he dreamed that there was a ladder set up on the earth, the top of it reaching to heaven; and the angels of God were ascending and descending on it. And the LORD stood beside him and said, "I am the LORD, the God of Abraham your father and the God of Isaac; the land on which you lie I will give to you and to your offspring; and your offspring shall be like the dust of the earth, and you shall spread abroad to the west and to the east and to the north and to the south; and all the families of the earth shall be blessed in you and in your offspring. Know that I am with you and will keep you wherever you go, and will bring you back to this land; for I will not leave you until I have done what I have promised you." Then Jacob woke from his sleep and said, "Surely the LORD is in this place—and I did not know it!" And he was afraid, and said, "How awesome is this place! This is none other than the house of God, and this is the gate of heaven."

Genesis 28:10–17 NRSV

God came one dark night. Jacob was on the run and everyone was against him. He'd deceived his elderly father in order to rob his brother of his birthright. His brother had then threatened to kill him. So his mother had arranged his escape, just as she'd arranged for him to steal the birthright. As he lay down to sleep that night alone and forsaken, perhaps he wondered whether that had been such a good idea after all and whether heading off toward his mom's relatives was such a good idea.

Sleeping with a rock for a pillow, he had weird dreams. When God promised him that everything would work out well, he just got scared again. This was his first encounter with God, but it would not be his last. Love casts out fear, and eventually he would learn to love God instead of being afraid of him. But it would take his whole life. When he promised God his devotion, he was responding to God as human beings always do: first with fear, then with love. He knew that though he was leaving his home, he wouldn't be alone after all. He was becoming part of God's plan, just as we become part of God's plan when we have a personal relationship with him.

I Will Go with You

Israel took his journey with all that he had, and came to Beersheba, and offered sacrifices to the God of his father Isaac. Then God spoke to Israel in the visions of the night, and said, "Jacob, Jacob!"

And he said, "Here I am."

So He said, "I am God, the God of your father; do not fear to go down to Egypt, for I will make of you a great nation there. I will go down with you to Egypt, and I will also surely bring you up again; and Joseph will put his hand on your eyes."

Then Jacob arose from Beersheba; and the sons of Israel carried their father Jacob, their little ones, and their wives, in the carts which Pharaoh had sent to carry him. So they took their livestock and their goods, which they had acquired in the land of Canaan, and went to Egypt, Jacob and all his descendants with him. His sons and his sons' sons, his daughters and his sons' daughters, and all his descendants he brought with him to Egypt.

Genesis 46:1–7 NKJV

What you think you know might be wrong. Jacob had sent his children to Egypt to get food because they were facing famine. When they returned, he discovered they'd been accused of being spies and one of his sons, Joseph, had been imprisoned. To get him out, Jacob would have to allow the last remaining son of his beloved Rachel to go down to Egypt. He repeated the list of all his troubles, from the fact that his favorite son was dead to what had just happened. Jacob then complained to his children, "Everything is against me." From his perspective, and from the perspective of his sons standing around him, Jacob's complaint was self-evidently true.

And yet, the fascinating thing about his words is that we know he couldn't have been more wrong! After having sent his sons back a second time, Jacob's world was turned upside down. The son he had thought was dead was not only alive, but he had also become the ruler of Egypt, the richest and most powerful country on earth. Jacob had been convinced that his life was awful. Suddenly, he found out that his life was wonderful and had always been wonderful. Until that moment, he hadn't been able to see it. He had forgotten that God was with him and would always be with him. How could it ever be better than that? As he readied himself to go see his son Joseph, God reassured Jacob of his care. God would never leave Jacob or his family. Like Jacob, we belong to God and will be with him forever.

What Do You Have to Worry About?

Moses spoke to the people: "Don't be afraid. Stand firm and watch GOD do his work of salvation for you today. Take a good look at the Egyptians today for you're never going to see them again.

GOD will fight the battle for you.

And you? You keep your mouths shut!"

GOD said to Moses: "Why cry out to me? Speak to the Israelites. Order them to get moving. Hold your staff high and stretch your hand out over the sea: Split the sea! The Israelites will walk through the sea on dry ground.

"Meanwhile I'll make sure the Egyptians keep up their stubborn chase—I'll use Pharaoh and his entire army, his chariots and horsemen, to put my Glory on display so that the Egyptians will realize that I am GOD."

The angel of God that had been leading the camp of Israel now shifted and got behind them. And the Pillar of Cloud that had been in front also shifted to the rear. The Cloud was now between the camp of Egypt and the camp of Israel. The Cloud enshrouded one camp in darkness and flooded the other with light. The two camps didn't come near each other all night.

Exodus 14:13–20 MSG

*W*hy are you worried? When God asked Moses, "Why do you cry to me?" God did not wonder why Moses asked for help. Instead, God asked, in essence, "Why are you yelling at me?" God questioned where the panic was coming from. Moses had just spent years standing before Pharaoh, the ruler of the most powerful nation on earth, and he'd seen God destroy the country with a series of ten plagues. And now Moses was going to let a little thing like a deep sea in the way make him think that they were doomed? God's wondering, "What? Did I go somewhere? You think I brought you this far just to let you fail? To get your hopes up and then dash them? Do you think that's what I'm all about?" But of course that's exactly what Moses and the Israelites were thinking. We humans commonly fear that God is going to let us down.

God's response to Moses and the Israelites was reassurance. God is neither capricious nor cruel. He wants us to know that we can stop worrying and just enjoy today.

Blessed Promise

"Behold, I send an Angel before you to keep you in the way and to bring you into the place which I have prepared. Beware of Him and obey His voice; do not provoke Him, for He will not pardon your transgressions; for My name is in Him. But if you indeed obey His voice and do all that I speak, then I will be an enemy to your enemies and an adversary to your adversaries. For My Angel will go before you and bring you in to the Amorites and the Hittites and the Perizzites and the Canaanites and the Hivites and the Jebusites; and I will cut them off. You shall not bow down to their gods, nor serve them, nor do according to their works; but you shall utterly overthrow them and completely break down their sacred pillars.

"So you shall serve the LORD your God, and He will bless your bread and your water. And I will take sickness away from the midst of you. No one shall suffer miscarriage or be barren in your land; I will fulfill the number of your days."

Exodus 23:20–26 NKJV

You're not on your own. God had been with the Israelites when they toiled in Egypt. And he had stayed with them through the wilderness. The word rendered *angel* in English is a transliteration of the Greek word meaning "messenger," which is also what the Hebrew word in Exodus meant. A messenger can be a human being working for a king or for God, or a messenger can be a supernatural agent working for God. In this passage, *messenger* represented something supernatural. The pillar of fire at night and the cloud during the day signified God's physical presence before his people. God assured the people they were not facing their problems alone. Wherever they went, his presence would be there.

God warned the people to obey the angel and to do whatever he said. Additionally, he warned them against the gods and religious practices of the Canaanites, the people already living in the promised land. Faithfulness to God would result in prosperity for the Israelites—full harvests, many children, and a full life span. The only thing the Israelites had to be afraid of was God, and then only if they disobeyed and failed to abide by the terms of the contract.

God did not promise the Israelites a life without problems. They spent forty years in the desert, and they fought a long war against strong enemies before they settled down in the land of promise. But every day and with every struggle, God was there. They weren't alone. Neither are we.

Occupying the Land

Israel moved in and lived in Amorite country. Moses sent men to scout out Jazer. They captured its villages and drove away the Amorites who lived there.

Then they turned north on the road to Bashan. Og king of Bashan marched out with his entire army to meet Moses in battle at Edrei.

GOD said to Moses, "Don't be afraid of him. I'm making a present of him to you, him and all his people and his land. Treat him the same as Sihon king of the Amorites who ruled in Heshbon."

So they attacked him, his sons, and all the people—there was not a single survivor. Israel took the land.

The People of Israel marched on and camped on the Plains of Moab at Jordan-Jericho.

Balak son of Zippor learned of all that Israel had done to the Amorites. The people of Moab were in a total panic because of Israel. There were so many of them! They were terrorized.

Moab spoke to the leaders of Midian: "Look, this mob is going to clean us out—a bunch of crows picking a carcass clean."

Numbers 21:31–22:4 MSG

God likes to give the unexpected bonus over and above his obligated promise. God also gives and takes away. What had belonged to one people, God took and gave away to the Israelites.

On the east side of the Jordan River, before the Israelites entered the land of Palestine, God gave them some bonus territories. Traveling north from the desert of Sinai, the Israelites faced the Amorites and their king Sihon. Their request that they be permitted to travel through the Amorite territory was rebuffed, and Sihon led his army to attack the Israelites. God let Israel conquer them. Next in their journey, the Israelites faced Og, the king of Bashan, and his army. God gave Og and his army as "a present" to Israel. The city of Jazar was probably located near Amman, the modern-day capital of the nation of Jordan. Bashan was a plateau in southern Syria to the east of the Sea of Galilee. Edrei would be just a bit south of Bashan, and east of the Jordan River, in the modern-day nation of Jordan.

Israel's stunning victories ended the Israelites' fears and filled the people with confidence as they faced the conquest of Canaan. But the victories had the opposite effect on the Moabites, who lived to the east of the Dead Sea. Ultimately, their king, Balak, would die at the hands of the Israelites.

As God showed the Israelites, he enjoys granting what his children need.

Day 8

All Will Be Well

GOD said to Moses, "Climb up into the Abarim Mountains and look over at the land that I am giving to the People of Israel. When you've had a good look you'll be joined to your ancestors in the grave—yes, you also along with Aaron your brother. This goes back to the day when the congregation quarreled in the Wilderness of Zin and you didn't honor me in holy reverence before them in the matter of the waters, the Waters of Meribah (Quarreling) at Kadesh in the Wilderness of Zin."

Moses responded to GOD: "Let GOD, the God of the spirits of everyone living, set a man over this community to lead them, to show the way ahead and bring them back home so GOD's community will not be like sheep without a shepherd."

GOD said to Moses, "Take Joshua the son of Nun—the Spirit is in him!—and place your hand on him. Stand him before Eleazar the priest in front of the entire congregation and commission him with everyone watching. Pass your magisterial authority over to him so that the whole congregation of the People of Israel will listen obediently to him. He is to consult with Eleazar the priest who, using the oracle-Urim, will prayerfully advise him in the presence of GOD. He will command the People of Israel, the entire community, in all their comings and goings."

Numbers 27:12–21 MSG

❀

*W*ho knows whether the one who comes after you will be wise or a fool?" said the author of Ecclesiastes. Moses knew he was going to die before he could lead the people of Israel into the promised land. Who would take his place? Would he be up to the task? Moses had been the one to stand before Pharaoh. He had prayed to God on Israel's behalf. He had stood up for Israel when even God seemed ready to give up on them. And now, just as they were about to reach the place God had promised them, Moses wasn't going to be there for them. Would his forty years of ministry be for nothing? Would it all fall apart without him?

God let Moses know who would take his place. God reassured him that just as he had been with Moses and had helped him lead a group of obstinate and difficult human beings through a nightmare, so God would be with Joshua. Just as Moses had succeeded because of God's presence, so Joshua would succeed for the same reason. The human leader might change, but the real leader—God—wasn't going anywhere. God can take care of things even when we're gone.

It Makes Sense to Be Scared

Every place on which the sole of your foot treads, I have given it to you, just as I spoke to Moses.

From the wilderness and this Lebanon, even as far as the great river, the river Euphrates, all the land of the Hittites, and as far as the Great Sea toward the setting of the sun will be your territory.

No man will be able to stand before you all the days of your life. Just as I have been with Moses, I will be with you; I will not fail you or forsake you.

Be strong and courageous, for you shall give this people possession of the land which I swore to their fathers to give them.

Only be strong and very courageous; be careful to do according to all the law which Moses My servant commanded you; do not turn from it to the right or to the left, so that you may have success wherever you go.

This book of the law shall not depart from your mouth, but you shall meditate on it day and night, so that you may be careful to do according to all that is written in it; for then you will make your way prosperous, and then you will have success.

Have I not commanded you? Be strong and courageous! Do not tremble or be dismayed, for the LORD your God is with you wherever you go.

Joshua 1:3–9 NASB

※

*F*right comes easily, suddenly, and without any effort or practice. It is often the smart response. Hope is a bit harder to make happen and can seem foolish. Moses was dead, and the promised land remained in enemy hands. Joshua was overwhelmed. It was up to him to lead more than two million people to a place he'd never been. He was scared. Not only did he face the burden of leading armies into battle against a powerful enemy, but he also had to face the Israelites, who he knew would be quick to compare him with the then-dead Moses. How could he ever hope to fill those shoes?

God appeared and reassured him that just as he had been with Moses, so he would be with Joshua. And since God would walk with him, he had nothing to fear. Fear exists in the land of doubt and in the shadow of trouble. God relieved Joshua's doubts. He promised to relieve his troubles. He told Joshua that he loved him and would stand with him. Joshua's courage was restored when he knew he was not facing the future alone.

You Should Eat

Manoah said to the angel of the LORD, "Allow us to detain you, and prepare a kid for you." The angel of the LORD said to Manoah, "If you detain me, I will not eat your food; but if you want to prepare a burnt offering, then offer it to the LORD." (For Manoah did not know that he was the angel of the LORD.) Then Manoah said to the angel of the LORD, "What is your name, so that we may honor you when your words come true?" But the angel of the LORD said to him, "Why do you ask my name? It is too wonderful."

So Manoah took the kid with the grain offering, and offered it on the rock to the LORD, to him who works wonders. When the flame went up toward heaven from the altar, the angel of the LORD ascended in the flame of the altar while Manoah and his wife looked on; and they fell on their faces to the ground. The angel of the LORD did not appear again to Manoah and his wife. Then Manoah realized that it was the angel of the LORD. And Manoah said to his wife, "We shall surely die, for we have seen God." But his wife said to him, "If the LORD had meant to kill us, he would not have accepted a burnt offering and a grain offering at our hands, or shown us all these things, or now announced to us such things as these."

Judges 13:15–23 NRSV

❀

God is not a computer that can't find the file just because you mistyped. God knows what you meant.

Samson's father, Manoah, was from the tribe of Dan. His wife was unable to have children. But then an angel promised that she would have a son who would be a Nazirite from birth. Manoah then asked God to send the angel back to repeat everything he had said to his wife.

The angel refused Manoah's offer of a nice meal. Instead, the angel told him to offer God a sacrifice. Although Manoah was not a descendant of Aaron, God accepted his offering. Realizing that the angel was actually God, Manoah was afraid that he would drop dead for having seen him. His wife pointed out that they'd already be dead if that had been God's intent. Besides, God had accepted the offering and had given them a promise about having a son that wouldn't come true if they died.

God seemed more concerned with attitude and sincerity than he did with the details of the law. The law boils down to two things: loving God and loving people. Do that, and the details will take care of themselves.

The Consistency of God

These are the last words
    of David the son of Jesse.
The God of Jacob chose David
    and made him a great king.
The Mighty God of Israel
    loved him.
When God told him to speak,
    David said:
The Spirit of the LORD
    has told me what to say.
Our Mighty Rock,
    the God of Jacob, told me,
    "A ruler who obeys God and does
    right is like the sunrise on a
    cloudless day, or like rain that
    sparkles on the grass."

I have ruled this way,
    and God will never break
    his promise to me.
God's promise is complete
    and unchanging;
    he will always help me
    and give me what I hope for.
But evil people are pulled up
    like thorn bushes.
They are not dug up by hand,
    but with a sharp spear
    and are burned on the spot.

2 Samuel 23:1–7 CEV

God doesn't love us because we're good. David referred to God as "the God of Jacob" because he wanted to make a point. Just as God had chosen Jacob despite all Jacob's faults, so God had chosen David. David was good at killing Philistines, but he was not good at raising his children: Amnon raped his sister Tamar; Absalom killed Amnon. Then Absalom rebelled against David, precipitated a civil war, and both he and many Israelites on both sides of the issue died in battle. David committed adultery with Bathsheba and then saw to it that her husband was killed in battle. Just before he died, like a mob boss, he told his son Solomon—the crown prince born to the woman he had committed adultery with—to settle accounts, old grudges, with everyone who had wronged him. But at the end of his life, David looked back on it all and said that he had been a king who obeyed God and did what was right.

How can we reconcile David's life with his claim to righteousness? And with God's words, that a king must be righteous? By remembering that righteousness came from David's relationship with God rather than from his behavior. David did not need to fear the wrath of God because God's wrath had been—or in David's case, would be—directed at the ultimate sacrifice. David was forgiven. God declared him righteous. That's how David could know he was a good man: his goodness was in God, not in himself. It's the same way we know we're righteous today.

Day 12

It Is Enough

When it was all done, David was overwhelmed with guilt because he had counted the people, replacing trust with statistics. And David prayed to GOD, "I have sinned badly in what I have just done. But now GOD forgive my guilt—I've been really stupid."

When David got up the next morning, the word of GOD had already come to Gad the prophet, David's spiritual advisor, "Go and give David this message: 'GOD has spoken thus: There are three things I can do to you; choose one out of the three and I'll see that it's done.'"

Gad came to deliver the message: "Do you want three years of famine in the land, or three months of running from your enemies while they chase you down, or three days of an epidemic on the country? Think it over and make up your mind. What shall I tell the one who sent me?"

David told Gad, "They're all terrible! But I'd rather be punished by GOD, whose mercy is great, than fall into human hands."

So GOD let loose an epidemic from morning until suppertime. From Dan to Beersheba seventy thousand people died. But when the angel reached out over Jerusalem to destroy it, GOD felt the pain of the terror and told the angel who was spreading death among the people, "Enough's enough! Pull back!"

The angel of GOD had just reached the threshing floor of Araunah the Jebusite. David looked up and saw the angel hovering between earth and sky, sword drawn and about to strike Jerusalem. David and the elders bowed in prayer and covered themselves with rough burlap.

2 Samuel 24:10–16 MSG

*E*rrors have a way of multiplying themselves. David had done something wrong when he conducted his census and God held him responsible. Because David was the king of Israel, what he did affected the nation. The prophet Gad offered David three choices for punishment. David noticed a difference between them. Certainly, they all came from the hand of God, but one required human involvement, while two were the actions of God alone. David decided that whatever the punishment, better that people not be a part of it. With God, mercy was possible. With people, mercy was unlikely. David knew he could trust God just as much as he knew he could not trust people.

So God sent the three-day plague, wiping out many people. Why did those men suffer for David's mistake? They had benefited from David's rule; likewise, they suffered for it. The king stood as representative for his people. What blessings or curses came to him, came to all. Our wrongdoings affect everyone around us, because our lives affect everyone around us.

Day 13

No More Impurity

The men of the city said to Elisha, "Behold now, the situation of this city is pleasant, as my lord sees; but the water is bad and the land is unfruitful."

He said, "Bring me a new jar, and put salt in it." So they brought it to him.

He went out to the spring of water and threw salt in it and said, "Thus says the LORD, 'I have purified these waters; there shall not be from there death or unfruitfulness any longer.' "

So the waters have been purified to this day, according to the word of Elisha which he spoke. Then he went up from there to Bethel; and as he was going up by the way, young lads came out from the city and mocked him and said to him, "Go up, you baldhead; go up, you baldhead!"

When he looked behind him and saw them, he cursed them in the name of the LORD. Then two female bears came out of the woods and tore up forty-two lads of their number. He went from there to Mount Carmel, and from there he returned to Samaria.

2 Kings 2:19–25 NASB

There is always something to complain about. The sun is shining, but the crops are withering. It's raining, but the picnic is spoiled. Elisha had become the chief prophet in Israel after Elijah had gone to heaven in a chariot. One day Elisha visited a city where conditions were good, but the people pointed out that their water supply was bad, rendering their land unproductive. Elisha responded by asking them to bring him a new jar filled with salt.

Why salt? Was Elisha a chemist who realized that the spring of water was missing a certain ingredient? No. He told the people that God purified the waters. The salt was symbolic, a picture to make it clear that God had intervened. Salt was used for preserving meat and adding flavor to what otherwise might be unpalatable. It was a symbol of purification. All grain offerings were required to have salt in them (Leviticus 2:13). A covenant of salt (Numbers 18:19) was an indissoluble covenant. Thus, the salt also signified that the water of the spring would remain good from that day forward.

Later, set upon by a mob cursing and mocking him, Elisha asked God to curse them. So God did. Bears attacked forty-two of the youths. God protects his people; they have no reason to be afraid. Only their enemies need be afraid. Were the city's bad water or the insulting youths major problems? Probably not. God solves the problems not because of their size but simply because they are ours. That's how much we matter to God.

Day 14

God Knows What's Going On

[Jahaziel] said, "Listen, all Judah and inhabitants of Jerusalem, and King Jehoshaphat: Thus says the LORD to you: 'Do not fear or be dismayed at this great multitude; for the battle is not yours but God's. Tomorrow go down against them; they will come up by the ascent of Ziz; you will find them at the end of the valley, before the wilderness of Jeruel. This battle is not for you to fight; take your position, stand still, and see the victory of the LORD on your behalf, O Judah and Jerusalem.' Do not fear or be dismayed; tomorrow go out against them, and the LORD will be with you."

Then Jehoshaphat bowed down with his face to the ground, and all Judah and the inhabitants of Jerusalem fell down before the LORD, worshiping the LORD. And the Levites, of the Kohathites and the Korahites, stood up to praise the LORD, the God of Israel, with a very loud voice.

2 Chronicles 20:15–19 NRSV

God has his own ways of taking care of things. No matter what methods he happens to use, all God's people have to do is believe him and do what he says. God makes it all work out.

Jehoshaphat was facing an invasion of the Moabites and Ammonites coming from Edom on the other side of the Dead Sea. He was the king. This was his responsibility. It was his job to do something. But Jehoshaphat didn't have any way of stopping the invasion. So he called all the people to fast. The people of Judah and Jerusalem came to Jerusalem and sought help from God. Jehoshaphat led them in prayer, concluding that "we have no power to face this vast army that is attacking us. We do not know what to do, but our eyes are upon you" (2 Chronicles 20:12 NIV).

God's spirit came upon one man, a Levite named Jahaziel, and God told him what to do. Jehoshaphat and the people responded by bowing down, worshipping God, and thanking him. Jehoshaphat then sent his army to face the enemies approaching Jerusalem. At the front of his army, people sang and praised God, and his army never had to face the enemy. Instead, God made the enemies fight among themselves. They destroyed one another. All Jehoshaphat's army had to do that day was gather the plunder left behind.

Since God is with us, we should never be afraid. When we understand that our own abilities are weak but that God is strong, and when we know in our hearts that what God wants is what we want, we can ask for and receive God's help.

What Are You Worried About?

Can you arrange stars in groups
  such as Orion and the Pleiades?
Do you control the stars
  or set in place the Big Dipper
  and the Little Dipper?
Do you know the laws
  that govern the heavens,
  and can you make them rule
  the earth?
Can you order the clouds
  to send a downpour,
  or will lightning flash
  at your command?
Did you teach birds to know
that rain or floods
  are on their way?
Can you count the clouds
  or pour out their water
  on the dry, lumpy soil?
When lions are hungry,
  do you help them hunt?
Do you send an animal
  into their den?
And when starving young ravens
  cry out to me for food,
  do you satisfy their hunger?

Job 38:31–41 CEV

When God asks a question, it isn't because he doesn't know the answer. Job had lost his family, his livelihood, and his health. He wondered why it had all happened, and his question made him doubt God's goodness. God responded by asking him other questions that Job wouldn't have answers for. An interesting question God asked Job was "Do you know the laws that govern the heavens and can you make them rule the earth?" When God asked Job the question, Job had no answer. Today, Job would have probably answered yes, thanks to the physicist Sir Isaac Newton. Newton discovered that the laws of nature are universal. What is true in the heavens is true on the earth. The falling of an apple is caused by the same force that keeps the moon swinging around the earth and the earth swinging around the sun.

But God's point was not to quiz Job about physics. God wanted Job to realize there was no difference between the questions God was asking and the question Job was asking. Not knowing how to arrange the stars didn't keep Job up at night questioning God's goodness. So why did not knowing why he suffered make him do that?

Job couldn't control the clouds. He didn't understand how they worked. He couldn't take care of hungry birds. But God does understand. God can take care of them. God's real point for Job was simple: "Why are you so worried and afraid? You don't know much and can't do much. But I do. I'm God, so relax."

The Only One to Fear Is God

The LORD spoke to me with mighty
power and instructed me not to walk
in the way of this people, saying,
"You are not to say, 'It is a conspiracy!'
In regard to all that this people
call a conspiracy,
And you are not to fear what they
fear or be in dread of it.
"It is the LORD of hosts whom you
should regard as holy.
And He shall be your fear,
And He shall be your dread.

"Then He shall become a sanctuary;
But to both the houses of Israel,
a stone to strike and a rock to
stumble over,
And a snare and a trap for the
inhabitants of Jerusalem.
"Many will stumble over them,
Then they will fall and be broken;
They will even be snared and
caught."

Isaiah 8:11–15 NASB

*P*eople are afraid of many things. A lot of those things don't even exist. They imagine dark conspiracies and worry about things that are unlikely, even as they happily ignore real dangers. The Israelites worshipped gods other than Yahweh and bent themselves beneath ridiculous superstitions, imagining that the motions of stars influenced their destinies or that animal innards and tossed piles of bones could give them answers. They gave money and attention to mediums and spiritists, carried lucky charms, and spoke magic incantations or waved their hands in special ways to ward off imagined curses.

Meanwhile, they ignored the real God, the one who could actually influence the events of their lives, the one who was about to bring his judgment against them. God told Jeremiah to ignore all the silliness that consumed the attention of the people around him. God alone was to be feared, and God alone, as a result, would be Jeremiah's sanctuary. God would protect him from the coming destruction of Judah, just as he had protected Moses from the plagues of Egypt. Judah would learn to fear God alone. As they came to understand God and his reasons for judgment, they would learn to love him. In that love, their other fears would fade away. They would come to know that God was the one who controlled their destinies rather than shadowy conspiracies or the motions of the stars. They would ultimately find great comfort in that realization, as should we. God can drive groundless fear away and give us minds and hearts at peace.

It Won't Be Long Now

Soon—and it will not be very long—
the forests of Lebanon will become a
fertile field, and the fertile field will
yield bountiful crops.
In that day the deaf will hear words
read from a book, and the blind will
see through the gloom and darkness.
The humble will be filled with fresh
joy from the LORD.
The poor will rejoice in the Holy One
of Israel.
The scoffer will be gone, the arrogant
will disappear, and those who plot
evil will be killed.
Those who convict the innocent by
their false testimony will disappear.
A similar fate awaits those who use
trickery to pervert justice and who
tell lies to destroy the innocent.

That is why the LORD, who redeemed
Abraham, says to the people of
Israel,
"My people will no longer be ashamed
or turn pale with fear.
For when they see their many children
and all the blessings I have given
them,
they will recognize the holiness of the
Holy One of Israel.
They will stand in awe of the God of
Jacob.
Then the wayward will gain under-
standing, and complainers will
accept instruction."

Isaiah 29:17–24 NLT

Sooner, rather than later, the people of Israel would get a clue. When Isaiah volunteered to become God's prophet, God told him that the people he went to would "be ever hearing, but never understanding; be ever seeing, but never perceiving" (Isaiah 6:9 NIV), and that it would remain thus until the nation was destroyed. But afterward, the blind would finally see and the deaf would finally hear, and then the wicked would finally be gone.

The forests of Lebanon were famous for their cedar trees, not for being good farmland. God used that as a metaphor. What you'd least expect to be possible is just what God can do. Those who were most disadvantaged in society—the handicapped, the poor, the humble of whatever sort—would find joy in God, while those who had oppressed them would be destroyed. The destruction of the wicked was not necessarily by their deaths, however. God explained that the wayward and complainers would gain understanding. The wicked would be destroyed by being transformed into the righteous. Some of the wicked would have their old hearts changed. They would die to their past way of life. They would be renewed in God. Their fear of destruction would become a fear of God, their redeemer who had saved them.

❈❈❈❈❈❈❈❈❈❈❈❈❈❈❈❈❈❈❈❈❈❈❈❈❈❈❈❈❈❈❈❈

Fading Flowers

Our God has said:
"Encourage my people!
Give them comfort.
Speak kindly to Jerusalem and
announce:
Your slavery is past; your punishment
is over.
I, the LORD, made you pay double for
your sins."
Someone is shouting:
"Clear a path in the desert!
Make a straight road for the LORD
our God.
Fill in the valleys; flatten every hill and
mountain.
Level the rough and rugged ground.

Then the glory of the LORD will appear
for all to see.
The LORD has promised this!"
Someone told me to shout, and I
asked, "What should I shout?"
We humans are merely grass, and we
last no longer than wild flowers.
At the LORD's command, flowers and
grass disappear, and so do we.
Flowers and grass fade away, but
what our God has said will
never change.

Isaiah 40:1–8 CEV

❈

*P*ayback time, with interest. With this chapter, the prophet Isaiah shifted gears. Where before he had predicted the necessary punishment against God's people Israel, he suddenly predicted what would come after the punishment. He told them that God intended to restore the relationship their idolatry had destroyed.

God promised his people that he would restore them just as surely as he had punished them. God was offering comfort to the Israelites. He was letting them know that their time in captivity was ending and that they would soon return to their land. Their sins had been paid for; their punishment was completed. Compared to God, the life of a human being was remarkably short. But God's purposes and promises, like God himself, would last forever.

The New Testament authors of the Gospels identified John the Baptist as the one calling in the wilderness to make a straight way for God. The one for whom John made a straight way was Jesus: the Messiah and the Son of God, whom the Gospel writers and John, by the use of this passage from Isaiah, identified with Yahweh, the God of Israel. How could that prophecy be applied by the New Testament authors to John the Baptist and Jesus? Just as God had rescued his people from exile in Babylon and forgiven them for all their unfaithfulness to him, so Jesus would rescue his people—all humanity—and forgive them. The forgiveness God offered to Israel he extends to all of us.

God's Chosen One

Hear, O Jacob my servant,
Israel whom I have chosen!
Thus says the LORD who made you,
who formed you in the womb and
will help you:
Do not fear, O Jacob my servant,
Jeshurun whom I have chosen.
For I will pour water on the thirsty land,
and streams on the dry ground;
I will pour my spirit upon your
descendants,
and my blessing on your
offspring.

They shall spring up like a green
tamarisk,
like willows by flowing streams.
This one will say, "I am the LORD's,"
another will be called by the name
of Jacob,
yet another will write on the hand,
"The LORD's,"
and adopt the name of Israel.

Isaiah 44:1–5 NRSV

God isn't just in heaven; he is everywhere—he lives with his people. Just before Babylon conquered Judah for its idolatry, the prophet Jeremiah predicted that a day would come when God's commands would be written on the hearts of Israel. Nearly seventy years before Jeremiah, Isaiah had also predicted the same thing, that God would send his Holy Spirit to live in his people. Their lives could never be the same after that. They would become fruitful and abundant. God compared his Spirit's coming infusion into his people to a stream watering willow trees.

Jeshurun was another name for Israel. It was used only in poetry. And even then, it was used only four times in the entire Bible, three times in Deuteronomy and once, here, in Isaiah. It was a diminutive, a term of endearment, taken from a Hebrew word that meant "upright." Jeshurun could therefore be translated as "little upright one."

Writing the words *The Lord's* on a hand was a reference to the original covenant between Israel and God, when God told the people they would write his law on their hands and forehead (Deuteronomy 6). In Jewish practice, this led to the phylacteries. Phylacteries were little boxes containing scripture that were tied about the hands and head when people prayed. Before the captivity, the people worshipped other gods and were distracted by everything else around them. After the captivity, they would have God as their focus. At last, they would be able to love both God and their neighbors as themselves when God came upon them. Our lives can never be the same after God puts himself in them.

Nothing Is Too Hard for God

The LORD says,
> Who formed Me from the womb
> to be His Servant,
> To bring Jacob back to Him,
> So that Israel is gathered to Him
> (For I shall be glorious in the eyes
> of the LORD,
> And My God shall be My
> strength),
> Indeed He says,
> "It is too small a thing that You
> should be My Servant
> To raise up the tribes of Jacob,
> And to restore the preserved ones
> of Israel;
> I will also give You as a light to
> the Gentiles,
> That You should be My salvation
> to the ends of the earth."
> Thus says the LORD,
> The Redeemer of Israel, their Holy
> One,
> To Him whom man despises,
> To Him whom the nation abhors,
> To the Servant of rulers:
> "Kings shall see and arise,
> Princes also shall worship,
> Because of the LORD who is
> faithful,
> The Holy One of Israel;
> And He has chosen You."

Isaiah 49:5–7 NKJV

※

*G*od is not in hiding. He is standing out in the open, shining brightly. The servant of this passage from Isaiah is someone other than Israel. And the servant is someone other than the prophet Isaiah, since Isaiah was not the one to "raise up the tribes of Jacob." Nor was Isaiah the one to give "light to the Gentiles." Paul quoted from this passage in Acts 13:47 and applied it to himself and Barnabas as missionaries to the Gentiles. In Acts 26:23, when he explained the gospel to King Agrippa, he said that the Messiah would suffer, rise from the dead, and "proclaim light to his own people and to the Gentiles" (NIV).

Simeon was an old man living in Jerusalem when Jesus was born. God had told him that he would live to see the Messiah with his own eyes. When Jesus' parents brought him to the temple to consecrate him to God and offer the sacrifices required of a newborn son, Simeon took the infant Jesus into his arms and quoted Isaiah's passage. He told Mary and Joseph that Jesus would bring the light of revelation to the Gentiles (Luke 2:29–32).

Jesus and his body and bride—the church—have done and are doing just what was predicted of them by God's words to the prophet Isaiah. They have brought the light of salvation to everyone.

Good Times Are Coming

"Never again will there be in [Jerusalem] an infant who lives but a few days, or an old man who does not live out his years; he who dies at a hundred will be thought a mere youth; he who fails to reach a hundred will be considered accursed.

They will build houses and dwell in them; they will plant vineyards and eat their fruit.

No longer will they build houses and others live in them, or plant and others eat.

For as the days of a tree, so will be the days of my people; my chosen ones will long enjoy the works of their hands.

They will not toil in vain or bear children doomed to misfortune; for they will be a people blessed by the LORD, they and their descendants with them.

Before they call I will answer; while they are still speaking I will hear.

The wolf and the lamb will feed together, and the lion will eat straw like the ox, but dust will be the serpent's food.

They will neither harm nor destroy on all my holy mountain," says the LORD.

Isaiah 65:20–25 NIV

⁂

People had lived in the dark for a long time. But the dawn finally came. The last of Isaiah's prophecies predicted new heavens and a new earth, a time when weeping would cease, when infants would not die, when people would live well into old age, when they would build houses, plant vineyards, and harvest the fruit, keeping it all for themselves instead of giving it to others.

When we read that God told his people about the "new heavens and a new earth" (Isaiah 65:17 NIV), we are tempted to imagine that God was talking about the eternal kingdom. When we read about the wolf and the lamb feeding together, the lion eating straw, and dust becoming the food of serpents, it is hard to think of anything else but the kingdom. But between those words that sound like the kingdom, God said that those who died at a hundred were dying young. God spoke about babies being born. Neither death nor birth seems to fit the usual notion about the kingdom of heaven. So what are we to make of the passage?

Are the blessings of the passage literal, or are they figurative? A clue comes from remembering that God chose to speak in poetry. This passage expressed the hope that was to come when God finally reigned in the lives of his people. The serpent eating dust reminds us of the curse in Genesis. God proclaimed victory over that old curse. The kingdom of heaven lives in our hearts. No matter what the world may throw at us today, God still reigns there.

What Good Is an Idol?

Hear the word that the LORD speaks to you, O house of Israel. Thus says the LORD:
> Do not learn the way of the nations, or be dismayed at the signs of the heavens; for the nations are dismayed at them.
> For the customs of the peoples are false:
> a tree from the forest is cut down, and worked with an ax by the hands of an artisan; people deck it with silver and gold; they fasten it with hammer and nails so that it cannot move.
> Their idols are like scarecrows in a cucumber field, and they cannot speak; they have to be carried, for they cannot walk.
> Do not be afraid of them, for they cannot do evil, nor is it in them to do good.

Jeremiah 10:1–5 NRSV

For most people in the modern world, idols are merely works of art. We are never tempted to worship them. Some art historians are dismayed that as Christians became dominant in the old Roman Empire, they destroyed the pagan temples and wrecked the images of the gods. Two thousand years later, it is easy to think only in terms of the destruction of art. Keep in mind, however, that for those who had turned from paganism to Christianity, idols held power. They symbolized something evil and wrong. They oppressed the hearts and minds of countless human beings, blinding them to the truth. People had devoted themselves, their money, and even their lives to things that were useless. Idols were a lie and a delusion.

Following the destruction of any totalitarian regime, whether that of Nazi Germany, Communism, or Saddam Hussein's dictatorship, the people freed from tyranny quickly destroyed statues and images of the hated regime. Statues of Stalin and Lenin were knocked down and dragged away; swastikas atop buildings in Berlin were dynamited; Saddam's statue in the center of Baghdad was toppled by tanks. Two thousand years from now, some might be appalled at the destruction of art and culture in these places, but those destroying the images were striking blows for freedom. For those who worshipped idols, the idols were not art. They were tyrants who had blinded their worshippers. Whatever idols oppress you today—fearful circumstances or material belongings—God has set you free from them. Your idols are nothing but objects made by men.

A Wall of Bronze

Jeremiah, get ready!
    Go and tell the people what I
      command you to say.
Don't be frightened by them, or I
    will make you terrified while
    they watch.
My power will make you strong like a
    fortress or a column of iron or a
    wall of bronze.
You will oppose all of Judah,
    including its kings and leaders, its
    priests and people.
They will fight back, but they
    won't win.

I, the LORD, give my word—I won't let
    them harm you.
The LORD told me to go to Jerusalem
    and tell everyone that he had said:
When you were my young bride, you
    loved me and followed me
    through the barren desert.
You belonged to me alone, like
    the first part of the harvest, and I
    severely punished those who
    mistreated you.

Jeremiah 1:17–2:3 CEV

God tells you how it is, not how you wish it were. God never promised Jeremiah that he wouldn't have problems. He didn't tell him his job would be easy or that anyone's mind would be changed by what he said. Instead, God told Jeremiah that those he confronted would fight back. But he also told him that they wouldn't win, and that they wouldn't harm him.

But God's definition of *harm* might have been a tad different from Jeremiah's definition. Jeremiah spent time in a miry pit, suffered repeated arrests, and endured blistering verbal attacks. Jeremiah did not have a nice house; nor did he make a lot of money. He didn't even get respect. But though his life was endangered, and though there were those who threatened to kill him, Jeremiah survived. His enemies didn't kill him or silence him. For God, *harm* did not mean trouble. For God, *harm* meant being rendered ineffective.

Jeremiah did exactly what God asked him to do every time. Despite his suffering, and despite the fact that no one believed his message or acted upon it, Jeremiah was successful. He had no way of knowing that his words would be preserved and studied by millions for more than twenty-five centuries. He did not change the minds of the people he first confronted, but his words have lived on to change people's minds. Live your life the way God wants you to, and you'll never suffer regret. You will ultimately realize true success.

Day 24

Behold, the Days Are Coming

"Woe to the shepherds who destroy and scatter the sheep of My pasture!" says the LORD. Therefore thus says the LORD God of Israel against the shepherds who feed My people: "You have scattered My flock, driven them away, and not attended to them. Behold, I will attend to you for the evil of your doings," says the LORD. "But I will gather the remnant of My flock out of all countries where I have driven them, and bring them back to their folds; and they shall be fruitful and increase. I will set up shepherds over them who will feed them; and they shall fear no more, nor be dismayed, nor shall they be lacking," says the LORD.

"Behold, the days are coming," says the LORD,
"That I will raise to David a Branch of righteousness;
    A King shall reign and prosper,
And execute judgment and righteousness in the earth.
    In His days Judah will be saved,
And Israel will dwell safely;
Now this is His name by which He will be called:
THE LORD OUR RIGHTEOUSNESS."

Jeremiah 23:1–6 NKJV

---

*I*t's hard to be the boss. Authority is a dangerous thing. The apostle James wrote that those who teach would be judged more harshly than others. Why? While each human being touches more people than he imagines, the impact of a teacher is far greater. A single teacher may train dozens, who then take the teacher's words to others, multiplying the effect exponentially. Similarly, "shepherds"—the leadership in Israel consisting of the king, the bureaucrats, and the religious establishment—affected the lives of all those around them.

The leaders of Israel had been made responsible for the spiritual safety of their people. But rather than leading them toward God, they led them away. They seduced them with other deities. God was going to take the power of the shepherds from them and pass it on to someone else, someone who would actually do right by those under them—a good shepherd.

Jeremiah prophesied while Zedekiah, whose name meant "righteousness of the Lord," ruled as the final king of Israel before Nebuchadnezzar took him into exile. God reassured the Israelites that one day they would have a king who actually lived up to that name, who would really be "the Lord our righteousness." God's words to Jeremiah found their fulfillment in Jesus, the son of David, the Good Shepherd (John 10:11).

God Has Plans for You

Thus says the LORD of hosts, the God of Israel, to all the exiles whom I have sent into exile from Jerusalem to Babylon, "Build houses and live in them; and plant gardens and eat their produce. Take wives and become the fathers of sons and daughters, and take wives for your sons and give your daughters to husbands, that they may bear sons and daughters; and multiply there and do not decrease. Seek the welfare of the city where I have sent you into exile, and pray to the LORD on its behalf; for in its welfare you will have welfare."

For thus says the LORD of hosts, the God of Israel, "Do not let your prophets who are in your midst and your diviners deceive you, and do not listen to the dreams which they dream. For they prophesy falsely to you in My name; I have not sent them," declares the LORD.

For thus says the LORD, "When seventy years have been completed for Babylon, I will visit you and fulfill My good word to you, to bring you back to this place. For I know the plans that I have for you," declares the LORD, "plans for welfare and not for calamity to give you a future and a hope. Then you will call upon Me and come and pray to Me, and I will listen to you. You will seek Me and find Me when you search for Me with all your heart."

Jeremiah 29:4–13 NASB

❧

*F*alse prophets predicted good times. They were quick to promise health, wealth, and prosperity. God warned his people not to listen to them because what they said simply wasn't going to be. Instead of good times, God, through Jeremiah, predicted that the false prophets were facing judgment and exile.

This news was hardly good, hardly comforting, and hardly what anyone wanted to hear. No wonder everyone was mad at the real prophets. They made the people think that God hated them and wanted to hurt them.

But God wanted to correct those misunderstandings. In the midst of the pain, God explained that his plans for them were good ones. They had a future to look forward to, and, oddly, in the midst of their misery they would turn to God, the one who seemed to be harming them. When the day came that they were genuinely sorry for what they had done, then he would listen to them and restore their fortunes.

Repentance is more than saying, "I'm sorry." Repentance is changed behavior. We have repented when we will do anything and take any punishment in order to make things right again.

❈❈❈❈❈❈❈❈❈❈❈❈❈❈❈❈❈❈❈❈❈❈❈❈❈❈❈❈❈❈❈❈

It Was for Your Own Good

This is what the LORD says:
"A cry is heard in Ramah—deep
  anguish and bitter weeping.
Rachel weeps for her children, refusing
  to be comforted—for her children
  are gone."
But now this is what the LORD says:
"Do not weep any longer, for I will
  reward you," says the LORD.
"Your children will come back to you
  from the distant land of the enemy.
There is hope for your future," says the
  LORD.
  "Your children will come again to
  their own land.

I have heard Israel saying,
'You disciplined me severely, like a calf
  that needs training for the yoke.
Turn me again to you and restore me,
  for you alone are the LORD my God.
I turned away from God,
  but then I was sorry.

I kicked myself for my stupidity!
  I was thoroughly ashamed of all I
  did in my younger days.'"

Jeremiah 31:15–19 NLT

❈

Augustus Caesar, the first emperor of Rome, once made a wry comment about Herod the Great, the man he had made into the king of Judea. He said, "It is better to be Herod's pigs than Herod's sons." Pigs were not kosher, so he wouldn't touch them. But Herod's family? Herod was paranoid and killed several sons he thought might be plotting against him.

When wise men from Persia came looking for a royal son, Herod was panic-stricken. None of his wives had recently given birth. He was not descended from David. If a new king had been born, then Herod had a rival. So he found out where the child had been born, and then he took care of things in his own inimitable style. He killed all the babies in Bethlehem who were close to the right age.

God's prophecy of Rachel's weeping because her children were no more was taken by Matthew and applied to Herod's slaughter. But Jeremiah's original intent was to prophesy about the deportation of the Jews to Babylon. "Rachel," of course, was Jacob's—Israel's—true love, the mother of Joseph and Benjamin. Rachel came to stand in as a poetic reference to the nation of Israel. Why did Matthew use a prophecy of the Babylonian captivity for Herod's slaughter? The thematic parallel in it—Babylon had failed to destroy Israel. Herod had failed to destroy Christ.

God reassured the Rachels of Jeremiah's day, the people of Israel, that those taken from them would one day return. For those murdered by Herod, the resurrection was coming. Those lost to us now will be with us forever someday. Our tears will be wiped away.

Them Bones, Them Bones

The hand of the LORD was on me, and He brought me out by His Spirit and set me down in the middle of the valley; it was full of bones. He led me all around them. There were a great many of them on the surface of the valley, and they were very dry. Then He said to me, "Son of man, can these bones live?"

I replied, "Lord GOD, [only] You know."

He said to me, "Prophesy concerning these bones and say to them: Dry bones, hear the word of the LORD! This is what the Lord GOD says to these bones: I will cause breath to enter you, and you will live. I will put tendons on you, make flesh grow on you, and cover you with skin. I will put breath in you so that you come to life. Then you will know that I am the LORD."

So I prophesied as I had been commanded. While I was prophesying, there was a noise, a rattling sound, and the bones came together, bone to bone.

Ezekiel 37:1–7 HCSB

※

*E*zekiel, an exile himself, prophesied to the exiles living in Babylon. The people in exile felt empty, abandoned, and hopeless. Despite the words of Jeremiah and Isaiah, who had promised that they would return home one day, they still doubted. They were unable to see any further than their current pain. So once again, God revealed the future.

God granted Ezekiel a vision of a vast field, filled with bones, metaphorically standing for the exiled nation. Then God restored the bones to life, a vast army, and told Ezekiel that they represented the Israelites who were saying, "Our bones are dried up, and our hope is gone; we are cut off." God intended to resurrect them. That is, he would bring them home, to the land of Israel.

God doesn't go back on his promises. But he makes allowances for human fear and weakness. Sometimes we may fear that God has abandoned us. We may fear that we've been too bad, we've gone too far from his will, and that for us it is too late. God reassured the Israelites—even after hundreds of years of their going too far and after years of exile—that it wasn't too late. Like Israel in the days of Ezekiel, even when we're nothing but dried bones, God still has a plan for us.

What Am I Going to Do with You?

People of Israel and Judah, what can I
do with you?
Your love for me disappears more
quickly than mist or dew
at sunrise.
That's why I slaughtered you with the
words of my prophets.
That's why my judgments blazed like
the dawning sun.
I'd rather for you to be faithful and to
know me than to offer sacrifices.
At a place named Adam, you betrayed
me by breaking our agreement.
Everyone in Gilead is evil; your
hands are stained with the blood
of victims.
You priests are like a gang of robbers
in ambush.
On the road to Shechem you murder
and commit other horrible crimes.
I have seen a terrible thing in Israel—
you are unfaithful and unfit to
worship me.
People of Judah, your time is
coming too.

Hosea 6:4–11 CEV

Human love can be fickle, vanishing over the least offense. Hosea married a prostitute because God told him to, so his wife spent most of her time elsewhere with other men. She didn't love Hosea. Likewise for God, Israel gave him lip service, but Israel's real passion was for the other gods, the ones she really cared about, since she spent all her time with them.

God listed three places where people had been unfaithful to him: Adam, which was near the Jordan River; Gilead, which was a region near Adam; and Shechem, which was in central Palestine. The people were guilty of unfaithfulness to God and unfaithfulness to one another. Even the priests, who were supposed to represent God, acted like a criminal gang. This was nothing new. Even in the days of Samuel, before Saul became king, the priests had taken advantage of those few people who had come to worship Yahweh.

But by the time of Hosea, God's patience was near an end. Hosea's wife wound up sold as a slave. Hosea bought her back from the slave market. The sad events of Hosea's life were pictures of what God intended for Israel. Israel would become captive in Babylon. Eventually God would redeem Israel from Babylon. Neither Hosea's wife nor Israel had done anything to merit being bought back. Hosea rescued his wife because he loved her, even if she didn't love him. God rescued Israel for the same reason. They were both redeemed because God's love is not fickle.

Obedience Is Better Than Sacrifice

In that day it shall be said
 to Jerusalem:
   "Do not fear;
   Zion, let not your hands be weak.
     The LORD your God in
       your midst,
   The Mighty One, will save;
   He will rejoice over you
     with gladness,
   He will quiet you with His love,
   He will rejoice over you
     with singing."
 "I will gather those who sorrow
     over the appointed assembly,
   Who are among you,
   To whom its reproach is a burden.
       Behold, at that time
   I will deal with all who afflict you;

I will save the lame,
 And gather those who were
   driven out;
 I will appoint them for praise
   and fame
 In every land where they were put
   to shame.
 At that time I will bring you back,
 Even at the time I gather you;
 For I will give you fame and praise
 Among all the peoples of
   the earth,
 When I return your captives before
   your eyes,"
 Says the LORD.

Zephaniah 3:16–20 NKJV

✻

$\mathcal{W}$e'd really like to do most of what tempts us. God tells us "Do not fear." It seems an unlikely commandment. But other things are equally unpleasant even though they may appear desirable or reasonable at first glance. Fear is that way, and Jerusalem certainly had many things to fear. Zephaniah prophesied during Josiah's reign in Judah. Jeremiah was prophesying then too. It was a time of revival, but the international situation was in flux. The balance of power was shifting to Babylon, and Josiah's revival had touched only a few. The rot in the heart of Israel remained festering. The return to exclusive worship of God stopped when he died. God had no solution left but exile. Captivity in Babylon became inevitable, the destruction of Jerusalem guaranteed. How could there be no fear in the face of that?

But Zephaniah pointed out that someday their punishment would be past tense. In that day, Jerusalem would stop being afraid. In that day, God's love would quiet them. Their hearts would grow calm and turn to joy. The captives would come home. Whether times are good or times are bad, we, like Jerusalem, are still with God. We do not need to be afraid. With God, we can capture the attitude of joy we will have tomorrow when the pain of today has become yesterday.

Love and Hate

Love is the theme of the Bible. God repeatedly told the Israelites to love him and each other. All God's other commandments are summarized by love. Hate desires what's worst for others. Sometimes hate is active, but mostly it just ignores other people and does nothing to relieve people's suffering. Love, on the other hand, is always energetic. It strives for what is best, regardless of the response. God is love, and how we perceive God's love often depends on where we are standing in our relationship with him. Though God's love toward one person or group might feel like hate to someone else, God is always love. How we perceive that love often depends on where we are standing in our relationship with him.

※

Love the Lord *your God with all*
your heart, all your soul, and all your strength.

Deuteronomy 6:5 NLT

God Chose You

The LORD said to Abram:

Leave your country, your family, and your relatives and go to the land that I will show you. I will bless you and make your descendants into a great nation. You will become famous and be a blessing to others. I will bless anyone who blesses you, but I will put a curse on anyone who puts a curse on you. Everyone on earth will be blessed because of you.

Abram was seventy-five years old when the LORD told him to leave the city of Haran. He obeyed and left with his wife Sarai, his nephew Lot, and all the possessions and slaves they had gotten while in Haran.

When they came to the land of Canaan, Abram went as far as the sacred tree of Moreh in a place called Shechem. The Canaanites were still living in the land at that time, but the LORD appeared to Abram and promised, "I will give this land to your family forever." Abram then built an altar there for the LORD.

Genesis 12:1–7 CEV

*J*ust because you think you know what to expect from life, doesn't mean you do. Abram was an old man when God called him from the city of Haran. By the world's standards, Abram's life was nearly done. It was past time to retire. He was just an ordinary man living in the Middle East, one of millions of people alive on the planet in that day. And God decided to pick him. What made Abram special was not who he was, but who God was. God did not choose Abram because he was extraordinary. Abram became extraordinary—even in his twilight years— because God chose him. God chose Abram because he loved him.

The promise that God gave Abram when he told him to pack up and move to what would someday be the land of Israel had no strings attached. Regardless of Abram's character or choices, God told him he was going to become famous, he'd be happy, and his descendants would grow to become a great nation. Moreover, God protected Abram and those who encountered him or his descendants—those who blessed Abram would themselves be blessed, and those who cursed him would be cursed. God takes care of those who belong to him, and woe to any who try to harm those God has chosen.

Abram responded to God's promise by going where God told him to go, and by building an altar to God. Abram didn't know much about God, but he paid attention to him. Like Abram, we never know when God might surprise us, or what God might have in store for us.

Perspective Matters

The LORD said to Moses, "I will bring one more plague upon Pharaoh and upon Egypt; afterwards he will let you go from here; indeed, when he lets you go, he will drive you away. Tell the people that every man is to ask his neighbor and every woman is to ask her neighbor for objects of silver and gold." The LORD gave the people favor in the sight of the Egyptians. Moreover, Moses himself was a man of great importance in the land of Egypt, in the sight of Pharaoh's officials and in the sight of the people.

Moses said, "Thus says the LORD: About midnight I will go out through Egypt. Every firstborn in the land of Egypt shall die, from the firstborn of Pharaoh who sits on his throne to the firstborn of the female slave who is behind the handmill, and all the firstborn of the livestock. Then there will be a loud cry throughout the whole land of Egypt, such as has never been or will ever be again. But not a dog shall growl at any of the Israelites—not at people, not at animals—so that you may know that the LORD makes a distinction between Egypt and Israel. Then all these officials of yours shall come down to me, and bow low to me, saying, 'Leave us, you and all the people who follow you.' After that I will leave." And in hot anger he left Pharaoh.

Exodus 11:1–8 NRSV

How you perceive God's actions depends on your point of view. God rescued his people from Egypt and set them free. The Israelites saw how much God loved them and cared about them when he slaughtered the firstborn of Egypt. The Egyptians, and especially the parents, probably didn't see it that way. One action gave rise to two points of view and two radically different interpretations of God.

The same fire that warms also burns. How you feel about the fire will depend on whether you're warming your hands on a cold night or you're being burned at the stake. The fire, however, has not changed. It is doing exactly the same thing, no matter how you feel about it. So it is with God. God is love. Whatever he does, he does because of love. He loves the world. And yet, when God showed his love, Egyptians died while Israelites rejoiced and were set free. God does not change. Love always motivates his actions. How we feel about what God does is up to us.

God Provided Despite the Attitude

[Moses] told them, "This is what the Lord has said: 'Tomorrow is a day of complete rest, a holy Sabbath to the Lord. Bake what you want to bake, and boil what you want to boil, and everything left over set aside to be kept until morning.'"

So they set it aside until morning as Moses commanded, and it didn't smell or have any maggots in it. "Eat it today," Moses said, "because today is a Sabbath to the Lord. Today you won't find any in the field. For six days you may gather it, but on the seventh day, the Sabbath, there will be none."

Yet on the seventh day some of the people went out to gather, but they did not find any. Then the Lord said to Moses, "How long will you refuse to keep My commands and instructions? Understand that the Lord has given you the Sabbath; therefore on the sixth day He will give you two days' worth of bread. Each of you stay where you are; no one is to leave his place on the seventh day." So the people rested on the seventh day.

The house of Israel named the substance manna. It resembled coriander seed, was white, and tasted like wafers [made] with honey.

Exodus 16:23–31 HCSB

✺

There's nothing to eat!" say our children when they can't find the one food item they are craving. Soon after, they may complain that we hate them and have ruined their lives if we don't immediately go to the grocery store and get what they want. Perhaps it's not so odd that God called his people the children of Israel. They complained about their hunger, which was not necessarily an unreasonable thing to do. But one day rather than simply announcing that they were hungry or asking how much longer before supper, they were sullen. They believed that they would never eat again and that in fact God had brought them to where they were for the express purpose of making them die miserable deaths. It was one thing to be hungry and let someone know about it. It was another thing entirely to accuse that someone of evil intent.

Despite that accusation, however, God fed his people—just as parents feed their sometimes-bratty children. We love our children and want what's best for them. We want them to be healthy, happy, and lacking for nothing. God loves his children, too, however annoying we might be. He loves us even when we break the rules.

Day 33

The Commandments

GOD spoke all these words: I am GOD, your God, who brought you out of the land of Egypt, out of a life of slavery.

No other gods, only me.

No carved gods of any size, shape, or form of anything whatever, whether of things that fly or walk or swim. Don't bow down to them and don't serve them because *I* am GOD, your God, and I'm a most jealous God, punishing the children for any sins their parents pass on to them to the third, and yes, even to the fourth generation of those who hate me. But I'm unswervingly loyal to the thousands who love me and keep my commandments.

No using the name of GOD, your God, in curses or silly banter; GOD won't put up with the irreverent use of his name.

Observe the Sabbath day, to keep it holy. Work six days and do everything you need to do. But the seventh day is a Sabbath to GOD, your God. Don't do any work—not you, nor your son, nor your daughter, nor your servant, nor your maid, nor your animals, not even the foreign guest visiting in your town. For in six days GOD made Heaven, Earth, and sea, and everything in them; he rested on the seventh day. Therefore GOD blessed the Sabbath day; he set it apart as a holy day.

Exodus 20:1–11 MSG

Doing what's right is all about love. The Ten Commandments can be broken down into two halves: the commandments that refer to God and the commandments that refer to people. Jesus pointed out that these Ten Commandments—and for that matter, all the rules and regulations of the Bible—can be summarized by two commandments: to love God and to love people.

God says that our actions have consequences for those around us. In the middle of the Ten Commandments, God explained that the iniquity of the fathers would pass on to the children. God simply meant that the effects of people's actions, for good or ill, have influence beyond them. The poor choices of a father affect his children, and the repercussions roll on to later generations, making life either harder or easier for others.

The commandments make life better. Before the Ten Commandments, people did not take a day off every week. Instead, they worked constantly, getting only the rare holiday. The Ten Commandments serve as an illustration of how God puts his love into practice in our lives.

Loving Other People

If someone steals an ox or a lamb and slaughters or sells it, the thief must pay five cattle in place of the ox and four sheep in place of the lamb. If the thief is caught while breaking in and is hit hard and dies, there is no bloodguilt. But if it happens after daybreak, there is bloodguilt.

A thief must make full restitution for what is stolen. The thief who is unable to pay is to be sold for his thieving. If caught red-handed with the stolen goods, and the ox or donkey or lamb is still alive, the thief pays double.

If someone grazes livestock in a field or vineyard but lets them loose so they graze in someone else's field, restitution must be made from the best of the owner's field or vineyard.

If fire breaks out and spreads to the brush so that the sheaves of grain or the standing grain or even the whole field is burned up, whoever started the fire must pay for the damages.

Exodus 22:1–6 MSG

※

*P*ayback hurts. Better not to owe it. When Nathan the prophet first confronted David for his affair with Bathsheba and the murder of her husband, Uriah, he told him a story about a rich man stealing a pet sheep from his impoverished neighbor and slaughtering it to feed his guests. David reacted angrily and pronounced that the man must pay back "four sheep" for the one stolen (2 Samuel 12:1–6).

The only place God gave the penalty for a stolen sheep is here, in this single passage. God had said that Israel's kings should, among other things, make a copy of God's law for themselves and read it regularly (Deuteronomy 17:18–19). Clearly, David had done so. He knew the Bible well, though it did not necessarily prevent him from doing wrong.

God made restitution the method for dealing with any sort of theft, whether intentional or accidental, as in the "theft" caused by letting one's animals get loose to steal grain from someone else's field, or by allowing a fire to get out of control and burn up the property of a neighbor. The principle envisioned was the practical outworking of the golden rule, to do to others as you'd have them do to you. If someone caused a loss, you'd wish that person to make restitution. The law, in all its varied detail, merely serves as a commentary explaining in specific circumstances how to love your neighbor as yourself.

Be Careful What You Eat

GOD spoke to Moses and Aaron: "Speak to the People of Israel. Tell them: Of all the animals on Earth, these are the animals that you may eat:

"You may eat any animal that has a split hoof, divided in two, and that chews the cud, but not an animal that only chews the cud or only has a split hoof. For instance, the camel chews the cud but doesn't have a split hoof, so it's unclean. The rock badger chews the cud but doesn't have a split hoof and so it's unclean. The rabbit chews the cud but doesn't have a split hoof so is unclean. The pig has a split hoof, divided in two, but doesn't chew the cud and so is unclean. You may not eat their meat nor touch their carcasses; they are unclean to you.

"Among the creatures that live in the water of the seas and streams, you may eat any that have fins and scales. But anything that doesn't have fins and scales, whether in seas or streams, whether small creatures in the shallows or huge creatures in the deeps, you are to detest. Yes, detest them. Don't eat their meat; detest their carcasses. Anything living in the water that doesn't have fins and scales is detestable to you."

Leviticus 11:1–12 MSG

It is said that we are what we eat. God's purpose in giving his people dietary restrictions was not to make their lives unpleasant or more difficult. Yet in the New Testament, the Jewish dietary restrictions were not imposed on the non-Jewish people who came to Jesus. If there were some health issues associated with the food restrictions, then freeing the Gentiles from them might be taken to mean that God didn't love the Gentiles as much as he loved the Jewish people. Since God loves everyone, health issues probably have nothing to do with it.

Why then were the Israelites allowed to eat some animals but not others? God's purpose was relational. Just as the prophets of God had to act out their prophetic messages—as when Hosea married a prostitute—so the people of Israel illustrated their relationship with God through their diet. God had told them that when they got up, when they went to sleep, when they walked along the road, and when they went about their day, he was always to be part of their thinking. So even in what they ate, they couldn't get away from God's presence in their lives. After Pentecost, with the arrival of his Holy Spirit, God began living inside his people. The external reminders of God were therefore no longer necessary. God is always with us now.

Obeying God

Do not steal.

Do not deceive or cheat one another.

Do not bring shame on the name of your God by using it to swear falsely. I am the LORD.

Do not defraud or rob your neighbor.

Do not make your hired workers wait until the next day to receive their pay.

Do not insult the deaf or cause the blind to stumble. You must fear your God; I am the LORD.

Do not twist justice in legal matters by favoring the poor or being partial to the rich and powerful. Always judge people fairly.

Do not spread slanderous gossip among your people.

Do not stand idly by when your neighbor's life is threatened. I am the LORD.

Do not nurse hatred in your heart for any of your relatives. Confront people directly so you will not be held guilty for their sin.

Do not seek revenge or bear a grudge against a fellow Israelite, but love your neighbor as yourself. I am the LORD.

Leviticus 19:11–18 NLT

✿

*T*here is more to righteousness than simply behaving well toward others. Outward actions, for good or ill, have their origins in what people are thinking, what their desires might be, or how they are feeling at any given moment. Bad decisions can grow from exhaustion, headache, or stress. Hate festers a long time before it results in outward violence. Evil is sometimes not an action but a failure to act. The mixing of things that shouldn't be mixed symbolizes the importance of not mixing evil with good or hatred with love. Some things should not be compromised.

It was common in Hebrew writing to have a summary statement followed by explanations or expansions upon that summary statement. And so the summary statement in this passage—"Do not steal"—is followed by explanations of what might constitute stealing: defrauding your neighbor, making hired day workers wait for their pay, gossip (which robs people of their reputations), and stealing the life of your neighbor through inaction when you could have saved it.

The passage concludes with the phrase upon which all the laws are built: to love your neighbor as yourself (Leviticus 19:18). The commandment to love comes in the context of when a person was least likely to feel affection for his neighbor, when he had wronged him and he wanted revenge. God asked us to love our neighbor, not when it was easy, but when it was hardest: when our natural reaction was only hate.

Respect for Everyone

You are to rise in the presence of the elderly and honor the old. Fear your God; I am the Lord.

When a foreigner lives with you in your land, you must not oppress him. You must regard the foreigner who lives with you as the native-born among you. You are to love him as yourself, for you were foreigners in the land of Egypt; I am the Lord your God.

You must not act unfairly in measurements of length, weight, or volume. You are to have honest balances, honest weights, an honest dry measure, and an honest liquid measure; I am the Lord your God, who brought you out of the land of Egypt. You must keep all My statutes and all My ordinances and do them; I am the Lord.

Leviticus 19:32–37 HCSB

*H*ow you treat those who can't do anything for you says a lot about you. Rising in the presence of the aged and showing respect costs you nothing and doesn't do a thing physically for them—it puts no money in their pockets and no food in their bellies. But it does something special for their souls.

How you treat those who are weak says something about you too. Those who are strangers, who do not belong to your people, should be treated as well as if they were old friends and part of your family. The Israelites had been treated poorly in the land of their sojourning. God reminded them not to act like the Egyptians; they were to instead show love.

In business, the customer depends on the honesty of the merchant. In the time of Moses, there was no such thing as money as we know it today. Gold and silver had to be weighed in order to make a payment. There were no standard-sized boxes or jars. Honest weights were critical for transactions, but a customer had no way of checking up on a merchant to know if his *ephah* and *hin* were accurate. An *ephah* and a *hin* were measurements of weight in ancient Israel. An *ephah* was a dry measure equal to about three-fifths of a bushel—think of the dry capacity of eleven two-liter soda bottles—and a *hin* was a liquid measure equivalent to about a gallon.

A merchant had power over his customers, and taking advantage of them was easy since the merchant owned all the scales, the baskets, and the weights. God told the Israelites to keep his commandments. Then he said simply that he was Yahweh. What did he mean by that? Just because no human being knows what you're doing does not mean there isn't someone who does: God. Who you are when no one is looking is who you really are.

God's Love Contract

This is what the LORD of Hosts says: I took you from the pasture and from following the sheep to be ruler over My people Israel. I have been with you wherever you have gone, and I have destroyed all your enemies before you. I will make a name for you like that of the greatest in the land. I will establish a place for My people Israel and plant them, so that they may live there and not be disturbed again. Evildoers will not afflict them as they have done ever since the day I ordered judges to be over My people Israel. I will give you rest from all your enemies.

The LORD declares to you: The LORD Himself will make a house for you. When your time comes and you rest with your fathers, I will raise up after you your descendant, who will come from your body, and I will establish his kingdom. He will build a house for My name, and I will establish the throne of his kingdom forever. I will be a father to him, and he will be a son to Me. When he does wrong, I will discipline him with a human rod and with blows from others. But My faithful love will never leave him as I removed it from Saul; I removed him from your way. Your house and kingdom will endure before Me forever, and your throne will be established forever.

2 Samuel 7:8–16 HCSB

God repairs what belongs to him. He doesn't throw it away. God's relationship with David was different from the relationship he had with Saul. Like those he would later have with the kings of the Northern Kingdom of Israel, his relationship with Saul was dependent upon Saul's performance. The contract was limited and temporary with no guarantees of renewal. This could be compared with the contract you make with your cell phone company—in exchange for a new phone, you agree to remain a customer for the next two years, but if you decide to leave early, you pay a penalty. But God's relationship with David was like a parent's with his child—it could not be undone.

There were still expectations, however. A failure to live up to them could never end the relationship, but it could result in discipline. Nevertheless, the house and kingdom of David would endure forever. How so? David surely thought it was a physical kingdom, with one of his descendants forever sitting on a physical throne. God understood—and later clarified in the New Testament—that his Son reigned on high in the hearts of men. The kingdom God promised to David lives on in the hearts and minds of his people.

Finding Love in All the Wrong Places

King Solomon loved many foreign women in addition to Pharaoh's daughter: Moabite, Ammonite, Edomite, Sidonian, and Hittite women from the nations that the LORD had told the Israelites about, "Do not intermarry with them, and they must not intermarry with you, because they will turn you away [from Me] to their gods." Solomon was deeply attached to these women and loved [them]. He had 700 wives who were princesses and 300 concubines, and they turned his heart away [from the LORD].

When Solomon was old, his wives seduced him [to follow] other gods. His heart was not completely with the LORD his God, as his father David's heart had been. Solomon followed Ashtoreth, the goddess of the Sidonians, and Milcom, the detestable idol of the Ammonites. Solomon did what was evil in the LORD's sight, and unlike his father David, he did not completely follow the LORD.

At that time, Solomon built a high place for Chemosh, the detestable idol of Moab, and for Milcom, the detestable idol of the Ammonites on the hill across from Jerusalem. He did the same for all his foreign wives, who were burning incense and offering sacrifices to their gods.

1 Kings 11:1–8 HCSB

*T*hose we love and care about can lead us astray. God knows what peer pressure does to us. We want to be loved, we want to be accepted, and we want to do what we can to make the people we're with happy. The fear of losing those we love combined with our desire to make them happy can lead us to make the wrong choices. It is easy to be influenced more by those we are with—those we can see and touch—than by someone as abstract to us as God usually is.

Human beings are social creatures, and we fear losing connection with those around us.

Solomon's relationships with many women were more complicated than most. Not only was the social dynamic at work—he genuinely cared for these women—but politics were at play as well. Marriages with foreign women, the daughters or sisters of neighboring rulers, solidified treaty obligations and guaranteed peace and trade. If Solomon didn't keep those women happy, not only might he lose their affections, but he also might lose money and prestige—and he might face war.

God understands the problems relationships can cause. That's why he warned Solomon and the Israelites. He warned them not to involve themselves in romantic relationships with non-Israelites who did not accept the exclusive worship of God. The people we are with influence us—for good or bad.

Why Serve God?

One day the sons of God came to present themselves before the LORD, and Satan also came with them. The LORD asked Satan, "Where have you come from?"

"From roaming through the earth," Satan answered Him, "and walking around on it."

Then the LORD said to Satan, "Have you considered My servant Job? No one else on earth is like him, a man of perfect integrity, who fears God and turns away from evil."

Satan answered the LORD, "Does Job fear God for nothing? Haven't You placed a hedge around him, his household, and everything he owns? You have blessed the work of his hands, and his possessions are spread out in the land. But stretch out Your hand and strike everything he owns, and he will surely curse You to Your face."

"Very well," the LORD told Satan, "everything he owns is in your power. However, you must not lay a hand on Job [himself]." So Satan went out from the LORD's presence.

Job 1:6–12 HCSB

o you serve God for what you think you'll get out of it, or because of what God will get out of it? That is, do you love yourself alone, or do you love God?

Satan is neither omniscient nor omnipresent. When Satan came before God, God asked him if he'd ever considered Job. God knew that Satan had already given Job considerable thought. That's why Satan knew who God was talking about. So what did Satan think about Job? Satan was certain that Job cared about God for the same reason most people care about anything, because of what he got out of it. Most relationships in the world are tit-for-tat—you scratch my back, I'll scratch yours. We spend time with people we like who like us back. We love people because, in some way, they're useful to us. They're fun, they make us laugh, or they benefit us. As soon as that benefit leaves—through disappointment, betrayal, mistreatment, withdrawal—we leave them in search of someone else. We find new friends who will treat us better.

So Satan had good reason to think Job would turn against God as soon as the pain started. Satan had a lot of experience with human beings, and he saw how people treated one another and why they usually related to one another. Satan didn't understand love. Job was a big surprise to him. Job was a man who served God because he loved God, not because he saw a payoff down the line for his love. Loving is not always the easy thing to do.

Day 41

Punishment Is Not Hate

I will love him and be kind to him
forever; my covenant with him will
never end. I will preserve an heir for
him; his throne will be as endless as
the days of heaven.

But if his descendants forsake my
instructions and fail to obey my
regulations, if they do not obey my
decrees and fail to keep my commands, then I will punish their sin
with the rod, and their disobedience
with beating.

But I will never stop loving him nor
fail to keep my promise to him.

No, I will not break my covenant; I
will not take back a single word I
said.

I have sworn an oath to David, and in
my holiness I cannot lie:

His dynasty will go on forever; his
kingdom will endure as the sun.

It will be as eternal as the moon, my
faithful witness in the sky!

Psalm 89:28–37 NLT

Some pain is the result of living in an imperfect world filled with imperfect creatures. The nature of freedom means the possibility of both good and bad. Some pain is the result of punishment. God's discipline, like that of an ideal parent, comes from love. When the neighbor children misbehave, I don't put them in time-out. I don't take their privileges from them. I don't send them to bed early. They're not mine. But my children I love, and so they will be punished if they misbehave. I care what sort of human beings they will grow up to become.

If God had just let his people do whatever they pleased whenever they pleased, he wouldn't have been showing them much love. God made a promise to David and his offspring: they would be his kings forever. But the fulfillment of that promise came at a cost. Because they belonged to him, God was responsible for their discipline. Discipline would save them. Only through discipline could God keep his promise that David's throne and kingdom would go on forever.

"Endure as the sun" and "as eternal as the moon" are not to be taken literally, since all physical things will have their end. But the timescale of the sun's and moon's existences, compared to human life spans and the transitory nature of all things human, serves as a useful picture of eternity. God's discipline is simply evidence of how much he loves us.

Love Is Not Stress-Free

If you make the Most High your dwelling—even the LORD, who is my refuge—then no harm will befall you, no disaster will come near your tent.
For he will command his angels concerning you to guard you in all your ways; they will lift you up in their hands, so that you will not strike your foot against a stone.
You will tread upon the lion and the cobra; you will trample the great lion and the serpent.

"Because he loves me," says the LORD, "I will rescue him; I will protect him, for he acknowledges my name.
He will call upon me, and I will answer him; I will be with him in trouble, I will deliver him and honor him.
With long life will I satisfy him and show him my salvation."

Psalm 91:9–16 NIV

t is odd, really, that human beings imagine that love can't hurt. God said, "I will rescue him." This implies a need for being rescued. If you need to be rescued, that means you're in a bad place, whether through poor choices or circumstances beyond your control.

God didn't say, "I'll never need to rescue you." God will not protect us from being uncomfortable, unhappy, lonely, disappointed, hungry, tired, short of cash, sick, or victimized. In the same breath that he said, "I will protect him," he said, "I will be with him in trouble."

We marvel when someone survives a disaster. We may comment on how God protected them. But why didn't God keep that bad thing from happening in the first place? We are impressed by how God preserved the lives of everyone in the plane that crashed in the Hudson River. But why did it crash in the first place? Wouldn't it have been easier to keep them all safe if the plane had just gone to its destination without incident?

God promised no harm (Psalm 91:10), and yet every day his people suffered death and destruction. How did that work? God promised long life, but he didn't promise we wouldn't die. After all, death isn't the worst thing that can happen to us. Whatever we face, God promises simply that he will be there with us. No matter what we face, we face nothing alone, no matter how much it hurts. "No harm" does not mean no pain. "No harm" means God's intentions are good, not evil.

Day 43

God's Love Song

I'll sing a ballad to the one I love,
    a love ballad about his vineyard:
The one I love had a vineyard,
    a fine, well-placed vineyard.
He hoed the soil and pulled the weeds,
    and planted the very best vines.
He built a lookout, built a winepress,
    a vineyard to be proud of.
He looked for a vintage yield of grapes,
    but for all his pains he got junk
      grapes.
"Now listen to what I'm telling you,
you who live in Jerusalem and
    Judah.
What do you think is going on
    between me and my vineyard?
Can you think of anything I could
    have done
    to my vineyard that I didn't do?
When I expected good grapes,
    why did I get bitter grapes?"

Isaiah 5:1–5 MSG

*U*nrequited love is unfulfilling. It is more painful than simple loneliness. But God is more familiar with unrequited love than any other kind. Sometimes God illustrated his messages by having his prophet perform an unusual action. In this passage, God told a parable. God pictured Israel as a carefully tended and protected vineyard. But despite all the efforts of the farmer, the vineyard yielded little but bitter grapes that were good for nothing.

It wasn't the farmer's fault that the vineyard was so bad. There was nothing more that the famer could have done. He did everything right; everything perfectly. He could have done nothing any better.

The point of God's parable was simple: Israel was without excuse. God was not demanding that they love him in the face of unrelenting misery. He did not ask them to return good for the evil being heaped upon them. He made it easy. He gave them anything they needed or asked for. He gave them everything and made them prosper. And what did God get back?

Most people respond to good gifts with at least a thank-you. They feel obligated to the person who has treated them well. But that wasn't so with God's people. The nicer he was to them, the worse they treated him. Like a bad vineyard, they gave him stuff that wouldn't even make good vinegar.

Despite the misery and evil Israel gave God, he always and forever did—and continued to do—what was good for them. God's love isn't dependent upon the actions of the ones he loves.

Covenant of Peace

"This is like the days of Noah to Me: when I swore that the waters of Noah would never flood the earth again, so I have sworn that I will not be angry with you or rebuke you.

Though the mountains move and the hills shake,
My love will not be removed from you and My covenant of peace will not be shaken," says your compassionate LORD.
"Poor [Jerusalem], storm-tossed, and not comforted, I will set your stones in black mortar, and lay your foundations in sapphires. I will make your battlements of rubies, your gates of sparkling stones, and all your walls of precious stones.
Then all your children will be taught by the LORD, their prosperity will be great, and you will be established on [a foundation of] righteousness.
You will be far from oppression, you will certainly not be afraid; you will be far from terror, it will certainly not come near you."

Isaiah 54:9–14 HCSB

When a judge offers a criminal mercy, his victim may feel that justice has not been served. God promised that he would never send a flood again to destroy the world. He did this despite the fact that the world's behavior didn't change; it remained just as wicked as before. Through the prophet Isaiah, God promised that he wouldn't be angry with Israel ever again. What he did to them that time, he'd never do to them again. He wouldn't ever repeat the punishment required by the covenant, their exile to Babylon. "Though the mountains move" and "the hills shake" he said, God's covenant of peace would not be shaken. It didn't matter how they acted now; they were his, and so everything would be fine.

God compared the captivity of Israel to the destruction of the world in the time of Noah. God destroyed Noah's world for its sins. Likewise, God destroyed Israel for its sins. In both cases, a remnant was preserved. And in both instances, God promised never to do it again. Israel's captivity in Babylon would not be repeated any more than there could be a rerun of Noah's Flood.

This was an illustration of God's grace. We are now at peace with God. Nothing is left of God's wrath, punishment, and anger to pour out on us. Whatever bad thing we do, however we act, God already punished us for it when Jesus accepted punishment for us. The covenant of peace stands because the punishment has already fallen. The fine has been paid, the sentence served.

Day 45

God Doesn't Think Like We Do

Come to me with your ears wide open.

Listen, and you will find life.

I will make an everlasting covenant with you.

I will give you all the unfailing love I promised to David . . .

Seek the Lord while you can find him.
Call on him now while he is near.
Let the wicked change their ways and banish the very thought of doing wrong.

Let them turn to the Lord that he may have mercy on them.
Yes, turn to our God, for he will forgive generously.
"My thoughts are nothing like your thoughts," says the Lord.
"And my ways are far beyond anything you could imagine.
For just as the heavens are higher than the earth, so my ways are higher than your ways and my thoughts higher than your thoughts."

Isaiah 55:3, 6–9 NLT

*E*very inclination of human beings is evil all the time. It was God's primary motivation for destroying the human race in the Flood (Genesis 6:5–6). The psalmist agreed that all human beings became corrupt and there was no one who did good, not even one (Psalm 14:1–3). If you're human, you fall into that characterization by God. We do not think as God thinks; we think selfishly. We tend to think and live and behave and do what we do, whether for God or for others, because of what we think we'll get out of it.

If we do good for God and think that he must therefore do something good for us, then we do not love God. And if we think God is waiting for certain good behavior before he'll bless us, then we think God does not love us. But God *does* love us, and that means he is good to us no matter what! He doesn't expect anything back.

The comfort for us is that God's thoughts and ways are nothing like ours. We love those who love us. It is easy for us to be nice to those who are nice to us. But how many people are nice to those who repay evil for good, who cause them pain, who harm them? How easy is it for us to forgive? But God's ways and his thoughts are not ours. Altruism is rare. We usually love only those who love us back. We get something out of our relationships, or we wouldn't maintain them. That's how we think. It isn't how God thinks. God is concerned only with what is best for us. He forgives us and asks us to change our thinking to be like his.

Redeeming Love

I will tell of the LORD's unfailing love.
I will praise the LORD for all he has
done.
I will rejoice in his great goodness to
Israel, which he has granted accord-
ing to his mercy and love.
He said, "They are my very own
people.
Surely they will not betray me again."
And he became their Savior.
In all their suffering he also suffered,
and he personally rescued them.
In his love and mercy he
redeemed them.

He lifted them up and carried them
through all the years.
But they rebelled against him and
grieved his Holy Spirit.
So he became their enemy and fought
against them.
Then they remembered those days of
old when Moses led his people out
of Egypt.
They cried out, "Where is the one who
brought Israel through the sea, with
Moses as their shepherd?
Where is the one who sent his Holy
Spirit to be among his people?"

Isaiah 63:7–11 NLT

According to Paul's definition of love, "Love always trusts" and "always hopes." That definition of love was reflected in what God said to his people through Isaiah. Surely they would never betray God again. God thought that because that's what love is like.

The first half of Isaiah's book relayed God's words of anger over their idolatry. He foretold Israel's coming exile for idolatry. But the last half of his book records God's words of hope and joy when he predicted a future where God forgave his people and reconciled them to him. God remembered the past with his people. He remembered how much they had suffered and how much that suffering hurt him. He remembered how much he loved them, and so he chose to forgive them one more time.

Such love seems unreasonable. The abused child, the beaten wife, and the kicked dog willingly return to the very ones who hurt them. They hope that it will be different next time. How foolish, how dangerous it appears to those of us outside watching. God forgives repeat offenders. He paid all our debts and didn't take away our credit card even as we tried to rack up more debt. He forgives all in perpetuity and forever. We can't max out God's credit card. That bill is always paid in full.

Unloved Prophet

The judges and the other people told the priests and prophets, "Since Jeremiah only told us what the LORD our God had said, we don't think he deserves to die."

Then some of the leaders from other towns stepped forward. They told the crowd that years ago when Hezekiah was king of Judah, a prophet named Micah from the town of Moresheth had said:

"I, the LORD All-Powerful, say Jerusalem will be plowed under and left in ruins.
Thorns will cover the mountain where the temple now stands." Then the leaders continued:

No one put Micah to death for saying that. Instead, King Hezekiah prayed to the LORD with fear and trembling and asked him to have mercy. Then the LORD decided not to destroy Jerusalem, even though he had already said he would. People of Judah, if Jeremiah is killed, we will bring a terrible disaster on ourselves.

After these leaders finished speaking, an important man named Ahikam son of Shaphan spoke up for me as well. And so, I wasn't handed over to the crowd to be killed.

Jeremiah 26:16–24 CEV

Governments, bureaucrats, and lawyers concern themselves with precedent—what has gone before. When confronted by the uncomfortable, inconvenient, and unpopular words of Jeremiah, their first thought was to get rid of those words by getting rid of the prophet himself. But then someone brought up the precedent of a previous inconvenient prophet named Micah. Since Micah had been left alive and free to go about his business, there was no reason for them to do anything to Jeremiah, either.

Precedent trumped what they had initially planned for Jeremiah, because a bureaucrat likes following the rules more than anything else. For them, the precedent of Micah meant they had fixed the problem of Jeremiah by letting him live.

So they did what was right with Jeremiah. But they did it not because they cared about what was right, not because they loved God, and certainly not because they loved Jeremiah. They did the right thing because the rules said they were supposed to. If the rules had told them to kill him, they'd have done so with no more passion than they had expended in freeing him.

Just because you do the right thing doesn't mean that you *are* righteous. Just because you did the loving thing, doesn't mean you *are* loving. It is easy to follow the rules, to follow the steps, to do what you're told. Following the rules is easy, but it never leads to righteousness.

Day 48

It's Because I Love You

The LORD appeared to us in the past,
saying: "I have loved you with an
everlasting love; I have drawn you
with loving-kindness.
I will build you up again and you will
be rebuilt, O Virgin Israel.
Again you will take up your tambou-
rines and go out to dance with the
joyful.
Again you will plant vineyards on the
hills of Samaria; the farmers will
plant them and enjoy their fruit.
There will be a day when watchmen
cry out on the hills of Ephraim,
'Come, let us go up to Zion, to the
LORD our God.' "
This is what the LORD says: "Sing with
joy for Jacob; shout for the foremost
of the nations.
Make your praises heard, and say,
'O LORD, save your people,
the remnant of Israel.'
See, I will bring them from the land of
the north and gather them from the
ends of the earth.
Among them will be the blind and
the lame, expectant mothers and
women in labor; a great throng will
return.
They will come with weeping; they will
pray as I bring them back.
I will lead them beside streams of
water on a level path where they will
not stumble, because I am Israel's
father, and Ephraim is my firstborn
son."

Jeremiah 31:3–9 NIV

❈

*L*ove is a fuzzy word in English. The first Hebrew word God used here for *love* has the same range of meaning as the English word. The word gets used for everything from how Abraham felt about his son Isaac to what Esau thought about his stew. And just as in English, it usually describes how husbands and wives feel about each other and about their children.

God promised to bring his people back home. Samaria was the capital city of Israel's Northern Kingdom. Zion was a hill in Jerusalem. Ephraim, the largest tribe of Israel, became a synonym for the nation as a whole. They would all return, no matter where or how far they might have wandered.

A second word in this passage is usually translated *loving-kindness*. Whereas people marry because they have "fallen in love," once married, they have obligations to one another that go beyond mere feelings that can ebb and flow. The word *loving-kindness* is used exclusively in that context. It refers to the obligations that exist between those bound by a contract like marriage. God's loving-kindness endures forever.

God Is Good

Yes, GOD's Message: "You're going to look at this place, these empty and desolate towns of Judah and streets of Jerusalem, and say, 'A wasteland. Unlivable. Not even a dog could live here.' But the time is coming when you're going to hear laughter and celebration, marriage festivities, people exclaiming, 'Thank GOD-of-the-Angel-Armies. He's so good! His love never quits,' as they bring thank offerings into GOD's Temple. I'll restore everything that was lost in this land. I'll make everything as good as new.' I, GOD, say so."

GOD-of-the-Angel-Armies says: "This coming desolation, unfit for even a stray dog, is once again going to become a pasture for shepherds who care for their flocks. You'll see flocks everywhere—in the mountains around the towns of the Shephelah and Negev, all over the territory of Benjamin, around Jerusalem and the towns of Judah—flocks under the care of shepherds who keep track of each sheep." GOD says so.

"Watch for this: The time is coming"—GOD's Decree—"when I will keep the promise I made to the families of Israel and Judah. When that time comes, I will make a fresh and true shoot sprout from the David-Tree. He will run this country honestly and fairly. He will set things right."

Jeremiah 33:10–15 MSG

*P*unishment is sometimes confusing. We forget all about the reason for our pain. In the middle of the sorrow, when the nation of Israel was a blasted wasteland and the cities were rubble piles, it was impossible for them to see the presence of God, to discern any hope. The hopeful words of the prophets were just so many empty platitudes. As hard as it had been during prosperity to hear God's promised judgment, so in the midst of judgment it was hard to hear his promise of renewal.

Our circumstances dictate what we hear, what we see, and what we think we know. When times are good, rejoicing comes naturally. The world is bright and happy. All circumstances are interpreted in the best possible way. At a basketball game, for instance, when the score is in our favor, we think every missed basket was "almost there." We think, *They're hot tonight.* But when the other team is ahead, the same missed basket becomes evidence that "they can't hit anything."

The "sprout from the David-Tree" was a promise fulfilled when the Messiah came and brought the kingdom of God into the hearts of his people. Just as everything was awful, God promised that someday everything would be wonderful. Do not let circumstances rob you of recognizing God's hand in your life.

A Fresh Start

"Here's what I'm going to do:
    I'm going to start all over again.
I'm taking her back out into the wilderness where we had our first date,
and I'll court her.
I'll give her bouquets of roses.
    I'll turn Heartbreak Valley into
    Acres of Hope.
She'll respond like she did as a young
girl, those days when she was fresh
out of Egypt.
"At that time"—this is God's Message still—"you'll address me, 'Dear
husband!'
Never again will you address me, 'My
slave-master!'
I'll wash your mouth out with soap,
get rid of all the dirty false-god
names, not so much as a whisper of
those names again.
At the same time I'll make a peace
treaty between you and wild animals
and birds and reptiles, and get rid of
all weapons of war.

Think of it! Safe from beasts and
bullies!
And then I'll marry you for good—
forever!
I'll marry you true and proper, in love
and tenderness.
Yes, I'll marry you and neither leave
you nor let you go.
You'll know me, God, for who I
really am.
"On the very same day, I'll answer"—
this is God's Message—"I'll answer
the sky, sky will answer earth, earth
will answer grain and wine and olive
oil, and they'll all answer Jezreel.
I'll plant her in the good earth.
    I'll have mercy on No-Mercy.
I'll say to Nobody, 'You're my dear
Somebody,'and he'll say 'You're
my God!'"

Hosea 2:14–23 MSG

God wanted to rekindle the spark that had gone out of his relationship with Israel. Despite Israel's infidelity with all the other gods and goddesses, God was willing to make a fresh start of it. He intended to sweep Israel off her feet once more, just as he had once done years before in those heady days when he rescued the Israelites from the slave masters of Egypt.

Jezreel in Hebrew means "God sows." Jezreel was the place where Jehu killed the priests, prophets, and followers of the false god Baal. God hoped it meant that Israel would finally turn to him and turn away from all the make-believe false gods.

Hosea's relationship with his prostitute wife, Gomer, served as the picture of what was going on between God and Israel. Hosea forgave Gomer's adultery. God forgave Israel's idolatry. The people of Israel meant more to God than the pain they had caused.

Day 51

Love Those Raisin Cakes

The LORD said to me, "Go again, love a woman who is loved by her husband, yet an adulteress, even as the LORD loves the sons of Israel, though they turn to other gods and love raisin cakes."

So I bought her for myself for fifteen shekels of silver and a homer and a half of barley.

Then I said to her, "You shall stay with me for many days. You shall not play the harlot, nor shall you have a man; so I will also be toward you."

For the sons of Israel will remain for many days without king or prince, without sacrifice or sacred pillar and without ephod or household idols.

Afterward the sons of Israel will return and seek the LORD their God and David their king; and they will come trembling to the LORD and to His goodness in the last days.

Hosea 3:1–5 NASB

🌼

*T*he world is bright and wonderful in the arms of love. Hosea loved his wife even though she was sleeping with other men, just as God loved Israel, even though they insisted on worshipping other deities. The raisin cakes, in this context, referred to the food used during the worship of other gods, such as Asherah.

Hosea's wife had left him, and she had fallen on hard times and become a slave.

Despite the fact that his wife had been and seemingly continued to be with other men, God instructed Hosea to buy her back. Hosea paid fifteen shekels of silver and a homer and a half of barley. Fifteen shekels was about six ounces of silver, while a homer and a half of barley was equivalent to fifteen ephahs, about 430 pounds. An ephah was usually worth about a shekel. So Hosea paid the equivalent of thirty shekels of silver for his wife, the standard price for a slave (Exodus 21:32). He told her she had to remain with him and that she could not continue to behave or live as a prostitute. In the same way, Israel would no longer have contact with those things that were part of their idolatrous relationships. That is, as Gomer must turn from other men, so Israel must turn away from other deities—from their idols, ephods, and pillars.

There was no sense here that Gomer had repented, any more than there was a sense that Israel had repented. Instead, they were being forced into a process that would *lead* them to repentance. Gomer was exiled from her lovers, and Israel was exiled from her land. Both exiles would lead to restoration. God's punishment transforms, restores, and beautifies.

Stealing and Adultery

Attention all Israelites! GOD's Message!
    GOD indicts the whole population:
"No one is faithful. No one loves.
    No one knows the first thing
      about God.
All this cussing and lying and killing,
    theft and loose sex, sheer anarchy,
    one murder after another!
And because of all this, the very land
    itself weeps and everything in it is
    grief-stricken—animals in the fields
    and birds on the wing, even the fish
    in the sea are listless, lifeless.
"But don't look for someone to blame.
    No finger pointing!
You, priest, are the one in the dock.
You stumble around in broad daylight,
And then the prophets take over and
    stumble all night.
    Your mother is as bad as you.
My people are ruined because they
    don't know what's right or true.
Because you've turned your back on
    knowledge, I've turned my back on
    you priests.
Because you refuse to recognize the
    revelation of God, I'm no longer
    recognizing your children."

Hosea 4:1–6 MSG

*H*ow can you have a relationship with someone you don't even know? If you don't love other people, then you don't love God—and vice versa. Not loving people results in all the crimes God listed in this passage. The crimes were merely symptoms of the underlying disease: an unfaithful and unloving heart.

Hosea prophesied during the reign of Jeroboam II of Israel, which corresponded to the reigns of Uzziah, Jotham, Ahaz, and Hezekiah in Judah. It was a prosperous time for the two kingdoms. Those who were in positions of leadership—particularly those tasked with the responsibility of teaching, had failed to live up to their calling. Priests and prophets had turned their back on God's revelation to his people. They did not concern themselves with what God had told them. They ignored the scripture and had no idea they mistreated the people around them. And they had no idea who God was, what he cared about, or what mattered to him.

What we know is what we will live. It is impossible for us to worship God in spirit and in truth if we know nothing about the one whom we claim to be worshipping. The religious establishment in Hosea's day had forgotten whom they were worshipping, and they imagined it didn't matter. They imagined that only enthusiasm, sincerity, and rituals counted. But what we know does matter. True worship is impossible without knowledge about the one being worshipped.

Unrequited Love

When Israel was a child, I loved him,
　　And out of Egypt I called My son.
　　　As they called them,
So they went from them;
They sacrificed to the Baals,
And burned incense to carved
　　images.
　　　I taught Ephraim to walk,
Taking them by their arms;
But they did not know that I
　　healed them.
　　　I drew them with gentle
　　　　cords,
　With bands of love,
And I was to them as those who
　　take the yoke from their neck.

I stooped and fed them.
　　He shall not return to the
　　　land of Egypt;
But the Assyrian shall be his king,
Because they refused to repent.
　　And the sword shall slash in
　　　his cities,
Devour his districts,
And consume them,
Because of their own counsels.
　　My people are bent on back-
　　　sliding from Me.
Though they call to the Most
　High,
None at all exalt Him.

Hosea 11:1–7 NKJV

✻

*G*od loved Israel as a father loves his son. Through Hosea, God compared his love for his people first to a betrayed husband, and then to a disappointed father. In context, Hosea's prophecy spoke to the fact that God had rescued his people from Egyptian bondage because of his great love, and that God would, for the same reason, send them to Assyria as punishment.

Matthew's gospel quoted the beginning of this passage in Hosea where God discussed what it was like raising his people from their childhood. Matthew applied the passage to the time Jesus' parents hid him in Egypt until Herod the Great was dead. Egypt and the bondage in slavery stood as a symbol of wickedness. How could Matthew apply this passage to Jesus? The New Testament authors used the exodus from Egypt as a picture of salvation. Even in the Old Testament, the prophets recognized that just as God had saved them from physical bondage, so also he had the power to rescue them from spiritual bondage. The exodus was Israel's salvation experience.

Israel's trip from Egypt, passing through the Red Sea, and receiving the commandments from God was paralleled in the life of Jesus' return from Egypt, being baptized in the Jordan by John, and then preaching about the kingdom. Raising children or saving humanity is not easy, but few worthwhile things are.

Love Rejoices Only in Good

Because of the violence you did to your close relatives in Israel, you will be filled with shame and destroyed forever.

When they were invaded, you stood aloof, refusing to help them.

Foreign invaders carried off their wealth and cast lots to divide up Jerusalem, but you acted like one of Israel's enemies.

You should not have gloated when they exiled your relatives to distant lands.

You should not have rejoiced when the people of Judah suffered such misfortune.

You should not have spoken arrogantly in that terrible time of trouble.

You should not have plundered the land of Israel when they were suffering such calamity.

You should not have gloated over their destruction when they were suffering such calamity.

You should not have seized their wealth when they were suffering such calamity.

You should not have stood at the crossroads, killing those who tried to escape.

You should not have captured the survivors and handed them over in their terrible time of trouble."

Obadiah 1:10–14 NLT

❀

*W*e're told to love our neighbors even if they're our enemies, but we tend to rejoice when bad things happen to our enemies. *Schadenfreude* is a German word that describes this paradox. Schadenfreude is the pleasure we experience when something bad happens to someone else, especially if we think that someone deserved it. But God told the Edomites not to rejoice when their enemy stumbled, and he criticized them for their reaction to Israel's punishment.

The Edomites were descendants of Esau, Israel's brother. Israel had deceived him and stolen his birthright. The prophet Obadiah brought God's message of judgment against the Edomites for rejoicing and plundering after the Babylonians destroyed Jerusalem. God condemned their attitude and their behavior and promised that consequently they would suffer his wrath. This was in keeping with God's promise to Abraham—those who blessed him would be blessed and those who cursed would be cursed. Although Esau and the Edomites were descended from Abraham, they were not in the line of promise. Israel alone had received Abraham's blessings.

God expects us to love our neighbors, even those neighbors who hate us. When our neighbors are in trouble, we're supposed to help them, whether they're nice to us or not. True love does not depend on the worthiness of the recipient.

Perseverance and Quitting

*I*f you're pounding on a rock with a sledge-hammer trying to break it, what happens if you stop one blow short of making it shatter? Or consider the Israelites who kept walking around Jericho even though the walls looked as strong as ever. It would have been easy to quit if all they thought of was their sore feet. It's hard not to give up when you're suffering. Yet suffering produces perseverance. When we recognize that suffering is the road to hope and not an end to itself but a journey, it changes everything. Don't stop one blow short.

※

The path of the righteous is like the light of dawn, shining brighter and brighter until midday.

Proverbs 4:18 HCSB

God Perseveres

Abram was ninety-nine years old when the LORD appeared to him again and said, "I am God All-Powerful. If you obey me and always do right, I will keep my solemn promise to you and give you more descendants than can be counted." Abram bowed with his face to the ground, and God said:

I promise that you will be the father of many nations. That's why I now change your name from Abram to Abraham. I will give you a lot of descendants, and in the future they will become great nations. Some of them will even be kings. I will always keep the promise I have made to you and your descendants, because I am your God and their God. I will give you and them the land in which you are now a foreigner. I will give the whole land of Canaan to your family forever, and I will be their God.

Genesis 17:1–8 CEV

Giving up is the easy way out. But it isn't God's way. God promised Abraham that he would have descendants who would become great nations with kings. The land of Canaan would be theirs.

The author of Genesis, writing after the exodus from Egypt, announced that it was Yahweh—translated as the word LORD in capital letters—who appeared to Abram when God promised him a son and changed his name to Abraham. *Abram* meant "exalted father," while *Abraham* meant "father of many." God changed Abram's name because Abraham would become the ancestor of more than one group of people, both the Jews and the Arabs.

The average life span is seventy years, give or take a bit. Abraham had to wait beyond a normal life span to receive what God had promised him. He had to wait until realistically all he had to look forward to was his own funeral. At that moment, however, God promised him a son. Abraham's descendants became the people of Israel—but not right away. Jacob's children would go to Egypt and have descendants who would be enslaved by Egypt for four hundred years.

Even after his people reached the promised land, God still would have to train them, leading them by prophet and punishment for centuries. It was not easy, and yet God never gave up on them. God persevered. He did not give up on Israel.

It is hard to keep working at a problem that never seems to be solved. Friends and family would probably support a decision to quit and turn back. They wouldn't want to see you suffer and be disappointed. But perseverance is a gift of God. Keep on going no matter how hard it is.

For the Foreseeable Future

God said to Abraham, "As for you, you shall keep my covenant, you and your offspring after you throughout their generations. This is my covenant, which you shall keep, between me and you and your offspring after you: Every male among you shall be circumcised. You shall circumcise the flesh of your foreskins, and it shall be a sign of the covenant between me and you. Throughout your generations every male among you shall be circumcised when he is eight days old, including the slave born in your house and the one bought with your money from any foreigner who is not of your offspring. Both the slave born in your house and the one bought with your money must be circumcised. So shall my covenant be in your flesh an everlasting covenant. Any uncircumcised male who is not circumcised in the flesh of his foreskin shall be cut off from his people; he has broken my covenant."

God said to Abraham, "As for Sarah your wife, you shall not call her Sarai, but Sarah shall be her name. I will bless her, and moreover I will give you a son by her. I will bless her, and she shall give rise to nations; kings of peoples shall come from her." Then Abraham fell on his face and laughed, and said to himself, "Can a child be born to a man who is a hundred years old? Can Sarah, who is ninety years old, bear a child?"

Genesis 17:9–17 NRSV

❀

*T*he symbol of God's relationship with Abraham and his descendants was a secret that only they could see. And only half his people carried it. Women were not circumcised. Were they not part of God's covenant? For them, the symbol of their connection to circumcision was secondary, made real in the marriage relationship when they became "one flesh." Their connection to the symbol also came from the fact that they were born of their fathers, related to their brothers, and mothers to their sons. The circumcised man would know he was circumcised. His father and mother and wife would know he was circumcised. No one else would ever see the circumcision. But it represented the connection between that person and his God. His life reflected the hidden symbol.

The symbol of our relationship with God is likewise hidden. More important than the symbol was the reality of a relationship with God, what God referred to as "circumcision of the heart," something that was true for both men and women. No one can see the interior circumcision either, except in the way it transforms a person. The evidence of a changed heart is demonstrated by how a life is lived.

Day 57

God Will Outlast You

God said to Moses: "Go to Pharaoh. I've made him stubborn, him and his servants, so that I can force him to look at these signs and so you'll be able to tell your children and grandchildren how I toyed with the Egyptians, like a cat with a mouse; you'll tell them the stories of the signs that I brought down on them, so that you'll all know that I am God."

Moses and Aaron went to Pharaoh and said to him, "God, the God of the Hebrews, says, 'How long are you going to refuse to knuckle under? Release my people so that they can worship me. If you refuse to release my people, watch out; tomorrow I'm bringing locusts into your country. They'll cover every square inch of ground; no one will be able to see the ground. They'll devour everything left over from the hailstorm, even the saplings out in the fields—they'll clear-cut the trees. And they'll invade your houses, filling the houses of your servants, filling every house in Egypt. Nobody will have ever seen anything like this, from the time your ancestors first set foot on this soil until today.'"

Then he turned on his heel and left Pharaoh.

Exodus 10:1–6 MSG

※

*J*ust as sometimes several whacks are needed to get a rock to break, so God knew it would take more than a single plague to get Pharaoh to break. Moses became discouraged at the beginning of the process, wondering why he didn't have immediate success in getting the people freed from their slavery. But thanks to God's instruction and encouragement, Moses kept confronting Pharaoh. Each time, the results were the same, with only minor variation. Every time, Pharaoh ended by telling Moses no.

Locust plagues weren't unusual in the ancient Middle East, though the severity of this particular plague was far above average. It was the worst such plague ever to have happened to Egypt. The timing of it was out of the ordinary also; it happened just when Moses said it would happen. Rather than the plague being a random event, it was clearly the hand of God.

The purpose of the plagues was not just to free the Israelites from Egyptian bondage. It also taught both Egyptians and Israelites that God was stronger than Pharaoh and all the many gods of Egypt. The plagues built their faith and helped prepare them—and their descendants—for the journey ahead. Don't be tempted to give up just because it's a long, hard trip.

Pay Attention to the Details

GOD spoke to Moses: "Tell the Israelites that they are to set aside offerings for me. Receive the offerings from everyone who is willing to give. These are the offerings I want you to receive from them: gold, silver, bronze; blue, purple, and scarlet material; fine linen; goats' hair; tanned rams' skins; dolphin skins; acacia wood; lamp oil; spices for anointing oils and for fragrant incense; onyx stones and other stones for setting in the Ephod and the Breastpiece. Let them construct a Sanctuary for me so that I can live among them. You are to construct it following the plans I've given you, the design for The Dwelling and the design for all its furnishings.

"First let them make a Chest using acacia wood: make it three and three-quarters feet long and two and one-quarter feet wide and deep. Cover it with a veneer of pure gold inside and out and make a molding of gold all around it. Cast four gold rings and attach them to its four feet, two rings on one side and two rings on the other. Make poles from acacia wood and cover them with a veneer of gold and insert them into the rings on the sides of the Chest for carrying the Chest. The poles are to stay in the rings; they must not be removed."

Exodus 25:1–15 MSG

※

*G*od cares about the details as well as he cares about the big picture. Just as God told Moses what to say regarding the plagues, so too God told Moses what decorations he wanted in the tabernacle. God explained the sorts of cloth to be used, details about the furniture, even the kinds of spices to be used for the anointing oils. He explained in detail how the ark was to be built and how it was to be carried. God had specific plans for how the Israelites were going to worship him formally.

Nothing is too small for God. Nothing is insignificant. God concerned himself with the number of gold rings to attach to the ark of the covenant, and he bothered to specify the kind of wood to use for the ark even when that wood was going to be covered over with a layer of gold. God concerned himself with those details knowing the finished box would wind up behind curtains that only one man once a year would even see. No matter how much you may think both you and your concerns are insignificant, they aren't. You are worth more to God than the choice of spices and the design of furniture.

Watching Hair Grow

The Lord said to Moses, "Give the following instructions to the people of Israel.

"If any of the people, either men or women, take the special vow of a Nazirite, setting themselves apart to the Lord in a special way, they must give up wine and other alcoholic drinks. They must not use vinegar made from wine or from other alcoholic drinks, they must not drink fresh grape juice, and they must not eat grapes or raisins. As long as they are bound by their Nazirite vow, they are not allowed to eat or drink anything that comes from a grapevine—not even the grape seeds or skins.

"They must never cut their hair throughout the time of their vow, for they are holy and set apart to the Lord. Until the time of their vow has been fulfilled, they must let their hair grow long. And they must not go near a dead body during the entire period of their vow to the Lord. Even if the dead person is their own father, mother, brother, or sister, they must not defile themselves, for the hair on their head is the symbol of their separation to God. This requirement applies as long as they are set apart to the Lord."

Numbers 6:1–8 NLT

Sometimes all you'll get out of a vow is distress. A Nazirite vow meant giving up haircuts and anything made out of grapes, among other things. People in the Bible who took a Nazirite vow include both Samson and Samuel, who were Nazirites from birth (Judges 13:7 and 1 Samuel 1:11). The apostle Paul took the vow as an adult, but only for a specified, limited period (Acts 18:18). Paul also paid for the ending ceremony for other Nazirites (Acts 21:17–26).

Why did God give the Israelites a spiritual discipline like the Nazirite vow? Did God delight in discomfort or deprivation? God is not brought nearer or better understood as a consequence of self-inflicted suffering. Rather, the discipline of the vow became the learning experience for the Nazirite—perseverance, seeing something through to the end. A person gets to know God better not in the pain but in the practice of God's qualities. A person who vows makes a promise that needs to be kept even when it is hard. To make a vow and to see it through to the end builds patience and perseverance, qualities that are valuable in life and in one's relationship with God. After all, God may not fulfill his promises instantly. His answers to our prayers often take time. We need to be patient.

Fire Snakes

They set out from Mount Hor by the way of the Red Sea, to go around the land of Edom; and the people became impatient because of the journey.

The people spoke against God and Moses, "Why have you brought us up out of Egypt to die in the wilderness? For there is no food and no water, and we loathe this miserable food."

The LORD sent fiery serpents among the people and they bit the people, so that many people of Israel died.

So the people came to Moses and said, "We have sinned, because we have spoken against the LORD and you; intercede with the LORD, that He may remove the serpents from us." And Moses interceded for the people.

Then the LORD said to Moses, "Make a fiery serpent, and set it on a standard; and it shall come about, that everyone who is bitten, when he looks at it, he will live."

And Moses made a bronze serpent and set it on the standard; and it came about, that if a serpent bit any man, when he looked to the bronze serpent, he lived.

Numbers 21:4–9 NASB

❈

*P*eople tend to give up on God at the first sign of trouble. On the other hand, they can praise him at the first hint of blessing. People can be fickle with their affections. The Israelites found it easy to complain about their condition. In fact, complaining is something that all humans everywhere are good at. The students at any school complain about the food in the cafeteria. Workers stand around the watercooler and gripe about the boss and all the work piling up. The unemployed grumble about the lines at the unemployment office and about how hard it is to find work. How much easier it would be to just lie down and die.

The Israelites had that chance. They were unhappy with their diet. They asked Moses why he had brought them out to the wilderness only to die. Snakes appeared and started biting people. Suddenly death was not merely a feared possibility—it was a present reality. God immediately provided an easy way to stay alive. The bronze snake became a cure for the poison. Those among the Israelites who were determined to die only had to close their eyes and give up. But persevering wasn't hard. The Israelites who didn't want to give up just had to alter their perspectives a little and look at the snake to know that God didn't want to kill them in the wilderness. God was near to them then just as he is near to us today. God never abandons his people.

Watch Where You're Going!

People of Israel, that's what the LORD
    has said to you.
But you don't have good sense, and
    you never listen to advice.
If you did, you could see where you
    are headed.
How could one enemy soldier chase a
    thousand of Israel's troops?
Or how could two of theirs pursue ten
    thousand of ours?
It can only happen if the LORD stops
    protecting Israel and lets the
    enemy win.
Even our enemies know that only our
    God is a Mighty Rock.

Our enemies are grapevines rooted in
    the fields of Sodom and
    Gomorrah.
The grapes they produce are full of
    bitter poison; their wine is more
    deadly than cobra venom.
But the LORD has written a list of their
    sins and locked it in his vault.
Soon our enemies will get what they
    deserve—suddenly they will
    slip, and total disaster will
    quickly follow.

Deuteronomy 32:28–35 CEV

The strongest person doesn't always win the race. At Jericho, God defeated the Midianite army of tens of thousands with barely three hundred Israelite men. The Midianites facing Gideon had no reason to think that they wouldn't be victorious against so small an army. But they lost all the same. But then there were times when Israel's forces severely outnumbered the enemy, and they lost all the same too.

Israel faced judgment. God had been warning his people for years that they would make mistakes. Nevertheless, those who stood arrayed against God's people didn't have a chance. In the end, no matter how good they looked, no matter how invincible, they were no better than Sodom and Gomorrah, the two cities that God had destroyed with fire and brimstone in a single day. God reassured his people that no matter what, God would avenge them. He was keeping track of all the wrongs they had done against his people. We may never see them judged, but we can trust that God will eventually call them to account.

Winning and losing are in God's hands, not in our own. We like to imagine we control our destinies, that our fate is ours to chose. But God is the one actually in charge, and no matter the odds, good or bad, God's way wins out.

Day 62

God Is Going to Be Around for a While

Indeed the LORD will vindicate his
people, have compassion on his
servants, when he sees that their
power is gone, neither bond nor free
remaining.
Then he will say: Where are their gods,
the rock in which they took refuge,
who ate the fat of their sacrifices,
and drank the wine of their
libations?
Let them rise up and help you, let
them be your protection!
See now that I, even I, am he; there is
no god beside me.
I kill and I make alive; I wound and I
heal; and no one can deliver from
my hand.
For I lift up my hand to heaven, and
swear:
As I live forever, when I whet my flash-
ing sword, and my hand takes hold
on judgment; I will take vengeance
on my adversaries, and will repay
those who hate me.
I will make my arrows drunk with
blood, and my sword shall devour
flesh—with the blood of the slain
and the captives, from the long-
haired enemy.

Deuteronomy 32:36–42 NRSV

All the king's horses and all the king's men couldn't put Humpty together again. God is neither a horse nor a king's man, but if the story were true, he could put Humpty together. Nothing is too hard for God. Just before the Israelites entered the land of Canaan, God repeated that he was the only God and the only one who could help them. The history of the Israelites ever after would largely consist of prophets and circumstances reminding them of what God said just before he gave them everything he'd ever promised.

When you have all the time in the world, you're not in much of a hurry. God is forever. God is all-powerful, so he can do whatever he wants, whenever he wants. In a contest between God's will and your will, God's will wins every time.

Moses had brought the Israelites to the promised land. Soon, Moses would die and the Israelites would begin fighting the Canaanites. God would make them victorious. But on the cusp of fulfilling their dreams, God warned them that they would quickly desert him. The Israelites would put their trust in other gods. They would devote time and treasure to them. And for what? When troubles came, their other gods wouldn't help. But even in the middle of their unfaithfulness, God would forgive them and rescue the Israelites. Be careful to place your trust in God. You can rely on him.

Whose Side Are You On?

It came to pass, when Joshua was by Jericho, that he lifted his eyes and looked, and behold, a Man stood opposite him with His sword drawn in His hand. And Joshua went to Him and said to Him, "Are You for us or for our adversaries?"

So He said, "No, but as Commander of the army of the LORD I have now come." And Joshua fell on his face to the earth and worshiped, and said to Him, "What does my Lord say to His servant?"

Then the Commander of the LORD's army said to Joshua, "Take your sandal off your foot, for the place where you stand is holy." And Joshua did so.

Now Jericho was securely shut up because of the children of Israel; none went out, and none came in. And the LORD said to Joshua: "See! I have given Jericho into your hand, its king, and the mighty men of valor. You shall march around the city, all you men of war; you shall go all around the city once. This you shall do six days. And seven priests shall bear seven trumpets of rams' horns before the ark. But the seventh day you shall march around the city seven times, and the priests shall blow the trumpets."

Joshua 5:13–6:4 NKJV

※

People like to believe that God is on their side. There is an abiding sense in most of us that if we believe what's right and do what's right, then God will have to back us. Wasn't God on the side of the Israelites when they went into their promised land? When Joshua asked the angel of the Lord that question, God's angel told him no.

The answer was puzzling. Weren't the Israelites God's chosen people? Hadn't he just rescued them from Egypt? How could God not be on their side?

God is on his own side. Joshua asked the wrong question. The real question for Joshua and the other freed slaves was the question for all of us: do we expect God to support our position and not that of our opposition? Or, to put it another way, do we expect God to back us, or do we expect to back God? God isn't on "our" side, whether it's a basketball game, a legal battle, or a war.

During the Civil War, Abraham Lincoln met with a group of civic leaders. One of them asked, "Mr. President, can we pray that God is on our side?" And Abraham Lincoln responded, "I won't join you in that prayer, but I'll join you in a prayer that we're on God's side."

Asking if God is on our side is the wrong question. The question we need to ask is more difficult: Are we on God's side?

My Heart in Perpetuity

After Solomon had completed building The Temple of GOD and his own palace, all the projects he had set his heart on doing, GOD appeared to Solomon again, just as he had appeared to him at Gibeon.

And GOD said to him, "I've listened to and received all your prayers, your ever-so-passionate prayers. I've sanctified this Temple that you have built: My Name is stamped on it forever; my eyes are on it and my heart in it always. As for you, if you live in my presence as your father David lived, pure in heart and action, living the life I've set out for you, attentively obedient to my guidance and judgments, then I'll back your kingly rule over Israel, make it a sure thing on a solid foundation. The same guarantee I gave David your father I'm giving you: 'You can count on always having a descendant on Israel's throne.'

"But if you or your sons betray me, ignoring my guidance and judgments, taking up with alien gods by serving and worshiping them, then the guarantee is off: I'll wipe Israel right off the map and repudiate this Temple I've just sanctified to honor my Name. And Israel will become nothing but a bad joke among the peoples of the world. And this Temple, splendid as it now is, will become an object of contempt; visitors will shake their heads, saying, 'Whatever happened here? What's the story behind these ruins?' Then they'll be told, 'The people who used to live here betrayed their GOD, the very God who rescued their ancestors from Egypt; they took up with alien gods, worshiping and serving them. That's what's behind this GOD-visited devastation.'"

1 Kings 9:1–7 MSG

*L*ove can hurt. God made a promise to Solomon that he would love Israel and Israel's king forever. It was up to Solomon and Solomon's offspring as to exactly how God would keep that promise. The Israelites were God's people, and their king was God's man. God was determined to fulfill his promise to love his people and his king no matter what. But there was an easy way and a hard way. One kind of love went directly to the blessings that Solomon and Israel most desired. But the other kind of love took a detour to discipline and pain.

Sadly, God had to show his love to Solomon's descendants and Israel through discipline—exile from the land and destruction of the monarchy because of the path God's king and people chose to take. After Nebuchadnezzar took King Zechariah into exile, no descendant of David ever sat on the throne in Jerusalem again.

Love never fails, and God never stopped loving his king or his people. That's why he disciplined them, after all. God will always love us the way we need to be loved.

Quitting Can Be Good

To this day they do according to the earlier customs: they do not fear the LORD, nor do they follow their statutes or their ordinances or the law, or the commandments which the LORD commanded the sons of Jacob, whom He named Israel; with whom the LORD made a covenant and commanded them, saying, "You shall not fear other gods, nor bow down yourselves to them nor serve them nor sacrifice to them.

"But the LORD, who brought you up from the land of Egypt with great power and with an outstretched arm, Him you shall fear, and to Him you shall bow yourselves down, and to Him you shall sacrifice.

"The statutes and the ordinances and the law and the commandment which He wrote for you, you shall observe to do forever; and you shall not fear other gods.

"The covenant that I have made with you, you shall not forget, nor shall you fear other gods.

"But the LORD your God you shall fear; and He will deliver you from the hand of all your enemies."

However, they did not listen, but they did according to their earlier custom.

So while these nations feared the LORD, they also served their idols; their children likewise and their grandchildren, as their fathers did, so they do to this day.

2 Kings 17:34–41 NASB

❈

*P*ractice makes perfect, but what if you're practicing the wrong way? You can get very good at swinging the bat with the wrong stance, the wrong grip, the wrong timing. Bad habits become hard to break. Perseverance in any direction, good or ill, becomes hard to stop.

Like father like son isn't necessarily a good thing. Perseverance isn't necessarily a good thing. God would like us to stop some of the things we keep doing. The nations that "feared the LORD" but also served their idols were Judah and Israel. God wanted them to quit their idolatry. But they persevered at the wrong thing. Hoshea, the last king of Israel, attempted to break free from Assyria and form an alliance with Egypt. The Assyrians responded by burning his capital to the ground and hauling him and many Israelites into exile. So God judged them for their persistent idolatry.

Bad habits are harder to give up than good ones. It is easier to keep doing the wrong thing than to keep doing the right thing. We seem more tempted to become weary in well-doing than in ill-doing. Generally you don't want to be a quitter. But sometimes a quitter is just what God wants you to be.

Love Is Forever

Once You spoke in vision to Your
godly ones,
> And said, "I have given help to
> one who is mighty;
> I have exalted one chosen from
> the people.
"I have found David My servant;
> With My holy oil I have
> anointed him,
With whom My hand will be
established;
> My arm also will strengthen him.

"The enemy will not deceive him,
> Nor the son of wickedness
> afflict him.
"But I shall crush his adversaries
before him,
> And strike those who hate him.
"My faithfulness and My lovingkindness will be with him,

> And in My name his horn will be
> exalted.
"I shall also set his hand on the sea
> And his right hand on the rivers.
"He will cry to Me, 'You are my Father,
> My God, and the rock of my
> salvation.'
"I also shall make him My firstborn,
> The highest of the kings of
> the earth.
"My lovingkindness I will keep for him
forever,
> And My covenant shall be con-
> firmed to him.
"So I will establish his descendants
forever
> And his throne as the days of
> heaven.

Psalm 89:19–29 NASB

❋

*D*oes God always keep his promises? God promised that David would always have a descendant ruling in Jerusalem. But the last descendant of David to sit on a throne was Zechariah, more than five hundred years before the birth of Jesus. Nebuchadnezzar dragged Zechariah to Babylon along with the people of Judah. There has not been a king in Jerusalem ever since. Even now, there are no genealogical records to connect any modern human beings with David.

God told David that his covenant had been established with him forever. God promised to crush his adversaries. But King Zechariah's sons were slaughtered in front of him just before he had his eyes poked out. The king of Israel was to be "the highest of the kings of the earth" and God's "firstborn," and yet Zechariah was dragged to Babylon in chains by Nebuchadnezzar.

So how did God keep his promise to David? Jesus Christ, the Messiah, the descendant of David, is the King and Creator of the universe: both son of David and Son of God. Jesus rules over God's people from heaven, sitting on David's throne there. We can't always see the promises that God keeps.

Stand by Me

He always stands by his covenant—the
   commitment he made to a thousand
   generations.
This is the covenant he made with
   Abraham and the oath he swore to
   Isaac.
He confirmed it to Jacob as a decree,
   and to the people of Israel as a
   never-ending covenant:
"I will give you the land of Canaan as
   your special possession."

He said this when they were few in
   number, a tiny group of strangers in
   Canaan.
They wandered from nation to nation,
   from one kingdom to another.
Yet he did not let anyone oppress
   them.
He warned kings on their behalf:
"Do not touch my chosen people,
   and do not hurt my prophets."

Psalm 105:8–15 NLT

*F*riends and family may let us down. There is no guarantee that they'll be there when we call. They may have had the best of intentions when they made promises, but things happen and circumstances change. They have their own problems to deal with. It just may not be a good time.

God wanted to make sure his people understood his commitment, and so he used symbols they understood. He spoke in their language. He borrowed things from their culture and turned them to his purposes. People made contracts with each other to make certain they'd keep their promises. Nations signed treaties. God took those images and used them to help his people understand the depth of his relationship with them. He bound himself to them. What he said was dependable. God was more than just a friend announcing he'd call back later.

Circumstances were never beyond God's control. Even when Israel was insignificant, barely more than a large family, God entered into a covenant—a treaty—with them. He kept his word then, when they were small, when they were barely anyone, when there was no reason even to give his word to them in the first place. It wasn't as if they had something to give to God. Nor was it as if he made promises so the people would give him something he didn't have. The Israelites didn't have to be concerned in their current circumstances. God protected his people in the past, took them through all their hard times, and didn't forsake them. There was no reason to think he would go back on his word.

God is consistent in how he treats his people. Look at what he did yesterday, and you'll see what he'll do for you tomorrow.

Day 68

Ever Hearing, Never Understanding

One of the seraphs flew to me with a live coal in his hand, which he had taken with tongs from the altar. With it he touched my mouth and said, "See, this has touched your lips; your guilt is taken away and your sin atoned for."

Then I heard the voice of the Lord saying, "Whom shall I send? And who will go for us?"
And I said, "Here am I. Send me!"
He said, "Go and tell this people:
"'Be ever hearing, but never understanding; be ever seeing, but never perceiving.'
Make the heart of this people calloused; make their ears dull and close their eyes.
Otherwise they might see with their eyes, hear with their ears, understand with their hearts, and turn and be healed."
Then I said, "For how long, O Lord?"
And he answered:
"Until the cities lie ruined and without inhabitant, until the houses are left deserted and the fields ruined and ravaged, until the LORD has sent everyone far away and the land is utterly forsaken.
And though a tenth remains in the land, it will again be laid waste.
But as the terebinth and oak leave stumps when they are cut down, so the holy seed will be the stump in the land."

Isaiah 6:6–13 NIV

"Never volunteer" is the old Army adage, but when someone's in love he's quick to do anything his beloved asks. Isaiah fell in love with God. So Isaiah volunteered to be God's prophet. He not only heard God's words but he also saw him and cried out that he was ruined. In John 12, the apostle John quoted Isaiah's words as an explanation for why many people didn't accept that Jesus was the Messiah.

The seraphs mentioned in this passage were a kind of angel mentioned only by Isaiah. He said they had three pairs of wings: one pair for flying, one pair for covering their faces, and one pair for covering their feet. Beyond that, we know nothing else about the seraphs. After the seraph told Isaiah his guilt was taken away, God spoke.

God told Isaiah to prophesy to the Israelites, but warned him that they would not pay any attention to him. Isaiah wanted to know how long he'd have to give them God's words if they weren't going to listen. God told Isaiah to keep talking until the nation was destroyed by the invading Assyrians. He added one note of comfort: Israel's devastation would not last forever. Isaiah had the strength to do the hard thing God had asked of him because his love for God carried him through. God's love can carry us through anything we have to face too.

Day 69

Never Tired

The holy God asks,
   "Who compares with me?
Is anyone my equal?"
Look at the evening sky!
   Who created the stars?
Who gave them each a name?
Who leads them like an army?
The Lord is so powerful that none of
   the stars are ever missing.
You people of Israel, say,
   "God pays no attention to us!
   He doesn't care if we are treated
   unjustly."
But how can you say that?
Don't you know?
Haven't you heard?

The Lord is the eternal God,
   Creator of the earth.
He never gets weary or tired; his
   wisdom cannot be measured.
The Lord gives strength to those who
   are weary.
Even young people get tired, then
   stumble and fall.
But those who trust the Lord will find
   new strength.
They will be strong like eagles soaring
   upward on wings; they will walk
   and run without getting tired.

Isaiah 40:25–31 CEV

The more we learn, the less we know, and the more insignificant we become. When Isaiah wrote about the stars, both he and his listeners had a limited sense of what they were and how many there were.

On any given clear night, far from city lights, an observer might be able to see, at most, six thousand stars. But that is but a tiny fraction of the number of stars that actually exist. Within just our own galaxy, the Milky Way, it is estimated that there are 200 billion stars. Our Milky Way galaxy is but one of at least 100 billion galaxies that are known to exist. There are actually more stars in the sky than there are grains of sand on all the seashores and deserts on earth. If you were to start taking a photograph of each star in just our galaxy, and took a photograph once every second, twenty-four hours a day, seven days a week, it would take more than thirty-one years just to photograph one billion stars. To take photos of all the stars in the Milky Way galaxy would take more than the length of all recorded human history. And then you'd have another 100 billion galaxies to go. Yet God created all those stars and keeps track of each one. No wonder his wisdom can't be measured!

The universe is immense, beyond human comprehension. Our place in it is vanishingly small. Our weakness is profound. But God is bigger than it all. His strength is beyond measure. And yet, that infinite God pays attention to us.

🌼🌼🌼🌼🌼🌼🌼🌼🌼🌼🌼🌼🌼🌼🌼🌼🌼🌼🌼🌼🌼🌼🌼🌼🌼🌼🌼🌼🌼🌼🌼

Ever Since You Were Born

Listen to me, descendants of Jacob, all
you who remain in Israel.
I have cared for you since you
were born.
Yes, I carried you before you
were born.
I will be your God throughout your
lifetime—until your hair is white
with age.
I made you, and I will care for you.
I will carry you along and save you.
To whom will you compare me?
Who is my equal?
Some people pour out their silver and-
gold and hire a craftsman to make a
god from it.

Then they bow down and worship it!
They carry it around on their shoul-
ders, and when they set it down, it
stays there.
It can't even move!
And when someone prays to it, there is
no answer.
It can't rescue anyone from trouble.
Do not forget this! Keep it in mind!
Remember this, you guilty ones.
Remember the things I have done in
the past.
For I alone am God!
I am God, and there is none like me.

Isaiah 46:3–9 NLT

🌼

*M*isplaced trust is disastrous. The Israelites had depended on their idols. They had ignored the one God who could have helped them. The Assyrians invaded Israel around 722 BC. They took captive a little fewer than thirty thousand people, mostly the upper classes and the well-to-do because they were most likely to lead an uprising. God spoke to the Israelites who were left behind after that destruction, who wondered what the future might hold.

Even though they might not have realized it, God had been taking care of them since before they were born, and he would continue caring for them until they were old and white-haired. There was no stage of their life where God was not present. They could not get away from him, no matter how hard they might try. There was no way that God had or ever would abandon them.

In contrast, the idols were nothing more than the wood, stone, or precious metals out of which they were manufactured. How could the Israelites ever compare God to them? They were worthless. We don't carry idols like those any longer, but we've made new ones of our jobs, our abilities, our technology. But if the economy goes bad, if we get sick or disabled, if the batteries run out, or we can't find a plug, what then? The new idols are as worthless as the wood, stone, and metal ones.

The End from the Beginning

Remember this, fix it in mind,
    take it to heart, you rebels.
Remember the former things, those of
    long ago;
    I am God, and there is no other;
    I am God, and there is none
        like me.
I make known the end from the begin-
    ning, from ancient times, what is
    still to come.
I say: My purpose will stand, and I will
    do all that I please.
From the east I summon a bird of
prey; from a far-off land, a man to
fulfill my purpose. What I have said,
that will I bring about; what I have
planned, that will I do.
Listen to me, you stubborn-hearted,
    you who are far from righteousness.
I am bringing my righteousness near,
    it is not far away; and my salvation
    will not be delayed. I will grant
    salvation to Zion, my splendor to
    Israel.

Isaiah 46:8–13 NIV

*G*od's sense of speed bears no resemblance to ours. So we need to have the mind of Christ.

God's people, the Israelites, had been conquered and captured by the Assyrians. Judah would soon follow when the Babylonians conquered them. But that exile would end when God rescued them with the Persians. Persia—modern-day Iran—was to the east of Israel. The "bird of prey" from the east, "a man to fulfill my purpose," was none other than Cyrus the Great. In Isaiah 45:1 God referred to Cyrus as his "anointed," from the Hebrew word *messiah.* The Jewish captivity in Babylon and Assyria would end because God would use Cyrus to destroy the Babylonian Empire and set his people free. God gave Isaiah the prophecy of Cyrus about a hundred years before it would happen, and yet God said that the fulfillment—the rescue—was going to happen soon.

When Isaiah prophesied, the Babylonians hadn't yet conquered or attacked Jerusalem. The seventy years of captivity were far in the future. Before the Jewish people even needed salvation from the Babylonians, God was already letting them know that he would save them. From a human standpoint, a hundred years doesn't seem to be very soon. We become impatient just waiting a couple of seconds for a Web page to come up or two minutes for our food to heat in a microwave. God's definition of *quick* is not nearly as rushed as ours.

Eagerly Waiting

The LORD says:
You are my people and nation!
    So pay attention to me.
My teaching will cause justice to shine
    like a light for every nation.
Those who live across the sea are
    eagerly waiting for me to
    rescue them.
I am strong and ready; soon I will
    come to save and to rule
    all nations.

Look closely at the sky!
    Stare at the earth.
The sky will vanish like smoke; the
    earth will wear out like clothes.
Everyone on this earth will die
    like flies.
But my victory will last; my saving
    power never ends.

Isaiah 51:4–6 CEV

God offers a lifetime warranty like no other. The earth wearing out like a garment is an image quoted by the author of Hebrews 1:11 as part of his exaltation of the Son of God, who created the universe and who, unlike the angels, always was and always will be.

Isaiah brought God's message to the Israelites who were facing the destruction of all they knew. The Assyrians were going to carry them far away to live as exiles. But they could not be separated from God no matter how far they went. Instead, he would ultimately defeat the Assyrians and bring his people back to their home. Someday the Israelites would accept God's truth and everything he had tried to teach them.

But God's salvation—his justice, his teaching—were not just for the people of Israel. Instead, God was for all people everywhere. He told the Israelites that soon he would reach out to everyone everywhere and rule over all the nations, not just over Israel. Israel had picked up the disease of their neighbors, the delusion that their God was small and ruled over only the lands that Israel called home. To be exiled from one's homeland was not just to be removed from what you had known, it was also to be removed from the care—and reach—of your god.

But God told them that he was more than just for the nations. Look at the sky, he told them, look at the earth. In Hebrew thinking, to refer to heaven and earth in the same passage meant "everything that there is." It was equivalent to our modern conception of the universe. God wanted them to see he ruled everywhere and through all time. The universe will end, but neither God nor his salvation will. We have a future with God.

My Deliverance Will Be Forever

Listen to me, you who know righteousness, you people who have my teaching in your hearts; do not fear the reproach of others, and do not be dismayed when they revile you.
For the moth will eat them up like a garment, and the worm will eat them like wool; but my deliverance will be forever, and my salvation to all generations.
Awake, awake, put on strength, O arm of the LORD!
Awake, as in days of old, the generations of long ago!

Was it not you who cut Rahab in pieces, who pierced the dragon?
Was it not you who dried up the sea, the waters of the great deep; who made the depths of the sea a way for the redeemed to cross over?
So the ransomed of the LORD shall return, and come to Zion with singing; everlasting joy shall be upon their heads; they shall obtain joy and gladness, and sorrow and sighing shall flee away.

Isaiah 51:7–11 NRSV

God promised Isaiah, and the remnant who had remained faithful to him, that they need not fear what their enemies said about them. The idolaters would soon be history. Even the Babylonians would someday be gone, just as every other enemy in the past had gone away. God had taken care of the Egyptians, and he would take care of the current bad guys too.

God used a familiar old story well known to the ancient world to make his point. It was a pagan story. Rahab was a mythological beast, a dragon in charge of chaos, that had become a symbol for Egypt in Isaiah's day. (This Rahab was not the Rahab of Jericho.) In the myth, this Rahab was chopped to bits by God, allowing God to then create the universe. In a similar way, Egypt had been overthrown by the plagues that God had sent against it, allowing God to make his people into a new nation. So God repurposed this old story and reapplied it.

God promised his people that just as he had delivered them from Egypt, so he would deliver them from the Assyrians and the Babylonians who had taken them captive. The current oppressors would meet the same end as all other oppressors who dared to rise up against God's people. Remembering how God has helped in the past can help us fight discouragement today.

Day 74

An Everlasting Name

Thus says the LORD:
 "Keep justice, and do
  righteousness,
 For My salvation is about to come,
 And My righteousness to
  be revealed.
 Blessed is the man who does this,
 And the son of man who lays hold
  on it;
 Who keeps from defiling
  the Sabbath,
 And keeps his hand from doing
  any evil."
Do not let the son of the foreigner
Who has joined himself to
 the LORD
Speak, saying,

 "The LORD has utterly separated
 me from His people";

Nor let the eunuch say,
 "Here I am, a dry tree."
For thus says the LORD:

 "To the eunuchs who keep
  My Sabbaths,
 And choose what pleases Me,
 And hold fast My covenant,
 Even to them I will give in
  My house
 And within My walls a place and
  a name
 Better than that of sons
  and daughters;
 I will give them an
  everlasting name
 That shall not be cut off."

Isaiah 56:1–5 NKJV

❈

God addressed people who had believed and obeyed him but who still felt estranged because of circumstances beyond their control, such as where they were born or of what had been done to them.

Non-Israelites who converted to Judaism often felt excluded. After the captivity, many were in fact cut off. The Samaritans and others who could not demonstrate a genealogy, a direct connection to Jewish ancestors, were excluded from participation in most aspects of worship. According to the Mosaic legislation, a descendant of Aaron who had "damaged testicles" (Leviticus 21:20 NLT) could not serve as a priest in the temple. Eunuchs—men who were castrated when they were young—would not even have testicles, of course, and so all eunuchs descended from Aaron would be excluded. Worse for them, of course, was the simple fact that they could never have children—no descendants. When they died, there would be nothing of them left behind. But God reassured them, as he reassured the foreign convert, that they belonged to God as much as anyone else might, and that if they had accepted God's covenant, they were as everlasting as God was. Our great-grandchildren might not remember our names, but God will never forget us. We'll be part of him forever.

From the Rising of the Sun

The LORD saw,
And it was displeasing in His sight
 that there was no justice.
And He saw that there was no man,
 And was astonished that there was
 no one to intercede;
 Then His own arm brought salva-
 tion to Him,
 And His righteousness
 upheld Him.
He put on righteousness like a
 breastplate,
 And a helmet of salvation on
 His head;
 And He put on garments of ven-
 geance for clothing
 And wrapped Himself with zeal as
 a mantle.
According to their deeds, so He
 will repay,
 Wrath to His adversaries, recom-
 pense to His enemies;

To the coastlands He will make
 recompense.
So they will fear the name of the LORD
 from the west
 And His glory from the rising of
 the sun,
 For He will come like a
 rushing stream
 Which the wind of the LORD drives.
"A Redeemer will come to Zion,
 And to those who turn from
 transgression in Jacob," declares
 the LORD.
"As for Me, this is My covenant with
 them," says the LORD: "My Spirit
 which is upon you, and My words
 which I have put in your mouth
 shall not depart from your mouth,
 nor from the mouth of your offspring, nor from the mouth of your
 offspring's offspring," says the LORD,
 "from now and forever."

Isaiah 59:15–21 NASB

Truth and justice are not as popular as some slogans might make us think. Instead, people would rather know what they're comfortable with.

God understands that the world of human relationships and activities sometimes fails to work the way he'd like. In the time of Isaiah, the Israelite government hated his message. Most of the people in the land also disliked what he had to say. The truth can be painful, unpopular, and make no one feel good. God predicted the destruction of his nation by the invasion of powerful neighbors. People were suffering, which is why God would bring judgment. Those who heard God's message accused Isaiah of being a traitor and of hating his own countrymen. They were wrong. He loved Israel just as God loved Israel.

But God's people needed the Babylonians in order to be saved. So God took the task of rescuing his people upon himself. Salvation was dependent upon him alone. He would see to it that his people came back from captivity in Babylon too.

Why Cling to Old Lies?

"In that day," says the LORD, "the enemy will break open the graves of the kings and officials of Judah, and the graves of the priests, prophets, and common people of Jerusalem. They will spread out their bones on the ground before the sun, moon, and stars—the gods my people have loved, served, and worshiped. Their bones will not be gathered up again or buried but will be scattered on the ground like manure. And the people of this evil nation who survive will wish to die rather than live where I will send them. I, the LORD of Heaven's Armies, have spoken!

"Jeremiah, say to the people, 'This is what the LORD says:

"When people fall down, don't they get up again?
When they discover they're on the wrong road, don't they turn back?

Then why do these people stay on their self-destructive path?
Why do the people of Jerusalem refuse to turn back?
They cling tightly to their lies and will not turn around.
I listen to their conversations and don't hear a word of truth.
Is anyone sorry for doing wrong?
Does anyone say, "What a terrible thing I have done"?
No! All are running down the path of sin as swiftly as a horse galloping into battle!
Even the stork that flies across the sky knows the time of her migration,
as do the turtledove, the swallow, and the crane.
They all return at the proper time each year.
But not my people!
They do not know the LORD's laws.

Jeremiah 8:1–7 NLT

※

*O*nce something becomes a habit, it's hard to break, even when we know that it's not good for us. Israel had been worshipping false gods for generations.

When Babylon invaded, they took their stuff. Part of an army's pay was the plunder. And since human beings tended to bury valuable items with their dead, armies commonly dug up the graves. For this reason, the bones of the dead wound up scattered beneath the sky. Those who had spent their lives worshipping the sun, moon, and stars were exposed to them until they rotted away.

Israel had repeatedly offered sacrifices and said prayers to their false gods. The rituals never satisfied and the gods never answered, but that didn't stop the Israelites because they knew nothing else.

We can't embrace lies and expect to discern the truth when we hear it.

Day 77

Running with Horses

Jeremiah, if you get tired in a race
against people, how can you possibly run against horses?
If you fall in open fields, what will
happen in the forest along the Jordan River?
Even your own family has turned
against you.
They act friendly, but don't trust them.
They're out to get you, and so is everyone else.
I loved my people and chose them as
my very own.
But now I will reject them and hand
them over to their enemies.
My people have turned against me and
roar at me like lions.
That's why I hate them.

My people are like a hawk surrounded
and attacked by other hawks.
Tell the wild animals to come and eat
their fill.
My beautiful land is ruined like a field
or a vineyard trampled by shepherds
and stripped bare by their flocks.
Every field I see lies barren, and no
one cares.
A destroying army marches along desert roads and attacks everywhere.
They are my deadly sword; no one is
safe from them.
My people, you planted wheat, but
because I was furious, I let only
weeds grow.
You wore yourselves out for nothing!

Jeremiah 12:5–13 CEV

*Y*ou think things are hard now? Sometimes it can be just the beginning—and for good reason. Jeremiah was just a man. Like any human being, he occasionally was worn down by the day-to-day grind. But God offered him neither commiseration nor relief. Rather, he added to Jeremiah's burden by letting him know that what he had experienced up until then was just the beginning. His previous experiences were nothing compared to what was coming. He had to learn to buck up.

What would Jeremiah face? He would be imprisoned in a cistern, he'd be mocked, and eventually he'd be taken as an unwilling captive down to Egypt by people who called him a liar when he told them something they didn't want to hear. But those people took him with them anyway because they believed he was a prophet who heard God. They just didn't believe he always told them what God had actually said.

If the people of Israel had turned against God, Jeremiah had no reason for surprise when they wouldn't listen to God's spokesperson. Jeremiah found strength to continue his work because he knew he and God were working toward the same thing. Like Jeremiah, we're not facing our lives alone even when every minute seems like a struggle.

You Don't Quit What You Love

You are saying about this city, "By the sword, famine and plague it will be handed over to the king of Babylon"; but this is what the LORD, the God of Israel, says: I will surely gather them from all the lands where I banish them in my furious anger and great wrath; I will bring them back to this place and let them live in safety. They will be my people, and I will be their God. I will give them singleness of heart and action, so that they will always fear me for their own good and the good of their children after them. I will make an everlasting covenant with them: I will never stop doing good to them, and I will inspire them to fear me, so that they will never turn away from me. I will rejoice in doing them good and will assuredly plant them in this land with all my heart and soul.

This is what the LORD says: As I have brought all this great calamity on this people, so I will give them all the prosperity I have promised them.

Jeremiah 32:36–42 NIV

*W*ho's your boss? Whom are you really working for? Israel's contract with God stipulated that they had to worship God exclusively and love their neighbors as themselves. But not long after the death of Moses, when they stood triumphant over the newly conquered promised land, Joshua found it necessary to ask them to choose whom they were going to serve—God or someone else. In the centuries that followed, God sent prophets who asked the same question Joshua had asked on the banks of the Jordan River: Whom will you serve? God sent them ever-escalating troubles for disobedience, just as the contract had stipulated.

The prophet Jeremiah's message was not only one of destruction, however. God also gave him messages of hope for the people of Judah. The judgment God was bringing by means of the Babylonians would solve his long-standing problem with his people. God could reassure them that everything would finally turn out for the best. They remained his people, and he had not torn up his contract with them. The reconciliation between God and his people would make the long struggle to achieve it worth the effort.

Most people quit the things they are doing as soon as they start to get uncomfortable. But some people find it easy to keep doing what they love, even if it's hard. God loved his people, so he kept working with them. You mean more to God than your problem.

You Cannot Change the Laws of Physics

The word of the LORD came to Jeremiah, saying,

"Thus says the LORD, 'If you can break My covenant for the day and My covenant for the night, so that day and night will not be at their appointed time, then My covenant may also be broken with David My servant so that he will not have a son to reign on his throne, and with the Levitical priests, My ministers. As the host of heaven cannot be counted and the sand of the sea cannot be measured, so I will multiply the descendants of David My servant and the Levites who minister to Me.' "

And the word of the LORD came to Jeremiah, saying,

"Have you not observed what this people have spoken, saying, 'The two families which the Lord chose, He has rejected them'? Thus they despise My people, no longer are they as a nation in their sight.

"Thus says the LORD, 'If My covenant for day and night stand not, and the fixed patterns of heaven and earth I have not established, then I would reject the descendants of Jacob and David My servant, not taking from his descendants rulers over the descendants of Abraham, Isaac and Jacob. But I will restore their fortunes and will have mercy on them.' "

Jeremiah 33:19–26 NASB

❀

*T*he creation is the mirror of the creator. The moral laws and the laws of nature are reflections of who and what God is. God links the permanence of the covenant with his people with the laws of the universe. The word translated as *patterns* is the word usually rendered *statute* or *ordinance*. That is, the laws. Breaking them is just as foolish as trying to count the sand or the stars.

God reassured his people that just as surely as the sun rose and set, and just as surely as the patterns of nature went about their courses, so God's promises to his people and their king were secure. Just because the people of Judah were being punished didn't mean God didn't love them anymore. And just because they were going into exile didn't mean God had rejected them. They would continue to be his people whether they remained in their land or not. God was not limited like the so-called gods who had power only within their own lands. God's domain was complete and absolute. God's laws are as unchangeable as the laws of physics, and just as the laws of physics cannot be broken, neither can God's love for his people be broken.

Whether They Listen or Not

All around him was a glowing halo, like a rainbow shining in the clouds on a rainy day. This is what the glory of the LORD looked like to me. When I saw it, I fell face down on the ground, and I heard someone's voice speaking to me.

"Stand up, son of man," said the voice. "I want to speak with you." The Spirit came into me as he spoke, and he set me on my feet. I listened carefully to his words. "Son of man," he said, "I am sending you to the nation of Israel, a rebellious nation that has rebelled against me. They and their ancestors have been rebelling against me to this very day. They are a stubborn and hard-hearted people. But I am sending you to say to them, 'This is what the Sovereign LORD says!' And whether they listen or refuse to listen—for remember, they are rebels—at least they will know they have had a prophet among them.

"Son of man, do not fear them or their words. Don't be afraid even though their threats surround you like nettles and briers and stinging scorpions. Do not be dismayed by their dark scowls, even though they are rebels. You must give them my messages whether they listen or not. But they won't listen, for they are completely rebellious! Son of man, listen to what I say to you. Do not join them in their rebellion. Open your mouth, and eat what I give you."

Ezekiel 1:28–2:8 NLT

*F*earing God means you have nothing else to be afraid of. While in some cases "fear of God" might mean something like "reverential awe," in most cases it simply means to be afraid. The Hebrew word for *fear* in "fearing God" is the same word used when an angel tells someone to "fear not." Being afraid of God is the first step in a relationship with him. Only as we realize God will forgive us can our fear turn to hope and love. Besides reassuring Ezekiel that he would protect him from all harm, God also told Ezekiel that even though the people would know he was a prophet, few would listen. Then God fed him a small scroll to symbolize that Ezekiel's prophetic message would come from God.

Most people would have a hard time digging a bunch of holes only to fill them in again. But essentially that's what Ezekiel faced in his ministry. Ezekiel was okay with that. He would persevere no matter how tough or unrewarding it got. He saw that his success came not in the reactions of his audience but in the performance of his duty. He trusted that God would work things out whether Ezekiel could see how or not.

Faith and Doubt

We don't doubt that the tire is flat when we can clearly see it. And we don't doubt that the tire is no longer flat when we can see it fixed. When we doubt God, doubt ourselves, and doubt our friends and family, we imagine that doubt undermines our faith. Many of us are afraid of doubt. But faith dwells in the shadow of doubt. Doubts can be doubted too. We need to recognize doubt for what it is—the soil in which faith grows. The flip side of doubt is faith.

❋

If you do not stand firm in your faith, then
you will not stand at all.
Isaiah 7:9 HCSB

Holy Ground

GOD saw that he had stopped to look. God called to him from out of the bush, "Moses! Moses!"

He said, "Yes? I'm right here!"

God said, "Don't come any closer. Remove your sandals from your feet. You're standing on holy ground."

Then he said, "I am the God of your father: The God of Abraham, the God of Isaac, the God of Jacob."

Moses hid his face, afraid to look at God.

GOD said, "I've taken a good, long look at the affliction of my people in Egypt. I've heard their cries for deliverance from their slave masters; I know all about their pain. And now I have come down to help them, pry them loose from the grip of Egypt, get them out of that country and bring them to a good land with wide-open spaces, a land lush with milk and honey, the land of the Canaanite, the Hittite, the Amorite, the Perizzite, the Hivite, and the Jebusite.

"The Israelite cry for help has come to me, and I've seen for myself how cruelly they're being treated by the Egyptians. It's time for you to go back: I'm sending you to Pharaoh to bring my people, the People of Israel, out of Egypt."

Exodus 3:4–10 MSG

❈

*T*he people of Israel were in slavery because God had put them there. God sent Joseph to Egypt so that he could save his family's lives and the lives of the Egyptians. Then God sent Jacob and the rest of Joseph's brothers to Egypt to live with him. With Moses, the time had come at last to rescue the Israelites from a bondage that had not come through disobedience but through obedience to God's commands. God wanted the Egyptians to know about him. He wanted the Israelites to learn about God's power and to give them a picture of salvation.

God intended to take the land of the Canaanites and give it to the Israelites. The Canaanites, Amorites, Perizzites, Hivites, and Jebusites all spoke a language similar to or in many cases the same as that of the Hebrews. The Hittites, however, spoke a language related to the languages of Europe and India. The people living in the promised land were disunited. Only their evil religion, a religion that included child sacrifice, bound them together. Israel would get their land because God needed to punish the Canaanites.

Sometimes doing what God wants might not be pleasant. We simply must trust that God knows what he is doing and that he is doing it for a very good reason.

Who Is This God Person?

Moses and Aaron came and said to Pharaoh, "Thus says the LORD, the God of Israel, 'Let My people go that they may celebrate a feast to Me in the wilderness.' "

But Pharaoh said, "Who is the LORD that I should obey His voice to let Israel go? I do not know the LORD, and besides, I will not let Israel go."

Then they said, "The God of the Hebrews has met with us. Please, let us go a three days' journey into the wilderness that we may sacrifice to the LORD our God, otherwise He will fall upon us with pestilence or with the sword."

But the king of Egypt said to them, "Moses and Aaron, why do you draw the people away from their work? Get back to your labors!"

Again Pharaoh said, "Look, the people of the land are now many, and you would have them cease from their labors!"

Exodus 5:1–5 NASB

✽

Speaking hard truth to power sometimes turns out poorly. Egyptian royalty had power and usually cared only about retaining it. They saw no reason to pay attention to the truth. After all, if people don't have power, how can they have anything useful to say?

Moses' request to set his people free made sense. But Pharaoh had a different perspective. What slave wouldn't like to get time off from his or her labors? What slave wouldn't want to be free? Moses told the pharaoh nothing the pharaoh didn't already know about slaves. So why should he pay any attention? So what if Moses had talked to the slaves' God and that God wanted the slaves to go free? If that God were so great, then why were his people slaves? Pharaoh believed himself a god. Given his circumstances, Pharaoh thought he was stronger than the slaves were and thus stronger than the slaves' God. He had no reason to pay any attention to Moses or the God he claimed to represent.

People are not quick to change their minds about anything—be it God or their favorite cola—until and unless it stops working for them. Those at ease, those who are in positions of power and wealth, are not likely to change their minds about much. A comfortable life would have to become uncomfortable before the truth Moses was speaking could be heard by the powerful Pharaoh. Our hearts can't be changed until we fully realize they need to be changed.

Jumping Frogs of Egypt

The LORD said to Moses, "Go back to Pharaoh and announce to him, 'This is what the LORD says: Let my people go, so they can worship me. If you refuse to let them go, I will send a plague of frogs across your entire land. The Nile River will swarm with frogs. They will come up out of the river and into your palace, even into your bedroom and onto your bed! They will enter the houses of your officials and your people. They will even jump into your ovens and your kneading bowls. Frogs will jump on you, your people, and all your officials.' "

Then the LORD said to Moses, "Tell Aaron, 'Raise the staff in your hand over all the rivers, canals, and ponds of Egypt, and bring up frogs over all the land.' " So Aaron raised his hand over the waters of Egypt, and frogs came up and covered the whole land! But the magicians were able to do the same thing with their magic. They, too, caused frogs to come up on the land of Egypt.

Then Pharaoh summoned Moses and Aaron and begged, "Plead with the LORD to take the frogs away from me and my people. I will let your people go, so they can offer sacrifices to the LORD."

Exodus 8:1–8 NLT

Tyrants are not quick to keep their promises. As his nation was overrun with frogs, Pharaoh recognized that they came from the God of the slaves, and he asked Moses to get his God to send them away. In exchange, Pharaoh promised to do just what the slaves' God said.

This was but the second plague that had come upon the land of Egypt, and like the plague before, though it was annoying, it wasn't exactly devastating to his kingdom. Frogs didn't bite. They just made noise and startled people by their presence. And they were messy, and, really, you didn't want them in your food or in bed with you.

But like many a tyrant after him, Pharaoh asked for concessions, and then when they were given, asked for more. He never did what he promised in return. And so the pharaoh was quick to give in to Moses. Once he got what he wanted, however, he felt no obligation to follow through on his promise. Pharaoh was contemptuous of his slaves and of their God. But Pharaoh underestimated the sort of god the slaves had. God cared about the oppressed and was willing—and able—to help them.

God Doesn't Play Fair

The LORD said to Moses, "Get up early in the morning and present yourself to Pharaoh when you see him going out to the water. Tell him: This is what the LORD says: Let My people go, so that they may worship Me. But if you will not let My people go, then I will send swarms of flies against you, your officials, your people, and your houses. The Egyptians' houses will swarm with flies, and so will the land where they live. But on that day I will give special treatment to the land of Goshen, where My people are living; no flies will be there. This way you will know that I, the LORD, am in the land. I will make a distinction between My people and your people. This sign will take place tomorrow."

And the LORD did this. Thick swarms of flies went into Pharaoh's palace and his officials' houses. Throughout Egypt the land was ruined because of the swarms of flies. Then Pharaoh summoned Moses and Aaron and said, "Go sacrifice to your God within the country."

But Moses said, "It would not be right to do that, because what we will sacrifice to the LORD our God is detestable to the Egyptians. If we sacrifice what the Egyptians detest in front of them, won't they stone us? We must go a distance of three days into the wilderness and sacrifice to the LORD our God as He instructs us."

Exodus 8:20–27 HCSB

God knows the best way to change a mind. He was in no hurry with Pharaoh's mind. God distinguished between his own and those who were not his own. This illustrated an important point about God's love. How his love is perceived depends on the relationship the object of God's love has with him. Those who love God will recognize God's hand as beneficial. Those who do not love God can't see it. The Egyptians suffered, but for the Israelites, the plague brought them one step closer to their liberation.

For the first time, Pharaoh's magicians found themselves unable to duplicate the plague and informed Pharaoh that clearly there was a god involved in events. But the plague went away the last time Pharaoh lied to Moses. Despite his refusal to keep his promise to Moses, the previous plague had not come back. Pharaoh believed the slaves' God was not as powerful as he was, so he didn't intend to back down. He needed the slaves.

God was patient, and though it might have seemed to both Pharaoh and the Israelites that nothing was changing, God's plan was in motion. It would work when and how it was supposed to.

The Plague

The LORD sent Moses with this message for the king of Egypt:

The LORD God of the Hebrews commands you to let his people go, so they can worship him. If you keep refusing, he will bring a terrible disease on your horses and donkeys, your camels and cattle, and your sheep and goats. But the LORD will protect the animals that belong to the people of Israel, and none of theirs will die. Tomorrow is the day the LORD has set to do this.

It happened the next day—all of the animals belonging to the Egyptians died, but the Israelites did not lose even one. When the king found out, he was still too stubborn to let the people go.

The LORD said to Moses and Aaron:

Take a few handfuls of ashes from a stove and have Moses throw them into the air. Be sure the king is watching. The ashes will blow across the land of Egypt, causing sores to break out on people and animals.

So they took a few handfuls of ashes and went to the king. Moses threw them into the air, and sores immediately broke out on the Egyptians and their animals. The magicians were suffering so much from the sores, that they could not even come to Moses. Everything happened just as the LORD had told Moses—he made the king too stubborn to listen to Moses and Aaron.

Exodus 9:1–12 CEV

※

*P*ain will get your attention if nothing else will. Egypt's plagues finally turned from mere annoyance to physical pain and financial devastation. With the fifth plague, Pharaoh's property was being lost. He didn't want to let the Jewish people go, because they were part of his wealth.

But then he started losing animals and people. The lost people cut into his nonslave labor pool as well as his army. The nation of Egypt depended on the sea and the desert to protect the kingdom. But with no soldiers able to fight, Egypt was vulnerable to possible attack. The danger posed by the slaves' God was suddenly becoming serious; the slaves were becoming a threat to his wealth.

Even so, he wasn't willing to give in to the slaves' God. He was Pharaoh, and Egypt was the most powerful nation on earth. Eventually, the gods of Egypt would rise up against Moses. Eventually, the world would make sense again and the slaves would know their place and stay there.

Pharaoh didn't yet understand that his sense of power was an illusion and that the slaves' God was the only real God. False gods may look good and work for a while, but they always and ultimately come up painfully short. The more you have invested in them, the more painful is the lesson.

What Have We Done?

The LORD said to Moses:

Tell the Israelites to turn back and camp in front of Pi-hahiroth, between Migdol and the sea, in front of Baal-zephon; you shall camp opposite it, by the sea. Pharaoh will say of the Israelites, "They are wandering aimlessly in the land; the wilderness has closed in on them." I will harden Pharaoh's heart, and he will pursue them, so that I will gain glory for myself over Pharaoh and all his army; and the Egyptians shall know that I am the LORD. And they did so.

When the king of Egypt was told that the people had fled, the minds of Pharaoh and his officials were changed toward the people, and they said, "What have we done, letting Israel leave our service?" So he had his chariot made ready, and took his army with him; he took six hundred picked chariots and all the other chariots of Egypt with officers over all of them. The LORD hardened the heart of Pharaoh king of Egypt and he pursued the Israelites, who were going out boldly. The Egyptians pursued them, all Pharaoh's horses and chariots, his chariot drivers and his army; they overtook them camped by the sea, by Pi-hahiroth, in front of Baal-zephon.

Exodus 14:1–9 NRSV

*W*ith the death of the firstborn, Pharaoh finally gave in to Moses and Moses' God. He granted the slaves—together with all their children and wives and all their livestock—permission to take three days off work to go somewhere to sacrifice to their God. Egypt was a mess; people were dead. For the benefit of the nation, he had to let the slaves' God have his way.

But after the three days had passed, the slaves didn't return. Pharaoh had to act. He'd been suspicious all along that Moses had in mind something more than just a worship service of singing, praying, and animal sacrifice. Pharaoh had lied repeatedly to Moses, but he now saw that Moses had been lying to him just as much. Pharaoh couldn't let Moses steal his property. He had to get it all back. He sent his army to track down and return the runaway slaves. Plagues or not, Pharaoh wasn't ready to lose his property for good.

Once again, however, Pharaoh underestimated God. He had lost his farms and his wealth, and he was about to lose his power. His army would be wiped out. Human power is no match for God's power.

How to Treat Your Slaves

When you buy a Hebrew slave, he is to serve for six years; then in the seventh he is to leave as a free man without paying anything. If he arrives alone, he is to leave alone; if he arrives with a wife, his wife is to leave with him. If his master gives him a wife and she bears him sons or daughters, the wife and her children belong to her master, and the man must leave alone.

But if the slave declares: "I love my master, my wife, and my children; I do not want to leave as a free man," his master is to bring him to the judges and then bring him to the door or doorpost. His master must pierce his ear with an awl, and he will serve his master for life.

When a man sells his daughter as a slave, she is not to leave as the male slaves do. If she is displeasing to her master, who chose her for himself, then he must let her be redeemed. He has no right to sell her to foreigners because he has acted treacherously toward her. Or if he chooses her for his son, he must deal with her according to the customary treatment of daughters.

Exodus 21:2–9 HCSB

❀

*S*lavery has been part of the human condition through all recorded history. God liked slavery no more than he liked divorce. But he knows the fallen condition of human beings, and so he set up regulations in order to protect the weak from the strong. In most cultures, slaves had no more rights than farm animals. In the Mosaic legislation, God required that his people treat slaves well: the need to love others extended to them too. Slavery was ordinarily a temporary status in Israel. As a person went into slavery, so they would leave slavery.

For those whose status changed while they were slaves—for instance in marriage—the slave could choose to make his condition permanent by means of a ceremony. Poking an awl through the slave's ear signified his decision to give up his freedom for good. Although piercing of ears and noses was not uncommon in ancient Israel, this piercing signified more than adornment.

A woman sold into slavery did not become a sex slave. If her master intended to use her sexually, then she had to be granted certain rights—the same rights as any other wife. If her husband married an additional wife, she retained her standing as his wife. And if she was divorced, then she had the same protections as any other divorced woman. She could no longer be considered a slave, nor did she have to pay for her freedom. It is God's desire that we act conscientiously and deal fairly with all people.

Show Me Your Way

Moses said to the Lord, "See, You say to me, 'Bring up this people.' But You have not let me know whom You will send with me. Yet You have said, 'I know you by name, and you have also found grace in My sight.' Now therefore, I pray, if I have found grace in Your sight, show me now Your way, that I may know You and that I may find grace in Your sight. And consider that this nation is Your people."

And He said, "My Presence will go with you, and I will give you rest."

Then he said to Him, "If Your Presence does not go with us, do not bring us up from here. For how then will it be known that Your people and I have found grace in Your sight, except You go with us? So we shall be separate, Your people and I, from all the people who are upon the face of the earth."

So the Lord said to Moses, "I will also do this thing that you have spoken; for you have found grace in My sight, and I know you by name."

And he said, "Please, show me Your glory."

Then He said, "I will make all My goodness pass before you, and I will proclaim the name of the Lord before you. I will be gracious to whom I will be gracious, and I will have compassion on whom I will have compassion."

Exodus 33:12–19 NKJV

There's always room for worry. No matter how clearly God acts, human beings will want more reassurance. Moses had seen many miracles. He regularly talked to God face-to-face. And yet, with all of that, he wondered who would be going with them to the promised land. He wondered if he knew for sure where they would be going and what they would be doing.

God did not berate Moses, did not criticize him, did not even ask him a pointed question. Instead, God quickly reassured Moses and told him again that he would be with him. Moses—who saw God in the burning bush, on Mount Sinai, and even in the Tent of Meeting where he talked to God as a man might converse with a friend—then asked God if he could see his glory. And God gave him what he asked!

No matter how close we think we are to God, it is easy to start taking our closeness with God for granted. We need a bigger fix just to feel normal and to know that God is still there. God accommodated Moses, so don't be afraid to tell God about the doubts and weariness you may be feeling.

Free at Last

You are to count seven sabbatic years, seven times seven years, so that the time period of the seven sabbatic years amounts to 49. Then you are to sound a trumpet loudly in the seventh month, on the tenth [day] of the month; you will sound it throughout your land on the Day of Atonement. You are to consecrate the fiftieth year and proclaim freedom in the land for all its inhabitants. It will be your Jubilee, when each of you are to return to his property and each of you to his clan. The fiftieth year will be your Jubilee; you are not to sow, reap what grows by itself, or harvest its untended vines. It is to be holy to you because it is the Jubilee; you may [only] eat its produce [directly] from the field.

In this Year of Jubilee, each of you will return to his property. If you make a sale to your neighbor or a purchase from him, do not cheat one another.

Leviticus 25:8–14 HCSB

God cares about those who have nothing left to give. In ancient Israel, people could sell their property or even themselves if they became impoverished. But every fifty years all the people enslaved were supposed to be freed during the year of Jubilee. Property was supposed to return to its original owner.

For the entire year of Jubilee, no plowing of fields, no planting of crops, and no harvesting were to be done. By taking a year off to do no work, they would face clearly what was always true: God was the source of their sustenance. Jubilee restored economic balance in the land. And it reminded the people that God really could provide for them—just as he had for the forty years of wandering in the wilderness after the exodus.

During the time of Moses and Joshua, the land had been distributed to the tribes and families of Israel. It was supposed to remain with those tribes and families for all time. Unfortunately, though God told the Israelites to "proclaim liberty throughout the land" (Leviticus 25:10 NRSV) every year of Jubilee, the harsh reality of Israelite society was that Jubilee never came.

Idolatry wasn't the only reason God brought the Babylonians against the Israelites. God also sent them into captivity because the powerful had oppressed the weak. The powerful never set anyone free. They never returned a bit of land. So the Babylonians took only a minority of Israelites into captivity—the upper classes who had oppressed the poor by denying them their Jubilees. Those whom they had oppressed were left behind. Freedom finally came as the oppressors were dragged away. God granted mercy with his judgment.

It Isn't About You

As Samuel grew old, he appointed his sons to be judges over Israel. Joel and Abijah, his oldest sons, held court in Beersheba. But they were not like their father, for they were greedy for money. They accepted bribes and perverted justice.

Finally, all the elders of Israel met at Ramah to discuss the matter with Samuel. "Look," they told him, "you are now old, and your sons are not like you. Give us a king to judge us like all the other nations have."

Samuel was displeased with their request and went to the LORD for guidance.

"Do everything they say to you," the LORD replied, "for it is me they are rejecting, not you. They don't want me to be their king any longer. Ever since I brought them from Egypt they have continually abandoned me and followed other gods. And now they are giving you the same treatment. Do as they ask, but solemnly warn them about the way a king will reign over them."

So Samuel passed on the LORD's warning to the people who were asking him for a king.

1 Samuel 8:1–10 NLT

*J*ust because people are good Christians and have good relationships with God doesn't mean their kids will too. Each person stands before God alone.

Samuel had been raised by Eli, whose children had been corrupt and evil. Sadly, Samuel's children turned out much as Eli's had. The people of Israel had no complaint with Samuel, but Samuel's children were clearly never going to be the spiritual leaders that he was. And so they asked that Samuel find someone else to become king for them.

Samuel was reluctant, and God warned the people that a king would not fix things. After all, a monarchy is hereditary; the king's children would take his place when he died. And if Samuel, as good as he was, produced children that the people didn't want ruling over them, what really made them think that getting a king, however good he might be, would solve that fundamental problem?

God compared their request for a new king with their continual problem with idolatry. Why? They kept looking to someone other than God to lead them and to fix their problems. They weren't willing to follow God at all. Samuel wasn't being rejected, even though their words hurt him and made him think that maybe they thought his life had not been worthwhile. The people were rejecting God. It wasn't about Samuel at all. God can use people to solve problems. The mistake comes in thinking that people can take the place of God altogether.

It's Good to Be King

[Samuel] said, "These are the rights of the king who will rule over you: He can take your sons and put them to his use in his chariots, on his horses, or running in front of his chariots. He can appoint them for his use as commanders of thousands or commanders of fifties, to plow his ground or reap his harvest, or to make his weapons of war or the equipment for his chariots. He can take your daughters to become perfumers, cooks, and bakers. He can take your best fields, vineyards, and olive orchards and give them to his servants. He can take a tenth of your grain and your vineyards and give them to his officials and servants. He can take your male servants, your female servants, your best young men, and your donkeys and use them for his work. He can take a tenth of your flocks, and you yourselves can become his servants. When that day comes, you will cry out because of the king you've chosen for yourselves, but the LORD won't answer you on that day."

The people refused to listen to Samuel. "No!" they said. "We must have a king over us. Then we'll be like all the other nations: our king will judge us, go out before us, and fight our battles."

Samuel listened to all the people's words and then repeated them to the LORD. "Listen to them," the LORD told Samuel. "Appoint a king for them."

Then Samuel told the men of Israel, "Each of you, go back to your city."

1 Samuel 8:11–22 HCSB

※

*T*he problems of the world cannot be solved simply by having a government, by changing the government, or by passing new legislation. People remain what they are, corrupt and corruptible, and putting some in charge of the others merely ensures that they will take advantage of those they rule.

Samuel let the people know exactly what they would get if they got a king. He let them know they would not be happy with him, that they would wish they could be freed from his tyranny. Despite Samuel's warning, they still insisted on having a king.

God was not surprised. Just as God does not like divorce, he still gave Moses the rules to regulate it in the law. He didn't like slavery, but he gave them the rules to regulate it. And he didn't like monarchy, but he gave them the rules for how a king should reign. He placed limits on the king's power. God works hard to protect the less powerful from the more powerful.

🌼🌼🌼🌼🌼🌼🌼🌼🌼🌼🌼🌼🌼🌼🌼🌼🌼🌼🌼🌼🌼🌼🌼🌼🌼🌼🌼

Hiding Among the Baggage

Samuel summoned the people to the LORD at Mizpah and said to them, "Thus says the LORD, the God of Israel, 'I brought up Israel out of Egypt, and I rescued you from the hand of the Egyptians and from the hand of all the kingdoms that were oppressing you.' But today you have rejected your God, who saves you from all your calamities and your distresses; and you have said, 'No! but set a king over us.' Now therefore present yourselves before the LORD by your tribes and by your clans."

Then Samuel brought all the tribes of Israel near, and the tribe of Benjamin was taken by lot. He brought the tribe of Benjamin near by its families, and the family of the Matrites was taken by lot. Finally he brought the family of the Matrites near man by man, and Saul the son of Kish was taken by lot. But when they sought him, he could not be found. So they inquired again of the LORD, "Did the man come here?" and the LORD said, "See, he has hidden himself among the baggage." Then they ran and brought him from there. When he took his stand among the people, he was head and shoulders taller than any of them. Samuel said to all the people, "Do you see the one whom the LORD has chosen? There is no one like him among all the people." And all the people shouted, "Long live the king!"

1 Samuel 10:17–24 NRSV

🌼

*S*amuel already knew who would become king. But he went through the motions of casting lots—in essence, rolling dice or flipping coins—because the people needed to understand that God had selected the king. As the lot was repeatedly cast, the field narrowed until the lot fell on the individual whom God had determined all along would become king—Saul.

Samuel had already told Saul that he would be king. And yet when the selection was made, Saul was hard to find, but not because he was busy. Saul had gone into hiding. Like Adam and Eve hiding from God in the garden of Eden after they had eaten from the forbidden fruit, Saul was hiding from God—and the people of Israel. He was not pleased with God's will for his life.

Abraham Lincoln compared being president to being tarred and feathered and said that if weren't for the honor of the thing, he'd have rather skipped it all together. Saul apparently could identify with that point of view.

But as Adam and Eve discovered, so Saul discovered: you can't hide from God, and you can't resist God's will.

You Think You're in Control?

When do mountain goats and deer
    give birth?
Have you been there when their young
    are born?
How long are they pregnant before
    they deliver?
Soon their young grow strong and
    then leave to be on their own.
Who set wild donkeys free?
I alone help them survive in salty
    desert sand.
They stay far from crowded cities and
    refuse to be tamed.
Instead, they roam the hills, searching
    for pastureland.

Would a wild ox agree to live in your
    barn and labor for you?
Could you force him to plow or to
    drag a heavy log to smooth out
    the soil?
Can you depend on him to use his
    great strength and do your
    heavy work?
Can you trust him to harvest your
    grain or take it to your barn from
    the threshing place?

Job 39:1–12 CEV

We don't have as much control over our lives as we think. We cannot control the day of our birth or the day of our death. We have no power over rain or drought, storm or earthquake, illness or health. But we'd like to be in control.

God confronted Job with how little he controlled. He couldn't make wild animals domesticated. He couldn't breed them or take their offspring for food or sacrifice. He couldn't rely on them to help him with his harvests.

Job's friends believed that good things came to the good and bad to the bad. They thought how people behaved determined the outcome of their lives. That's why they insisted that Job had to be bad. If the circumstances of life were not dependent upon their choices of behavior, that meant they couldn't prevent bad things from happening to them. Their lives were in God's hands, not theirs. They didn't like that. And really, Job didn't like it either. He—and his friends—thought his life to be in his own hands more than in God's. God pointed out to him that was both silly and foolish. Whose hands were better—the hands of Job, who knew and understood little, or the hands of God, who knew and understood everything? So what if Job didn't understand why the bad stuff had happened to him. Job didn't understand a lot of things. What else was new?

Our desire to control and manipulate our environment leads us to absurdities. We become superstitious, imagining that certain rituals, certain objects, can somehow allow us to control those things that we otherwise cannot. But if you ask God to reveal these absurdities to you, he will.

Who's the Boss?

Why do the nations rage,
  And the people plot a vain thing?
The kings of the earth set themselves,
  And the rulers take counsel
    together,
Against the Lord and against His
  Anointed, saying,
"Let us break Their bonds in
  pieces
And cast away Their cords
  from us."

He who sits in the heavens shall laugh;
  The Lord shall hold them in
    derision.
Then He shall speak to them in His
    wrath,
And distress them in His deep
  displeasure:
"Yet I have set My King
  On My holy hill of Zion."

Psalm 2:1–6 NKJV

✽

*R*esistance is futile. It is wasted effort to fight God and his "Anointed." Neither the author nor the moment in time when this psalm was composed are known. But it seems most likely that it was written during a time when Israel had a monarch sitting on the throne. Both kings and priests were anointed with oil when they took their positions of authority. Any king or priest could be called an anointed one. For that matter, it could be applied to anyone who was wholly devoted to God's service, of whatever sort. But the word *anointed* is a translation of the Hebrew word that also comes into English as "Messiah" or "Christ." The apostles Peter and John applied this psalm to Jesus (Acts 4:25–26). The psalmist pictured both the king of Israel on his physical throne as well as the Son of God on his heavenly throne. People—the nations around Israel—wanted to break free from what they perceived to be God's unreasonable demands. God's response was derisive laughter. His demands were not unreasonable, unless they found a parachute strapped to their back or a seat belt across their lap and shoulders too restraining. The so-called constraints were hardly that; they existed for their benefit. They made life better, not worse.

Some people decided to reject God because they thought he stood in the way of human pleasure. Only after they burned themselves out, like the prodigal son, would they come to realize that perhaps the "old man" wasn't so stupid after all and may have been giving them guidelines for their own good. That could have saved them a lot of pain along the way.

God wants what is best for us. But often we'd rather listen to ourselves or other people, who know next to nothing. We find it hard to believe that God really knows what is best, but the Bible's cloud of witnesses tells us that he unquestionably does.

God Is Not Silent

The Mighty One, God, the LORD, has
spoken,
    And summoned the earth from
      the rising of the sun to its
      setting.
Out of Zion, the perfection of beauty,
    God has shone forth.
May our God come and not keep
silence;
    Fire devours before Him,
    And it is very tempestuous
      around Him.

He summons the heavens above,
    And the earth, to judge His
      people:
"Gather My godly ones to Me,
    Those who have made a covenant
      with Me by sacrifice."
And the heavens declare His
righteousness,
    For God Himself is judge.

Psalm 50:1–6 NASB

Just because someone talks doesn't mean anyone is listening. It is easy for people to fail to notice that God is speaking or to misunderstand him or to explain him away. Sometimes what God says is not what we want to hear; so it is easy, at such a moment, to decide that we didn't hear anything at all.

Human failure does not prevent God from communicating with us. God has ways of getting our attention. He is also patient and willing to repeat himself until we get it.

The time when human beings are least likely to hear what God says is when everything is falling apart. It's during the dark times, when all seems lost, when people are dying and suffering, that people are most tempted to believe that prayers are going unheard, that maybe God is not there or doesn't care.

Through four hundred years of slavery in Egypt, God heard every cry, noticed every wince of pain, finally answered those prayers, and spoke clearly through Moses. Was the lack of deliverance for four hundred years indicative of God's lack of care? No. God was there, and he was speaking. He walked beside every slave, and he whispered encouragement to every struggling individual, whether that person understood or knew God was speaking. Even when the slave seemed most alone and abandoned, God's words had an impact on him. Some died or were abused to the point of death, but God met them in heaven.

God shows himself to us every day, when we rise, when we eat, when we take each breath. God speaks through each life we touch. With each breeze, with each ray of sunlight, and with each star at night, God whispers. The world constantly declares how much God cares if only we would pay attention.

If You Would Only Listen

But no, my people wouldn't listen.
  Israel did not want me around.
So I let them follow their own stubborn desires, living according to
  their own ideas.
Oh, that my people would listen to
  me!
Oh, that Israel would follow me, walking in my paths!
How quickly I would then subdue
  their enemies!

How soon my hands would be upon
  their foes!
Those who hate the LORD would cringe
  before him; they would be doomed
  forever.
But I would feed you with the finest
  wheat.
I would satisfy you with wild honey
  from the rock.

Psalm 81:11–16 NLT

Sometimes when you can't get something to work, it's because you chose to ignore the instructions. In life, it is easy to decide we don't need to pay attention to what God told us. Our circumstances are different, this is special, we know better, times are different now—the excuses are endless and always the same. As are the results. This psalm is attributed to Asaph, a musician who sang at the dedication of Solomon's temple. But King Solomon, as he grew older, began worshipping other gods in addition to Yahweh. He even built high places for them.

From the time of Moses to the time Israel fell to Babylonian conquest, at least six hundred years went by. God's people lived their lives, grew their crops, and traded their goods. They married and they gave in marriage. Kings good and bad rose and fell. God let them do mostly just as they wished, intervening only now and then with a word here, a bit of help there. He gave them rain, and sometimes he gave them drought.

God hadn't been silent; he'd sent his prophets to the Israelites. Before that, he'd sent Moses, who gave them a contract and laid out quite clearly and precisely what God expected. It wasn't complicated: love God; love people.

But people had better ideas, they thought, of what was best for their lives. They thought they knew what would bring them real happiness in contrast to what they imagined God was going to give them. God was patient. He let them have their way, knowing that eventually they would recognize their mistake and come back to him. He would be waiting with open arms. He made us free to do as we please. But he knows that sooner or later we'll decide to do as he pleases.

Who Wants to Be a Prophet?

In the year that the supreme commander, sent by Sargon king of Assyria, came to Ashdod and attacked and captured it—at that time the Lord spoke through Isaiah son of Amoz. He said to him, "Take off the sackcloth from your body and the sandals from your feet." And he did so, going around stripped and barefoot.

Then the Lord said, "Just as my servant Isaiah has gone stripped and barefoot for three years, as a sign and portent against Egypt and Cush, so the king of Assyria will lead away stripped and barefoot the Egyptian captives and Cushite exiles, young and old, with buttocks bared—to Egypt's shame. Those who trusted in Cush and boasted in Egypt will be afraid and put to shame.

In that day the people who live on this coast will say, 'See what has happened to those we relied on, those we fled to for help and deliverance from the king of Assyria! How then can we escape?' "

Isaiah 20:1–6 NIV

A prophet's life was never dull. It was also rarely comfortable. When God asked Isaiah to be a prophet, Isaiah probably had no idea what he was willingly volunteering for or just how uncomfortable God would make him. His life regularly served as a prop for God.

When Isaiah began prophesying, the Assyrian Empire had risen to become a major player on the world stage. Only Egypt seemed able to hold the Assyrians in check. Israel relied on Egypt to protect them from Assyria. God wanted to show Israel that this was a mistake. Egypt wouldn't even be able to protect itself from the Assyrians, let alone be able to help Israel. Egypt was no longer as powerful as it seemed. Trusting in everything and everyone but God would prove embarrassing. The Egyptians would see exile, and those who witnessed their leaving would see more than they bargained for.

God recognized that giving speeches wasn't the only way to communicate. There was also storytelling, acting, and art. So Isaiah became a living parable to illustrate the message God wanted to get across. God was good at communicating, and he knew how to get an audience's attention. Having Isaiah run around without clothes certainly got people's attention—especially since he did it for three years. Why did he do it for so long? Perhaps, like any other message from God, even a naked prophet tended to be ignored. We don't always like to listen to God, no matter how well he tells the story. Sometimes God asks us to do things we don't understand, but we know he'll never tell us to do the wrong thing.

God to the Rescue

When the poor and needy are dying
  of thirst and cannot find water, I,
  the LORD God of Israel, will come to
  their rescue.
I won't forget them.
I will make rivers flow on mountain
  peaks.
I will send streams to fill the valleys.
Dry and barren land will flow with
  springs and become a lake.

I will fill the desert with all kinds of
  trees—cedars, acacias, and myrtles;
  olive and cypress trees; fir trees and
  pines.
Everyone will see this and know that I,
  the holy LORD God of Israel, created
  it all.

Isaiah 41:17–20 CEV

❈

*I*saiah prophesied both before and during the time that the northern ten tribes—Israel—went into Assyrian captivity. He continued prophesying through the reign of Hezekiah, the king of Judah, and into the reign of Hezekiah's son Manasseh. Tradition says that Manasseh murdered Isaiah by sawing him in half.

Like all God's prophets, Isaiah didn't proclaim a new message; rather, his message was an old one. It was the message of Moses. The prophets told God's people that there was but one God and that he was everyone's God. They told the people that they should love God and love one another, not simply because it was the right thing to do, but because it was what they had promised to do. The prophets warned the people just to keep their word.

When the Israelites were taken captive by their enemies, it was no surprise. God had warned them of the coming calamity and made it clear to them that they were being punished, much as a parent would give his child the rules, warn him of impending punishment, and then carry it out. But like a parent, God did not disown his child. God did not mete out punishment in order to ruin the lives of his people. Rather, God had the best of intentions and reassured his people that he would still provide for their needs. They didn't need to fear they would dry up and blow away.

While the nation was in captivity and oppressed, the fields of their homeland were left fallow. The places that needed irrigation were left dry. But that changed when God's people returned. The barren places bloomed once again, the water flowed, and everyone had plenty to eat and drink.

God's Gentle Servant

Behold! My Servant whom I uphold,
  My Elect One in whom My soul
    delights!
  I have put My Spirit upon Him;
  He will bring forth justice to the
    Gentiles.
      He will not cry out, nor raise
        His voice,
  Nor cause His voice to be heard in
    the street.
      A bruised reed He will not
        break,
And smoking flax He will not
  quench;
He will bring forth justice for
  truth.
He will not fail nor be
  discouraged,
Till He has established justice in
  the earth;
And the coastlands shall wait for
  His law.

Isaiah 42:1–4 NKJV

It's one thing to feel bad; it's another thing to quit. Real discouragement is not merely a feeling. God predicted the coming of his Son through the prophet Isaiah. Matthew quoted the words from God through Isaiah and applied them to Jesus. The people of Israel were looking for a political, military savior who would rescue them from the oppression of the Roman Empire by defeating it in a great war of conquest. Instead, Jesus came quietly and peacefully, without raising his voice. He did not intend to lead a rebellion. He would raise no weapons. His concern was to bring justice to the Gentiles—the last people that the Israelites of his day cared about. The last people they wanted to receive justice.

Jesus did not quit or become discouraged in his mission; he stuck with it till the end. Discouragement is not just a feeling of gloom or being unhappy about current circumstances. Jesus prayed, wishing there were some other way. On the cross, he cried out in pain over feeling abandoned by God. But Jesus never stopped doing God's will. We can be down and still move on; we can wonder about whether we'll be able to finish, even as we keep on marching forward. Discouragement is not just a feeling; it is the act of giving up. Jesus never gave up. He finished what God sent him to do.

By his actions, Jesus brought God's justice and his law, not only to Israel but also to the world as a whole. The law that had been written only on stone and papyrus has been written on the human heart, thanks to Jesus.

Setting the Prisoners Free

Thus says God the LORD,
Who created the heavens and
stretched them out,
Who spread out the earth and its
offspring,
Who gives breath to the people
on it
And spirit to those who walk in it,
"I am the LORD, I have called you in
righteousness,
I will also hold you by the hand
and watch over you,
And I will appoint you as a cov-
enant to the people,
As a light to the nations,

To open blind eyes,
To bring out prisoners from the
dungeon
And those who dwell in darkness
from the prison.
"I am the LORD, that is My name;
I will not give My glory to
another,
Nor My praise to graven images.

"Behold, the former things have come
to pass,
Now I declare new things;
Before they spring forth I proclaim
them to you."

Isaiah 42:5–9 NASB

When God sets us free, no human being can ever enslave us again. God identified himself as the Creator and promised his people that he was still with them in their captivity. Better, he promised them they would come out of their captivity. The day would arrive when they would be free.

God released the Israelites from their place of exile, and they returned home to their land during the time of Ezra and Nehemiah. Such physical freedom had been on the minds of those who had first heard Isaiah's prophecy. But God was thinking of something far more precious than physical freedom. In fact, the nation of Israel was never again a free and independent people. When Cyrus allowed the captives to return to their homes, they were still part of his Persian Empire. When Alexander the Great conquered the Persians, the Israelites became part of the Greek Empire, and when the Romans took over, they remained part of the Roman Empire.

God's goal was not to set them free from foreign domination, since that never happened. God hoped his people would understand what kind of freedom he meant when their physical situation remained unchanged. He freed his people's minds, releasing them from the wreckage of their broken lives. He restored relationships; broke down the barriers between classes, nations, and genders; and ended the division between them and God.

Oppressing the Oppressor

"Come down, virgin daughter of Babylon, and sit in the dust.
For your days of sitting on a throne have ended.
O daughter of Babylonia, never again will you be the lovely princess, tender and delicate.
Take heavy millstones and grind flour.
Remove your veil, and strip off your robe.
Expose yourself to public view.
You will be naked and burdened with shame.
I will take vengeance against you without pity."
Our Redeemer, whose name is the LORD of Heaven's Armies, is the Holy One of Israel.

"O beautiful Babylon, sit now in darkness and silence.
Never again will you be known as the queen of kingdoms.
For I was angry with my chosen people and punished them by letting them fall into your hands.
But you, Babylon, showed them no mercy.
You oppressed even the elderly.
You said, 'I will reign forever as queen of the world!'
You did not reflect on your actions or think about their consequences.
Listen to this, you pleasure-loving kingdom, living at ease and feeling secure.
You say, 'I am the only one, and there is no other.
I will never be a widow or lose my children.'
Well, both these things will come upon you in a moment: widowhood and the loss of your children.
Yes, these calamities will come upon you, despite all your witchcraft and magic."

Isaiah 47:1–9 NLT

※

*A*rrogance is not a good look for anyone. God disciplined his people by using other people. The Babylonians destroyed Jerusalem and burned down God's temple. They acted as God's instruments in his hands.

Nevertheless, the Babylonians behaved arrogantly and cruelly, and so God pronounced his judgment against them. Although Nebuchadnezzar, the great king of Babylon who had destroyed Jerusalem, turned to God, his nation and his descendants did not. And so God's judgment came upon the Babylonian Empire. The Persians slaughtered Nebuchadnezzar's grandson and destroyed his army. Never again would Babylon matter to the world.

A few stone ruins are all that remain of what was once the most powerful and important city on the planet. God promised that those who oppressed or harmed his people would in turn be harmed. The city that Babylon destroyed, Jerusalem, was rebuilt, and it prospers until this day.

Answered Prayers

This is what the LORD says:
I will answer your prayers because I
    have set a time when I will help by
    coming to save you.
I have chosen you to take my promise
    of hope to other nations.
You will rebuild the country from its
    ruins, then people will come and
    settle there.
You will set prisoners free from dark
    dungeons to see the light of day.
On their way home, they will find
    plenty to eat, even on barren hills.

They won't go hungry or get thirsty;
    they won't be bothered by the
    scorching sun or hot desert winds.
I will be merciful while leading them
    along to streams of water.
I will level the mountains and make
    roads.
Then my people will return from dis-
    tant lands in the north and the west
    and from the city of Syene.

Isaiah 49:8–12 CEV

*T*here is no doubt that God will answer our prayers. But God has his own time and way of doing it. Israel was destroyed by the Assyrians and then the Babylonians. Seventy years of captivity followed. People prayed for deliverance, just as their ancestors had prayed for deliverance from the Egyptians—for four hundred long years. Sometimes there is a gap between when a prayer is offered and when it is answered.

We pray for healing. We pray that those we love will be restored and protected. We pray they will not die or be hurt. When our loved ones die, when they don't come home from war, when the bank forecloses, when the job is lost, when whatever we fear most comes upon us, we may think that God has forsaken us, that he didn't hear our prayer.

God has a time and way of answering that is nothing like we expect. We live such short lives and see so little of the overall plan of God. There is more to eternity than the seventy years of a human life span. God has all the time in the world—all the time in eternity—to answer your prayer. Your loved ones who believed in God will be resurrected and walk on streets of gold. God has prepared rooms in his mansion just for those who believe in him. Believers' dreams will come true. We just need to broaden our perspective and widen our expectations. We expect too little of God.

Drunk on Their Own Blood

Thus says the LORD:
"Even the captives of the mighty shall be taken away,
And the prey of the terrible be delivered;
For I will contend with him who contends with you,
And I will save your children.

I will feed those who oppress you with their own flesh,
And they shall be drunk with their own blood as with sweet wine.
All flesh shall know
That I, the LORD, am your Savior,
And your Redeemer, the Mighty One of Jacob."

Isaiah 49:25–26 NKJV

God has more in mind than we do. Israel wanted to be delivered from their enemies, and God promised them that deliverance. God also told them that every human being would know that God was the mighty one of Israel.

The powerful empires of Mesopotamia, first Assyria and then Babylonia, had conquered and destroyed the kingdoms of God's people, Israel and Judah. God used Isaiah both to warn his people of their coming disaster and to explain to them its meaning—that it was to correct their insatiable desire to worship idols.

Through Isaiah, God also spoke the message of a hope yet to be. The Mesopotamian empires that had destroyed them would themselves be destroyed. And that destruction, which would lead to the restoration of Israel to their homeland, would change not just Israel for the better, but the world as a whole when it saw how God had rescued Israel.

Why should everyone know of God's deliverance? God was not going to save only the people of Israel. God's goal was to rescue everyone. The restoration of Israel to their land set the stage for the coming Messiah. And so the rescue of Israel was not just, or even primarily, a physical rescue. His concern was not just to send a captive people back home to their promised land. Rather, the physical rescue served as a parable for the real task that God had envisioned. The story of God's people would become the story of salvation. God's ability to rescue his people from their physical trials was proof of his ability to save them from their spiritual trials. Their bondage to idols and other wickedness could be broken just as easily as their physical chains.

But God loved even those who were not yet his people, and he intended to transform them from enemies into friends. By bringing his people back home, he would make it possible for everyone to come home to God.

What Certificate of Divorce?

Thus says the LORD,
"Where is the certificate of divorce
By which I have sent your mother
away?
Or to whom of My creditors did I
sell you?
Behold, you were sold for your
iniquities,
And for your transgressions your
mother was sent away.
"Why was there no man when I came?
When I called, why was there
none to answer?

Is My hand so short that it cannot
ransom?
Or have I no power to deliver?
Behold, I dry up the sea with My
rebuke,
I make the rivers a wilderness;
Their fish stink for lack of water
And die of thirst.
"I clothe the heavens with blackness
And make sackcloth their
covering."

Isaiah 50:1–3 NASB

*I*f you're in time-out, you probably know why you're there. In the midst of their punishment, the Israelites had started to think that God had abandoned them forever. God asked them a series of pointed questions to let them know that there was a good reason for their suffering: they were being disciplined.

The break in the relationship between God and Israel was not because God had divorced them, however. Nor had he sold them to pay a debt. A man was not allowed to remarry a woman after divorcing her if she remarried. Just as marriage was designed to be lifelong, so was divorce. The break in their relationship existed because the Israelites had turned away from God, but God had not turned away from them. The marriage had not ended. So Israel's relationship with God was not permanently broken. The prophets had already explained the issue between God and his people when they repeatedly compared Israel to an adulterous wife chasing after other men in her insatiable lust.

But it was unreasonable for his people to imagine that God was unable to save them regardless of the mess they had created for themselves. He reminded them of past care when they had faced the impossible and God had come through for them. "Dry up the sea" was a reference to the Red Sea crossing by Moses and the Israelites. "Make the rivers a wilderness" likely refers to the time when the Israelites, under Joshua, crossed the blocked-up Jordan River to go conquer the promised land.

God's power to rescue his people from Egyptian bondage demonstrated his ability to rescue them from their bondage to sin.

Set Free

I, even I, am He who comforts you.
Who are you that you are afraid of
man who dies
And of the son of man who is
made like grass,
That you have forgotten the LORD your
Maker,
Who stretched out the heavens
And laid the foundations of the
earth,
That you fear continually all day
long because of the fury of the
oppressor,
As he makes ready to destroy?
But where is the fury of the op-
pressor?

The exile will soon be set free, and will
not die in the dungeon, nor will his
bread be lacking.

For I am the LORD your God, who stirs
up the sea and its waves roar (the
LORD of hosts is His name).

I have put My words in your mouth
and have covered you with the
shadow of My hand, to establish the
heavens, to found the earth, and to
say to Zion, "You are My people."

Isaiah 51:12–16 NASB

✻

Free at last! free at last! Thank God Almighty, we are free at last!" Through the prophet Isaiah, God tried to comfort the people who remained in the land following the Assyrian conquest of Israel. He reassured them that those who had been deported were not gone for good. God pointed out a contrast for the Israelites, a contrast between their perception of things and the reality of those things. Where they cringed in fear before their Assyrian oppressors, God wondered why. Had they forgotten that their oppressors were merely humans who were weak and mortal? The Israelites would likely have pointed out that the description of the oppressors as human fit the Israelites as well.

But God went on and reminded them that they weren't alone in opposing their oppressors. God was part of the mix, and that's always a game changer. God reminded his people that he would release them from their captivity in Mesopotamia. Those who oppressed them would not keep them from eating. The Israelites would not die in dungeons. Everything really would be okay because the same God who had created the universe was the God who was standing with them.

It is so easy, in the midst of hard times, to lose sight of reality. We are God's children, and we will spend an eternity with God in paradise. From the perspective of eternity, any troubles in our temporary, temporal existence are microscopic.

You Like Being Slaves?

This is what the LORD says:
"When I sold you into exile,
    I received no payment.
Now I can redeem you
    without having to pay for you."

This is what the Sovereign LORD says: "Long ago my people chose to live in Egypt. Now they are oppressed by Assyria. What is this?" asks the LORD. "Why are my people enslaved again? Those who rule them shout in exultation. My name is blasphemed all day long. But I will reveal my name to my people, and they will come to know its power. Then at last they will recognize that I am the one who speaks to them."

Isaiah 52:3–6 NLT

*W*hat's a nice person like you doing in a place like this?" God pointed out that his people were where they were because of their own free choice. They went to Assyria because of their idolatry and because of their mistreatment of the poor and powerless. They had been warned prior to their exile that if they kept up their bad behavior, the Assyrians would come and take them away. They had freely chosen to ignore both Moses and the prophets after him.

Through the prophet Isaiah, God addressed Jerusalem. When Israel and his family had left their homeland at God's command and gone into Egypt in the time of Joseph, they had gone as guests of the Egyptians. Only later, through circumstances beyond their control, had the Egyptians turned them into slaves. But the Assyrians and Babylonians had dragged them away from their homeland involuntarily and turned them into slaves right away. And it was because the Israelites had disobeyed God. Their slavery to idols manifested itself in their slavery to conquerors.

No problem, however. God would rescue them anyway, just as he had from the Egyptians, if for no other reason than to silence those who blasphemed and rejoiced over the suffering of his people. Both the new slave masters and his enslaved people would come to know God's power—once again. And once again, they would recognize the one true God. Never again would the Israelites worship any God other than Yahweh.

God will rescue us, and not just because we don't want to hurt anymore, but because of what we mean to him. It really is all about God.

Just Ask

You will call, and the LORD will answer;
  you will cry for help, and he will
  say: Here am I.
  "If you do away with the yoke of
  oppression, with the pointing
  finger and malicious talk,

and if you spend yourselves in behalf
  of the hungry and satisfy the needs
  of the oppressed, then your light
  will rise in the darkness, and your
  night will become like the noonday.

The LORD will guide you always; he
  will satisfy your needs in a sun-
  scorched land and will strengthen
  your frame. You will be like a well-
  watered garden, like a spring whose
  waters never fail.

Your people will rebuild the ancient
  ruins and will raise up the age-old
  foundations; you will be called
  Repairer of Broken Walls, Restorer of
  Streets with Dwellings.

"If you keep your feet from breaking the Sabbath and from doing as
  you please on my holy day, if you
  call the Sabbath a delight and the
  LORD's holy day honorable, and if
  you honor it by not going your own
  way and not doing as you please or
  speaking idle words,

then you will find your joy in the
  LORD, and I will cause you to ride on
  the heights of the land and to feast
  on the inheritance of your father
  Jacob."

The mouth of the LORD has spoken.

Isaiah 58:9–14 NIV

All the Israelites had to do was ask and God would respond. But what exactly did God mean by "asking"? Offering warm words to someone who needs a warm meal won't help him. Sentiment is not the same as accomplishment. Asking was not just about using the right words. It was about doing the right things. God would know that they had asked him for help—and he would hear them—when they started loving one another, when they started loving God, when they gave aid to the poor, and when they kept the Sabbath.

Giving aid to the poor meant not taking advantage of them. Keeping the Sabbath meant taking God seriously. In both cases, rather than thinking only about themselves, they'd be thinking about those outside themselves, whether human or God. The focus of their attention, the aim of their efforts, would all be on others, rather than on what they could get for themselves, how they could make things work to their advantage.

God cares about us. He'd like us to care about him and everyone he cares about. Caring about others shows just how much we care about God, because we're paying attention then to what God cares about most.

You Broke Your Promise

Those slave owners changed their minds and forced their former slaves back into slavery.

That's when the LORD told me to say to the people:

I am the LORD God of Israel, and I made an agreement with your ancestors when I brought them out of Egypt, where they had been slaves. As part of this agreement, you must let a Hebrew slave go free after six years of service.

Your ancestors did not obey me, but you decided to obey me and do the right thing by setting your Hebrew slaves completely free. You even went to my temple, and in my name you made an agreement to set them free. But you have abused my name, because you broke your agreement and forced your former slaves back into slavery.

You have disobeyed me by not giving your slaves their freedom. So I will give you freedom—the freedom to die in battle or from disease or hunger. I will make you disgusting to all other nations on earth.

You asked me to be a witness when you made the agreement to set your slaves free. And as part of the ceremony you cut a calf into two parts, then walked between the parts. But you people of Jerusalem have broken that agreement as well as my agreement with Israel. So I will do to you what you did to that calf.

Jeremiah 34:11–18 CEV

Although God did not forbid slavery, he did regulate it heavily. The law of Moses stipulated that such slavery was supposed to be temporary. After seven years, slaves had to be set free. Unfortunately, the Israelites never abided by that limitation. Instead, they kept their fellow Israelites in permanent bondage.

God sent his prophets, like Jeremiah, to the Israelites with a very simple message that he had them repeat again and again. God said there were two fundamental problems for the Israelites. First, the Israelites were guilty of worshipping other gods when they were supposed to worship Yahweh exclusively. Second, the Israelites were guilty of taking advantage of the people among them who were least able to protect themselves.

Zedekiah, the last king of Judah, was in power, and the Babylonians were laying siege to Jerusalem when God sent Jeremiah to warn the Israelites to repent of what they had done with their slaves.

The Israelites seemed to have problems following through on their promises to God. When they worshipped in the temple, they vowed to obey him. But later on, they wouldn't do it. God wants us to do what we promise.

Digging a Hole

The word of the LORD came to me: Mortal, you are living in the midst of a rebellious house, who have eyes to see but do not see, who have ears to hear but do not hear; for they are a rebellious house. Therefore, mortal, prepare for yourself an exile's baggage, and go into exile by day in their sight; you shall go like an exile from your place to another place in their sight. Perhaps they will understand, though they are a rebellious house. You shall bring out your baggage by day in their sight, as baggage for exile; and you shall go out yourself at evening in their sight, as those do who go into exile. Dig through the wall in their sight, and carry the baggage through it. In their sight you shall lift the baggage on your shoulder, and carry it out in the dark; you shall cover your face, so that you may not see the land; for I have made you a sign for the house of Israel.

I did just as I was commanded. I brought out my baggage by day, as baggage for exile, and in the evening I dug through the wall with my own hands; I brought it out in the dark, carrying it on my shoulder in their sight.

Ezekiel 12:1–7 NRSV

*H*ouses in the ancient Middle East were usually built with bricks made of clay mixed with straw. Digging through such a brick wall was as easy as digging a shallow hole in the ground. But nobody ever did this, and so Ezekiel's peculiar behavior of digging through the wall would have attracted attention—which of course was God's point in having him do it.

God used Ezekiel to illustrate the words he had spoken to his people. Ezekiel was living in Babylon. Back in Jerusalem, Zedekiah was sitting on David's throne. He had been put there by Nebuchadnezzar, king of Babylon, after Zedekiah's nephew Jehoiachin had rebelled. Learning nothing from his predecessor, Zedekiah rebelled, too, and so Nebuchadnezzar attacked. Zedekiah tried sneaking away by night. Nebuchadnezzar captured him, killed his children, and then blinded him before hauling him away in chains back to Babylon. Nebuchadnezzar burned Jerusalem and its temple to the ground.

Zedekiah had refused to listen to Jeremiah. The exiles in Babylon paid about as much attention to Ezekiel. God is speaking even now, whether we choose to listen to him or not. We'd do well to listen.

God Believed

God spoke: "Light!"
    And light appeared.
God saw that light was good
    and separated light from dark.
God named the light Day,
    he named the dark Night.
It was evening, it was morning—
Day One.

God spoke: "Sky! In the middle of the
    waters; separate water from water!"

God made sky.
He separated the water under sky
    from the water above sky.

And there it was:
    he named sky the Heavens;
It was evening, it was morning—
Day Two.

God spoke: "Separate!
    Water-beneath-Heaven, gather
      into one place;
Land, appear!"
    And there it was.
God named the land Earth.
    He named the pooled water
      Ocean.
God saw that it was good.

Genesis 1:3–10 MSG

❈

*G*od brought light to a dark place. The phrase "It was evening, it was morning" occurs nowhere else in the Bible. Within these first verses, the word *day* is used as a designation for "light," while the word *night* is used as the designation for "darkness." God spent the beginning of creation making light and separating it from darkness, just as he separated the waters into various locations. He repeatedly saw that his creation was "good."

The author of Genesis carefully selected his structure and his words in order to create a contrast between what the Israelites believed and what the nations around them believed. The nations believed in many gods. They believed that the ocean, the stars, the moon, and the sun were all deities. In Genesis, the author carefully made it clear that there is but one God and that the moon, the stars, the sun, and the ocean are merely created objects devoid of personality and designed to benefit humanity.

Where the nations around Israel believed that their gods were geographically limited and belonged to individual nations exclusively, the Israelites were presented with a God who was universal, and with all humanity united as one family.

If the God you worship was able to create the universe, then it is easier to believe he has the power to help you through your current crisis, however gloomy it might seem just now.

Heir Apparent

The word of the LORD came to Abram in a vision, saying, "Do not be afraid, Abram. I am your shield, your exceedingly great reward."

But Abram said, "Lord GOD, what will You give me, seeing I go childless, and the heir of my house is Eliezer of Damascus?" Then Abram said, "Look, You have given me no offspring; indeed one born in my house is my heir!"

And behold, the word of the LORD came to him, saying, "This one shall not be your heir, but one who will come from your own body shall be your heir." Then He brought him outside and said, "Look now toward heaven, and count the stars if you are able to number them." And He said to him, "So shall your descendants be."

And he believed in the LORD, and He accounted it to him for righteousness.

Then He said to him, "I am the LORD, who brought you out of Ur of the Chaldeans, to give you this land to inherit it."

Genesis 15:1–7 NKJV

God has not forgotten your dreams. Abram was an old man; his wife was an old woman. Despite a successful and prosperous life, something important was lacking. Abram was not slow to let God know of his disappointment. For the ancient Jewish people, nothing was more important than having heirs to carry on their names. Abram would do anything for a proper heir.

According to ancient tablets unearthed in Iraq at a place called Nuzi, there were two things that a couple like Abram and Sarai who were unable to have children could do back then. First, they could designate someone, usually a servant, to become their heir. In essence, they adopted the servant. Second, the husband could marry a second wife and get her pregnant. The child born to the second wife would become the son of the first wife and then become the heir.

So Abram followed the customs of his culture and made his servant, Eliezer of Damascus, his heir. But it didn't satisfy him. Eliezer had all the rights and privileges of a firstborn son. Only Sarai giving birth could change that.

When God told Abram that the designated heir would be unnecessary because Abram would have a flesh-and-blood son, Abram's reaction was one of joy. He believed what God had told him.

Because Abram believed, God considered him righteous. Righteousness does not begin in how we act but in what we believe.

Don't Go Anywhere

There was another famine in the land in addition to the one that had occurred in Abraham's time. And Isaac went to Abimelech, king of the Philistines, at Gerar. The LORD appeared to him and said, "Do not go down to Egypt. Live in the land that I tell you about; stay in this land as a foreigner, and I will be with you and bless you. For I will give all these lands to you and your offspring, and I will confirm the oath that I swore to your father Abraham. I will make your offspring as numerous as the stars of the sky, I will give your offspring all these lands, and all the nations of the earth will be blessed by your offspring, because Abraham listened to My voice and kept My mandate, My commands, My statutes, and My instructions." So Isaac settled in Gerar.

Genesis 26:1–6 HCSB

*I*n the ancient world, no one worried about being too fat. Rather, people regularly worried about starving to death. Famine was common, and it remained common through most of human history. Obesity was certainly not an epidemic.

As famine came once again to the land where Isaac was living, it was only natural for him to think about traveling to a place where food was more abundant. He first moved to the land of the Philistines along the southern coast of Palestine. That put him on the road pointing toward Egypt. Gerar was one of the major trading cities along that route, situated near modern-day Gaza. Thanks to the Nile River, Egypt rarely suffered famines, so it was only natural that Isaac would think about relocating there, much as a modern family might move for a job. But when God told Isaac to stay where he was, Isaac simply believed what God told him and acted on that belief. God didn't want Isaac to go to Egypt simply because it wasn't time yet. The journey to Egypt was meant for Isaac's grandson Joseph, not Isaac. Even though Isaac didn't know that future, he accepted that God knew what he was doing and that things would work out according to God's own timing.

The promise that God made to Isaac was the same one he had made to Abraham earlier (Genesis 12:1–3). And so Isaac didn't rely on himself and on what he alone thought best. He trusted God to take care of him because he knew that God had cared for both him and his father, Abraham, in the past. Faith grows from experience.

How God Signs a Contract

[Abram] said, "Lord God, how can I know that I will possess it?"

[God] said to him, "Bring Me a three-year-old cow, a three-year-old female goat, a three-year-old ram, a turtledove, and a young pigeon."

So he brought all these to Him, split them down the middle, and laid the pieces opposite each other, but he did not cut up the birds. Birds of prey came down on the carcasses, but Abram drove them away. As the sun was setting, a deep sleep fell on Abram, and suddenly a terror and great darkness descended on him.

Then the Lord said to Abram, "Know this for certain: Your offspring will be strangers in a land that does not belong to them; they will be enslaved and oppressed 400 years. However, I will judge the nation they serve, and afterwards they will go out with many possessions. But you will go to your fathers in peace and be buried at a ripe old age. In the fourth generation they will return here, for the iniquity of the Amorites has not yet reached its full measure."

When the sun had set and it was dark, a smoking fire pot and a flaming torch appeared and passed between the divided [animals]. On that day the Lord made a covenant with Abram, saying, "I give this land to your offspring, from the brook of Egypt to the Euphrates River."

Genesis 15:8–18 HCSB

❖

A picture is worth a thousand words. God tried to communicate with people in ways that would make sense to them. So why did Abram decorate the ground with the dead carcasses of animals that he had cut in half? God promised Abram that he would have a child. Abram "believed God," but wanted proof, and so God granted Abram's request for certainty.

In Abram's day, when kings made treaties with one another, they would take some animals and cut them in half. They would then lay the pieces out in parallel rows. Together, the two kings would then walk between the carcasses. It was a picture: the kings were announcing that if they didn't fulfill the treaty they had just made, then what had happened to the animals would happen to them. So after God—as symbolized by the smoking firepot—passed between the dead animals, Abram knew God would do what he had promised. He had made just such a treaty with him.

If God and Abram were making a treaty like this today, the symbolism would have been different, to fit modern cultural expectations. God wants us to understand what he has to say. He does not try to confuse or elude us.

❈❈❈❈❈❈❈❈❈❈❈❈❈❈❈❈❈❈❈❈❈❈❈❈❈❈❈❈❈❈

It's Unbelievable!

Abraham hurried into the tent to Sarah. He said, "Hurry. Get three cups of our best flour; knead it and make bread."

Then Abraham ran to the cattle pen and picked out a nice plump calf and gave it to the servant who lost no time getting it ready. Then he got curds and milk, brought them with the calf that had been roasted, set the meal before the men, and stood there under the tree while they ate.

The men said to him, "Where is Sarah your wife?"

He said, "In the tent."

One of them said, "I'm coming back about this time next year. When I arrive, your wife Sarah will have a son." Sarah was listening at the tent opening, just behind the man.

Abraham and Sarah were old by this time, very old. Sarah was far past the age for having babies. Sarah laughed within herself, "An old woman like me? Get pregnant? With this old man of a husband?"

God said to Abraham, "Why did Sarah laugh saying, 'Me? Have a baby? An old woman like me?' Is anything too hard for GOD? I'll be back about this time next year and Sarah will have a baby."

Sarah lied. She said, "I didn't laugh," because she was afraid.

But he said, "Yes you did; you laughed."

Genesis 18:6–15 MSG

❈

*G*uess who's coming to dinner? One day three men showed up, and Abraham invited them to his home. But they were not ordinary men. Two would turn out to be angels, while the third was God himself. As was customary, Abraham offered the men food and drink, and they accepted his hospitality. Abraham asked Sarah to make some bread, while he hurried to select a calf from his pen. He then got a servant to slaughter, butcher, and cook it. The three visitors were there for several hours before the meal was finally served.

Though Sarah had not joined them in the meal, she was listening to what was going on. But she could not believe what she had heard, and so she laughed within herself. But they knew anyway. Embarrassed, her first instinct was to lie: it was rude to laugh at guests like that. She was afraid of what they would think and of how her husband would react.

What did the man who turned out to be God do in the face of her silent laugh? Did he berate her, condemn her, strike her down? Take back the promised blessing? No, he simply reminded her that nothing was beyond God's capabilities. God will bless us even if we can't believe it.

Will That Be on the Test?

After all this, God tested Abraham. God said, "Abraham!"

"Yes?" answered Abraham. "I'm listening."

He said, "Take your dear son Isaac whom you love and go to the land of Moriah. Sacrifice him there as a burnt offering on one of the mountains that I'll point out to you." Abraham got up early in the morning and saddled his donkey. He took two of his young servants and his son Isaac. He had split wood for the burnt offering. He set out for the place God had directed him. On the third day he looked up and saw the place in the distance. Abraham told his two young servants, "Stay here with the donkey. The boy and I are going over there to worship; then we'll come back to you."

Abraham took the wood for the burnt offering and gave it to Isaac his son to carry. He carried the flint and the knife. The two of them went off together.

Isaac said to Abraham his father, "Father?"

"Yes, my son."

"We have flint and wood, but where's the sheep for the burnt offering?"

Abraham said, "Son, God will see to it that there's a sheep for the burnt offering." And they kept on walking together.

Genesis 22:1–8 MSG

❈

*A*braham should have gotten the willies. What God asked Abraham to do contradicted all that we know about God. So why did God ask Abraham to sacrifice his son?

It was a test. In Abraham's day the sacrifice of children to the gods was commonplace. God wanted to see if Abraham understood that God was different. Although Abraham's faith that God could restore Isaac was commendable, it was never God's will that Isaac should be sacrificed. In the end, God stopped Abraham.

Abraham probably should have responded to God's request with a no, just as Moses did years later. When Moses went to get the Ten Commandments and returned to find a golden calf, God asked Moses to stand aside while he destroyed the Israelites and replaced them with Moses's descendants. Instead, Moses begged God to forgive them (Exodus 32:9–14). What we see from Abraham's test is that Abraham still didn't understand who God was or how much he differed from the false gods he'd grown up with. Abraham learned about God's character, thanks to this test and its outcome. Every test in our lives is a learning experience. God will help us pass them all, one way or another.

What Did You Say Your Name Was?

Moses said to God, "Who am I that I should go to Pharaoh, and bring the Israelites out of Egypt?" He said, "I will be with you; and this shall be the sign for you that it is I who sent you: when you have brought the people out of Egypt, you shall worship God on this mountain."

But Moses said to God, "If I come to the Israelites and say to them, 'The God of your ancestors has sent me to you,' and they ask me, 'What is his name?' what shall I say to them?" God said to Moses, "I AM WHO I AM." He said further, "Thus you shall say to the Israelites, 'I AM has sent me to you.'" God also said to Moses, "Thus you shall say to the Israelites, 'The LORD, the God of your ancestors, the God of Abraham, the God of Isaac, and the God of Jacob, has sent me to you':

> This is my name forever,
> and this my title for all
> generations.

Go and assemble the elders of Israel, and say to them, 'The LORD, the God of your ancestors, the God of Abraham, of Isaac, and of Jacob, has appeared to me, saying: I have given heed to you and to what has been done to you in Egypt.'"

Exodus 3:11–16 NRSV

✻

*G*od doesn't need a name. Moses and the Israelites in Egypt lived in a world filled with many gods and goddesses. That there was but one God was something they only gradually comprehended. Although he accepted that this was the same God that Abraham, Isaac, and Jacob had worshipped, he wanted a name to take back to the people. Names were important because they conferred power: if someone called your name, you looked up to see who had used your name. Moses wanted that with God.

God thought that Moses' question was odd. It showed God how little Moses really understood. Names are necessary when there are many examples of something: for instance, there are many human beings, and names keep us from becoming confused. But what need had God of a name? He is all there is, the only God. Therefore, he responded, "I AM WHO I AM." How else could he answer that question? So Moses went back to the Israelites and told them that "I AM" had sent him. The Hebrew pronunciation of that phrase is "Yahweh," which is sometimes rendered in English as "Jehovah."

We don't need God's name in order to get him to respond to our prayers. We don't need a special incantation worded just right. He responds to our prayers because he loves us, not because we used the right name.

Signs and Wonders

Moses answered and said, "But suppose they will not believe me or listen to my voice; suppose they say, 'The LORD has not appeared to you.'"

So the LORD said to him, "What is that in your hand?"

He said, "A rod."

And He said, "Cast it on the ground." So he cast it on the ground, and it became a serpent; and Moses fled from it. Then the LORD said to Moses, "Reach out your hand and take it by the tail" (and he reached out his hand and caught it, and it became a rod in his hand), "that they may believe that the LORD God of their fathers, the God of Abraham, the God of Isaac, and the God of Jacob, has appeared to you."

Furthermore the LORD said to him, "Now put your hand in your bosom." And he put his hand in his bosom, and when he took it out, behold, his hand was leprous, like snow. And He said, "Put your hand in your bosom again." So he put his hand in his bosom again, and drew it out of his bosom, and behold, it was restored like his other flesh.

Exodus 4:1–7 NKJV

If you claim to be from God, people will want some proof. When Moses stood before Pharaoh, he was applying, as it were, for the job of "rescuer from slavery" for the people of Israel. Both the slave master, Pharaoh, and the enslaved people, the Israelites, would have expected some references. Neither would have any particular reason for believing Moses when he showed up and said, "Let my people go." The references God gave Moses to outwardly show that he was a legitimate spokesperson for God were what you might expect: miracles.

Moses responded as any human being might to the unexpected appearance of a snake: he ran away from it. After all, one of the most common human phobias is a fear of snakes. Moses could now turn his shepherd's staff into a snake, or pick it up and turn it back again. Likewise, he could take his hand and make it diseased with one of the most feared diseases in the ancient world and then, just as easily, make the disease go away. Leprosy scared people because of the consequences of the disease: disfigurement, banishment from one's family and community, and the loss of any way to make a living.

God had given Moses power over what people feared most. God was reiterating for Moses that he had nothing to be afraid of at all. When God is with us, we never need to be afraid.

Please Send Someone Else

"If they will not believe you and will not respond to the evidence of the first sign, they may believe the evidence of the second sign. And if they don't believe even these two signs or listen to what you say, take some water from the Nile and pour it on the dry ground. The water you take from the Nile will become blood on the ground."

But Moses replied to the LORD, "Please, Lord, I have never been eloquent—either in the past or recently or since You have been speaking to Your servant—because I am slow and hesitant in speech."

The LORD said to him, "Who made the human mouth? Who makes him mute or deaf, seeing or blind? Is it not I, the LORD? Now go! I will help you speak and I will teach you what to say."

Moses said, "Please, Lord, send someone else."

Then the LORD's anger burned against Moses, and He said, "Isn't Aaron the Levite your brother? I know that he can speak well. And also, he is on his way now to meet you. When he sees you, his heart will rejoice. You will speak with him and tell him what to say. I will help both you and him [to speak], and will teach you both what to do. He will speak to the people for you. He will be your spokesman, and you will serve as God to him. And take this staff in your hand that you will perform the signs with."

Exodus 4:8–17 HCSB

※

*G*od won't take no for an answer. Although an Israelite, Moses had been raised by the daughter of Egypt's pharaoh. At the age of forty, angry at the mistreatment of his people by a slave master, he murdered the slave master and fled. Moses spent the next forty years living in exile as a shepherd. When he was eighty years old, God unexpectedly appeared to him in a burning bush and asked him to rescue the Israelite slaves from their Egyptian oppressors.

Moses doubted himself and he doubted God, even though he was standing in his presence. The task seemed impossible. When Moses tried to tell God to find someone else, God did not strike him down with a lightning bolt. Instead, God helped Moses recognize that he really could do the job. God removed Moses' doubts, not by giving him faith, but by giving him certainty. Over time, Moses' faith grew as he saw God consistently transform his hopes into reality. Rather than face each new crisis with hopelessness, Moses faced it secure in the knowledge that since God had helped him in the past, he'd continue to help him in the future.

I'm Still Hurting, God

Moses went back to the LORD and protested, "Why have you brought all this trouble on your own people, Lord? Why did you send me? Ever since I came to Pharaoh as your spokesman, he has been even more brutal to your people. And you have done nothing to rescue them!"

Then the LORD told Moses, "Now you will see what I will do to Pharaoh. When he feels the force of my strong hand, he will let the people go. In fact, he will force them to leave his land!"

And God said to Moses, "I am Yahweh— 'the LORD.' I appeared to Abraham, to Isaac, and to Jacob as El-Shaddai—'God Almighty'—but I did not reveal my name, Yahweh, to them. And I reaffirmed my covenant with them. Under its terms, I promised to give them the land of Canaan, where they were living as foreigners. You can be sure that I have heard the groans of the people of Israel, who are now slaves to the Egyptians. And I am well aware of my covenant with them.

"Therefore, say to the people of Israel: 'I am the LORD. I will free you from your oppression and will rescue you from your slavery in Egypt. I will redeem you with a powerful arm and great acts of judgment.'"

Exodus 5:22–6:6 NLT

*W*hat if you pray and do what God asks and your problem is still there? When Moses reluctantly returned to Egypt, he did exactly what God told him: he demanded the Egyptian pharaoh allow the Israelites a holiday to worship God. The three-day retreat was a ruse designed to let the Israelites escape from slavery. To help Moses convince the pharaoh, God had given him impressive miracles to perform.

His weak confidence was shattered, however, when Pharaoh not only turned down his request but also made life even more difficult for the Israelites. The pharaoh punished his slaves for daring to request a vacation, and he made sure they knew Moses was to blame. Angry and upset, Moses complained to God about the apparent defeat.

But God did not berate Moses. Instead, God reassured him. He reaffirmed his identity, pointing out Moses' privilege of knowing God's name, and reminding Moses that he had already promised to save the Israelites. Just because the problem was still there—or had even gotten worse—did not mean God wasn't on top of it. God was going to rescue the slaves, but it would take ten plagues and at least a year. A great story and a witness to God's power came out of this difficulty. Sometimes our pain and struggles are necessary to work things out for our good and God's glory.

Miracles Won't Make You Believe

GOD said to Moses, "Go to Pharaoh and tell him, 'GOD, the God of the Hebrews, says: Release my people so they can worship me. If you refuse to release them and continue to hold on to them, I'm giving you fair warning: GOD will come down hard on your livestock out in the fields—horses, donkeys, camels, cattle, sheep—striking them with a severe disease. GOD will draw a sharp line between the livestock of Israel and the livestock of Egypt. Not one animal that belongs to the Israelites will die.' "

Then GOD set the time: "Tomorrow GOD will do this thing."

And the next day GOD did it. All the livestock of Egypt died, but not one animal of the Israelites died. Pharaoh sent men to find out what had happened and there it was: none of the livestock of the Israelites had died—not one death. But Pharaoh stayed stubborn. He wouldn't release the people.

Exodus 9:1–7 MSG

※

Some people think that if they could see God perform a miracle, they would believe him. But Pharaoh was not so easily convinced by Moses. Not until ten plagues devastated his nation did Pharaoh reluctantly—and temporarily—grant Moses' request to let his people go.

The plague on the livestock was the fifth out of ten—the halfway point. It was also the second plague where God had made a distinction between Israel and Egypt. It clarified that the disasters were not just coincidences.

The plagues were not simply inconveniences. They were not merely attacks on water, land, and property. They were far more. They were also attacks on the Egyptian gods and goddesses (Exodus 12:12). Why should Pharaoh, himself a god according to Egyptian belief, pay the slightest attention to Yahweh, God of slaves?

But with plague after plague, Egyptian god after Egyptian god was laid low. The bull was the symbol of Apis, a protector of the diseased. The cow was the symbol of Hathor, the goddess of love, beauty, and joy. A common title for the pharaoh was "strong bull of his mother Hathor." That their animals should be so slaughtered could be interpreted by the Egyptians only as a victory of Yahweh over those gods.

But there were many gods in Egypt. That's why Pharaoh didn't give in easily. His attitude was, so what if Yahweh could beat a few of them? A lost battle did not mean a lost war. It took many plagues before Israel's God could convince Pharaoh of the error of his ways. It may likewise take God a long time to convince us to change something in our lives that we'd rather not.

Day 121

Angel Food

The LORD spoke to Moses, "I have heard the complaints of the Israelites. Tell them: At twilight you will eat meat, and in the morning you will eat bread until you are full. Then you will know that I am the LORD your God."

So at evening quail came and covered the camp. In the morning there was a layer of dew all around the camp. When the layer of dew evaporated, there on the desert surface were fine flakes, as fine as frost on the ground. When the Israelites saw it, they asked one another, "What is it?" because they didn't know what it was.

Moses told them, "It is the bread the LORD has given you to eat. This is what the LORD has commanded: 'Gather as much of it as each person needs to eat. You may take two quarts per individual, according to the number of people each of you has in his tent.'"

Exodus 16:11–16 HCSB

Hungry people are unhappy people. There's nothing unusual in that. God's response was not to let them starve, despite the fact that their words and concern grew out of disbelief and distrust of God's intentions toward them. They were quick to assume the worst, which is also a common human failing. It would have been one thing for them to ask, "How much longer?" in the midst of a crisis. It was quite another to accuse God of not loving them and of wanting them to starve. One attitude expresses a belief that God does care and will act, however long it might take. The other attitude expresses a belief that God doesn't care at all or maybe isn't even there in the first place. The second is the most common response to any crisis.

God's actions toward the people he loved were always the same. He was good and loving toward them. He gave them quail for meat and manna for bread. Some have speculated that manna was a honeydew secretion from insects that ate the sap of the tamarisk trees that grew in the Sinai. However, this explanation fails to explain why the manna appeared only six days a week.

The Hebrew word for "What is it?" was pronounced the same as manna, and so that became the name of what was appearing on the ground six days a week. What began as strange and wonderful soon became as ordinary as gravity. People quickly took it for granted, a part of nature no different from the daily rising and setting of the sun. It's easy to stop noticing God's common daily blessings in our lives.

They're Bigger than We Are

The LORD said to Joshua, "Do not fear or be dismayed; take all the fighting men with you, and go up now to Ai. See, I have handed over to you the king of Ai with his people, his city, and his land. You shall do to Ai and its king as you did to Jericho and its king; only its spoil and its livestock you may take as booty for yourselves. Set an ambush against the city, behind it."

So Joshua and all the fighting men set out to go up against Ai. Joshua chose thirty thousand warriors and sent them out by night with the command, "You shall lie in ambush against the city, behind it; do not go very far from the city, but all of you stay alert. I and all the people who are with me will approach the city. When they come out against us, as before, we shall flee from them. They will come out after us until we have drawn them away from the city; for they will say, 'They are fleeing from us, as before.' While we flee from them, you shall rise up from the ambush and seize the city; for the LORD your God will give it into your hand. And when you have taken the city, you shall set the city on fire, doing as the LORD has ordered; see, I have commanded you."

Joshua 8:1–8 NRSV

*I*f at first you don't succeed, try again. The Canaanites were not a unified nation. Instead, they were a conglomeration of competing cities scattered across hundreds of square miles. Each city had to be defeated separately. The war that Joshua had begun at Jericho would have to continue until every Canaanite city was defeated. There were hundreds of cities, some small, some large, ranging in population from a few hundred to a hundred thousand. Ai was just a tiny village. Joshua had thought it would be an easy victory. But at Jericho, one of his soldiers by the name of Achan had stolen plunder that belonged to God. As a result, when the Israelites attacked Ai, they lost the battle. Many Israelites died. It was the first time Israel had ever lost, and Joshua was afraid. But God told him to punish Achan and then to go ahead and attack the city a second time. He reassured Joshua that the second battle would turn out differently.

Achan's sin, their previous loss, and their subsequent fear did not mean that God was not with them. Victory was certain despite how things looked because victory was not dependent upon them or the size of their faith. It was dependent upon the size of their God.

Who Am I?

The Angel of the LORD came and sat under the terebinth tree which was in Ophrah, which belonged to Joash the Abiezrite, while his son Gideon threshed wheat in the winepress, in order to hide it from the Midianites. And the Angel of the LORD appeared to him, and said to him, "The LORD is with you, you mighty man of valor!"

Gideon said to Him, "O my lord, if the LORD is with us, why then has all this happened to us? And where are all His miracles which our fathers told us about, saying, 'Did not the LORD bring us up from Egypt?' But now the LORD has forsaken us and delivered us into the hands of the Midianites."

Then the LORD turned to him and said, "Go in this might of yours, and you shall save Israel from the hand of the Midianites. Have I not sent you?"

So he said to Him, "O my Lord, how can I save Israel? Indeed my clan is the weakest in Manasseh, and I am the least in my father's house."

And the LORD said to him, "Surely I will be with you, and you shall defeat the Midianites as one man."

Judges 6:11–16 NKJV

✹

*S*ometimes low self-esteem has a basis in fact. Gideon didn't think much of himself or his abilities. He belonged to an insignificant family in a small tribe. He was just an ordinary person trying to survive, wondering why God didn't rescue his people from their dire conditions: they had been oppressed for seven years by Midianite raiders who had stolen crops and impoverished them. The Midianites were descendants of Abraham, through one of his sons born to his wife Keturah, whom he'd married after Sarah died. The Midianites were the ones who had sold Joseph into slavery in Egypt (Genesis 37:25-28, 36; 39:1). Moses' first wife, Zipporah, was the daughter of a priest of Midian (Exodus 2:16; 3:1).

God had rescued the Israelites from Egypt, but what had he done for them since? It seemed to Gideon that they had merely exchanged one set of chains for another. Slavery was slavery, even if they weren't in Egypt anymore. And while Gideon expected God to raise up a new Moses to save them, the last thing he imagined was that God would ask him to fill that role.

But God was not dependent upon Gideon's sense of his own importance, nor was he dependent upon Gideon's having enormous faith. God can use whomever he wants, and those he picks are invariably changed as a result. Heroes are made, not born.

I Have a Dream

The 300 men took the people's provisions and their trumpets into their hands. And Gideon sent all the other men of Israel, each to his tent, but retained the 300 men; and the camp of Midian was below him in the valley.

Now the same night it came about that the LORD said to him, "Arise, go down against the camp, for I have given it into your hands.

"But if you are afraid to go down, go with Purah your servant down to the camp, and you will hear what they say; and afterward your hands will be strengthened that you may go down against the camp." So he went with Purah his servant down to the outposts of the army that was in the camp.

Now the Midianites and the Amalekites and all the sons of the east were lying in the valley as numerous as locusts; and their camels were without number, as numerous as the sand on the seashore.

When Gideon came, behold, a man was relating a dream to his friend. And he said, "Behold, I had a dream; a loaf of barley bread was tumbling into the camp of Midian, and it came to the tent and struck it so that it fell, and turned it upside down so that the tent lay flat."

His friend replied, "This is nothing less than the sword of Gideon the son of Joash, a man of Israel; God has given Midian and all the camp into his hand."

When Gideon heard the account of the dream and its interpretation, he bowed in worship. He returned to the camp of Israel and said, "Arise, for the LORD has given the camp of Midian into your hands."

Judges 7:8–15 NASB

The word of God was not sufficient for Gideon. He also needed words from his enemies. Why? Adam had God as a constant companion, but God said it wasn't good for him to be alone. Although God had spoken through prophets for centuries, he had to become human to really get humanity's attention. We sometimes trust people we can see more than God, whom we can't.

The Amalekites were descended from Amalek, the grandson of Isaac's son Esau (Genesis 36:15–16). Together with the Midianites, they were a source of suffering for the Israelites during the time of Gideon.

After his army had been reduced to a mere three hundred, Gideon's confidence in God's mission was at a low ebb. For most of us, hearing God tell us to do something would seem like enough. But Gideon needed to hear an enemy's dream. God knows what we need, and he makes sure we get it.

Night Whispers

The boy Samuel served the LORD by assisting Eli. Now in those days messages from the LORD were very rare, and visions were quite uncommon.

One night Eli, who was almost blind by now, had gone to bed. The lamp of God had not yet gone out, and Samuel was sleeping in the Tabernacle near the Ark of God. Suddenly the LORD called out, "Samuel!"

"Yes?" Samuel replied. "What is it?" He got up and ran to Eli. "Here I am. Did you call me?"

"I didn't call you," Eli replied. "Go back to bed." So he did.

Then the LORD called out again, "Samuel!"

Again Samuel got up and went to Eli. "Here I am. Did you call me?"

"I didn't call you, my son," Eli said. "Go back to bed."

Samuel did not yet know the LORD because he had never had a message from the LORD before . . .

Then Eli realized it was the LORD who was calling the boy. So he said to Samuel, "Go and lie down again, and if someone calls again, say 'Speak, LORD, your servant is listening.'"

1 Samuel 3:1–9 NLT

God's people hear his voice, but they don't always recognize it. Samuel heard a voice in the night and responded, but he didn't know who was calling him. Oddly, God did not identify himself. He let Samuel repeatedly run to Eli to wake him up.

Eli had not heard God's voice, but he realized it was God. This was so despite the fact that he was not in the habit of listening to God.

Samuel's mother was unable to have children, and so she promised God that if he gave her a son, she would dedicate him to God. Once Samuel was weaned, she brought him to the tabernacle and placed him in Eli's care. Eli had essentially adopted Samuel as his own.

Visions and messages from God had become rare because God saw no point in wasting his breath for someone who wouldn't listen anymore. So God decided to raise up a prophet. If Eli wouldn't or couldn't hear God directly, he would have no trouble hearing Samuel. And if Eli wouldn't proclaim God to the people of Israel, then Samuel would.

God's people still recognize him, no matter how far they may have drifted or how long they may last have talked to him. Like glimpsing an old friend after years of separation, Eli knew whom Samuel had heard.

Believing What You Want to Hear

The old prophet answered, "I am a prophet, too, just as you are. And an angel gave me this command from the LORD: 'Bring him home with you so he can have something to eat and drink.'" But the old man was lying to him. So they went back together, and the man of God ate and drank at the prophet's home.

Then while they were sitting at the table, a command from the LORD came to the old prophet. He cried out to the man of God from Judah, "This is what the LORD says: You have defied the word of the LORD and have disobeyed the command the LORD your God gave you. You came back to this place and ate and drank where he told you not to eat or drink. Because of this, your body will not be buried in the grave of your ancestors."

After the man of God had finished eating and drinking, the old prophet saddled his own donkey for him, and the man of God started off again. But as he was traveling along, a lion came out and killed him. His body lay there on the road, with the donkey and the lion standing beside it.

1 Kings 13:18–24 NLT

※

*N*obody's perfect. God sent a prophet to deliver a message to Jeroboam, king of Israel. Jeroboam was standing by the false altar in Bethel when the prophet arrived. He told Jeroboam that the false priests would be slaughtered and that their bones would be burned on that very altar by Josiah, a future king of Judah. As proof of his words, the prophet said that the altar would split and the ashes would be spilled. As Jeroboam yelled and pointed at the prophet, his hand shriveled up. He begged the prophet to heal him, which he did. Jeroboam then offered him a meal, but the prophet refused. God had told him that he must not eat or drink anything until he got home.

On his journey back, another prophet offered him hospitality. He lied to him and said God had given him a new message: it was now okay to eat and drink.

Doubtless hungry, he accepted the prophet's hospitality. But when God tells someone to do something, he doesn't change his mind later just because carrying out his instructions might have become inconvenient. It is important to believe what God said, even if we'd rather he had said something else.

The prophet died because he believed a stranger, whom he had never met before, instead of God. It is all too easy to let the shadows of life distract us from the light of God.

Food from the Sky

Elijah the Tishbite, from among the settlers of Gilead, confronted Ahab: "As surely as GOD lives, the God of Israel before whom I stand in obedient service, the next years are going to see a total drought—not a drop of dew or rain unless I say otherwise."

GOD then told Elijah, "Get out of here, and fast. Head east and hide out at the Kerith Ravine on the other side of the Jordan River. You can drink fresh water from the brook; I've ordered the ravens to feed you."

Elijah obeyed GOD's orders. He went and camped in the Kerith canyon on the other side of the Jordan. And sure enough, ravens brought him his meals, both breakfast and supper, and he drank from the brook.

1 Kings 17:1–6 MSG

God uses ordinary people. There aren't any other kind. God made Elijah a prophet to the Northern Kingdom of Israel. There was nothing special about him. He simply believed whatever it was God told him.

Elijah's name means "my God is Yahweh." He lived and prophesied during the reign of the kings Ahab and his son Ahaziah. The first time Elijah shows up in the Bible is when he confronts Ahab about the coming drought. Elijah was the only person in the Bible referred to as a Tishbite. The word translated as *settlers* was taken by the ancient Greek translation of the Bible known as the Septuagint to be the name of a city, Tishbe, Elijah's home village.

Ahab was the king of Israel. He had married Jezebel, a non-Israelite. Ahab and his wife encouraged the people to worship gods other than just Yahweh. So Elijah delivered God's message to Ahab: because of your sin, no more rain.

When God told Elijah to run away from Ahab, he obeyed that command just as quickly as he'd obeyed the previous. God's message to Ahab included the assurance that the rain would stay away until Elijah said otherwise. Elijah understood what Ahab might do to him if he stayed.

Ahab's response to Elijah tells us something unexpected about Ahab. Although he was ruthless and despicable, he believed God, and believed what Elijah had told him. Ahab wouldn't have waited for drought before arresting poor Elijah. He knew already that Elijah was a prophet. He knew already what God could and would do. Which also tells us something about faith: it doesn't necessarily make people behave well or choose wisely. Faith without actions is dead. Just about anyone can have faith, but what's critical is that faith is accompanied by doing what's right.

An Unreasonable Request

Ravens brought him bread and meat twice a day, and he drank water from the creek. But after a while, it dried up because there was no rain.

The LORD told Elijah, "Go to the town of Zarephath in Sidon and live there. I've told a widow in that town to give you food."

When Elijah came near the town gate of Zarephath, he saw a widow gathering sticks for a fire. "Would you please bring me a cup of water?" he asked. As she left to get it, he asked, "Would you also please bring me a piece of bread?"

The widow answered, "In the name of the living LORD your God, I swear that I don't have any bread. All I have is a handful of flour and a little olive oil. I'm on my way home now with these few sticks to cook what I have for my son and me. After that, we will starve to death."

Elijah said, "Everything will be fine. Do what you said. Go home and fix something for you and your son. But first, please make a small piece of bread and bring it to me. The LORD God of Israel has promised that your jar of flour won't run out and your bottle of oil won't dry up before he sends rain for the crops."

1 Kings 17:6–14 CEV

*B*ecause of the drought, people were starting to starve. Why was there a drought? King Ahab's wife Jezebel, the daughter of the king of Sidon, had introduced the worship of her Phoenician gods into Israel. So God told Elijah to pray that there would be no more rain. God answered his prayer. But where did God then send Elijah to live when the stream he'd been living beside had run out of water? To a widow who lived just a few miles from Jezebel's old hometown of Sidon! She was a Phoenician just like Jezebel herself. When Elijah approached that poor widow—at God's command because the stream he'd been living beside had run out of water—she was teetering on the edge of starvation. Elijah demanded the last bit of food from this miserable, desperate woman.

There were many widows in Israel, and many of God's people were suffering the consequences of the drought God had sent to punish Ahab and Jezebel. But Elijah went to only one hungry person: that widow in Zarephath, in the region of Sidon. She was less likely than an Israelite to be a worshipper of Yahweh. And yet it was to this unhappy woman that the prophet went. His request was unreasonable. But she believed God and took Elijah in. Because she did this, she prospered in the dark times. Faith is a gift of God that he grants to whom he will, even the least likely. It isn't given on the basis of merit.

Someone Just Like Us

After a long time, the word of the LORD came to Elijah in the third year: "Go and present yourself to Ahab. I will send rain on the surface of the land." So Elijah went to present himself to Ahab.

The famine was severe in Samaria. Ahab called for Obadiah, who was in charge of the palace. Obadiah was a man who greatly feared the LORD and took 100 prophets and hid them, 50 men to a cave, and provided them with food and water when Jezebel slaughtered the LORD's prophets. Ahab said to Obadiah, "Go throughout the land to every spring of water and to every wadi. Perhaps we'll find grass so we can keep the horses and mules alive and not have to destroy any cattle." They divided the land between them in order to cover it. Ahab went one way by himself, and Obadiah went the other way by himself.

While Obadiah was [walking] along the road, Elijah suddenly met him. When Obadiah recognized him, he fell with his face [to the ground] and said, "Is it you, my lord Elijah?"

"It is I," he replied. "Go tell your lord, 'Elijah is here!'"

1 Kings 18:1–8 HCSB

✻

*Y*ou can't hide forever. Sooner or later, you must face the problem. Elijah had spent months hiding from Ahab. But God told him at last that the time had come to confront the king of Israel and tell him that the drought was over. He headed toward Samaria, the capital of Israel, where Ahab lived. Ahab's name meant "father's brother." His father had been Omri, noted in the Bible only for his wickedness. The other nations, however, thought so highly of Omri that ever after they called Israel "Omriland."

On Obadiah's way to meet Ahab in Samaria, God brought an old friend to meet him along the way. Obadiah (not to be confused with the prophet by the same name) had been put in charge of Ahab's palace. Obadiah's name meant "servant of Yahweh," and that is certainly what he was. Elijah didn't have to face his enemy alone. He had a mediator in Obadiah. He had a man he could trust and whom the king trusted as well. Obadiah would be the one to let the king know that Elijah was back.

Elijah's faith was nothing remarkable. He was, after all, merely human. But he had learned that he could believe what God said, and so he acted accordingly. We all have to face the same issue: will we hide from our problems, or will we decide that God is as real and as trustworthy as our closest friend? We don't have to face our lives alone.

God, You Just Don't Understand

"Go out and stand on the mountain," the LORD replied. "I want you to see me when I pass by."

All at once, a strong wind shook the mountain and shattered the rocks. But the LORD was not in the wind. Next, there was an earthquake, but the LORD was not in the earthquake. Then there was a fire, but the LORD was not in the fire.

Finally, there was a gentle breeze, and when Elijah heard it, he covered his face with his coat. He went out and stood at the entrance to the cave. The LORD asked, "Elijah, why are you here?" Elijah answered, "LORD God All-Powerful, I've always done my best to obey you. But your people have broken their solemn promise to you. They have torn down your altars and killed all your prophets, except me. And now they are even trying to kill me!"

The LORD said:

> Elijah, you can go back to the desert near Damascus. And when you get there, appoint Hazael to be king of Syria. Then appoint Jehu son of Nimshi to be king of Israel, and Elisha son of Shaphat to take your place as my prophet. Hazael will start killing the people who worship Baal. Jehu will kill those who escape from Hazael, and Elisha will kill those who escape from Jehu. But seven thousand Israelites have refused to worship Baal, and they will live.

1 Kings 19:11–18 CEV

Doesn't God understand how bad things are? Why doesn't he do something? Jezebel, the foreign queen of Israel, had executed as many prophets of God as she could find. Baal worship was rampant. Elijah, one of God's remaining prophets, challenged Baal's prophets to a contest to see who was most powerful: God or Baal. God won, of course.

Jezebel responded by threatening to kill Elijah, and so he ran away. For weeks Elijah, exhausted and discouraged, hid in the wilderness. Finally, while Elijah was sitting in a cave, God told him that he was about to pass by. Elijah anticipated glorious things. But Elijah's thinking needed to be changed, and God began the process by arriving in a whisper rather than in a spectacle. Elijah thought God just didn't understand his situation. By his silence, followed by his simple question, God showed Elijah that he was the one who really didn't understand. Enlightenment came to Elijah only as illusions were shattered and he was forced to see things as they actually were. Sometimes the reason we don't see God's solution is simply because we're looking the wrong way.

Miracle in the Desert

Jehoshaphat said, "Isn't there a prophet of the LORD here? Let's inquire of the LORD through him."

One of the servants of the king of Israel answered, "Elisha son of Shaphat, who used to pour water on Elijah's hands, is here."

Jehoshaphat affirmed, "The LORD's words are with him." So the king of Israel and Jehoshaphat and the king of Edom went to him.

However, Elisha said to King [Joram] of Israel, "We have nothing in common. Go to the prophets of your father and your mother!"

But the king of Israel replied, "No, because it is the LORD who has summoned us three kings to hand us over to Moab."

Elisha responded, "As the LORD of Hosts lives, I stand before Him. If I did not have respect for King Jehoshaphat of Judah, I would not look at you; I wouldn't take notice of you. Now, bring me a musician."

While the musician played, the LORD's hand came on Elisha. Then he said, "This is what the LORD says: 'Dig ditch after ditch in this wadi.' For the LORD says, 'You will not see wind or rain, but the wadi will be filled with water, and you will drink—you and your cattle and your animals.' This is easy in the LORD's sight. He will also hand Moab over to you. Then you must attack every fortified city and every choice city. You must cut down every good tree and stop up every spring of water. You must ruin every good piece of land with stones."

2 Kings 3:11–19 HCSB

*W*ho are you going to call when you really need help? Since Joram worshipped Baal and had priests and prophets of Baal working for him, the prophet Elisha couldn't understand why Joram didn't seek guidance from them. Joram's insistence on hearing from Elisha indicated that he understood Baal was useless. Like his father, Ahab, he didn't take Baal as seriously as he did Yahweh, the one true God.

God does not speak loud. Elisha's master, the prophet Elijah, had once discovered that God did not speak in earthquakes and that instead he spoke in a "still small voice" (1 Kings 19:12). Elisha was angry. He did not like Joram, a wicked king, and he did not like the king of Edom, a pagan king. Following the example of King Saul, who had David play music for him when he felt bad, Elisha listened to music in order to calm himself and get himself out of his bad mood long enough that he could focus on listening to God instead of listening to his own raging thoughts.

Life can be noisy. God is quiet. Sometimes it takes extra effort to find a quiet place where we can hear him.

No Food for You

Elisha was sitting in his house, and the elders were sitting with him. And the king sent a man ahead of him, but before the messenger came to him, he said to the elders, "Do you see how this son of a murderer has sent someone to take away my head? Look, when the messenger comes, shut the door, and hold him fast at the door. Is not the sound of his master's feet behind him?" And while he was still talking with them, there was the messenger, coming down to him; and then the king said, "Surely this calamity is from the LORD; why should I wait for the LORD any longer?"

Then Elisha said, "Hear the word of the LORD. Thus says the LORD: 'Tomorrow about this time a seah of fine flour shall be sold for a shekel, and two seahs of barley for a shekel, at the gate of Samaria.'"

So an officer on whose hand the king leaned answered the man of God and said, "Look, if the LORD would make windows in heaven, could this thing be?"

And he said, "In fact, you shall see it with your eyes, but you shall not eat of it."

2 Kings 6:32–7:2 NKJV

✳

*D*oubt can kill you. Elijah had ascended by chariot into heaven, but Ahab was still the king. Due to a siege against Samaria by Ben Hadad, the king of Aram, the capital city of the Northern Kingdom of Israel was nearly out of food. Some had resorted to cannibalism. Ahab blamed Elisha and wanted him dead. Elisha had been Elijah's servant, but with Elijah's departure, he became prophet in his place. He was as much a critic of Ahab as Elijah had been.

God predicted that the famine would end by the next day. One of the king's officers couldn't see how, and he even suggested God couldn't do it.

That night, four men with leprosy decided that they'd rather be killed by the Arameans than starve. So they sneaked out and found the Aramean camp deserted. God had convinced the Aramean army that they were being attacked by the Hittites and Egyptians—and so they had fled, abandoning their provisions, their tents, their horses and donkeys.

The lepers filled their bellies. They gathered gold and silver and hid it. Then they decided they should return to the city with the news. In the mad rush of desperate people leaving the city for the suddenly available food, the doubting officer was trampled to death. He saw God's words come true, but he was never able to benefit from them.

Day 133

❀❀❀❀❀❀❀❀❀❀❀❀❀❀❀❀❀❀❀❀❀❀❀❀❀❀❀❀❀❀❀❀❀❀

The Gates of Death

The LORD answered Job out of the
whirlwind and said . . .
"Have you entered into the
springs of the sea
Or walked in the recesses of
the deep?
"Have the gates of death been
revealed to you,
Or have you seen the gates of
deep darkness?
"Have you understood the ex-
panse of the earth?
Tell Me, if you know all this.

"Where is the way to the dwelling
of light?
And darkness, where is its
place,
That you may take it to its territory
And that you may discern the
paths to its home?
"You know, for you were born
then,
And the number of your days
is great!"

Job 38:1, 16–21 NASB

❀

*G*od's response to Job's flagging faith was sarcasm. Job had lost his family and his health, and he was beginning to lose his belief in God's love.

Job lived in the land of Uz and was an Israelite. Since he apparently performed sacrifices for his children, it's possible he was a priest, and thus a Levite. When did Job live? God's name, Yahweh, appears repeatedly in the book of Job. It's a name that was not used prior to Moses. Since the exodus from Egypt is also mentioned in the book of Job (Job 26:12), it seems obvious that Job and his troubles dated from a time after Israel had entered the promised land.

After Job's family, wealth, and health had been devastated, he faced his friends, who accused him of being guilty of a major sin. Job insisted he had done nothing to deserve his suffering, even though he had no explanation for it.

God asked Job a series of questions that he knew Job would not be able to answer. Why did God respond to Job's suffering by gently teasing him?

God wondered why Job's inability to fathom an explanation for his suffering was any different from Job's inability to explain where light lived or where the gates of death might be. Job had concluded that there was no good reason for his pain and so God must hate him or be bad or unreasonable. That made as much sense as concluding that his ignorance about light meant God hated him. Job learned that God wouldn't necessarily answer all the questions he wondered about. In fact, the answers he got might not even be to the questions he was asking. He learned that too often he didn't even know what the right questions might be. Just because we are confused doesn't mean that God is.

Catching Monsters

The LORD answered Job from the whirl-wind: . . .

"Can you catch Leviathan with a hook or put a noose around its jaw?

Can you tie it with a rope through the nose or pierce its jaw with a spike?

Will it beg you for mercy or implore you for pity?

Will it agree to work for you, to be your slave for life?

Can you make it a pet like a bird, or give it to your little girls to play with?

Will merchants try to buy it to sell it in their shops?

Will its hide be hurt by spears or its head by a harpoon?

If you lay a hand on it, you will certainly remember the battle that follows.

You won't try that again!

No, it is useless to try to capture it.

The hunter who attempts it will be knocked down.

And since no one dares to disturb it, who then can stand up to me?

Who has given me anything that I need to pay back?

Everything under heaven is mine."

Job 40:6; 41:1–11 NLT

❄

*G*od compared himself to a monster. In the mythology of Ugarit, a Canaanite city just north of Israel, Leviathan was a sea monster that battled the god Baal. His ally was Mot, the god of the underworld. Leviathan was defeated. For the Israelites, the monster's death became a symbol for the death of the wicked. It was also used figuratively to represent the Egyptians, since God had drowned them in the Red Sea (Psalm 74:14; Isaiah 27:1). Moreover, the monster was recognized as something that only God could defeat or control.

God adapted the myth to his own purposes, pointing out that neither Job nor any other human being could control such a sea monster. Job thought he could stand up to God and legitimately question God's choices. But God is all powerful and owns everything.

Did God owe Job something? Had God somehow missed the past-due bill? Job had no business questioning God's goodness. If he wouldn't bother a sea monster or ask it questions, then how could Job dare question God? If he feared a monster, he should fear even more the one who created it. If God can control a sea monster, he can control our lives.

Nothing to Fear

It was told to the house of David, saying, "Syria's forces are deployed in Ephraim." So his heart and the heart of his people were moved as the trees of the woods are moved with the wind.

Then the LORD said to Isaiah, "Go out now to meet Ahaz, you and Shear-Jashub your son, at the end of the aqueduct from the upper pool, on the highway to the Fuller's Field, and say to him: 'Take heed, and be quiet; do not fear or be fainthearted for these two stubs of smoking firebrands, for the fierce anger of Rezin and Syria, and the son of Remaliah. Because Syria, Ephraim, and the son of Remaliah have plotted evil against you, saying, "Let us go up against Judah and trouble it, and let us make a gap in its wall for ourselves, and set a king over them, the son of Tabel"—'thus says the Lord GOD:

> "It shall not stand,
> Nor shall it come to pass.
> For the head of Syria is Damascus,
> And the head of Damascus is
>   Rezin.
> Within sixty-five years Ephraim
>   will be broken,
> So that it will not be a people.
> The head of Ephraim is Samaria,
> And the head of Samaria is Rema-
>   liah's son.
> If you will not believe,
> Surely you shall not be
>   established."'"

Isaiah 7:2–9 NKJV

※

It's hard to trust someone you can't see when you're faced with a threat you can see. Ahaz, the king of Judah from about 735 BC to 715 BC, didn't trust God much. He was being threatened by nations to the north: Israel, ruled by Pekah, had allied itself with Rezin, king of the Arameans in Syria. Thanks to that alliance, Syria had moved its troops into Israel. So Ahaz and his officials were understandably concerned.

But the Assyrian Empire under Tiglath-Pileser would soon invade the region and conquer both Syria and Israel, carrying them into captivity around 722 BC, barely two years after Isaiah's prophecy.

God promised to destroy the enemies Ahaz was so worried about. Ahaz should have been comforted. He should have had confidence in God. Instead, he was more willing to put his trust in everything and everyone else. He burned his son and offered other sacrifices to false gods (2 Kings 16:3–4).

He turned his back on God. But despite his disbelief, God took care of him and protected the people of God anyway. God is with you even when you don't feel his presence, even when you don't think he can do anything, and even if you make all the wrong choices.

Give God a Test

The LORD spoke to Ahaz, "Ask the LORD your God for a sign, whether in the deepest depths or in the highest heights."

But Ahaz said, "I will not ask; I will not put the LORD to the test."

Then Isaiah said, "Hear now, you house of David! Is it not enough to try the patience of men? Will you try the patience of my God also? Therefore the Lord himself will give you a sign: The virgin will be with child and will give birth to a son, and will call him Immanuel. He will eat curds and honey when he knows enough to reject the wrong and choose the right. But before the boy knows enough to reject the wrong and choose the right, the land of the two kings you dread will be laid waste. The LORD will bring on you and on your people and on the house of your father a time unlike any since Ephraim broke away from Judah—he will bring the king of Assyria."

Isaiah 7:10–17 NIV

When God asks you to take a test drive, you should get in the car. God told Ahaz to ask for a sign, but Ahaz refused.

Ahaz claimed he didn't want to test God. But really, Ahaz simply didn't want to do God's will. He thought his own plans would take care of his problems. He did not trust God because he did not have a right belief about God. Like many people in his time, Ahaz believed that gods had authority only over their own nations and that conflicts between nations were conflicts between those nations' gods. Ahaz thought that his enemies' gods might be stronger than his, and he wasn't willing to risk his kingdom based just on what Judah's God told him.

God gave him a sign anyway. Sometimes, God doesn't take no for an answer. God told him that a virgin would give birth. The virgin who would have the promised child was identified as a prophetess (Isaiah 8:3). God promised Ahaz that before the child was old enough to tell right from wrong, the two kings that he feared—Pekah of Israel and Rezin of Syria—would be dead. God would do what he intended, regardless of Ahaz's beliefs.

God can reveal himself miraculously, perform great wonders, and give you what you want most in the world, even when you lack faith and have a bad attitude. God will always do what needs to be done for you.

The Hidden God

Thus says the LORD:

The wealth of Egypt and the merchandise of Ethiopia,
and the Sabeans, tall of stature,
shall come over to you and be yours,
they shall follow you;
they shall come over in chains and
bow down to you.
They will make supplication to you,
saying,
"God is with you alone, and there
is no other;
there is no god besides him."
Truly, you are a God who hides
himself,

O God of Israel, the Savior.
All of them are put to shame and
confounded,
the makers of idols go in
confusion together.
But Israel is saved by the LORD
with everlasting salvation;
you shall not be put to shame or
confounded
to all eternity.

Isaiah 45:14–17 NRSV

*W*hat you see isn't always what you get. Egypt and Ethiopia were close to each other in Africa. Sometimes the Egyptians ruled the Ethiopians. Sometimes the Ethiopians ruled the Egyptians. Sebea, or Sheba, from which the Sabeans came, was located on the coast of the Arabian Peninsula in what is today called Yemen. Sheba also may have established colonies along the coast of Ethiopia. One of their queens once visited Solomon.

Alone among the peoples of the world, the Jews did not make physical representations of their God. The God of Israel was not visible, nor was he ever to be made visible. While the other gods had visible representations, they were powerless and did nothing. The God of Israel was invisible, but he was powerful and did everything. The hidden God became visible in what he accomplished. The Israelites could place their faith in him because of the evidence of his actions.

Isaiah predicted that the people of Egypt, Ethiopia, and Sabea would turn to worshipping the God of Israel. But they wouldn't do it because of beautiful idols stationed in a beautiful temple. The God of Israel was something far more than just a pretty statue. When we can't see our friends, it's because they aren't around. But God is different. He's around even when we can't see him.

Believing Won't Make It Happen

Stand now with your enchantments
  And the multitude of your
    sorceries,
  In which you have labored from
    your youth—
Perhaps you will be able to profit,
Perhaps you will prevail.
You are wearied in the multitude
  of your counsels;
Let now the astrologers, the
  stargazers,
And the monthly prognosticators
Stand up and save you
From what shall come upon you.
Behold, they shall be as stubble,

The fire shall burn them;
They shall not deliver themselves
From the power of the flame;
It shall not be a coal to be
  warmed by,
Nor a fire to sit before!
Thus shall they be to you
With whom you have labored,
Your merchants from your youth;
They shall wander each one to his
  quarter.
No one shall save you.

Isaiah 47:12–15 NKJV

*W*hat you put your faith in matters. Israel had turned to other gods, hoping that they would provide the answers to the puzzles of life. The Israelites had been poorly influenced by the peoples around them. Their neighbors worshipped the moon, the stars, the sun, and the sea with their enchanters and astrologers. But the Israelites believed that wisdom dwelled in the ancient mysteries the people of Canaan trusted.

But God had repeatedly sent prophets to the people of Israel to warn them to turn from the beliefs and practices of the Canaanites. The prophets did not bring the Israelites new words. They merely repeated the old words that God had already spoken through Moses. Isaiah and Micah were the last prophets to bring God's warning before he finally punished the northern tribes by sending them into exile.

Lies cannot be transformed into reality just because you believe hard enough. Astrologers imagined that the placement of the planets among the stars and the placement of the stars in the sky somehow influenced the paths of human beings. They thought that the motions of the sky could predict the directions of people on earth.

But the conquering Assyrians were not stopped by the horoscopes that the Israelites consulted. When the bad times came, the enchanters and false gods proved incapable of rescuing the Israelites. Only the real God can be completely trusted to do what he says.

Day 139

Listening to God

"Listen to me, you who pursue
   righteousness,
      Who seek the LORD:
      Look to the rock from which you
         were hewn
      And to the quarry from which you
         were dug.

"Look to Abraham your father
      And to Sarah who gave birth to
         you in pain;
      When he was but one I
         called him,
      Then I blessed him and
         multiplied him."

Indeed, the LORD will comfort Zion;
      He will comfort all her
         waste places.
      And her wilderness He will make
         like Eden,
      And her desert like the garden of
         the LORD;
      Joy and gladness will be found
         in her,
      Thanksgiving and sound of
         a melody.

Isaiah 51:1–3 NASB

God comforts the troubled. The Israelites went into captivity for their sin: the North to Assyria and the South to Babylon. In captivity, the Israelites turned away from their sin and back to God. God told them to get back on the path where they had first gone astray. He told them to pay attention to the lessons of their past. They needed to discover what God had actually said and how God had actually acted. God's words to Isaiah were reiterated in the New Testament when Jesus enjoined his listeners to "seek first the kingdom of God and His righteousness" (Matthew 6:33 NKJV).

Those who seek God's righteousness should remember those before them who did the same. God sent Abraham from his home into a land that wasn't his and gave him promises, many of which he never lived to see. Abraham waited decades before the promise of an heir was fulfilled, far past the time when it even seemed possible. The fulfillment of Abraham's hopes didn't come until he was a very old man. He lived most of his life without experiencing the reality of any of God's promises.

Those seeking righteousness can have confidence in God. But the need for comfort grows from suffering. It is easy to focus on the promised land that will be like Eden. We forget that the wilderness preceded the milk and the honey. The Israelites wandered for forty years before they entered the promised land, and even then, they faced years of hardship and war. The path of righteousness, the search for God, is sometimes a hard one.

Your Limitations Don't Bother God

The LORD gave me this message: "I knew you before I formed you in your mother's womb.
Before you were born I set you apart
and appointed you as my prophet to the nations."

"O Sovereign LORD," I said, "I can't speak for you! I'm too young!"
The LORD replied, "Don't say, 'I'm too young,' for you must go wherever I send you and say whatever I tell you. And don't be afraid of the people, for I will be with you and will protect you.

I, the LORD, have spoken!" Then the LORD reached out and touched my mouth and said,
"Look, I have put my words in your mouth!
Today I appoint you to stand up against nations and kingdoms.
Some you must uproot and tear down, destroy and overthrow.
Others you must build up and plant."

Jeremiah 1:4–10 NLT

❄

*I*t's good to know yourself. Do you know God? Jeremiah was the son of Hilkiah, a Levite descended from Aaron. That meant Jeremiah was a member of the priestly line. It is possible that he was a descendant of Abiathar, David's priest during his exile while he was running for his life from Saul. Jeremiah had a realistic picture of himself. But he did not have a realistic picture of God. Jeremiah believed God was calling him. Jeremiah believed that God needed to do something about all the wickedness in the land. But Jeremiah doubted that he could be the one through whom God chose to work. Jeremiah's lack of faith in himself and his lack of faith in God's ability to transform him into the mighty prophet he became did not slow God down. Jeremiah already had a tongue, and he could already talk. Getting Jeremiah up and running was not nearly so hard as creating a universe from scratch.

Jeremiah lived in a prosperous time. But a shadow hung over the land of milk and honey: the Babylonians were rising at the same time Egypt was declining. The balance of power in the world was shifting. But the real problem had nothing to do with international relations. Instead, God's concern lay with matters of the heart. His people had continued their love affair with other gods, and they didn't believe God would do anything about it, any more than Jeremiah believed that God could use him. Both God's people and Jeremiah would learn otherwise. God is never limited by human doubts.

Yes, This Might Hurt

Jeremiah said to Zedekiah, "Thus says the LORD, the God of hosts, the God of Israel: 'If you surely surrender to the king of Babylon's princes, then your soul shall live; this city shall not be burned with fire, and you and your house shall live. But if you do not surrender to the king of Babylon's princes, then this city shall be given into the hand of the Chaldeans; they shall burn it with fire, and you shall not escape from their hand.' "

And Zedekiah the king said to Jeremiah, "I am afraid of the Jews who have defected to the Chaldeans, lest they deliver me into their hand, and they abuse me."

But Jeremiah said, "They shall not deliver you. Please, obey the voice of the LORD which I speak to you. So it shall be well with you, and your soul shall live.

But if you refuse to surrender, this is the word that the LORD has shown me: 'Now behold, all the women who are left in the king of Judah's house shall be surrendered to the king of Babylon's princes, and those women shall say:

"Your close friends have set upon you
And prevailed against you;
Your feet have sunk in the mire,
And they have turned away again."

'So they shall surrender all your wives and children to the Chaldeans. You shall not escape from their hand, but shall be taken by the hand of the king of Babylon. And you shall cause this city to be burned with fire.' "

Jeremiah 38:17–23 NKJV

※

*G*od's goodness and mercy follow us all the days of our lives because we spend so many of those days running away from them. Nebuchadnezzar placed Zedekiah on the throne after conquering Jerusalem, but Zedekiah decided to rebel. The result was just what God had warned: Nebuchadnezzar attacked, and Zedekiah tried to run away but was captured. Nebuchadnezzar then executed Zedekiah's sons just before blinding Zedekiah. Afterward, Nebuchadnezzar took Zedekiah in chains to Babylon. Nebuchadnezzar burned Jerusalem and its temple to the ground. The people of God spent the next seventy years in captivity.

Zedekiah could have spared himself all these horrors. His people did not have to suffer. But he decided not to believe God. Instead, he believed he could maneuver things to his liking, get the Egyptians to help him, and somehow stand against the Chaldeans, that is, the Babylonians. He didn't like God's will for his life. Too often, we think God's will is designed to make us miserable. In actuality, however, he wants to make our lives wonderful. We simply have to resist our own will and give in to his.

I Reject Your Reality and Substitute My Own

They said to Jeremiah, "Let GOD be our witness, a true and faithful witness against us, if we don't do everything that your GOD directs you to tell us. Whether we like it or not, we'll do it. We'll obey whatever our GOD tells us. Yes, count on us. We'll do it."

Ten days later God's Message came to Jeremiah. He called together Johanan son of Kareah and all the army officers with him, including all the people, regardless of how much clout they had.

He then spoke: "This is the Message from GOD, the God of Israel, to whom you sent me to present your prayer. He says, 'If you are ready to stick it out in this land, I will build you up and not drag you down, I will plant you and not pull you up like a weed. I feel deep compassion on account of the doom I have visited on you. You don't have to fear the king of Babylon. Your fears are for nothing. I'm on your side, ready to save and deliver you from anything he might do. I'll pour mercy on you. What's more, *he* will show you mercy! He'll let you come back to your very own land.'"

Jeremiah 42:5–12 MSG

❋

*W*hat if God's answer to your question is the last thing you'd want to hear? Zedekiah, the last descendant of David, was blind and living in Babylon. The city of Jerusalem had been destroyed. Most of the rich and powerful of the land had been taken away to captivity. But Jeremiah and the rest of the people of Judah were still there. Nebuchadnezzar had appointed Gedaliah as governor over those who remained.

Both Gedaliah (2 Kings 25:24) and God, through Jeremiah, told the people to settle down and relax. They explained all would be well for those who remained in Judah if they didn't resist the Babylonians.

A group of concerned citizens went to Jeremiah pretending to seek God's will. But what they really wanted was for God to bless their will. So they rejected what God said through Jeremiah. God's will wasn't what they wanted at all. They wanted to fight for freedom. They wanted to restore the kingdom of Judah and get rid of the occupying troops. They wanted to rebel against the Babylonians. They wanted to go to Egypt, and so they did. They murdered Gedaliah (2 Kings 25:25–26) and then fled to Egypt, dragging Jeremiah with them. People usually want God to bless their decisions. They don't want to be blessed by God's decisions, because they don't trust God as much as they trust themselves. But it's best to start your decision-making process with God in the first place.

Loyalty and Betrayal

Betrayal disappoints our expectations. It comes as a surprise when the one we love doesn't love us back, or when cruelty is the response to our kindness. Loyalty, by contrast, fulfills expectations. Loyalty is faithfulness to one's commitments, the consequence of promises made regardless of actions on the part of another. Ruth's loyalty to her mother-in-law is an excellent example. Loyalty is indistinguishable from love, while betrayal is the same as hate.

✻

Please don't tell me to leave you and return home!
I will go where you go, I will live where you live;
your people will be my people,
your God will be my God.

Ruth 1:16 CEV

A Father Betrayed

God said to Noah, "This is the sign of the covenant which I have established between Me and all flesh that is on the earth."

Now the sons of Noah who went out of the ark were Shem, Ham, and Japheth. And Ham was the father of Canaan. These three were the sons of Noah, and from these the whole earth was populated.

And Noah began to be a farmer, and he planted a vineyard. Then he drank of the wine and was drunk, and became uncovered in his tent. And Ham, the father of Canaan, saw the nakedness of his father, and told his two brothers outside. But Shem and Japheth took a garment, laid it on both their shoulders, and went backward and covered the nakedness of their father. Their faces were turned away, and they did not see their father's nakedness.

So Noah awoke from his wine, and knew what his younger son had done to him. Then he said:

"Cursed be Canaan;
A servant of servants
He shall be to his brethren."

Genesis 9:17–25 NKJV

✺

*G*od judged the world for its wickedness by sending the great Flood. Afterward, the world was just as wicked as ever. Nevertheless, God made a new contract with the remnants of humanity—Noah and his family—and all the animals. The world would never again suffer as it had, and the rainbow would be proof.

How wicked was the post-Flood world? Noah soon planted a vineyard and drank too much. Ham saw the nakedness of his father and told his brothers about it. Shem and Japheth covered their father's nakedness. Noah found out what Ham had done to him, and he cursed one of Ham's sons: Canaan.

Why did Noah curse Canaan? Why didn't he curse Ham?

The phrase "saw the nakedness of his father" is a Hebrew idiom. It doesn't mean that Ham saw his father naked. The phrase "to see" or "to uncover" the nakedness of a man meant having sexual intercourse with that man's wife (Leviticus 18:7–8; 20:20–21). "His nakedness" was a reference to his wife. It meant that Ham slept with Noah's wife. Canaan, then, was the result of Ham's affair. Canaan was an illegitimate child born of incest and the betrayal of a father by his own son. Covering up Noah's nakedness meant covering up Noah's wife. Ordinarily children received a blessing from their parents or grandparents. Canaan, given his illegitimate status, could not be blessed, only cursed.

Sin's repercussions spread to everyone around, sometimes for generations. Our poor choices affect our families.

❀❀❀❀❀❀❀❀❀❀❀❀❀❀❀❀❀❀❀❀❀❀❀❀❀❀❀❀❀❀❀❀

Keeping Promises

The LORD said to Moses, "Cut two tablets of stone like the first ones, and I will write on these tablets the words that were on the first tablets which you broke. So be ready in the morning, and come up in the morning to Mount Sinai, and present yourself to Me there on the top of the mountain. And no man shall come up with you, and let no man be seen throughout all the mountain; let neither flocks nor herds feed before that mountain."

So he cut two tablets of stone like the first ones. Then Moses rose early in the morning and went up Mount Sinai, as the LORD had commanded him; and he took in his hand the two tablets of stone.

Now the LORD descended in the cloud and stood with him there, and proclaimed the name of the LORD. And the LORD passed before him and proclaimed, "The LORD, the LORD God, merciful and gracious, long-suffering, and abounding in goodness and truth, keeping mercy for thousands, forgiving iniquity and transgression and sin, by no means clearing the guilty, visiting the iniquity of the fathers upon the children and the children's children to the third and the fourth generation."

Exodus 34:1–7 NKJV

❀

*V*iolating God's commandments works out as well as violating the laws of physics. Angry at the Israelites' sudden idolatry and his brother Aaron's collusion in it, Moses smashed the tablets bearing the Ten Commandments. But God made replacements for the lost commandments. God will now allow his word to be destroyed or undone by human actions.

God explained that he was a merciful and forgiving God. But he also announced that he would bring the iniquity of the fathers upon their children and later descendants. That not only seems unjust, but it also appears to contradict what God had told Moses elsewhere, that children could not be punished for the crimes of their parents (Deuteronomy 24:16). So how did that jibe with the fact that the iniquity of the fathers would be visited upon the children and the children's children down to the third and fourth generations?

God meant that no one was an island. A person's actions would affect not just himself, but also all of those around him, including family and descendants. If the father violated the covenant with God, he would go into exile, and his children would be in exile also, along with their descendants. The repercussions of bad behavior reverberated for a long time. Israel's exile in Babylon for violating the covenant affected the people of God for generations. Just as a pebble dropped into a pool sends out ripples, so do our actions, good or bad.

We Have to Wear Shades

GOD said to Moses: "Now write down these words, for by these words I've made a covenant with you and Israel."

Moses was there with GOD forty days and forty nights. He didn't eat any food; he didn't drink any water. And he wrote on the tablets the words of the covenant, the Ten Words.

When Moses came down from Mount Sinai carrying the two Tablets of The Testimony, he didn't know that the skin of his face glowed because he had been speaking with GOD. Aaron and all the Israelites saw Moses, saw his radiant face, and held back, afraid to get close to him.

Moses called out to them. Aaron and the leaders in the community came back and Moses talked with them. Later all the Israelites came up to him and he passed on the commands, everything that GOD had told him on Mount Sinai.

When Moses finished speaking with them, he put a veil over his face, but when he went into the presence of GOD to speak with him, he removed the veil until he came out. When he came out and told the Israelites what he had been commanded, they would see Moses' face, its skin glowing, and then he would again put the veil on his face until he went back in to speak with GOD.

Exodus 34:27–35 MSG

✿

God made the Israelites an offer they couldn't refuse. His contract with them established their relationship with him. Where before the Israelites had been slaves to Egypt with Egypt as their master, they then entered bondage to God. God would be their new master—and they would be his slaves. But servitude to God meant freedom, not oppression. God would never use whips on his people or force them to make bricks without straw.

Moses brought the people the "ten words"—what we know as the Ten Commandments. The Ten Commandments were written on two stone tablets. The first five commandments concerned God, the last five concerned people. The "ten words" can be summed up by just two commandments: to love God and to love other people.

When Moses came back from Mount Sinai the second time, he did not return to judge the people or punish them for their misbehavior. Instead, he came back with something wonderful. His time with God had left its mark on him: in fact, he reflected so much of God's glory that it frightened his brother and the people. Moses had to cover his face.

Moses was changed by his time with God. It was a change that everyone could see. Those who spend time with God will likewise be transformed.

Promises, Promises

The LORD said to Moses, "Soon you will lie down with your ancestors. Then this people will begin to prostitute themselves to the foreign gods in their midst, the gods of the land into which they are going; they will forsake me, breaking my covenant that I have made with them. My anger will be kindled against them in that day. I will forsake them and hide my face from them; they will become easy prey, and many terrible troubles will come upon them. In that day they will say, 'Have not these troubles come upon us because our God is not in our midst?' On that day I will surely hide my face on account of all the evil they have done by turning to other gods. Now therefore write this song, and teach it to the Israelites; put it in their mouths, in order that this song may be a witness for me against the Israelites. For when I have brought them into the land flowing with milk and honey, which I promised on oath to their ancestors, and they have eaten their fill and grown fat, they will turn to other gods and serve them, despising me and breaking my covenant. And when many terrible troubles come upon them, this song will confront them as a witness, because it will not be lost from the mouths of their descendants. For I know what they are inclined to do even now, before I have brought them into the land that I promised them on oath."

Deuteronomy 31:16–21 NRSV

God isn't surprised by betrayal. In fact, he expected the Israelites' betrayal and made plans to deal with it. He even had Moses teach them a song about it. God knew that song would not keep them from going after the other gods. But he wanted them to know the song so it would bear witness against them.

God knew he would be angered by their betrayal. But no matter what they did, he would not be the one to break the contract. In fact, when God punished them, he was keeping part of the very contract he had made with them. God's loyalty to them was never at issue. God obligated himself to his people even though he knew they couldn't reciprocate.

God did not enter the contract with them so they could fail. But he made allowance for the fact that they would fail. And God provided a way of success for them, dependent upon God's faithfulness instead of theirs. God expects us to be human. He can help us anyway. He has a plan for it.

Do It for the Kids

"It shall be that if you earnestly obey My commandments which I command you today, to love the LORD your God and serve Him with all your heart and with all your soul, then I will give you the rain for your land in its season, the early rain and the latter rain, that you may gather in your grain, your new wine, and your oil. And I will send grass in your fields for your livestock, that you may eat and be filled." Take heed to yourselves, lest your heart be deceived, and you turn aside and serve other gods and worship them, lest the LORD's anger be aroused against you, and He shut up the heavens so that there be no rain, and the land yield no produce, and you perish quickly from the good land which the LORD is giving you.

Therefore you shall lay up these words of mine in your heart and in your soul, and bind them as a sign on your hand, and they shall be as frontlets between your eyes. You shall teach them to your children, speaking of them when you sit in your house, when you walk by the way, when you lie down, and when you rise up. And you shall write them on the doorposts of your house and on your gates, that your days and the days of your children may be multiplied in the land of which the LORD swore to your fathers to give them, like the days of the heavens above the earth.

Deuteronomy 11:13–21 NKJV

God's will for your life is no mystery. What are the commandments that God gave his people? To love him and to love one another. It really wasn't that complicated. In exchange for abiding by those simple terms of the contract, God assured his people of his blessings. Making God's words to be signs on their hands and between their eyes encouraged the people to put his words front and center in their lives: to live them in what they thought, what they saw, and what they did. They were to live in the presence of God.

But they missed the point God was making and created a ritual instead. It is much easier to put the word of God in a little box that can be bound around the head and attached to the hands or attached to the sides of the doors in one's house than it is to actually read what the words say and put them into practice. Living God's words every day is hard, just as saying that you love someone is far easier than actually putting your words into practice. But when you do, powerful things start to happen.

Just Going Through the Motions

This is the word that came to Jeremiah from the LORD: "Stand at the gate of the LORD's house and there proclaim this message:

"'Hear the word of the LORD, all you people of Judah who come through these gates to worship the LORD. This is what the LORD Almighty, the God of Israel, says: Reform your ways and your actions, and I will let you live in this place. Do not trust in deceptive words and say, "This is the temple of the LORD, the temple of the LORD, the temple of the LORD!" If you really change your ways and your actions and deal with each other justly, if you do not oppress the alien, the fatherless or the widow and do not shed innocent blood in this place, and if you do not follow other gods to your own harm, then I will let you live in this place, in the land I gave your forefathers for ever and ever. But look, you are trusting in deceptive words that are worthless.

"Will you steal and murder, commit adultery and perjury, burn incense to Baal and follow other gods you have not known, and then come and stand before me in this house, which bears my Name, and say, "We are safe"—safe to do all these detestable things? Has this house, which bears my Name, become a den of robbers to you? But I have been watching! declares the LORD.'"

Jeremiah 7:1–11 NIV

※

The prophets of God, like Jeremiah, were the annoying "bill collectors" of their day. Israel had failed to keep their agreement with God, and God sent the prophets to remind his people of their obligation. God's agreement with the people stipulated that they must love God and love one another. Instead, the powerful and wealthy took advantage of the poor and disadvantaged. They mistreated resident aliens, even though God had implored them to remember how bad it had been for them as foreigners in Egypt. God didn't want them to become like the Egyptians.

Instead, the Israelites failed utterly to love other people, breaking all the commandments that affected human beings. They likewise failed to love God. They instead adopted the religious practices and gods of their pagan neighbors.

The Israelites found the rituals of God worship easy to maintain. It took no thought to visit the temple, to perform a sacrifice, to wave some incense, to sing a hymn, to drop some money in the coffer—as if that's all worshipping God meant. God disagreed. True worship means loving other people and loving God. But that got in the way of how the Israelites wanted to live.

The Day of Flint Knives

At that time GOD said to Joshua, "Make stone knives and circumcise the People of Israel a second time." So Joshua made stone knives and circumcised the People of Israel at Foreskins Hill.

This is why Joshua conducted the circumcision. All the males who had left Egypt, the soldiers, had died in the wilderness on the journey out of Egypt. All the people who had come out of Egypt, of course, had been circumcised, but all those born in the wilderness along the way since leaving Egypt had not been. The fact is that the People of Israel had walked through that wilderness for forty years until the entire nation died out, all the men of military age who had come out of Egypt but had disobeyed the call of GOD. GOD vowed that these would never lay eyes on the land GOD had solemnly promised their ancestors to give us, a land flowing with milk and honey. But their children had replaced them. These are the ones Joshua circumcised. They had never been circumcised; no one had circumcised them along the way.

When they had completed the circumcising of the whole nation, they stayed where they were in camp until they were healed.

GOD said to Joshua, "Today I have rolled away the reproach of Egypt." That's why the place is called The Gilgal. It's still called that.

Joshua 5:2–9 MSG

✻

_D_etails are easily forgotten. Because the Egyptians practiced circumcision, the people born in Egypt had all been circumcised, and it would have been hard to avoid being circumcised. But in the wilderness, they didn't think to circumcise any more than they thought to remember any of God's other commandments, for that matter.

When it was time to enter the land and conquer it, Joshua forced the people to start paying attention to the agreement they had with God. Circumcision was the first step. Joshua hoped that by performing even the most simple of rituals, particularly a painful one, perhaps the people would start to think more about God. God told Joshua that the circumcision removed Egypt's "reproach." Circumcision was a reminder that the Israelites belonged to God rather than Egypt. They commemorated the operation that symbolized their freedom by naming the place "Gilgal," that is, "Rolled Away." They no longer belonged to Egypt. Certainly the men who endured the operation would have time to reflect on the significance of what had happened while they healed. God has different, and sometimes unusual, ways of trying to get our attention.

Get Up and Do Something

The LORD said to Joshua, "Rise up! Why is it that you have fallen on your face?

"Israel has sinned, and they have also transgressed My covenant which I commanded them. And they have even taken some of the things under the ban and have both stolen and deceived. Moreover, they have also put them among their own things.

"Therefore the sons of Israel cannot stand before their enemies; they turn their backs before their enemies, for they have become accursed. I will not be with you anymore unless you destroy the things under the ban from your midst.

"Rise up! Consecrate the people and say, 'Consecrate yourselves for tomorrow, for thus the LORD, the God of Israel, has said, "There are things under the ban in your midst, O Israel. You cannot stand before your enemies until you have removed the things under the ban from your midst."

"'In the morning then you shall come near by your tribes. And it shall be that the tribe which the LORD takes by lot shall come near by families, and the family which the LORD takes shall come near by households, and the household which the LORD takes shall come near man by man.

"'It shall be that the one who is taken with the things under the ban shall be burned with fire, he and all that belongs to him, because he has transgressed the covenant of the LORD, and because he has committed a disgraceful thing in Israel.'"

Joshua 7:10–15 NASB

※

God had been clear in his instructions about how Jericho was to be treated, and he had warned what the consequences would be if anyone violated those rules. Jericho was to be "devoted to God," meaning that, like a burnt offering, nothing was to be left.

Joshua thought attacking Ai, a small city, would be an easy victory compared to Jericho, and he didn't pray first. He sent only a small group against Ai. After the defeat, there was little point in praying.

One man had decided to take a little for himself from Jericho. Because of that theft, when the Israelites went up against Ai, God did not let them win.

Praying can sometimes be used as a way of just looking busy. Praying for people instead of helping them is simple laziness. Joshua didn't need to pray. He needed to call people to account.

The man who had stolen from God and betrayed his trust and by whose actions the nation had suffered was caught and disciplined. Then the nation went on to defeat the city of Ai.

Broken Promise

The angel of the LORD went up from Gilgal to Bokim and said to the Israelites, "I brought you out of Egypt into this land that I swore to give your ancestors, and I said I would never break my covenant with you. For your part, you were not to make any covenants with the people living in this land; instead, you were to destroy their altars. But you disobeyed my command. Why did you do this? So now I declare that I will no longer drive out the people living in your land. They will be thorns in your sides, and their gods will be a constant temptation to you."

When the angel of the LORD finished speaking to all the Israelites, the people wept loudly. So they called the place Bokim (which means "weeping"), and they offered sacrifices there to the LORD.

Judges 2:1–5 NLT

❈

*B*roken promises hurt. And the person whose trust is betrayed isn't the only one who gets hurt; the one who betrays him also suffers. Joshua had led the Israelites in battle against the indigenous population of the promised land, the Canaanites. But in his time, not all the promised land had been conquered. Not all the Canaanites had been eliminated. The people still had a job to do. They had reaffirmed the covenant with God, but they had failed to act on it. They had not obeyed God. Why did Israel betray God and not abide by the contract they had with him? They thought they knew better. They made treaties with the people of the land of Canaan rather than wiping them all out. God told them what needed to be done, but they thought they could do better.

Israel didn't want to destroy all their enemies. They thought they could negotiate with them instead. So their wish became God's command. He let them learn the hard way why he asked them to destroy the Canaanites. The Canaanites led his people to sin. The Israelites started mixing the religious practices of the Canaanites with their own religious practices, and they started worshipping the gods of the Canaanites.

Their rejection of God, already incipient in their refusal to follow his instructions, would grow. Since God had no choice but to abide by his own promises to them, he would ultimately have to bring discipline upon them. God's discipline would range from famine and other suffering to the ultimate pain of exile from their homeland in Babylon and being witness to the destruction of Jerusalem and the sacred temple. God always gets his way. Whether it is the easy way or the hard way, the choice is ours.

Keeping a Promise

Hiram king of Tyre sent ambassadors to Solomon when he heard that he had been crowned king in David's place. Hiram had loved David his whole life. Solomon responded, saying, "You know that David my father was not able to build a temple in honor of GOD because of the wars he had to fight on all sides, until GOD finally put them down. But now GOD has provided peace all around—no one against us, nothing at odds with us.

"Now here is what I want to do: Build a temple in honor of GOD, my God, following the promise that GOD gave to David my father, namely, 'Your son whom I will provide to succeed you as king, he will build a house in my honor.' And here is how you can help: Give orders for cedars to be cut from the Lebanon forest; my loggers will work alongside yours and I'll pay your men whatever wage you set. We both know that there is no one like you Sidonians for cutting timber."

When Hiram got Solomon's message, he was delighted, exclaiming, "Blessed be GOD for giving David such a wise son to rule this flourishing people!"

1 Kings 5:1–7 MSG

✳

*S*olomon wrote, "A friend loves at all times" (Proverbs 17:17 NASB). David loved God, and despite all his faults, his loyalty to God was absolute. He wanted to serve God with everything he had. He was completely devoted to him. One day, after he had built his palace, he felt bad that the place for worshipping God was merely a tent. He decided that he needed to do something to change that. But God told David that while the desire to build a permanent temple for God was a good thing, it was not something for him to build. Instead, the task of building a temple would be left to his son Solomon, who would reign in his place.

David let Solomon know what he desired for God. And David made plans. He gathered the materials and even purchased the land for the temple. But David wound up having to trust his son to do what he had set his heart on. It was not an ill-placed trust. Solomon fulfilled the promise he made to his father and built the temple. And he got David's friend Hiram, the king of Tyre who had loved him his whole life, to help.

It doesn't necessarily mean that it is God's will for you just because you want to do it, just because it is a good thing, and just because it is God who wants it done. Sometimes God's will for you is merely to watch, to pray, or to encourage those who will do it.

❀❀❀❀❀❀❀❀❀❀❀❀❀❀❀❀❀❀❀❀❀❀❀❀❀❀❀❀❀❀

Talking the Talk

To the wicked God says:
> "What right have you to recite my
> statutes, or take my covenant on
> your lips?
For you hate discipline, and you cast
my words behind you.
You make friends with a thief when
you see one, and you keep company
with adulterers.

"You give your mouth free rein
for evil, and your tongue frames
deceit.
You sit and speak against your kin;
you slander your own mother's
child.

These things you have done and I have
been silent; you thought that I was
one just like yourself.
But now I rebuke you, and lay the
charge before you.

"Mark this, then, you who forget God,
or I will tear you apart, and there
will be no one to deliver.
Those who bring thanksgiving as their
sacrifice honor me; to those who go
the right way I will show the salvation of God."

Psalm 50:16–23 NRSV

❀

*S*o the wicked thought God was just one of the guys? Since he hadn't commented on their behavior for a long time, they thought he must agree with them? He had already told them, "Do not murder." Did he have to say it all over again when they killed their neighbors? Didn't they already know what he thought? Or did they expect God to be a nag?

Asaph, the author of this psalm, was a Levite. He also became a musician in the tabernacle during the reign of King David. He was described as a "seer," that is, a prophet of God, demonstrated by how he quoted God's words to the wicked.

Asaph wrote that God's silence should not be taken as agreement. Quoting God's commandments is fine, but God doesn't like being quoted by those who disagree with everything he stands for. Those caught in crimes who talk about how much they love God are doing nothing but piling up reasons for God's judgment.

Not only were they guilty of wickedness, but they also insulted God. They brought his name into disrepute, giving ammunition to scoffers who delighted in pointing out the vile deeds of the self-righteous. When Satan stands before God and accuses the saints, he doesn't have to make stuff up. We give him all the ammunition he needs.

Wearing the Crown

God gave David his word,
   he won't back out on this
      promise:
"One of your sons
   I will set on your throne;
If your sons stay true to my Covenant
   and learn to live the way I
      teach them,
Their sons will continue the line—
   always a son to sit on your throne.
Yes—I, God, chose Zion,
   the place I wanted for my shrine;
This will always be my home;
   this is what I want, and I'm here
      for good.

I'll shower blessings on the pilgrims
  who come here,
and give supper to those who arrive hungry;
I'll dress my priests in salvation
  clothes;
   the holy people will sing their
    hearts out!
Oh, I'll make the place radiant for
  David!
   I'll fill it with light for my
    anointed!
I'll dress his enemies in dirty rags,
   but I'll make his crown sparkle
    with splendor."

Psalm 132:11–18 MSG

✻

Treaties and other contracts are simple things. They lay out the expectations that two parties have for each other. In a treaty with God, there should be great confidence that he'll do exactly what he says he'll do. His promise regarding Zion—another name for Jerusalem—should have put the people at ease.

All the Israelites had to do was love God. How hard was that when all he offered them was prosperity and happiness?

And yet human beings are perverse creatures. We love ourselves, but we're afraid no one else does. We devote ourselves to looking out for our best interests or what we think are our best interests. God's people trusted only themselves, and so they went off on their own, forgetting what God had promised.

He had not promised them happiness no matter what. He had promised them happiness in exchange for their loyalty. If they betrayed him, well, he had made a promise about that, too, a promise that was the opposite of happiness. God keeps all his promises, both those with positive consequences and those with negative ones.

No matter how far the people strayed from him, he guaranteed them that he would bring them back and fulfill every good thing he had ever promised. Ultimately, no matter how far they ran, no matter how hard they tried to get away, God chased after them and blessed them.

Do You Really Want to Know God's Will?

The LORD told me to write down his message for his people, so that it would be there forever. They have turned against the LORD and can't be trusted. They have refused his teaching and have said to his messengers and prophets:

Don't tell us what God has shown you and don't preach the truth. Just say what we want to hear, even if it's false. Stop telling us what God has said! We don't want to hear any more about the holy God of Israel.

Now this is the answer of the holy God of Israel:
"You rejected my message, and you trust in violence and lies.
This sin is like a crack that makes
  a high wall quickly crumble and
  shatter like a crushed bowl.
There's not a piece left big enough
  to carry hot coals or to dip out
  water."

The Holy Lord God of Israel
  has told all of you,
  "I will keep you safe
  if you turn back to me
  and calm down.
  I will make you strong
  if you quietly trust me."

Isaiah 30:8–15 CEV

❈

*J*ust as they really don't want to know the future, people rarely want to know God's will. Sure, they'd like to know they will be rich and famous in the future, but they don't want to be told about the failed relationships yet to come, the illnesses to be endured, the financial hardships that will keep them up at night with worry. Similarly, people fear that God's will for them will mean that they will wind up living in a hut somewhere on the Amazon and preaching in a foreign language. People don't want the truth. They want what makes them feel good today. Sometimes people ask for advice when all they want is approval.

Isaiah's audience knew that God wanted them to change. And they knew that if they didn't change, God's judgment would force them to change anyway. The destruction of their nation would invariably impact their lifestyles. But they preferred their delusions to reality.

God pointed out that rejecting his message meant a self-betrayal. The consequence of going one's own way instead of God's way is inevitably disastrous. Not only does God love his people, but he also knows what they really want and what will really make them happy—and that's what he'll give them.

The Inheritance

Some time after this conversation, Joseph was told, "Your father is ill." He took his two sons, Manasseh and Ephraim, and went to Jacob. When Jacob was told, "Your son Joseph has come," he roused himself and sat up in bed.

Jacob said to Joseph, "The Strong God appeared to me at Luz in the land of Canaan and blessed me. He said, 'I'm going to make you prosperous and numerous, turn you into a congregation of tribes; and I'll turn this land over to your children coming after you as a permanent inheritance.' I'm adopting your two sons who were born to you here in Egypt before I joined you; they have equal status with Reuben and Simeon. But any children born after them are yours; they will come after their brothers in matters of inheritance. I want it this way because, as I was returning from Paddan, your mother Rachel, to my deep sorrow, died as we were on our way through Canaan when we were only a short distance from Ephrath, now called Bethlehem."

Genesis 48:1–7 MSG

☸

God doesn't take back the gifts he gives. God gave the land of the Canaanites to the Jewish people because, among the promises that God gave Abraham, there was the promise that the land he wandered in would belong to him and his offspring forever (Genesis 13:14–17). God later extended that same promise to Isaac, and then to Jacob, to whom twelve sons were born. God's promise became increasingly focused. God didn't give the promise to all the descendants of Abraham. It didn't go to his son Ishmael or to the many other children born to wives he married after Sarah's death. Isaac alone was the son of promise. And the promise did not extend to both sons of Isaac, but only to Jacob and his twelve sons, who became the fathers of the twelve tribes.

Jacob's son Joseph became ruler in Egypt. As a result, he was able to rescue his family from starvation and bring them to live with him in Egypt. When Jacob became sick, Joseph presented his two sons before him. Jacob did something special. He adopted Joseph's sons. Why? The descendants of one of his other sons, Levi, would be separated from the other tribes of Israel. They would receive no land (Deuteronomy 10:9). By splitting Joseph into two tribes, the land that God gave to the nation of Israel could still be divided twelve ways. Though the Levites were given no territory at all, Joseph would get a double portion, divided between Ephraim and Manasseh. Whatever God has given you belongs to you from now on.

God Puts Up with It a Lot

I have held My peace a long time,
I have been still and restrained Myself.
Now I will cry like a woman in labor,
I will pant and gasp at once.
I will lay waste the mountains and
  hills,
And dry up all their vegetation;
I will make the rivers coastlands,
And I will dry up the pools.
I will bring the blind by a way they did
  not know;
I will lead them in paths they have not
  known.
I will make darkness light before them,
And crooked places straight.
These things I will do for them,
And not forsake them.
They shall be turned back,
They shall be greatly ashamed,
Who trust in carved images,
Who say to the molded images,
"You are our gods."
Hear, you deaf;
And look, you blind, that you may see.
Who is blind but My servant,
Or deaf as My messenger whom I
  send?
Who is blind as he who is perfect,
And blind as the LORD's servant?
Seeing many things, but you do not
  observe;
Opening the ears, but he does not
  hear.

Isaiah 42:14–20 NKJV

*G*od has feelings. He is passionate; he is expressive; he is not ashamed to let people see his heart. God can be patient; he can outwait anyone. For the longest time it may seem as if he isn't there or that he doesn't care. But sometimes he is merely restraining himself. Because of his intense love for his people, he would like to act immediately. But because he is also wise, he waits for the right moment. Like a parent who keeps the wonderful present hidden until Christmas morning, no matter how much the parent would like the child to enjoy it early, God restrains his excitement and joy.

Israel was God's servant, designed by God to serve as the world's priests (Exodus 19:5–6). He had hoped they would lead the world to him. Instead, the world led Israel astray. God told them their idols were blind and deaf. Likewise, the Israelites had become just as blind and deaf. But God would soon lead those in darkness back into the light. God knows what those he loves most need, and he knows when they need it. He waits until just the right moment to give what is most needed. Sometimes it may seem God is doing nothing, but the reality is that he is indeed busy.

꙳꙳꙳꙳꙳꙳꙳꙳꙳꙳꙳꙳꙳꙳꙳꙳꙳꙳꙳꙳꙳꙳꙳꙳꙳꙳꙳꙳꙳꙳꙳꙳꙳꙳꙳

The Only God

Thus says the LORD,
who created the heavens
    (he is God!),
who formed the earth and made it
    (he established it;
he did not create it a chaos,
    he formed it to be inhabited!):
I am the LORD, and there is no other.
I did not speak in secret,
    in a land of darkness;
I did not say to the offspring of Jacob,
    "Seek me in chaos."
I the LORD speak the truth,
    I declare what is right.
Assemble yourselves and come
  together,
    draw near, you survivors of the
      nations!
They have no knowledge—
    those who carry about their
      wooden idols,
and keep on praying to a god
    that cannot save.
Declare and present your case;
    let them take counsel together!
Who told this long ago?
    Who declared it of old?
Was it not I, the LORD?
    There is no other god besides me,
a righteous God and a Savior;
    there is no one besides me.

Isaiah 45:18–21 NRSV

꙳

God isn't living in the dark. He isn't invisible. He isn't unorganized. He is not hard to find. His words are not so complex and difficult that no one can understand them. There are no secret mysteries, quests, maps, or complicated ideas to get God's love or blessing. There is no secret handshake or magical ritual.

The Israelites, in accepting the gods of their neighbors, had accepted a belief system that was inherently confused and chaotic. A false god might become angry on a whim and lash out, only to regret his action a moment later. The false gods were utterly dependent upon their worshippers for their sustenance. Israel's God, the true God, was nothing at all like the false gods.

God stood out in the light, calling to people, ready to bless them, but oddly, they ran away from him instead. They sought him everywhere but where he was. They prayed to everything else but him. They worshipped inanimate objects, muttering at the rocks and sticks of wood and behaving like complete idiots, all the while imagining they were deep, spiritual, and holy. They thought that finding God and knowing God intimately had to be deserved, that being close to God was granted only to those who strove hardest or who made the most pilgrimages.

But there is only one God, and he alone can save. No one else can rescue you—not your neighbor, not a special ritual, and not yourself. Only the obvious God.

I Am Strong and Righteous

Look to Me, and be saved,
All you ends of the earth!
For I am God, and there is no
other.
I have sworn by Myself;
The word has gone out of My
mouth in righteousness,
And shall not return,
That to Me every knee shall bow,
Every tongue shall take an oath.
He shall say,

"Surely in the LORD I have righ-
teousness and strength.
To Him men shall come,
And all shall be ashamed
Who are incensed against Him.
In the LORD all the descendants of
Israel
Shall be justified, and shall glory."

Isaiah 45:22–25 NKJV

❈

I swear to God," some people will say when they want to convince you that they are telling the truth. Isaiah, with the other prophets, repeated God's words that were so difficult for the Israelites to understand: there was just one God, and he always kept his promises.

In the ancient world, no nations anywhere believed that. People everywhere were certain that just as the earth was filled with many people, so the heavens had to be populated by many gods. Simply looking at the busy, changing sky was proof enough. What everyone saw everywhere was a plurality of beings. Likewise, since the promises of people were untrustworthy, because people changed their minds or because other people thwarted their good intentions, everyone came to believe that the gods must face the same limitations. But the real God was not so limited.

God simply swears by himself: his own word is trustworthy. He doesn't need to try to convince anyone that he'll do what he says.

Although Israel was going into captivity in Babylon, they would not have to stay there forever. They would be sent back to their homeland to rebuild it, and at that time, the Israelites who might have wondered if God had forgotten them would finally praise him and thank him. God said that "every knee shall bow" and "take an oath." In context, God was speaking to the people of Israel, letting them know that despite their suffering they would once again acknowledge God and respond to him, reaffirming the contract that he had with them. They weren't loyal to God, but God's loyalty to them never wavered. Likewise, God will remember you even when you forget all about him.

Loving Their Bed

Behind the door and the doorpost
> You have set up your sign;
>> Indeed, far removed from Me, you have uncovered yourself,
>> And have gone up and made your bed wide.
>> And you have made an agreement for yourself with them,
>> You have loved their bed,
>> You have looked on their manhood.

You have journeyed to the king with oil
>> And increased your perfumes;
>> You have sent your envoys a great distance

And made them go down to
> Sheol.

You were tired out by the length of your road,
>> Yet you did not say, "It is hopeless."
>> You found renewed strength,
>> Therefore you did not faint.

Isaiah 57:8–10 NASB

✳

*P*eople can cause God pain. God graphically described the disloyalty of his people, trying to get them to understand just how much they had hurt him. "Uncovering," "looked on their manhood," and "looked at their nakedness" were Hebrew idioms indicating sexual activity. Israel's worship of other gods was described in terms of sexual infidelity.

Israel worshipped a wide variety of gods and goddesses. Molech, an Ammonite god, was worshipped by sacrificing children to him. Asherah was a popular deity among the Israelites as well. She was a fertility goddess whose wooden poles—phallic symbols—stood on hills and other high places throughout the land. Those who worshipped her engaged in sympathetic magic: sleeping with the priestesses devoted to her.

The Israelites felt no shame. In fact, they ridiculed those who insisted on worshipping God alone, and they laughed in God's face. They arrogantly insisted on their own ways. They insisted on doing what they wanted to do regardless of the pain they caused God. They broke God's heart, but they felt no guilt over their betrayal. Because God loves us, we can hurt him.

Returning Evil for Good

"When I brought you into a fruitful land to enjoy its bounty and goodness, you defiled my land and corrupted the possession I had promised you.
The priests did not ask, 'Where is the LORD?'
Those who taught my word ignored me, the rulers turned against me, and the prophets spoke in the name of Baal, wasting their time on worthless idols.

Therefore, I will bring my case against you," says the LORD.
"I will even bring charges against your children's children in the years to come."

Jeremiah 2:7–9 NLT

❀

*P*eople take God for granted during the good times. He's easy to ignore. Jeremiah began prophesying to the Israelites in the few years left before they went into captivity in Babylon. God dared his people to try to justify their behavior. What, exactly, he wondered, could they say against him?

But they continued with the same behavior, ignoring everything Jeremiah said. God told them how they were mistreating him. He told them the way they were acting made no sense. When someone is kind and helpful, when someone gives gifts, the normal human response is gratitude. Even the worst of human beings are usually nice to those who are nice to them, if for no other reason than a selfish desire to maintain the benefits.

Loving regardless of how someone treats you is rare, while tit for tat is common. But God's people couldn't muster even that. In the face of God's goodness, they responded by chasing after other gods. Israel acted like a wife inexplicably cheating on a good and loving husband, heaping insults upon him even as she throws herself at her lovers. Those entrusted with leading the people—the priests and the rulers—were first in the line leading away from God.

When things are bad, we are quick to blame God. When things are good, it's easy to ignore him. But God loves us anyway, good times or bad, no matter how we treat him.

Trash for Treasure

"Cross over to the coasts of Kittim
and look,
send to Kedar and observe closely;
see if there has ever been anything
like this:
Has a nation ever changed its gods?
(Yet they are not gods at all.)
But my people have exchanged
their Glory
for worthless idols.
Be appalled at this, O heavens,
and shudder with great horror,"
declares the LORD.
"My people have committed two sins:
They have forsaken me,
the spring of living water,
and have dug their own cisterns,
broken cisterns that cannot
hold water.

Is Israel a servant, a slave by birth?
Why then has he become plunder?
Lions have roared;
they have growled at him.
They have laid waste his land;
his towns are burned and
deserted.
Also, the men of Memphis and
Tahpanhes
have shaved the crown of
your head.
Have you not brought this on
yourselves
by forsaking the LORD your God
when he led you in the way?"

Jeremiah 2:10–17 NIV

❀

For hundreds of years, the people of Canaan, Mesopotamia, and Egypt worshipped multiple gods that didn't exist. Even though the Babylonians had never seen Marduk do anything, they worshipped him faithfully all the same.

Some scholars identify Kittim with Syria. Other scholars identify Kittim with the Philistines or the islands of the Aegean. Kedar refers to a confederation of Arab tribes in northern Arabia. *Memphis* and *Tahpanhes* refer to the two cities in Egypt. Memphis was the capital of Egypt, and Tahpanhes is where Jeremiah would be taken by those who fled the Babylonians (Jeremiah 43:7). God's point was this: no matter where you look, could anyone find people that have abandoned their own gods?

God compared himself to springwater. Idols were like broken, empty cisterns. Cisterns were holes in the ground lined with bricks that caught rainwater runoff. Given a choice between a spring and a cistern, no one would chose a cistern, let alone one that was broken and empty.

Sin is irrational. People turn from God, who is real, to gods who are fake. As the Israelites' lives spiraled down, they exchanged treasure for trash.

Crazed Camel

How can you say, "I am not defiled,
    I have not gone after the Baals"?
Look at your way in the valley;
    know what you have done—
a restive young camel interlacing her
    tracks, a wild ass at home in the
    wilderness, in her heat sniffing the
    wind!
    Who can restrain her lust?
None who seek her need weary
    themselves;
    in her month they will find her.
Keep your feet from going unshod
    and your throat from thirst.
But you said, "It is hopeless,
    for I have loved strangers,
    and after them I will go."
As a thief is shamed when caught,
    so the house of Israel shall be
    shamed—

they, their kings, their officials,
    their priests, and their prophets,
who say to a tree, "You are my father,"
    and to a stone, "You gave me
    birth."
For they have turned their backs to me,
    and not their faces.
But in the time of their trouble
    they say,
    "Come and save us!"
But where are your gods
    that you made for yourself?
Let them come, if they can save you,
    in your time of trouble;
for you have as many gods
    as you have towns, O Judah.
Why do you complain against me?
    You have all rebelled against me,
    says the LORD.

Jeremiah 2:23–29 NRSV

✻

God compared his people to animals governed by their instincts, but the animals looked more reasonable than his people did. First, the people tried to pretend they hadn't forsaken God, even when the evidence was obvious. Then they claimed they couldn't help themselves. They claimed they were helplessly in love with "strangers." The "strangers" were the gods they had turned to instead of Yahweh. All God's people could offer him were excuses.

People sometimes ignore friends who have stood by them in the past, who have been there for them during previous crises. Instead, they turn to those who are actually leading them astray. But as soon as the bottom drops out and desperation sets in, they turn back to those they had scorned. God asked his people why they were suddenly turning to him.

The people quickly blamed God for the problems they had caused themselves. They depended on what was undependable, and they suffered the consequences. Nevertheless, God was willing to forgive. All they needed to do was ask. God loves us and will forgive us immediately, no matter how wretchedly we've treated him.

Day 164

The Needed Discipline

The LORD said also to me in the days of Josiah the king: "Have you seen what backsliding Israel has done? She has gone up on every high mountain and under every green tree, and there played the harlot. And I said, after she had done all these things, 'Return to Me.' But she did not return. And her treacherous sister Judah saw it. Then I saw that for all the causes for which backsliding Israel had committed adultery, I had put her away and given her a certificate of divorce; yet her treacherous sister Judah did not fear, but went and played the harlot also. So it came to pass, through her casual harlotry, that she defiled the land and committed adultery with stones and trees. And yet for all this her treacherous sister Judah has not turned to Me with her whole heart, but in pretense," says the LORD.

Then the LORD said to me, "Backsliding Israel has shown herself more righteous than treacherous Judah. Go and proclaim these words toward the north, and say:

'Return, backsliding Israel,' says
  the LORD;
'I will not cause My anger to fall
  on you.
For I am merciful,' says the LORD;
'I will not remain angry forever.'"

Jeremiah 3:6–12 NKJV

❈

*G*od sometimes gives people exactly what they want. Of course, it usually doesn't take long for them to realize they didn't really know what they wanted after all. Eve desperately wanted a certain fruit that for some inexplicable reason God was "cruelly" withholding from her. Only after she got it were her eyes opened to just how big a mistake she had made.

God's words to Jeremiah arrived during the reign of Josiah, one of the most righteous kings Judah ever had. He restored the temple. He got rid of the idols and high places. He worshipped Yahweh exclusively. But nothing much had really changed. Josiah's public reforms had transformed few private hearts. With his death, his son Jehoiakim reverted to idols, idols everywhere.

Israel and Judah wanted to worship other gods. They didn't care about Yahweh anymore. So God gave them up, sent them away, left them to their own devices. But unlike human beings, who are willing to write off those who betray them, God was always willing to take her back. In fact, the "divorce" was really part of his plan, the final discipline that he knew she needed in order for true repentance to take place. God knows exactly what his people need, even if they don't see it themselves. His discipline is always perfect and always achieves his goal: the restoration of the relationship.

Fess Up!

"Go and proclaim these words toward the north and say . . .
'Only acknowledge your iniquity,
> That you have transgressed against the LORD your God
> And have scattered your favors to the strangers under every green tree,
> And you have not obeyed My voice,' declares the LORD.
'Return, O faithless sons,' declares the LORD;
> 'For I am a master to you,
> And I will take you one from a city and two from a family,
> And I will bring you to Zion.'

"Then I will give you shepherds after My own heart, who will feed you on knowledge and understanding.

"It shall be in those days when you are multiplied and increased in the land," declares the LORD, "they will no longer say, 'The ark of the covenant of the LORD.' And it will not come to mind, nor will they remember it, nor will they miss it, nor will it be made again.

"At that time they will call Jerusalem 'The Throne of the LORD,' and all the nations will be gathered to it, to Jerusalem, for the name of the LORD; nor will they walk anymore after the stubbornness of their evil heart.

"In those days the house of Judah will walk with the house of Israel, and they will come together from the land of the north to the land that I gave your fathers as an inheritance."

Jeremiah 3:12–18 NASB

❋

*C*onfession is good for the soul. It is also the only way that repentance can happen, since repentance can happen only with knowledge of the wrong done. Children learn to say "sorry" if they fear they will get in trouble. But that kind of "sorry" is an empty word tossed like a charm to ward off pain. Real confession and real repentance are possible only when the child acknowledges what he or she has done. A genuinely repentant heart offers up no excuses, balks at no punishment, and complains about no restitution.

Someday, God said, that would happen to his people. God assured them they would come back to him transformed and he would restore their land.

Though in the time of Jeremiah people spoke of the ark of the covenant as if it were magic, the time would come when it would be gone for good and no one would care. Obsession about sacred objects and places is misguided. What matters are people, because people are the true sacred objects of God (John 4:21–24).

A Burning Wind

Then I said, "O Sovereign LORD,
the people have been deceived by
what you said,
for you promised peace for Jerusalem.
But the sword is held at their
throats!"

The time is coming when the LORD will
say to the people of Jerusalem,
"My dear people, a burning wind is
blowing in from the desert,
and it's not a gentle breeze useful
for winnowing grain.
It is a roaring blast sent by me!
Now I will pronounce your
destruction!"

Our enemy rushes down on us like
storm clouds!
His chariots are like whirlwinds.
His horses are swifter than eagles.
How terrible it will be, for we are
doomed!
O Jerusalem, cleanse your heart
that you may be saved.
How long will you harbor
your evil thoughts?
Your destruction has been announced
from Dan and the hill country of
Ephraim.

Jeremiah 4:10–15 NLT

Jeremiah told God that he had deceived his people. Was he calling God a liar? Not at all. He was pointing out that the people of Israel had listened only selectively to what God had said. They comforted themselves with God's promises of blessing and conveniently ignored what they had to do to get them. And they forgot the promised curses that were inevitable for disobedience.

The imagery that God employed for the coming destruction—the burning wind and horses swifter than eagles—was lifted from the threatened curses that God had put in his covenant, his treaty with Israel: the book of Deuteronomy (28:45–57). God reminded his people there was more to his promises than what they had chosen to remember. Their deception was not because God had lied to them. Instead, they had lied to themselves. The Israelites, like most of us, heard more clearly what they wanted to hear and ignored what didn't fit their preferences.

When a betrayed wife serves her cheating husband divorce papers, he might protest, "But you said you would love me and honor me and always be there for me, in sickness and in health." Similarly, the Israelites seemed unable to understand how the bad things they faced had anything to do with how they had betrayed God. Just as God had promised peace for Jerusalem, so he also had promised its destruction. The Israelites needed to realize what they were doing and repent. It was up to the Israelites to decide which promises they were going to get. The same is true for us. When we honor God, he will honor us.

You Like Being Oppressed?

"Among my people are wicked men who lie in wait like men who snare birds and like those who set traps to catch men.

Like cages full of birds, their houses are full of deceit; they have become rich and powerful and have grown fat and sleek.

Their evil deeds have no limit; they do not plead the case of the fatherless to win it, they do not defend the rights of the poor.

Should I not punish them for this?" declares the LORD.
"Should I not avenge myself on such a nation as this?

"A horrible and shocking thing has happened in the land:
The prophets prophesy lies, the priests rule by their own authority, and my people love it this way.
But what will you do in the end?"

Jeremiah 5:26–31 NIV

The false prophets predicted never-ending success and peace. The priests served the highest bidders. And since life was comfortable for them, they came to believe they were blessed by God. After all, since they were so rich and prosperous, they must be doing something right.

Catching a bird in a snare takes effort and subterfuge. Snaring men is the same. The world works according to rules and according to those who interpret those rules. The religious establishment knew all the rules, and they found it easy to manipulate them to their advantage. They defended the cause of the poor, making themselves look good and upright, even as they lined their own pockets and left only scraps for the poor. They cared only for the money and the acclaim that came from standing up for what was right, without actually having to do what was right.

God loves people and wants people to love one another. All societies, from the earliest Sumerians on, record how their rulers protected the orphans and widows. The reality was always something quite different. Those in power knew what they were supposed to do. They always gave lip service to it. But in Israel's case, God held them to it: God expected their deeds to match their words. If they did otherwise, God promised that those who betrayed the weak would soon find themselves weak. We need to love in deeds, and not simply in words.

Can't You at Least Blush?

"'Here's what will happen to the
know-it-alls:
I'll make them wifeless and
homeless.
Everyone's after the dishonest dollar,
little people and big people alike.
Prophets and priests and everyone
in between twist words and doctor
truth.
My dear Daughter—my people—broken, shattered, and yet they put on
band-aids,
Saying, "It's not so bad. You'll be just
fine."
But things are not "just fine"!

Do you suppose they are embarrassed
over this outrage?
Not really. They have no shame.
They don't even know how to
blush.
There's no hope for them. They've hit
bottom
and there's no getting up.
As far as I'm concerned, they're
finished.'" GOD has spoken.

Jeremiah 8:9–12 MSG

It is easy to overestimate one's knowledge. A college student in his or her second year is called a sophomore. It comes from two Greek words: *sophos*, "wise," and *mõros*, "stupid." A little knowledge is a dangerous thing because people easily believe they know more than they really do. When they see how much more they know than others, they become proud.

The student acquires a genuine education when he realizes how little he knows—and how little he can ever know. Humility is the consequence of genuine knowledge, because only then can we see how small we are and how big the subject matter is.

The Israelites had mistakenly imagined they knew it all. Instead, they knew nothing. And what little they did know, they didn't use. They simply patted themselves on the back for what they'd gotten. But they had missed altogether the important things like love of neighbor and love of God, and doing rather than simply saying.

God concluded that they didn't deserve their scholarship anymore. He would send them back to captivity in Babylon. They hadn't learned anything yet—and their test scores were abysmal. Sometimes God has to teach the same lessons repeatedly, but God is patient. His school of hard knocks works.

What the Contract Stipulates

The LORD God told me to say to the people of Judah and Jerusalem:

I, the LORD, am warning you that I will put a curse on anyone who doesn't keep the agreement I made with Israel. So pay attention to what it says. My commands haven't changed since I brought your ancestors out of Egypt, a nation that seemed like a blazing furnace where iron ore is melted. I told your ancestors that if they obeyed my commands, I would be their God, and they would be my people. Then I did what I had promised and gave them this wonderful land, where you now live.

"Yes, LORD," I replied, "that's true."

Jeremiah 11:1–5 CEV

*P*eople change their minds. They make promises, but then circumstances arise and they find it easy to alter the agreement. They had good intentions, but how were they to know what would happen?

The prophets were not innovators. They did not bring a new message from God. Instead, they preached the old story, repeating what God expected: his people would love him and love one another.

The book of Deuteronomy contained the formal agreement between God and Israel. The outline and structure of Deuteronomy matched the ancient treaties of the era. Such treaties were usually made as a consequence of war, when one nation defeated another in battle. In the Israelites' case, however, they had been rescued rather than beaten.

Such ancient treaties began with a summary of recent events that explained the reason for the treaty. Following that were regulations that governed the relationship between the two nations. Then the treaty listed all the benefits that would come if agreements were properly kept, followed by the horrible curses that would befall those who dared violate the terms of the agreement. Finally, witnesses were called upon to confirm the treaty.

Israel had agreed to that treaty with God in the time of Moses. They promised to do whatever God said. They had not been forced under duress to agree to the contract. He rescued them from Egypt before he offered it to them. They were out of danger. And that was when they had decided to agree to the contract.

God reminded his people that he had not changed. They were comforted to know that God does what he promises.

Without a Prayer

The LORD said to me: Proclaim all these words in the cities of Judah, and in the streets of Jerusalem: Hear the words of this covenant and do them. For I solemnly warned your ancestors when I brought them up out of the land of Egypt, warning them persistently, even to this day, saying, Obey my voice. Yet they did not obey or incline their ear, but everyone walked in the stubbornness of an evil will. So I brought upon them all the words of this covenant, which I commanded them to do, but they did not.

And the LORD said to me: Conspiracy exists among the people of Judah and the inhabitants of Jerusalem. They have turned back to the iniquities of their ancestors of old, who refused to heed my words; they have gone after other gods to serve them; the house of Israel and the house of Judah have broken the covenant that I made with their ancestors. Therefore, thus says the LORD, assuredly I am going to bring disaster upon them that they cannot escape; though they cry out to me, I will not listen to them. Then the cities of Judah and the inhabitants of Jerusalem will go and cry out to the gods to whom they make offerings, but they will never save them in the time of their trouble. For your gods have become as many as your towns, O Judah; and as many as the streets of Jerusalem are the altars you have set up to shame, altars to make offerings to Baal.

As for you, do not pray for this people, or lift up a cry or prayer on their behalf, for I will not listen when they call to me in the time of their trouble.

Jeremiah 11:6–14 NRSV

Sometimes it is simply too late. Israel's idolatry was endemic. Shrines to deities dotted the hillsides. Yahweh was simply one among the many gods worshipped by the Israelites.

They thought superstitiously in terms of ritual and sacred objects. The god of one town was useless in the town next to it. False gods were not much to be feared, but not much help either. That's why the Israelites had so many gods—there was supposed strength in numbers.

God told Jeremiah that it was too late. There was no solution to the problem of idolatry other than exile. There was no prayer left for these people. Only judgment. Unfortunately, sometimes judgment—discipline—is the only thing that can fix us. God knows when that time comes. Thankfully, it's always for our good, never for our harm.

People Are Untrustworthy

Thus says the LORD:
"Cursed is the man who trusts
in man
And makes flesh his strength,
Whose heart departs from the
LORD.
For he shall be like a shrub in
the desert,
And shall not see when good
comes,
But shall inhabit the parched
places in the wilderness,
In a salt land which is not
inhabited.

"Blessed is the man who
trusts in the LORD,
And whose hope is the LORD.
For he shall be like a tree
planted by the waters,
Which spreads out its roots by the
river,
And will not fear when heat
comes;
But its leaf will be green,
And will not be anxious in the
year of drought,
Nor will cease from yielding fruit."

Jeremiah 17:5–8 NKJV

God alone is completely trustworthy. The land of Israel is dry in many places, but it has streams called wadis. During the rainy season they fill with water, but during the summer and during droughts they dry up. But beneath the parched soil, the water is still there if you dig for it. Trees planted near such wadis will never lack for water, regardless of the changing seasons.

God said the one who trusted in a person was cursed. Why? Because the people of Jeremiah's time had turned away from God and instead relied on themselves. The God of Israel was not visible. He had no images. Some people found it hard to trust what could not be seen or touched. But because we can see people, it is easier to put faith in them, despite the fact that people are flawed, inconsistent, and often fail to meet their well-intentioned obligations—just like the water in a wadi. God pointed out that putting our trust in the strength of our own flesh was likewise a mistake, since we will fail ourselves: we will become guilty of the one thing we could never imagine ourselves being guilty of. We will lose the job that seemed so perfect. Our bodies will age, we will grow sick, and our memories will fail us. And all too often, our hearts drift far from God. We must admit that we, too, are just as unreliable as any wadi.

But God never tires, never gets sick, never has a short temper. The events of his day never ruin his mood or turn him grumpy.

God will always be ready for us, like the deep water of a river; he is the one person that we can always rely on.

Mind Tricks

"The heart is more deceitful than all else
And is desperately sick;
Who can understand it?
"I, the LORD, search the heart,
I test the mind,
Even to give to each man according to his ways,
According to the results of his deeds.
"As a partridge that hatches eggs which it has not laid,
So is he who makes a fortune, but unjustly;
In the midst of his days it will forsake him,
And in the end he will be a fool."
A glorious throne on high from the beginning
Is the place of our sanctuary.
O LORD, the hope of Israel,
All who forsake You will be put to shame.
Those who turn away on earth will be written down,
Because they have forsaken the fountain of living water, even the LORD.

Jeremiah 17:9–13 NASB

Our minds can play tricks on us. The Hebrew word commonly translated into English as *heart* in the Old Testament rarely refers to the physical organ. Rather, it refers to the mind, the seat of the intellect. The mind is the source of who we are, the place where personality and all experiences are stored. From the mind come the dark thoughts and the good thoughts, the emotions, the feelings of hatred and love. Actions grow from and are directed by the mind, and the mind can fool us, deceive us, and lead us into the wrong paths. The mind can help justify our actions, however reprehensible, and the mind can help us see reason and lead us to repentance.

Regarding those who had forsaken God, God said that they "on earth will be written down." That is, those who turned from God would be like writing on the dust or in the dirt; it wouldn't last long, and neither would they. In contrast, it was said that God was enthroned between the cherubim in the sanctuary—the Holy Place—of God (Psalm 99:1). But that was mere symbol. God's true sanctuary was in heaven, where he could guarantee the safety of his people.

Consider how easy it is to be fooled. A stage magician can convince us we've witnessed the impossible. An optical illusion easily confuses us. We lie to ourselves. We easily jump to conclusions. Our biases warp our perceptions of reality. The mind betrays us on a regular basis.

But God understands us even when we don't understand ourselves.

Just Making It Up as You Go Along

Am I a God near by, says the LORD, and not a God far off? Who can hide in secret places so that I cannot see them? says the LORD. Do I not fill heaven and earth? says the LORD. I have heard what the prophets have said who prophesy lies in my name, saying, "I have dreamed, I have dreamed!" How long? Will the hearts of the prophets ever turn back—those who prophesy lies, and who prophesy the deceit of their own heart? They plan to make my people forget my name by their dreams that they tell one another, just as their ancestors forgot my name for Baal. Let the prophet who has a dream tell the dream, but let the one who has my word speak my word faithfully. What has straw in common with wheat? says the LORD. Is not my word like fire, says the LORD, and like a hammer that breaks a rock in pieces? See, therefore, I am against the prophets, says the LORD, who steal my words from one another. See, I am against the prophets, says the LORD, who use their own tongues and say, "Says the LORD." See, I am against those who prophesy lying dreams, says the LORD, and who tell them, and who lead my people astray by their lies and their recklessness, when I did not send them or appoint them; so they do not profit this people at all, says the LORD.

Jeremiah 23:23–32 NRSV

People tend to make God in their own image. In the ancient world, therefore, most gods were limited. They oversaw a particular plot of land, a particular profession, a particular city. The Israelites came to view Yahweh in a restricted way. But God tried to remind them that he was not so limited.

God's reminders had implications for one particular group of people: those who claimed, without warrant, to speak for God. Rather than speaking what God said, they would hear the words of a real prophet and simply repeat them. What they couldn't plagiarize, they just made up. They pretended they had a line to God so they could charge money for sitting around all day and doing nothing. Such false prophets were misleading the people, turning them away from God, and endangering people by giving them false comfort and false information. Their lies made their hearers less likely to take seriously the true prophets. How were they to know when a real prophet was standing before them? What would keep them from turning away from God entirely? People, circumstances, and the distractions of life tend to shrink God—but your God is bigger than your problems.

God Doesn't Have a Lawyer

"This is the new covenant I will make with the people of Israel on that day," says the LORD. "I will put my instructions deep within them, and I will write them on their hearts. I will be their God, and they will be my people. And they will not need to teach their neighbors, nor will they need to teach their relatives, saying, 'You should know the LORD.' For everyone, from the least to the greatest, will know me already," says the LORD. "And I will forgive their wickedness, and I will never again remember their sins."

It is the LORD who provides the sun to light the day and the moon and stars to light the night, and who stirs the sea into roaring waves.
His name is the LORD of Heaven's Armies, and this is what he says:
"I am as likely to reject my people Israel as I am to abolish the laws of nature!"
This is what the LORD says:
"Just as the heavens cannot be measured and the foundations of the earth cannot be explored, so I will not consider casting them away for the evil they have done. I, the Lord, have spoken!"

Jeremiah 31:33–37 NLT

When God rescued Israel from Egypt, he made a covenant, a contract, with them. For the people of Israel, it signaled their change of ownership. They now belonged to God, whereas before they had been slaves to Egypt. So they agreed to do what he told them. The details of the contract were laid out in the book of Deuteronomy, the actual treaty between God and Israel. The people of Israel became obligated to worship God exclusively and to treat one another in a loving way.

Although God's promises are more certain than tomorrow's sunrise, his people's promises were not. That's why human beings have contracts—and lawyers. But God doesn't have fine print in his contracts, nor does he have a band of lawyers working to get him out of them. Instead, God wants to keep his contracts—and he wants to help his people keep theirs. But the Israelites had a hard time remembering what God expected of them. It was difficult for them even to think about God at all.

To solve the ongoing problem of his people breaking their promises, God decided at last to write a new covenant—a new contract—inside them. He wanted to make the new covenant a part of them so it could never be erased, lost, or forgotten. He wrote this new covenant on our hearts.

Why Can't You Do What I Say?

The word of the LORD came to Jeremiah, saying: "This is what the LORD Almighty, the God of Israel, says: Go and tell the men of Judah and the people of Jerusalem, 'Will you not learn a lesson and obey my words?' declares the LORD. 'Jonadab son of Recab ordered his sons not to drink wine and this command has been kept. To this day they do not drink wine, because they obey their forefather's command. But I have spoken to you again and again, yet you have not obeyed me. Again and again I sent all my servants the prophets to you. They said, "Each of you must turn from your wicked ways and reform your actions; do not follow other gods to serve them. Then you will live in the land I have given to you and your fathers." But you have not paid attention or listened to me. The descendants of Jonadab son of Recab have carried out the command their fore-father gave them, but these people have not obeyed me.'

"Therefore, this is what the LORD God Almighty, the God of Israel, says: 'Listen! I am going to bring on Judah and on everyone living in Jerusalem every disaster I pronounced against them. I spoke to them, but they did not listen; I called to them, but they did not answer.' "

Then Jeremiah said to the family of the Recabites, "This is what the LORD Almighty, the God of Israel, says: 'You have obeyed the command of your forefather Jonadab and have followed all his instructions and have done everything he ordered.' Therefore, this is what the LORD Almighty, the God of Israel, says: 'Jonadab son of Recab will never fail to have a man to serve me.' "

Jeremiah 35:12–19 NIV

❈

The Recabites were a peculiar group of people. Jonadab, the son of Recab, had told his children not to drink wine, build houses, sow seed, or plant vineyards. Instead, they always had to live in tents (Jeremiah 35:7). Ever after, all descendants of Jonadab obeyed his words, despite the fact that the instructions were, to put it mildly, rather nonsensical.

In contrast to the weird Recabites, who strictly adhered to the most peculiar rules, the Israelites ignored the reasonable instructions of God. God wondered how a mere human being could get generations of people to abide by his idiosyncratic beliefs but the Israelites wouldn't listen to wisdom given to them by God himself. They were crazier than the Recabites ever were.

God did something remarkable: he promised that because of their faithfulness he would make sure that there would always be descendants of the Recabites to serve God. God appreciates loyalty and rewards it.

Increasing Promiscuity

"After all your evil—Woe, woe to you!"—the declaration of the Lord GOD—"you built yourself a mound and made yourself an elevated place in every square. You built your elevated place at the head of every street and turned your beauty into an abomination. You spread your legs to everyone who passed by and increased your prostitution. You engaged in promiscuous acts with Egyptian men, your well-endowed neighbors, and increased your prostitution to provoke Me to anger.

"Therefore, I stretched out My hand against you and reduced your provisions. I gave you over to the desire of those who hate you, the Philistine women, who were embarrassed by your indecent behavior. Then you engaged in prostitution with the Assyrian men because you were not satisfied. Even though you did this with them, you were still not satisfied. So you extended your prostitution to Chaldea, the land of merchants, but you were not even satisfied with this!

"How your heart was inflamed [with lust]"—the declaration of the Lord GOD—"when you did all these things, the acts of a brazen prostitute, building your mound at the head of every street and making your elevated place in every square. But you were unlike a prostitute because you scorned payment."

Ezekiel 16:23–31 HCSB

Sometimes people need to be shocked. Ezekiel had problems with getting the people of God to hear what he was saying. They paid as much attention to his words as the average person pays to the lyrics of a song (Ezekiel 33:32). But God wanted his people to understand how their worship of other gods was making him feel, and so he made use of explicit language. He compared Judah to an adulterous wife who prostituted herself, expending her wealth on false gods. In fact, Judah wasn't even a prostitute who at least got paid for what she did. God wanted his people to recognize just how vulgar they had become. The underlying Hebrew that is translated "offering your body with increasing promiscuity to anyone who passed by" is very graphic. Bible scholars give us the literal translation, "You spread your legs for everyone who comes by."

God was shocked by what Israel and Judah had done, how badly they had betrayed him. They were the same as an adulterous wife turned to prostitution. They had fallen into the arms of every other god but him. God was hurt. God's heart was broken. And God was furious. He hoped that shocking them with graphic images would finally get their attention.

God has feelings. If being betrayed hurts us, how can we imagine that it is any less painful for God?

Gods Don't Die

The LORD God said:

Ezekiel, son of man, tell the king of Tyre that I am saying: You are so arrogant that you think you're a god and that the city of Tyre is your throne. You may claim to be a god, though you're nothing but a mere human. You think you're wiser than Daniel and know everything. Your wisdom has certainly made you rich, because you have storehouses filled with gold and silver. You're a clever businessman and are extremely wealthy, but your wealth has led to arrogance!

You compared yourself to a god, so now I, the LORD God, will make you the victim of cruel enemies. They will destroy all the possessions you've worked so hard to get. Your enemies will brutally kill you, and the sea will be your only grave.

When you face your enemies, will you still claim to be a god? They will attack, and you will suffer like any other human. Foreigners will kill you, and you will die the death of those who don't worship me. I, the LORD, have spoken.

Ezekiel 28:1–10 CEV

*T*he king of Tyre believed that he was a god, as did many other monarchs of the ancient world. God sarcastically pointed out that reality would have an unpleasant way of clarifying things for him. Mortality had a habit of reminding people that they really weren't divine beings, no matter how prideful, rich, and powerful they might be. And certainly the city of Tyre was wealthy, powerful, and prosperous, thanks to its widespread Mediterranean trade.

God said that the king of Tyre believed he was as wise as Daniel, whose reputation as a wise official had spread beyond Babylon (Daniel 1:20; 5:11–12). But unlike Daniel, the king of Tyre betrayed the trust of his people, amassing wealth and power while doing nothing for the poor and disadvantaged. The sacrifice of children as burnt offerings was common in Tyre. Worse, the upper classes did not sacrifice their own children. They purchased the children of the poor.

During the time of Alexander the Great, the city of Tyre was flattened. But many of the inhabitants fled. They established Carthage, a new city on the northern coast of Africa. Some years later, the Romans attacked. As they lay under the Roman siege, the upper classes decided that their sacrifices of poor children were not enough, and so they started sacrificing their own. But the Romans destroyed them anyway.

We need to be careful not to think more of ourselves than we should. The wiser we become, the more human, and therefore limited, we realize we are—and the closer we want to be to God.

The Unfaithful Wife

The Lord said, "Hosea, Israel has betrayed me like an unfaithful wife. Marry such a woman and have children by her." So I married Gomer the daughter of Diblaim, and we had a son. Then the Lord said, "Hosea, name your son Jezreel, because I will soon punish the descendants of King Jehu of Israel for the murders he committed in Jezreel Valley. I will destroy his kingdom, and in Jezreel Valley I will break the power of Israel." Later, Gomer had a daughter, and the Lord said, "Name her Lo-Ruhamah, because I will no longer have mercy and forgive Israel. But I am the Lord God of Judah, and I will have mercy and save Judah by my own power—not by wars and arrows or swords and cavalry." After Gomer had stopped nursing Lo-Ruhamah, she had another son. Then the Lord said, "Name him Lo-Ammi, because these people are not mine, and I am not their God."

Someday it will be impossible to count the people of Israel, because there will be as many of them as there are grains of sand along the seashore. They are now called "Not My People," but in the future they will be called "Children of the Living God." Israel and Judah will unite and choose one leader. Then they will take back their land, and this will be a great day for Jezreel.

Hosea 1:2–11 CEV

Hosea may have thought the worst job in the world was to be God's prophet. The Israelites had betrayed God and chased after other gods, and God used the prophet's life to illustrate his words. God had Hosea purposely find a woman who would behave toward him just as the Israelites had behaved toward God. In marrying Gomer, Hosea had no illusions about what he was getting himself into. And from the very first day, Gomer continued to live and act like the prostitute she was.

The performance art extended to his children. The name Jezreel was given to his son as a symbol of God's displeasure with what Jehu had done. The name Lo-Ruhamah means "unloved," while Lo-Ammi means "not my people," standing for what Israel had become.

After repentance and restoration, however, the Israelites would be "as many as the grains of sand on the seashore." The phrase is hyperbole, not literal. It simply means that there will be a lot of Israelites. Hosea's wife would one day become faithful to him, just as one day Israel would become faithful to God. God honors his commitments.

The Time of Reaping Approaches

For you also, O Judah, a harvest is appointed.
When I would restore the fortunes
of my people, when I would heal
Israel, the corruption of Ephraim is
revealed, and the wicked deeds of
Samaria; for they deal falsely, the
thief breaks in, and the bandits raid
outside.
But they do not consider that I remember all their wickedness.
Now their deeds surround them,
they are before my face.
By their wickedness they make the
king glad, and the officials by their
treachery.
They are all adulterers; they are like a
heated oven, whose baker does not
need to stir the fire, from the kneading of the dough until it is leavened.
On the day of our king the officials
became sick with the heat of wine;
he stretched out his hand with
mockers.
For they are kindled like an oven, their
heart burns within them; all night
their anger smolders; in the morning
it blazes like a flaming fire.
All of them are hot as an oven,
and they devour their rulers.
All their kings have fallen;
none of them calls upon me.

Hosea 6:11–7:7 NRSV

*H*arvests were happy times of celebration in ancient agrarian societies because they meant that the people didn't have to worry about starving that year. A good autumn harvest meant there would be enough seed to plant the next spring.

God used the image of the harvest as a metaphor for his judgment on his people. From the perspective of the crops harvested, the reaping was a painful thing. The crops were mowed down and threshed, and the leftover chaff was burned. Harvests were inherently violent. Animals were slaughtered and their meat smoked or salted to preserve it during the long dark winter.

But harvests are not destructive. They are not designed to harm. They are for the benefit of all concerned, ensuring the continuation of life. A harvest captures clearly the true nature of judgment. God loved his people. He disciplined them for their own good.

God always acts in love, but how his actions are perceived depends on whether you look at things from the perspective of the chopped and threshed grain or from the perspective of the joyful villagers who benefit from the bounty.

Just Deserts

They sow the wind,
  And reap the whirlwind.
  The stalk has no bud;
  It shall never produce meal.
  If it should produce,
  Aliens would swallow it up.
    Israel is swallowed up;
  Now they are among the Gentiles
  Like a vessel in which is no
    pleasure . . .

Because Ephraim has made many
  altars for sin,
They have become for him altars
  for sinning.
I have written for him the great
  things of My law,
But they were considered a strange
  thing.

For the sacrifices of My offerings
  they sacrifice flesh and eat it,
But the LORD does not accept
  them.
Now He will remember their iniq-
  uity and punish their sins.
They shall return to Egypt.
For Israel has forgotten his Maker,
And has built temples;
Judah also has multiplied fortified
  cities;
But I will send fire upon his cities,
And it shall devour his palaces.

Hosea 8:7–8, 11–14 NKJV

*J*ust as a farmer will harvest the sort of crop that he planted back in the spring, so the nation of Israel was going to harvest what it had planted. They had put their trust and dependence in vapor. When the Assyrians invaded, the Israelites' nonexistent gods rendered the aid of the pretend, and so Israel returned to captivity. Metaphorically speaking, the Israelites were back in Egypt. Once there, they would eventually figure out their mistake and repent, and God would once more forgive and rescue them from their mistake.

Hosea prophesied at the same time that Isaiah and Amos did, before either the Northern Kingdom of Israel, also called Ephraim, or the Southern Kingdom of Judah had been judged by God and sent away into exile. Both were going to harvest the fruits of the sins they had sown.

The word for *sin* and the word for *sin offering* were the same in the Hebrew language of the Old Testament. The sin offering was identified with the sin, became one with the sin, and so as the sin offering was offered to God and burned up in the sacrifice, the sin was purged away, destroyed, and forgiven.

When God gives his forgiveness, there is nothing left to feel guilty about. We can be secure in his forgiveness.

Come, Holy Spirit!

You will have plenty to eat and
  be satisfied
    And praise the name of the Lord
      your God,
    Who has dealt wondrously
      with you;
    Then My people will never be put
      to shame.
Thus you will know that I am in the
  midst of Israel,
    And that I am the Lord your God,
    And there is no other;
    And My people will never be put
      to shame.
It will come about after this
    That I will pour out My Spirit on
      all mankind;
    And your sons and daughters will
      prophesy,
    Your old men will dream dreams,
    Your young men will see visions.

Even on the male and female servants
    I will pour out My Spirit in
      those days.
I will display wonders in the sky and
    on the earth,
      Blood, fire and columns of smoke.
The sun will be turned into darkness
    And the moon into blood
    Before the great and awesome day
      of the Lord comes.
And it will come about that whoever
  calls on the name of the Lord
    Will be delivered;
    For on Mount Zion and in
      Jerusalem
    There will be those who escape,
    As the Lord has said,
    Even among the survivors whom
      the Lord calls.

Joel 2:26–32 NASB

*L*et the good times begin. God told his people that the famine was over. The Israelites would have plenty to eat, both physically and spiritually. Joel often quoted the prophets who came before him: Isaiah, Micah, and Amos. The "day of the Lord" was not automatically a reference to the end of the world. Rather, it described whenever God judged his people.

The sun becoming dark and the moon turning to blood were descriptions of what happened when a city was burned down. The smoke blackened the sky and dimmed the light from the heavenly bodies.

In the time of Moses, the Spirit empowered a select few to build the tabernacle or to join with Moses in leadership. In the time of the judges, God's Spirit fell on those he had chosen to rescue his people from oppression. But through Joel, God promised that a time would come when his Spirit would be poured out on everyone, young and old, and not on just a few. One day, everyone who calls on God's name will be delivered.

Looking Out for Number One

The word of the LORD came by Haggai the prophet, saying, "Is it time for you yourselves to dwell in your paneled houses, and this temple to lie in ruins?" Now therefore, thus says the LORD of hosts: "Consider your ways!

"You have sown much, and bring in little;
You eat, but do not have enough;
You drink, but you are not filled with drink;
You clothe yourselves, but no one is warm;
And he who earns wages,
Earns wages to put into a bag with holes."

Thus says the LORD of hosts: "Consider your ways! Go up to the mountains and bring wood and build the temple, that I may take pleasure in it and be glorified," says the LORD. "You looked for much, but indeed it came to little; and when you brought it home, I blew it away. Why?" says the LORD of hosts. "Because of My house that is in ruins, while every one of you runs to his own house. Therefore the heavens above you withhold the dew, and the earth withholds its fruit. For I called for a drought on the land and the mountains, on the grain and the new wine and the oil, on whatever the ground brings forth, on men and livestock, and on all the labor of your hands."

Haggai 1:3–11 NKJV

※

People often fail to recognize what is actually in their best interests. Upon returning to Palestine after seventy years of captivity in Babylon, the Israelites came home to find their cities in ruins and their farms overgrown with weeds. They set about repairing them. But despite their best efforts to repair their land, nothing seemed to be working out quite right.

God, through the prophet Haggai, identified their problem. Their ancestors had gotten them into this mess in the first place by ignoring God. Already, they were acting like their ancestors again. They had focused on themselves and their needs, instead of on God. Once again, God pointed to the treaty and said, "Look, if you seek God and his righteousness, all these things will be added unto you." By rebuilding the temple, performing the sacrifices, genuinely loving God and loving others, the stuff they wanted and needed—all those necessities of life like food, drink, clothing, and shelter—would come. But if they ignored God and focused on the stuff, then their lives would continue to be unfulfilling. Focusing on God first is practical—it's the way to make life better.

Worthless Sacrifices

The LORD of Heaven's Armies says to the priests: "A son honors his father, and a servant respects his master. If I am your father and master, where are the honor and respect I deserve? You have shown contempt for my name!

"But you ask, 'How have we ever shown contempt for your name?'

"You have shown contempt by offering defiled sacrifices on my altar.

"Then you ask, 'How have we defiled the sacrifices?'

"You defile them by saying the altar of the LORD deserves no respect. When you give blind animals as sacrifices, isn't that wrong? And isn't it wrong to offer animals that are crippled and diseased? Try giving gifts like that to your governor, and see how pleased he is!" says the LORD of Heaven's Armies.

"Go ahead, beg God to be merciful to you! But when you bring that kind of offering, why should he show you any favor at all?" asks the LORD of Heaven's Armies.

"How I wish one of you would shut the Temple doors so that these worthless sacrifices could not be offered! I am not pleased with you," says the LORD of Heaven's Armies, "and I will not accept your offerings. But my name is honored by people of other nations from morning till night. All around the world they offer sweet incense and pure offerings in honor of my name. For my name is great among the nations," says the LORD of Heaven's Armies.

Malachi 1:6–11 NLT

❋

God wanted the temple shut down. He was tired of offerings that were meaningless because they were thoughtless. Those offerings were merely empty ritualism that grew out of superstition rather than genuine devotion to God. The Israelites performed the rituals because they thought that in so doing they could get God to perform. They thought they could manipulate God. For that reason, God wanted the Israelites to stop sacrificing to him.

The prophet said that God's name was honored by people of other nations and that they worshipped him. While some have suggested that this referred to the Jewish people already in exile in Babylon and Assyria, the more likely understanding is that this was a prophecy of what was going to happen: the Gentiles, those who were not Jewish, would see the light and become worshippers of God. The temple would then be destroyed, ending the sacrificial system once and for all. The temple was destroyed by the Romans during the summer of AD 70. True worshippers worship not at a temple, but in spirit and truth.

No Respect

"I the LORD do not change. So you, O descendants of Jacob, are not destroyed. Ever since the time of your forefathers you have turned away from my decrees and have not kept them. Return to me, and I will return to you," says the LORD Almighty.

"But you ask, 'How are we to return?'

"Will a man rob God? Yet you rob me.

"But you ask, 'How do we rob you?'

"In tithes and offerings. You are under a curse—the whole nation of you—because you are robbing me. Bring the whole tithe into the storehouse, that there may be food in my house. Test me in this," says the LORD Almighty, "and see if I will not throw open the floodgates of heaven and pour out so much blessing that you will not have room enough for it. I will prevent pests from devouring your crops, and the vines in your fields will not cast their fruit," says the LORD Almighty. "Then all the nations will call you blessed, for yours will be a delightful land," says the LORD Almighty.

"You have said harsh things against me," says the LORD.

"Yet you ask, 'What have we said against you?'

"You have said, 'It is futile to serve God. What did we gain by carrying out his requirements and going about like mourners before the LORD Almighty? But now we call the arrogant blessed. Certainly the evildoers prosper, and even those who challenge God escape.' "

Malachi 3:6–15 NIV

*G*od's character is consistent. He is patient; he is not easily angered. God keeps no record of wrongs, rejoices with the truth, always protects, and never fails. God is love, and because of who he is, God did not destroy Israel. From the time of the exodus until the time the prophet quoted God's words in this passage, the Israelites had been rebellious and disobedient. They had chased after false gods. Instead of being concerned with others, they were concerned only with themselves. They were oblivious to their attitude and didn't understand why their behavior would bother God. But despite their sin, God's love for them never faltered.

The Israelites were unconvinced that it was in their best interests to serve God. Because the rain falls on the just and the unjust, they thought it didn't matter which they were. They forgot that they weren't to be righteous in order to get God's blessing or to miss God's punishment. They were to be righteous because God loved them.

Companionship and Isolation

Companionship is part of what it means to be human. It is not possible to express love if you are isolated. Individuals remain important, however, not just the group or the community. The Bible has genealogies, lists of the artisans responsible for building the tabernacle, lists of those who returned from exile, and lists of the great people of faith. Individuals matter, as they relate to one another. Isolation apart from community, however, can have a negative effect. Companionship is made up of people we love and who love us.

❈

GOD said, "It's not good for the Man to be alone."
Genesis 2:18 MSG

Never Alone

God said, "Let Us make man in Our image, according to Our likeness; let them have dominion over the fish of the sea, over the birds of the air, and over the cattle, over all the earth and over every creeping thing that creeps on the earth." So God created man in His own image; in the image of God He created him; male and female He created them. Then God blessed them, and God said to them, "Be fruitful and multiply; fill the earth and subdue it; have dominion over the fish of the sea, over the birds of the air, and over every living thing that moves on the earth."

And God said, "See, I have given you every herb that yields seed which is on the face of all the earth, and every tree whose fruit yields seed; to you it shall be for food. Also, to every beast of the earth, to every bird of the air, and to everything that creeps on the earth, in which there is life, I have given every green herb for food"; and it was so.

Genesis 1:26–30 NKJV

The greatest commandment is to love God. But the second is equal to it: love your neighbor as yourself. From the beginning, human beings were designed to live together with others and to be involved with one another. The very word for *man* in the first chapter of Genesis has a collective sense to it; that's why most modern translations normally translate it as "human beings." Notice that *man* means male and female humans together. By creating them as male and female—as more than one—they became the image of God, not as individuals, but as a collective whole.

To make this point, God referred to himself with plural pronouns, *we* and *us*. The only other place he did this was in the Tower of Babel incident, when the collective nature of *man* or *humanity* is an important part of the story. God's use of plural pronouns indicates a plurality within God himself, an Old Testament hint about the nature of the Trinity. Humanity was made male and female because it took more than one individual to make humanity like God.

It was never God's will for human beings to be alone or isolated. It is only together that we are like God and reflect his image. Living a life as a hermit, living without reaching out to one's fellow man, or being concerned only with oneself is less than God's design for people. After all, how can we love people if we're always alone or if we think only about what's best for ourselves, as if we are alone? Love requires an object beyond self.

Nothing Is Impossible

At one time all the people of the world spoke the same language and used the same words. As the people migrated to the east, they found a plain in the land of Babylonia and settled there.

They began saying to each other, "Let's make bricks and harden them with fire." (In this region bricks were used instead of stone, and tar was used for mortar.) Then they said, "Come, let's build a great city for ourselves with a tower that reaches into the sky. This will make us famous and keep us from being scattered all over the world."

But the LORD came down to look at the city and the tower the people were building. "Look!" he said. "The people are united, and they all speak the same language. After this, nothing they set out to do will be impossible for them! Come, let's go down and confuse the people with different languages. Then they won't be able to understand each other."

In that way, the LORD scattered them all over the world, and they stopped building the city. That is why the city was called Babel, because that is where the LORD confused the people with different languages. In this way he scattered them all over the world.

Genesis 11:1–9 NLT

❁

*T*he Hebrew word used for the *tower* in the Tower of Babel story was used of watchtowers. Such towers were placed on city walls so that guards could watch for approaching enemies. That it "reaches into the sky" simply meant that it was tall; it didn't mean that the people were attempting to reach heaven. The goal of the people in Babel was to make a name for themselves and to stay together in one place. Pride and fear of isolation were the motivation for building the city of Babel.

The joke in the narrative is that while they built a tall tower, God "came down" to take a look at it. But God made a remarkable statement regarding human capability—he said that nothing would be impossible for people to accomplish. This story of Babel is one of only two places in the Bible where God used the plural pronoun *we* or *us* in reference to himself. The other place was in the creation account when God created people in his image and likeness. A humanity of many parts reflected who and what God is. The Tower of Babel story demonstrates that only God can limit us. Out potential as humans is limitless if we choose to work with God rather than for our own selfish gain.

Never Abandoned

Early in the morning Abraham got up, took bread and a waterskin, [put them] on Hagar's shoulders, and sent her and the boy away. She left and wandered in the Wilderness of Beer-sheba. When the water in the skin was gone, she left the boy under one of the bushes. Then she went and sat down nearby, about a bowshot away, for she said, "I can't [bear to] watch the boy die!" So as she sat nearby, she wept loudly.

God heard the voice of the boy, and the angel of God called to Hagar from heaven and said to her, "What's wrong, Hagar? Don't be afraid, for God has heard the voice of the boy from the place where he is. Get up, help the boy up, and sustain him, for I will make him a great nation." Then God opened her eyes, and she saw a well of water. So she went and filled the waterskin and gave the boy a drink. God was with the boy, and he grew; he settled in the wilderness and became an archer. He settled in the Wilderness of Paran, and his mother got a wife for him from the land of Egypt.

Genesis 21:14–21 HCSB

*I*t's hard to see through our tears. That's why God keeps trying to wipe them away. Abraham was unhappy about sending his son and maidservant Hagar away from him. But he did because his wife, Sarah, told him to. God did too. With her son, Ishmael, Hagar went off into the southern desert of Israel beyond Beersheba. She and her boy soon ran out of water, and Hagar was certain they would die.

God noticed her son crying and intervened on his behalf. He comforted Hagar in that moment. Not only did he provide for their immediate, physical need of water, but he also answered her other concerns as an exile, disowned and cast from her home. The circumstances were grim, but the future for her and the future for her son were no longer grim. God told her that worry about the morrow was unfounded. Her son would live under God's blessing and prosper.

Ishmael's home in the Desert of Paran was most likely in the region around Mount Sinai. It was a mostly barren wilderness. Hagar was from Egypt, so it was natural that she would find a wife for her son from her homeland.

How can we be alone or without hope so long as God is with us? No matter how bleak the circumstances, with God things are never as they seem to be.

Wrestlemania

Jacob was left alone; and a Man wrestled with him until the breaking of day. Now when He saw that He did not prevail against him, He touched the socket of his hip; and the socket of Jacob's hip was out of joint as He wrestled with him. And He said, "Let Me go, for the day breaks."

But he said, "I will not let You go unless You bless me!"

So He said to him, "What is your name?"

He said, "Jacob."

And He said, "Your name shall no longer be called Jacob, but Israel; for you have struggled with God and with men, and have prevailed."

Then Jacob asked, saying, "Tell me Your name, I pray."

And He said, "Why is it that you ask about My name?" And He blessed him there.

So Jacob called the name of the place Peniel: "For I have seen God face to face, and my life is preserved." Just as he crossed over Penuel the sun rose on him, and he limped on his hip. Therefore to this day the children of Israel do not eat the muscle that shrank, which is on the hip socket, because He touched the socket of Jacob's hip in the muscle that shrank.

Genesis 32:24–32 NKJV

*W*restling with God in prayer became more than a metaphor for Jacob. On the dark night when he ran from his brother, Jacob had strange dreams of angels going up and down a ladder. God promised him then that he would always be with him.

After spending more than twenty years with his uncle Laban, and after gaining four wives and nearly a dozen sons, Jacob ran from his uncle much as he'd run from his brother.

In that context, on another dark night, he found himself wrestling a man who wouldn't give up his name. The man beat him in the struggle by putting Jacob's hip out of joint. As the sun was starting to rise, the man asked Jacob to let him go, but Jacob refused unless the man blessed him. So the man blessed him and gave him a new name. *Israel* means "he wrestles with God." Jacob had a lot to struggle with God over. And God was okay with that.

In the morning, Jacob called the place where he had wrestled *Peniel*, which means "face of God." Jacob realized that it wasn't just a man he'd fought, but God himself. He had discovered that it was okay to fight with God because God always wins (as he did by putting Jacob's hip out of joint). And that's what we really need and desire: a God who can overcome our fears and problems.

The Reunion

The LORD said to Aaron, "Go into the wilderness to meet Moses." So he went; and he met him at the mountain of God and kissed him. Moses told Aaron all the words of the LORD with which he had sent him, and all the signs with which he had charged him. Then Moses and Aaron went and assembled all the elders of the Israelites. Aaron spoke all the words that the LORD had spoken to Moses, and performed the signs in the sight of the people. The people believed; and when they heard that the LORD had given heed to the Israelites and that he had seen their misery, they bowed down and worshiped.

Exodus 4:27–31 NRSV

People who need people are not just the luckiest people—they're normal people. Moses had seen God in a burning bush. He'd received miracles he could perform whenever he needed. God had answered all his questions. But it had taken the offer of his brother's help to overcome his continued reluctance to do the task God had assigned. Moses knew that his big brother Aaron would stand with him, and so he would face the job God had given him.

At the same time God was recruiting Moses, God was also recruiting his brother. Moses did not have to talk Aaron into helping him. God had already paved the way. God had let Aaron know what was going on and had sent him off on the long journey from Egypt to meet his brother on the mountain of God. The "mountain of God" was Mount Sinai, where Moses would later return with the Israelites to receive the Ten Commandments. Traditionally, Mount Sinai is identified with *Jebel Musa*—Arabic for "mountain of Moses"—located on the Sinai Peninsula. The Greek Orthodox Saint Catherine's Monastery was built there in the sixth century near the supposed site of the burning bush.

When Aaron met Moses, Moses told him everything that God had told him to say, and he told him all about the miracles and signs that God had given him to perform.

Moses did not have to face his return to Egypt alone. He did not have to face the other Israelites alone. He didn't have to face Pharaoh alone. From the beginning, his big brother acted as his spokesperson. All Moses had to do was perform the miracles. When the people heard and saw how much God cared, they bowed down in worship. If the work that God calls us to is more than we can do alone, God will already have made provision for any help we'll need. For God, failure is not an option.

Love Your Family

Dedicate yourselves to me and be holy because I am the LORD your God. I have chosen you as my people, and I expect you to obey my laws.

If you curse your father or mother, you will be put to death, and it will be your own fault.

If any of you men have sex with another man's wife, both you and the woman will be put to death.

Having sex with one of your father's wives disgraces him. So both you and the woman will be put to death, just as you deserve. It isn't natural to have sex with your daughter-in-law, and both of you will be put to death, just as you deserve. It's disgusting for men to have sex with one another, and those who do will be put to death, just as they deserve. It isn't natural for a man to marry both a mother and her daughter, and so all three of them will be burned to death. If any of you have sex with an animal, both you and the animal will be put to death, just as you deserve.

Leviticus 20:7–16 CEV

✻

*C*an't people just get along? God had chosen his people, rescued them from Egypt, and entered into a binding covenant with them. This treaty meant that where before they had been subject to Egypt, they were now subject to God. Because of the relationship that God now had with them, he expected them to obey him. Obedience was a result of God in their lives, not the cause. God then prohibited a variety of bad behavior, ranging from the cursing of parents to inappropriate sexual activities. What all these bad behaviors had in common was their penalty—death.

Given that the overall principle in punishment according to God was an eye for an eye—that is, the penalty for a crime must not exceed the crime—why were cursing parents, committing adultery, and having intercourse with animals treated the same way that murdering someone was treated?

Murder was punished by death because human beings were created in the image of God. A man and woman became one flesh in marriage and produced offspring who were in their image and likeness. Sexual intercourse outside that pattern broke the image of God just as much as murder did. Cursing parents was like cursing one's own existence, and it threatened one's very survival.

God knows the importance of relationships and family. For human beings to survive and prosper, they must get along. God treated all threats to the survival and prosperity of his people harshly. Love isn't just a pleasant feeling. It ensures our continued existence.

Even You Count

Then the LORD spoke to Moses in the Wilderness of Sinai, saying: "Number the children of Levi by their fathers' houses, by their families; you shall number every male from a month old and above."

So Moses numbered them according to the word of the LORD, as he was commanded. These were the sons of Levi by their names: Gershon, Kohath, and Merari. And these are the names of the sons of Gershon by their families: Libni and Shimei. And the sons of Kohath by their families: Amram, Izehar, Hebron, and Uzziel. And the sons of Merari by their families: Mahli and Mushi. These are the families of the Levites by their fathers' houses.

From Gershon came the family of the Libnites and the family of the Shimites; these were the families of the Gershonites. Those who were numbered, according to the number of all the males from a month old and above—of those who were numbered there were seven thousand five hundred.

Numbers 3:14–22 NKJV

When Moses was on Mount Sinai receiving the Ten Commandments from God, God told him to take a census of the Israelites by family and tribe, including all the Levites, the tribe to which Moses and his brother Aaron belonged. Moses and Aaron were descended from Kohath, the second born of Levi's three sons. Amran was the father of Aaron and Moses. Amran's wife was Kohath's sister, Jochebed. Thus, Moses' mother was also his great aunt. This may seem strange, but the prohibitions on marrying close relatives came into practice only after God gave the law to Moses. Until then, it was common for people to marry relatives. While the information contained in genealogies was interesting to the family members involved, most people think the genealogies in the Bible are boring. So why did God tell Moses to create them?

They served as a reminder that each individual mattered to God. Human organizations—whether civilizations, secular clubs, denominations, corporations, or nonprofits—are all mortal. Nothing lasts forever except for individual human souls. Since individuals count, God had Moses count them.

Why count only the males from a month old and up? It probably had to do with mortality rates that were very high until the advent of antibiotics in the mid-twentieth century.

We are more than just numbers or names on a list. All of us are worth the effort to keep track of. We matter to one another, and we matter to God.

Representatives for the Whole

The LORD spoke to Moses saying,

"Send out for yourself men so that they may spy out the land of Canaan, which I am going to give to the sons of Israel; you shall send a man from each of their fathers' tribes, every one a leader among them."

So Moses sent them from the wilderness of Paran at the command of the LORD, all of them men who were heads of the sons of Israel.

These then were their names: from the tribe of Reuben, Shammua the son of Zaccur; from the tribe of Simeon, Shaphat the son of Hori; from the tribe of Judah, Caleb the son of Jephunneh; from the tribe of Issachar, Igal the son of Joseph; from the tribe of Ephraim, Hoshea the son of Nun; from the tribe of Benjamin, Palti the son of Raphu; from the tribe of Zebulun, Gaddiel the son of Sodi; from the tribe of Joseph, from the tribe of Manasseh, Gaddi the son of Susi; from the tribe of Dan, Ammiel the son of Gemalli; from the tribe of Asher, Sethur the son of Michael; from the tribe of Naphtali, Nahbi the son of Vophsi; from the tribe of Gad, Geuel the son of Machi.

These are the names of the men whom Moses sent to spy out the land; but Moses called Hoshea the son of Nun, Joshua.

Numbers 13:1–16 NASB

God believes in the power of people working together. God brought the people of Israel out of Egypt to bring them back to the land he had promised to Abraham. Then God told Moses to select twelve people to go check it out.

The importance of people in groups remains a constant throughout the Bible. Rather than sending a single individual, God sent a group of men already in positions of authority and leadership and they marched out together.

God knew that human beings like to experience things for themselves. Moreover, these particular human beings, the Israelites, had repeatedly demonstrated the all too human tendency to live by sight and not by faith. They had shown a remarkable inability to put much trust in God or believe what he said. A report from twelve people would be believed where God's report would not.

If we can find out something on our own, God isn't going to tell it to us. God doesn't allow himself to become a shortcut for laziness or a way to shirk our responsibility. He is willing to let us learn things the hard way.

Day 193

Family Duty

The LORD said to Aaron: "You, your sons, and your relatives from the tribe of Levi will be held responsible for any offenses related to the sanctuary. But you and your sons alone will be held responsible for violations connected with the priesthood.

"Bring your relatives of the tribe of Levi—your ancestral tribe—to assist you and your sons as you perform the sacred duties in front of the Tabernacle of the Covenant. But as the Levites go about all their assigned duties at the Tabernacle, they must be careful not to go near any of the sacred objects or the altar. If they do, both you and they will die. The Levites must join you in fulfilling their responsibilities for the care and maintenance of the Tabernacle, but no unauthorized person may assist you.

"You yourselves must perform the sacred duties inside the sanctuary and at the altar. If you follow these instructions, the LORD's anger will never again blaze against the people of Israel. I myself have chosen your fellow Levites from among the Israelites to be your special assistants. They are a gift to you, dedicated to the LORD for service in the Tabernacle. But you and your sons, the priests, must personally handle all the priestly rituals associated with the altar and with everything behind the inner curtain. I am giving you the priesthood as your special privilege of service. Any unauthorized person who comes too near the sanctuary will be put to death."

Numbers 18:1–7 NLT

Aaron and his descendants were priests. They alone were allowed to perform the sacrifices. The tribe they belonged to, the tribe of Levi, was given the responsibility to help them perform their duties. It was like the difference between the pilots who fly the airplanes and those who do the maintenance, monitor the radar, and work the radios.

Why did God threaten death for those who didn't follow the rules of the tabernacle? The priests were responsible for maintaining the Israelite's relationship with God. They performed the sacrifices that atoned for sin. They were the ones who stood between God and the people. The priests were not merely performing rituals. The very lives of God's people were in their hands. So God held them personally responsible. Life for life.

Being on the front lines of worshipping God was a dangerous position and was much like the pilots who fly into enemy territory. Those back at the base, like the Levites, had their own dangers to worry about.

Everyone has a role to play for God. When we work together, we can reach our goal and achieve God's ultimate purpose for his people.

The Importance of Daughters

The daughters of Zelophehad approached; [Zelophehad was the] son of Hepher, son of Gilead, son of Machir, son of Manasseh from the clans of Manasseh, the son of Joseph. These were the names of his daughters: Mahlah, Noah, Hoglah, Milcah, and Tirzah. They stood before Moses, Eleazar the priest, the leaders, and the entire community at the entrance to the tent of meeting and said, "Our father died in the wilderness, but he was not among Korah's followers, who gathered together against the LORD. Instead, he died because of his own sin, and he had no sons. Why should the name of our father be taken away from his clan? Since he had no son, give us property among our father's brothers."

Moses brought their case before the LORD, and the LORD answered him, "What Zelophehad's daughters say is correct. You are to give them hereditary property among their father's brothers and transfer their father's inheritance to them. Tell the Israelites: When a man dies without having a son, transfer his inheritance to his daughter. If he has no daughter, give his inheritance to his brothers. If he has no brothers, give his inheritance to his father's brothers. If his father has no brothers, give his inheritance to the nearest relative of his clan, and he will take possession of it. This is to be a statutory ordinance for the Israelites as the LORD commanded Moses."

Numbers 27:1–11 HCSB

❀

God heard the women of the Bible. The five daughters of Zelophehad wanted to protect their father's name, and they wanted to protect themselves. It was important for the Israelites that their names and property be passed down to future generations. In their patriarchal society, if a man had no sons, then some other male relative gained his inheritance. Zelophehad's daughters thought that was wrong. They were his children as much as any son could be, so why couldn't they get the inheritance? God agreed with them. God told Moses that from then on, children, regardless of gender, took priority over other male relatives. Only if there were no children at all could the next closest male relative of the extended family inherit a dead man's property.

In a patriarchal society, women were dependent upon the men around them for their survival. Without a male relative to support her, a woman was likely to end up starving or having to work as a prostitute. God saw to it that daughters could not be deprived of what was rightly theirs. Gender does not trump an individual's humanity. Regardless of what Moses or the other men might have thought, God insisted that women mattered. No one is unimportant to God.

A Place of Refuge

The LORD spoke to Moses, saying: Speak to the Israelites, and say to them: When you cross the Jordan into the land of Canaan, then you shall select cities to be cities of refuge for you, so that a slayer who kills a person without intent may flee there. The cities shall be for you a refuge from the avenger, so that the slayer may not die until there is a trial before the congregation.

The cities that you designate shall be six cities of refuge for you: you shall designate three cities beyond the Jordan, and three cities in the land of Canaan, to be cities of refuge. These six cities shall serve as refuge for the Israelites, for the resident or transient alien among them, so that anyone who kills a person without intent may flee there.

Numbers 35:9–15 NRSV

*R*evenge is a dish best served cold. In ancient Israel, there were no police officers, no detectives, no CSI, no FBI. Instead, family and friends were responsible for avenging the victim of a violent crime. Justice was dependent upon the victim's family. Unfortunately, vigilante justice is notoriously imprecise. The wrong person was frequently fingered for a crime. Accidents were magnified into malevolence. An injured party was not interested in the notion that the accused was innocent until proven guilty. They just wanted satisfaction—string him up now and ask questions later.

God established refuges for those accused of violent crimes. An accused person could flee to any one of six cities where they would be protected from vengeance. But it was up to the accused to seek safety. If he or she didn't reach one of those cities, there was no recourse, no second chance, no appeal. Once the accused was safe within one of the cities of refuge, however, the vengeful relatives could do nothing more than bring charges against the person before the city leadership. Ideally, those leaders could then dispassionately investigate the matter.

If the accused was found not guilty, the accused could stay in the city indefinitely, safe from a vengeful family who might not be satisfied by a pronouncement of innocence. That meant permanent exile from home, but better that than death. The law of refuge was the same, whether the person was a citizen or not. God decided that justice was best served by those not lost in the heat of their emotions so that only the guilty would actually be punished. Revenge is not just about making the victim feel better. Our emotions can get in the way of what's right. God wants to protect us from ourselves.

Respect the Son

I will tell the promise that the LORD
made to me:
"You are my son, because today I have
become your father.
Ask me for the nations, and every
nation on earth will belong
to you.
You will smash them with an iron rod
and shatter them like dishes
of clay."

Be smart, all you rulers, and pay close
attention.
Serve and honor the LORD; be glad
and tremble.
Show respect to his son because if you
don't, the LORD might become
furious and suddenly destroy you.
But he blesses and protects everyone
who runs to him.

Psalm 2:7–12 CEV

How long do you want to live? It depends on your relationship with God's Son. David, and those who ascended the throne in Jerusalem after him, became sons of God—his representatives on earth to the people of Israel. God first told David that he would become God's son when David told God his desire to build a permanent temple for him. After Nathan the prophet told David he wasn't the man to build the temple, God made a covenant with him. God told him that there would always be someone to sit on his throne (2 Samuel 7:5–16).

But God had in mind more than just an endless string of human rulers. Some day there would be an ultimate ruler of Israel and of all the nations of the world. Who that might be and how it would happen were unclear to the author of the psalm.

In a monarchy, the king was supreme and deserved respect in a way that is alien to those of us living in a democratic society. But even so, the king of Israel was not like the rulers in the other nations around Israel, whose mere whims had the force of law. The Israelite king was constrained by the law of God as much as any other Israelite. He was a limited monarch—a righteous monarch—prevented by God from becoming capricious or cruel. He was not even allowed to consider himself better than the other Israelites (Deuteronomy 17:20). The king, like the people of Israel, stood beneath God and God's laws given by Moses.

God promised that those who mistreated David or his descendants would suffer, just as those who blessed him would prosper. The promise of protection and blessing extends to all who come to God.

❈❈❈❈❈❈❈❈❈❈❈❈❈❈❈❈❈❈❈❈❈❈❈❈❈❈❈❈❈❈❈❈❈

God Loves Your Enemies

In that day there will be an altar to the LORD in the midst of the land of Egypt, and a pillar to the LORD at its border. And it will be for a sign and for a witness to the LORD of hosts in the land of Egypt; for they will cry to the LORD because of the oppressors, and He will send them a Savior and a Mighty One, and He will deliver them. Then the LORD will be known to Egypt, and the Egyptians will know the LORD in that day, and will make sacrifice and offering; yes, they will make a vow to the LORD and perform it. And the LORD will strike Egypt, He will strike and heal it; they will return to the LORD, and He will be entreated by them and heal them.

In that day there will be a highway from Egypt to Assyria, and the Assyrian will come into Egypt and the Egyptian into Assyria, and the Egyptians will serve with the Assyrians.

In that day Israel will be one of three with Egypt and Assyria—a blessing in the midst of the land, whom the LORD of hosts shall bless, saying, "Blessed is Egypt My people, and Assyria the work of My hands, and Israel My inheritance."

Isaiah 19:19–25 NKJV

❈

*G*od doesn't love only us; he also loves those who hate us. Egypt had enslaved the Israelites for more than four hundred years, and Egypt became a picture of transgression. The exodus from Egyptian slavery became a picture of God's salvation. Assyria was a place of bondage and exile too. Assyria was a brutal dictatorship noted for its cruelty in war, and it was a place destined to be judged by God for its mistreatment of his people.

But despite all that, God loved the Egyptians and the Assyrians no less than he loved anyone else. He offered forgiveness and salvation to them, just as he had offered it to his own people, the Israelites. Surprisingly, just like the Israelites, God announced that the Assyrians and the Egyptians would repent and become as much God's people as the Israelites.

God's words through the prophet Isaiah were not new. From the first chapter of Genesis, God had made clear that he was the God of everyone and that everyone was part of one family. Those of us who are not Jewish by birth can become one with all of God's people. Even the enemies of God, the enemies of his people, were offered—and then granted—God's love. We might as well love our enemies, since God already does. In God, enemies come together and even political differences vanish.

Rebellious Children

"Woe to the rebellious children,"
  declares the LORD,
    "Who execute a plan, but
      not Mine,
    And make an alliance, but not of
      My Spirit,
    In order to add sin to sin;
Who proceed down to Egypt
  Without consulting Me,
  To take refuge in the safety
    of Pharaoh
  And to seek shelter in the shadow
    of Egypt!
"Therefore the safety of Pharaoh will
  be your shame
And the shelter in the shadow of
  Egypt, your humiliation.
"For their princes are at Zoan
  And their ambassadors arrive
    at Hanes.
"Everyone will be ashamed because of
  a people who cannot profit them,
  Who are not for help or profit,
    but for shame and also
    for reproach."

Isaiah 30:1–5 NASB

🎋

The people of Israel feared the rising power of the Assyrians and the Babylonians. To counter the very real threat, they attempted to make an alliance with the Egyptians. The Egyptians had long served as a counterweight to the power of Mesopotamia, with Israel balanced precariously between the two of them. God pointed out that in seeking help from Egypt, the Jewish people were rejecting help from God. They trusted the power of an Egypt they could see and distrusted the God they could not see. Rather than consulting God, rather than praying, or rather than studying the Word of God, they relied on themselves.

Like children who find it easier to depend on the friends they are with rather than their parents who are not there, the Israelites operated by what they could see. Children make decisions based on what they think is best and on their understanding of things. But children lack both the brain development and the experience base that adults have. What seems like a perfectly reasonable plan of action to a child can be incredibly stupid in reality. The child could be spared much grief if he or she talked to his or her parents first. Likewise, Israel should have turned to God for advice instead of to an alliance with Egypt. God had already warned them not to go back to Egypt (Deuteronomy 17:16). God was willing to provide proper guidance to his people. He was willing to take care of them, and he was far more powerful than the Egyptians. But they trusted themselves more than they trusted him, and they lost everything because of that. God understands our problems better than we do. Why not let him make the plans?

He'll Come If You Call

This is what the Sovereign LORD, the Holy One of Israel, says:
"Only in returning to me and resting in me will you be saved.
In quietness and confidence is your strength.
But you would have none of it.
You said, 'No, we will get our help from Egypt.
They will give us swift horses for riding into battle.'
But the only swiftness you are going to see
is the swiftness of your enemies chasing you!
One of them will chase a thousand of you.
Five of them will make all of you flee.
You will be left like a lonely flagpole on a hill
or a tattered banner on a distant mountaintop."
So the LORD must wait for you to come to him so he can show you his love and compassion.
For the LORD is a faithful God.
Blessed are those who wait for his help.
O people of Zion, who live in Jerusalem, you will weep no more.
He will be gracious if you ask for help.
He will surely respond to the sound of your cries.

Isaiah 30:15–19 NLT

❋

*Y*ou can do things your way or God's way. Like a small child telling his father, "I can do it myself," so the children of Israel were not interested in what God had to offer them. They were convinced they had a good plan and everything was under control. God pointed out that they were mistaken, but he let them try it their way first.

In the time of Moses, God promised his people that if they were faithful, one person could make a thousand enemies flee. If they were not faithful, God promised that one enemy would make a thousand Israelites flee. Five hundred years later, God used Isaiah to remind them of those old promises.

The Israelites had not been faithful to God or to one another. Since they had walked away from God, all God could do was wait for them to walk back. The Israelites lived in a dangerous part of the world. The only highway between the two most powerful nations on earth at the time, Egypt and the Assyrian Empire, passed right through the middle of Israel.

God promised his people that whenever they finally called out to him for help, whenever it was that they finally realized they really couldn't do it themselves, he would be there to help them pick up the pieces. God is always near, always ready to help us, no matter how many bad choices we've made.

God Made You

Descendants of Jacob,
I, the LORD, created you and
formed your nation.
Israel, don't be afraid.
I have rescued you.
I have called you by name; now you
belong to me.
When you cross deep rivers, I will be
with you, and you won't drown.
When you walk through fire, you
won't be burned or scorched by
the flames.
I am the LORD, your God, the Holy
One of Israel, the God who
saves you.
I gave up Egypt, Ethiopia, and the
region of Seba in exchange
for you.

To me, you are very dear, and I
love you.
That's why I gave up nations and
people to rescue you.
Don't be afraid! I am with you.
From both east and west I will bring
you together.
I will say to the north and to the
south,
"Free my sons and
daughters!
Let them return from distant lands.
They are my people—I created each of
them to bring honor to me."

Isaiah 43:1–7 CEV

The writer of Proverbs pointed out that children need discipline, but the rod of discipline will not kill the child. The Israelites were suffering because they had violated the terms of God's contract with them. They were suffering justly. They were being punished because they had worshipped other gods and mistreated the weak. By this time, in exile, they understood why they were suffering. The words of the prophets had finally sunk in. But the Israelites were certain that God had abandoned them for all time and that they were in exile in Babylon or Assyria because God hated them and never wanted to see them again.

Children often take any bad situation and magnify it beyond recognition. The children of Israel were no different. But God reassured his people that no matter what they went through, he would be with them and would protect them. He still loved them. It was all for the best, and in the end, they'd be glad for the experience.

God created his people, and not only did he love them despite their unfaithfulness and their many failures, he told them they were still his people and he had created them to bring him honor. Remarkably, God is honored to know us, because he made us.

Who Can Hinder God?

Bring forth the people who are blind,
yet have eyes, who are deaf, yet have
ears!
Let all the nations gather together, and
let the peoples assemble.
Who among them declared this, and
foretold to us the former things?
Let them bring their witnesses to
justify them, and let them hear and
say, "It is true."
You are my witnesses, says the LORD,
and my servant whom I have
chosen, so that you may know and
believe me and understand that I
am he.
Before me no god was formed,
nor shall there be any after me.
I, I am the LORD, and besides me there
is no savior.
I declared and saved and proclaimed,
when there was no strange god
among you; and you are my witnesses, says the LORD.
I am God, and also henceforth I
am He; there is no one who can deliver from my hand; I work and who
can hinder it?

Isaiah 43:8–13 NRSV

❊

*I*t was hard for the Israelites to accept what seems obvious to us today: there is only one God.

The Egyptian civilization out of which Israel had been rescued and the Mesopotamian civilization into which they had settled was polytheistic. They had many deities—deities for each city, deities for each profession, deities for the seasons, even deities for individual households. This reflected the very nature of civilization itself, which depends upon a division of labor; not every-one farms, not everyone manufactures tools, not everyone is a scribe, and not everyone is a king or governor or other bureaucratic official.

The concept that there was but one God in charge of everything was hard for the Israelites to wrap their heads around. Additionally, as the time passed from those who had seen the miracles of the exodus, the very reality of God seemed to fade. How could they rely on a God without symbols, without images? At least the gods they knew from the people around them were visible, even if their power was nonexistent and their effectiveness in question. How could a God who was invisible do anything for them? Or against them?

It took the captivity of seventy years in Babylon for God to get through to the Israelites. God is real. He can—and he will—remind us of his involvement in our lives. God never leaves us alone.

Don't Be Afraid

Thus says the LORD, the King of Israel,
And his Redeemer, the LORD of hosts:
"I am the First and I am the Last;
Besides Me there is no God.
And who can proclaim as I do?
Then let him declare it and set it in
   order for Me,
Since I appointed the ancient people.
And the things that are coming and
   shall come,
Let them show these to them.
Do not fear, nor be afraid;
Have I not told you from that time,
   and declared it?
You are My witnesses.
Is there a God besides Me?
Indeed there is no other Rock;
I know not one."

Isaiah 44:6–8 NKJV

No one can stop God. When the Israelites conquered the promised land, many of the indigenous people, the Canaanites, remained behind because God left them there to test the Israelites' faithfulness. The Israelites failed the test and quickly joined the Canaanites in their false religion.

The Israelites' neighbors, the Canaanites (not to mention Egypt and Mesopotamia), believed there were many gods—and since there were many, they believed they were in conflict with one another. According to Canaanite mythologies, each god had his or her own agenda. The myths recounted that the gods did not get along. The gods were like squabbling bureaucrats, each striving for advantage and prestige. In the myths, people sometimes got caught in the cross fire between the gods. And in the stories, the gods were often thwarted. Just because a god wanted something to happen didn't mean that some other god couldn't stop it. Not surprisingly, the people of Canaan believed that just because you faithfully obeyed your god didn't mean some other god might not get mad at you.

The Israelites had adopted this Canaanite theology. But God told them that all the supposed power and attributes of all the gods that the Israelites knew of from the people around them were combined into just him—their God Yahweh—the only God that really existed. Furthermore, God reassured his people they had to contend only with him. Unlike the nonexistent gods their neighbors and all too often the Israelites worshipped, Yahweh was firmly reliable. He was strong, he was a single Deity without rivals, and he would take care of them in a consistent way. No imaginary god could thwart his goals.

God's will is going to happen. Because God knows what he is doing, we have nothing to worry about.

A Dried-Up, Childless Tree

Don't let foreigners who commit
themselves to the LORD say,
"The LORD will never let me be
part of his people."
And don't let the eunuchs say,
"I'm a dried-up tree with no children and no future."
For this is what the LORD says:
I will bless those eunuchs
who keep my Sabbath days holy
and who choose to do what
pleases me
and commit their lives to me.
I will give them—within the walls
of my house—
a memorial and a name
far greater than sons and daughters could give.
For the name I give them is an everlasting one.
It will never disappear!

I will also bless the foreigners who
commit themselves to the LORD,
who serve him and love his name,
who worship him and do not desecrate the Sabbath day of rest,
and who hold fast to my
covenant.
I will bring them to my holy mountain
of Jerusalem
and will fill them with joy in my
house of prayer.
I will accept their burnt offerings
and sacrifices,
because my Temple will be called
a house of prayer for all nations.
For the Sovereign LORD,
who brings back the outcasts of
Israel, says:
I will bring others, too,
besides my people Israel.

Isaiah 56:3–8 NLT

It's human nature to exclude the outsider. It is also human nature to fear being excluded when experiencing a new job, a new school, a new place. Both foreigners and eunuchs were outsiders in Israel. Foreigners had different customs and behaviors. They spoke with accents. Levites who were eunuchs weren't allowed to enter the temple.

Despite God's words to Moses requiring the Israelites to be kind to outsiders, that was a hard lesson for the Jewish people to learn. Their reluctance to bring God's message of hope to the Gentiles—the outsiders—continued from Jonah's reluctance to go to Nineveh to an early church's doubts that Gentiles could ever become followers of Christ.

God granted the future to eunuchs, those who had no way of passing their memory beyond the present since they were forever childless. Their future depended on their relationship with an eternal God who could never forget them.

God is not exclusive. God welcomes all, and we are not allowed to exclude anyone. Everyone is good enough for God.

Your Sun Will Never Set

Although you have been forsaken and hated, with no one traveling through, I will make you the everlasting pride and the joy of all generations.

You will drink the milk of nations and be nursed at royal breasts.

Then you will know that I, the LORD, am your Savior, your Redeemer, the Mighty One of Jacob.

Instead of bronze I will bring you gold, and silver in place of iron.

Instead of wood I will bring you bronze, and iron in place of stones. I will make peace your governor and righteousness your ruler.

No longer will violence be heard in your land, nor ruin or destruction within your borders, but you will call your walls Salvation and your gates Praise.

The sun will no more be your light by day, nor will the brightness of the moon shine on you, for the LORD will be your everlasting light, and your God will be your glory.

Your sun will never set again, and your moon will wane no more; the LORD will be your everlasting light, and your days of sorrow will end.

Then will all your people be righteous and they will possess the land forever.

They are the shoot I have planted, the work of my hands, for the display of my splendor.

The least of you will become a thousand, the smallest a mighty nation. I am the LORD; in its time I will do this swiftly.

Isaiah 60:15–22 NIV

God promised hope and change to those who needed it most desperately. The Israelites in foreign captivity in Assyria and Babylonia felt lost and abandoned. But God told them that what had failed them would become their hope. The city of Jerusalem, then scattered and broken, would rise again as a fortress of protection. Within seventy years, the Israelites would rebuild it all and once again worship God with their sacrifices. They would never again abandon God.

The sun and the moon would fade from their consciousness. God would take the place of the sun and moon, and unlike the false deities he would never fade to a crescent sliver. No cloud would cover him, no shifting phases, no dark nights ever again. God would always be there, a steady light of joy and hope free of sorrow.

A Discouraging Word

Now Shephatiah son of Mattan, Gedaliah son of Pashhur, Jehucal son of Shelemiah, and Pashhur son of Malkijah heard what Jeremiah had been telling the people. He had been saying, "This is what the LORD says: 'Everyone who stays in Jerusalem will die from war, famine, or disease, but those who surrender to the Babylonians will live. Their reward will be life. They will live!' The LORD also says: 'The city of Jerusalem will certainly be handed over to the army of the king of Babylon, who will capture it.' "

So these officials went to the king and said, "Sir, this man must die! That kind of talk will undermine the morale of the few fighting men we have left, as well as that of all the people. This man is a traitor!"

King Zedekiah agreed. "All right," he said. "Do as you like. I can't stop you."

So the officials took Jeremiah from his cell and lowered him by ropes into an empty cistern in the prison yard. It belonged to Malkijah, a member of the royal family. There was no water in the cistern, but there was a thick layer of mud at the bottom, and Jeremiah sank down into it.

Jeremiah 38:1–6 NLT

Jeremiah was an enemy of the state. From the perspective of his government, God's words as relayed by the prophet sounded treasonous: he was encouraging the people in a time of war against an existential threat, Babylon, to surrender. Jeremiah was arguing that God had turned against Judah and they would lose the war. In fact, Jeremiah reported that God was fighting on the side of Babylon! The only ones who could come out well from this disaster would be those who were least patriotic, least loyal, and least devoted to their nation. Those who were cowards, who surrendered to the invader, were the ones who would prosper.

The government decided that something had to be done—Jeremiah should be executed. He was arrested and put into a cistern full of mud to rot until they got around to killing him, assuming he didn't die there and save them all the trouble.

Sometimes God's message will seem obviously wrong to us. We will be tempted, like Jeremiah's government, to reject it. We will want to attack those who are reporting it to us. God is not always particularly popular. God does not always sound like he's on our side, because sometimes he isn't. Sometimes what we really need is a trip to the woodshed, not a trip to the candy store.

One Stick Instead of Two

The word of the LORD came to me: "Son of man, take a single stick and write on it: Belonging to Judah and the Israelites associated with him. Then take another stick and write on it: Belonging to Joseph—the stick of Ephraim—and all the house of Israel associated with him. Then join them together into a single stick so that they become one in your hand. When your people ask you: Won't you explain to us what you mean by these things?—tell them: This is what the Lord GOD says: I am going to take the stick of Joseph—which is in the hand of Ephraim—and the tribes of Israel associated with him, and put them together with the stick of Judah. I will make them into a single stick so that they become one in My hand.

"When the sticks you have written on are in your hand and in full view of the people, tell them: This is what the Lord GOD says: I am going to take the Israelites out of the nations where they have gone. I will gather them from all around and bring them into their own land. I will make them one nation in the land, on the mountains of Israel, and one king will rule over all of them. They will no longer be two nations and will no longer be divided into two kingdoms."

Ezekiel 37:15–22 HCSB

*M*ore than three hundred years before Ezekiel was born, the northern tribes of Israel had rebelled against the son of Solomon and established a separate nation, with a different king. For all those years, they had maintained their independence—until the Assyrians arrived, destroyed their capital, and took nearly thirty thousand of them away to Nineveh. When Ezekiel prophesied, the Northern Kingdom had been in Assyrian captivity for over a hundred years. The Southern Kingdom, ruled by a descendant of Solomon, was then in the process of being destroyed and also taken into captivity in Babylon, where they were destined to remain for seventy years.

In the midst of this division and destruction, God announced that both the captivity in foreign lands and the divisions between the people of Israel were ending. The shattered Israelites, both northerners and southerners, would together rebuild the desolate cities and find rest under a single king.

God's words to Ezekiel began to come true when Cyrus, the Persian king, issued his decree permitting all the captives to go back home. They became fully true when the Holy Spirit united all believers everywhere into one body in Christ.

God never intended for his people to be estranged, and he intends to restore harmony wherever it has gone missing.

More Than a Two-Minute Warning

People of Israel,
   I rescued you from Egypt.
Now listen to my judgment
   against you.
Of all nations on earth,
   you are the only one
   I have chosen.
That's why I will punish you
   because of your sins.

Can two people walk together
   without agreeing to meet?
Does a lion roar in the forest
   unless it has caught a victim?
Does it growl in its den
   unless it is eating?
How can anyone catch a bird
   without using a net?

Does a trap spring shut
   unless something is caught?
Isn't the whole city frightened
   when the trumpet
   signals an attack?
Isn't it the LORD who brings
   disaster on a city?
Whatever the LORD God
   plans to do,
   he tells his servants,
   the prophets.
Everyone is terrified
   when a lion roars—
and ordinary people
   become prophets
   when the LORD God speaks.

Amos 3:1–8 CEV

God punishes those he loves. God told his people, whom he loved, that just as two people couldn't walk along together unless there was some agreement between them, so the Israelites were going to have to agree with God. Moreover, just as a lion roars only when he has his prey, and just as trumpets are blown to signal an attack, so God did not act without warning. Ordinary people would become prophets when God spoke. God didn't need anyone special to serve as his spokesperson. Amos was not a professional prophet. He was just a shepherd and farmer. He had never planned to speak on God's behalf, but when God came to him, he obeyed. He warned Israel, Judah, and the surrounding nations of God's intent and their need to repent.

How was a person to know when what was happening was the hand of God? Prophets interpreted the circumstances and explained the reasons for them. They pointed at how in the past, in the time of Moses, God had already warned them. Disaster does not come from God without his issuing a warning. It isn't going to be a mystery; people won't be wondering whether it was God or not. A trumpet blast, a roaring lion, a snare catching a bird are all obvious and easy to recognize. Likewise, the acts of God in our lives are obvious when we've been warned.

Slavery to Sin

The LORD replied:
"Write down the revelation
and make it plain on tablets
so that a herald may run with it.
For the revelation awaits an
appointed time;
it speaks of the end
and will not prove false.
Though it linger, wait for it;
it will certainly come and will
not delay.
See, he is puffed up;
his desires are not upright—

but the righteous will live by
his faith—indeed, wine
betrays him;
he is arrogant and never at rest.

Because he is as greedy as the grave
and like death is never satisfied,he
gathers to himself all the nations
and takes captive all the peoples."

Habakkuk 2:2–5 NIV

*I*t isn't what you do that makes you a good person. It is what God has done to you. Habakkuk lived in the time before the Babylonians came to punish Israel for their idolatry. He had wondered why God hadn't done something about the wickedness of the Israelites. He saw the problems of idolatry and oppression that plagued his nation. The Israelites were unfaithful to God and unjust to people. Given the nature of God's covenant with Israel, Habakkuk thought it peculiar that God hadn't done anything yet, and it didn't look like God was planning to do anything.

God reassured Habakkuk that he had the situation well in hand and that the Babylonians were coming to punish the Israelites. The news did not encourage Habakkuk, who rightly pointed out that the Babylonians were far worse than the Israelites and needed judgment themselves so much more. How could God use people so wicked to judge the more righteous Israelites? It made no sense to him, but he wrote it all down anyway.

God told Habakkuk to keep the words of his prophecy simple and short enough to fit on tablets. Tablets were small, pillow-shaped clay slabs.

Babylon had to punish Israel in order for God to save them. But God agreed with Habakkuk that the Babylonians were evil and should be judged. God contrasted them with the righteous. And who were the righteous, according to God? The righteous were the ones who lived by faith. So Habakkuk chose to trust God even though he didn't fully understand and couldn't quite make sense of what God was telling him. God gives us understanding when we put our faith in him and not in ourselves.

※※※※※※※※※※※※※※※※※※※※※※※※※※※※※※

Thirty Shekels of Silver

In one month I disposed of the three shepherds, for I had become impatient with them, and they also detested me. So I said, "I will not be your shepherd. What is to die, let it die; what is to be destroyed, let it be destroyed; and let those that are left devour the flesh of one another!" I took my staff Favor and broke it, annulling the covenant that I had made with all the peoples. So it was annulled on that day, and the sheep merchants, who were watching me, knew that it was the word of the LORD. I then said to them, "If it seems right to you, give me my wages; but if not, keep them." So they weighed out as my wages thirty shekels of silver. Then the LORD said to me, "Throw it into the treasury"—this lordly price at which I was valued by them. So I took the thirty shekels of silver and threw them into the treasury in the house of the LORD. Then I broke my second staff Unity, annulling the family ties between Judah and Israel.

Then the LORD said to me: Take once more the implements of a worthless shepherd. For I am now raising up in the land a shepherd who does not care for the perishing, or seek the wandering, or heal the maimed, or nourish the healthy, but devours the flesh of the fat ones, tearing off even their hoofs.

Zechariah 11:8–16 NRSV

※

Zechariah worked as a shepherd, and as was common for prophets, his life and circumstances became parables. The prophet got rid of three bad shepherds, but Zechariah was unpopular for doing that. So he quit and broke his shepherd's staff since he wouldn't need it anymore. He'd given the staff the name "Favor." The merchants paid Zechariah a miserable pittance equivalent to the price of a slave, which he cast away. And he broke his other staff, "Unity," which he likewise no longer needed.

God had been like a shepherd to the people of Israel, taking care of them and pouring out his blessings, his "favor." But the Israelites wanted a different shepherd. So in God's place would come a shepherd who would not treat them well: the Babylonians. God also warned that the breaking of staffs and the casting away of money were images that illustrated the disunity and captivity of Israel and Judah in Mesopotamia.

The shepherds Zechariah tried to get rid of didn't care for flocks of sheep, just as the Babylonians didn't care for anyone other than themselves. Looking to powerful people and material things will disappoint us in the end.

Struck Shepherd, Scattered Sheep

"Awake, O sword, against My
  Shepherd,
Against the Man who is My
  Companion,"
Says the LORD of hosts.
"Strike the Shepherd,
And the sheep will be scattered;
Then I will turn My hand against the
  little ones.
And it shall come to pass in all
  the land,"
Says the LORD,
"That two-thirds in it shall be cut off
  and die,

But one-third shall be left in it:
I will bring the one-third through
  the fire,
Will refine them as silver is refined,
And test them as gold is tested.
They will call on My name,
And I will answer them.
I will say, 'This is My people';
And each one will say, 'The LORD is
  my God.' "

Zechariah 13:7–9 NKJV

*T*he prophecies in the last chapters of Zechariah were actually composed by the earlier prophet Jeremiah. Through the prophet, God told his people that the shepherd—meaning the king of Israel—would be struck. And so he was. Zedekiah, the last king of Judah, was blinded and taken captive back to Babylon by Nebuchadnezzar. After that, the people of the land scattered. Many went into Babylonian captivity, but many others fled to Egypt and beyond, to other parts of the Mediterranean world. Even Jeremiah was taken away. What came to be called the *Diaspora*—"the scattering"—had begun. By the time Cyrus, the king of Persia, allowed the captives to return to rebuild Jerusalem and the temple, Jewish people were living as far away as Spain to the west. A thriving community in Alexandria would translate the Bible into Greek so that even more people than ever before could read God's words.

The scattering from the promised land did not mean a scattering from God. God would purge them in the lands to which they were scattered. Somehow, far from home and without a temple, they would become more firmly God's people than ever before. Where before the Diaspora the Israelites had worshipped many gods, afterward they would be faithful only to Yahweh. They had finally learned that their God was not bound by time or space.

They realized that their relationship with God was not dependent upon their home address. Just because we leave family, friends, and everyone else who is familiar to us does not mean we are alone. God is with us.

Mercy and Judgment

Abraham Lincoln argued that "the best way to destroy your enemy is to make him your friend." God's purpose in judgment is likewise transformative. *Judgment* and *mercy* are closely related. Mercy is withholding from a person the judgment that is deserved. By its nature, God's mercy is unjust and profoundly disturbing to those who have been wronged. But his mercy is a relief to those who have themselves done wrong. Fortunately, God can be trusted as both judge and jury, doing what's best for everyone involved.

⁂

Where is another God like you, who pardons the
guilt of the remnant, overlooking the sins of
his special people? You will not stay angry
with your people forever, because you
delight in showing unfailing love.

Micah 7:18 NLT

Cursed by Pain

To the woman he said, "I will greatly increase your pains in childbearing; with pain you will give birth to children.
Your desire will be for your husband, and he will rule over you."

To Adam he said, "Because you listened to your wife and ate from the tree about which I commanded you, 'You must not eat of it,'
"Cursed is the ground because of you;
through painful toil you will eat of it all the days of your life.
It will produce thorns and thistles for you, and you will eat the plants of the field.
By the sweat of your brow you will eat your food until you return to the ground, since from it you were taken; for dust you are and to dust you will return."

Genesis 3:16–19 NIV

God wants you to have a good life. Two special trees stood in the garden of Eden: the Tree of Life and the Tree of Knowledge of Good and Evil. Sadly, Adam and Eve ate from the forbidden Tree of Knowledge of Good and Evil. They believed the serpent's lie: God was holding out on them; he was keeping back something good. Ever since, human beings have doubted God's intentions.

God pronounced a series of judgments against Adam and Eve, but he wrapped mercy around the judgments. Though the woman's childbirth would be painful, she would still want to become pregnant. Though the man's work would be hard, he would still be able to grow food. And though they would die, their deaths would make their ultimate redemption possible.

God barred them from the Tree of Life to keep them mortal. Why? So that when the Son of God became a human being, he could be mortal as well. The greatest judgment against the human race—mortality—was also the greatest gift. Mortality provides the key to salvation. What God does for us and what God keeps from us are always what is best for us.

God Had a Reason

The earth also was corrupt before God, and the earth was filled with violence. So God looked upon the earth, and indeed it was corrupt; for all flesh had corrupted their way on the earth.

And God said to Noah, "The end of all flesh has come before Me, for the earth is filled with violence through them; and behold, I will destroy them with the earth. Make yourself an ark of gopherwood; make rooms in the ark, and cover it inside and outside with pitch. And this is how you shall make it: The length of the ark shall be three hundred cubits, its width fifty cubits, and its height thirty cubits. You shall make a window for the ark, and you shall finish it to a cubit from above; and set the door of the ark in its side. You shall make it with lower, second, and third decks. And behold, I Myself am bringing flood-waters on the earth, to destroy from under heaven all flesh in which is the breath of life; everything that is on the earth shall die. But I will establish My covenant with you; and you shall go into the ark—you, your sons, your wife, and your sons' wives with you. And of every living thing of all flesh you shall bring two of every sort into the ark, to keep them alive with you; they shall be male and female. Of the birds after their kind, of animals after their kind, and of every creeping thing of the earth after its kind, two of every kind will come to you to keep them alive. And you shall take for yourself of all food that is eaten, and you shall gather it to yourself; and it shall be food for you and for them."

Genesis 6:11–21 NKJV

❀

For every cloud there seems to be a silver lining. Despite God's dismay over a creation that no longer seemed good, God found a bright spot in Noah. Noah "found favor in the eyes of the LORD" and "walked with God" (Genesis 6:8–9 NIV). *To find favor* is a Hebrew idiom meaning that God "liked" Noah.

God told Noah the reason why the disaster was coming. And he gave Noah plenty of time to prepare.

In the midst of the judgment against the world, God offered mercy to one man, his family, and certain animals. God preserved a future for humanity and the life of the planet. God will always stand with and protect his people. God will take you through the darkest times and deliver you safe on the other side.

Death Penalty

God blessed Noah and his sons and said to them, "Be fruitful and multiply and fill the earth. The fear and terror of you will be in every living creature on the earth, every bird of the sky, every creature that crawls on the ground, and all the fish of the sea. They are placed under your authority. Every living creature will be food for you; as [I gave] the green plants, I have given you everything. However, you must not eat meat with its lifeblood in it. I will require the life of every animal and every man for your life and your blood. I will require the life of each man's brother for a man's life.

Whoever sheds man's blood,
his blood will be shed by man,
for God made man
in His image.

But you, be fruitful and multiply; spread out over the earth and multiply on it."

Genesis 9:1–7 HCSB

※

*Y*ou're more than what you eat. From the time of Adam until Noah's Flood, everyone was a vegetarian. With the Flood, God judged the world, wiping out most of the human race and most of the animals. After the rain stopped and the water went down, Noah, his family, and the animals left the ark.

God then made a covenant—a contract—with those who had survived. God told them some old things and some new things. They were to repopulate the world—the same thing God had told Adam and Eve. Then there was a twist on an old thing: Adam and Eve had been given all the plants to eat with one restriction: they could not eat from the Tree of Knowledge of Good and Evil. After the Flood, however, God told Noah and his family that from then on, in addition to all the plants, they could eat all the animals too. There was only one restriction: they could not eat the blood. Why? The Tree of Knowledge of Good and Evil represented death. Good and evil were supposed to be known only to God. Blood represented life. Likewise, only God was allowed to have the blood, when it was poured out for a sin offering.

The blood of human beings was not to be shed. Anyone, whether human or animal, who took the life of a human being would forfeit his own life, because human beings were created in the image of God. You reflect aspects of God by virtue of your humanity.

No Joke

God said to Abraham, "As for you, you shall keep my covenant, you and your offspring after you throughout their generations. This is my covenant, which you shall keep, between me and you and your offspring after you: Every male among you shall be circumcised. You shall circumcise the flesh of your foreskins, and it shall be a sign of the covenant between me and you. Throughout your generations every male among you shall be circumcised when he is eight days old, including the slave born in your house and the one bought with your money from any foreigner who is not of your offspring. Both the slave born in your house and the one bought with your money must be circumcised. So shall my covenant be in your flesh an everlasting covenant. Any uncircumcised male who is not circumcised in the flesh of his foreskin shall be cut off from his people; he has broken my covenant." . . .

Then Abraham took his son Ishmael and all the slaves born in his house or bought with his money, every male among the men of Abraham's house, and he circumcised the flesh of their foreskins that very day, as God had said to him. Abraham was ninety-nine years old when he was circumcised in the flesh of his foreskin. And his son Ishmael was thirteen years old when he was circumcised in the flesh of his foreskin. That very day Abraham and his son Ishmael were circumcised; and all the men of his house, slaves born in the house and those bought with money from a foreigner, were circumcised with him.

Genesis 17:9–14, 23–27 NRSV

*D*isbelief doesn't deter God. Sarah did not believe it when she overheard God tell her husband that within a year she'd be pregnant. In fact, she disbelieved so much that she laughed. But she was not alone in her laughter. Abraham laughed as well. And they had good reason to laugh because they were both past the age when people could have children.

In less than a year, however, their disbelieving laughter would be transformed to the laughter of joy. They called their son *Isaac*, which means "laughter."

God promised that the contract he had made with Abraham would be extended to Isaac and not Ishmael or anyone else. God's original promise to Abraham was exclusive to just one of his sons, not both. Ultimately, the promise would focus on the Jewish people exclusively. They alone would have a special relationship with God. From them would come the Messiah.

God simply told Abraham how it would be. God has ways of making us believe when we focus on what God says.

Letting His Friend In on It

The LORD said to himself, "I should tell Abraham what I am going to do, since his family will become a great and powerful nation that will be a blessing to all other nations on earth. I have chosen him to teach his family to obey me forever and to do what is right and fair. Then I will give Abraham many descendants, just as I promised."

The LORD said, "Abraham, I have heard that the people of Sodom and Gomorrah are doing all kinds of evil things. Now I am going down to see for myself if those people really are that bad. If they aren't, I want to know about it."

The men turned and started toward Sodom. But the LORD stayed with Abraham, who asked, "LORD, when you destroy the evil people, are you also going to destroy those who are good? Wouldn't you spare the city if there are only fifty good people in it? You surely wouldn't let them be killed when you destroy the evil ones. You are the judge of all the earth, and you do what is right."

The LORD replied, "If I find fifty good people in Sodom, I will save the city to keep them from being killed."

Abraham answered, "I am nothing more than the dust of the earth. Please forgive me, LORD, for daring to speak to you like this. But suppose there are only forty-five good people in Sodom. Would you still wipe out the whole city?"

"If I find forty-five good people," the LORD replied, "I won't destroy the city."

Genesis 18:17–28 CEV

※

*G*od and Abraham were on speaking terms. God ate a meal with Abraham and made him promises. Then God told him he intended to destroy the cities of Sodom and Gomorrah.

Abraham was upset, not because he loved those wicked cities, but because he knew his nephew Lot and Lot's family lived there. Abraham didn't request mercy for the guilty cities. But he believed that God would punish only those who deserved it. So he got God to promise he would spare the city if there were but ten righteous living there.

Although it turned out that there were far fewer than ten righteous there, Abraham was right in thinking that God wouldn't destroy the innocent with the guilty. But Abraham forgot that the innocent could simply be moved out of the way. God's judgment hit only the guilty. Lot and two of his daughters were spared, though even Lot's wife lost her life to God's judgment. God loves those you love as much as you do, so don't worry about them. God will protect them better than you could.

Messenger of Death

I will pass through the land of Egypt that night, and I will strike down every firstborn in the land of Egypt, both human beings and animals; on all the gods of Egypt I will execute judgments: I am the LORD. The blood shall be a sign for you on the houses where you live: when I see the blood, I will pass over you, and no plague shall destroy you when I strike the land of Egypt.

This day shall be a day of remembrance for you. You shall celebrate it as a festival to the LORD; throughout your generations you shall observe it as a perpetual ordinance.

Seven days you shall eat unleavened bread; on the first day you shall remove leaven from your houses, for whoever eats leavened bread from the first day until the seventh day shall be cut off from Israel. On the first day you shall hold a solemn assembly, and on the seventh day a solemn assembly; no work shall be done on those days; only what everyone must eat, that alone may be prepared by you.

Exodus 12:12–16 NRSV

God's judgment on Egypt would be harsh: the firstborn would die. The firstborn of Egypt's Pharaoh was believed to be an incarnation of the sun god, Ra, the chief god of Egypt. That Pharaoh's firstborn should die was a blow not just against the political leader, but also against the religious system of Egypt—as had been all the plagues. The attack was about more than physical things or people. It was a systematic attack upon a belief system. God was against those things in which the Egyptians had put their trust.

The judgment of God against Pharaoh and his people was a great victory for the Israelites. From that time forward every year, the people of Israel would remember what God had done and would celebrate it as their day of deliverance. The annual Jewish celebration of Passover gets its name from what God told Moses, that he would "pass over" them when he saw the blood. What was judgment for the Egyptians was loving salvation for the Israelites.

But mercy was attainable even for the Egyptians. The Israelites weren't the only ones who could protect their loved ones by putting blood on their doorposts. Any Egyptian who so chose could put blood on his doorpost or joined with an Israelite who had and gained the same protection, the same benefit, the same relief from God's judgment. Repentance is an option for anyone (Jeremiah 18:5–8). God's mercy is available to everyone who seeks it.

A Nice Meal with God

Moses took the blood, sprinkled it on the people, and said, "This is the blood of the covenant which the LORD has made with you according to all these words."

Then Moses went up, also Aaron, Nadab, and Abihu, and seventy of the elders of Israel, and they saw the God of Israel. And there was under His feet as it were a paved work of sapphire stone, and it was like the very heavens in its clarity. But on the nobles of the children of Israel He did not lay His hand. So they saw God, and they ate and drank.

Then the LORD said to Moses, "Come up to Me on the mountain and be there; and I will give you tablets of stone, and the law and commandments which I have written, that you may teach them."

Exodus 24:8–12 NKJV

※

*L*ike Father, like Son. The Son of God is as much God as his Father is God. Nadab and Abihu, like their father, Aaron, were priests. They, along with Aaron's brother, Moses, and seventy other Israelites, all went up on a mountain. They saw God there and suffered no ill effects for it. What they saw was something that Isaiah and Ezekiel would later see as well: God on his throne. But God told Moses that no one could see God and live (Exodus 33:20). So how could Moses, his family, and the leaders of Israel see God and eat with him? God is a Trinity: Father, Son, and Holy Spirit. While no one has seen the Father, the Son showed himself throughout the Bible.

Joel 2:32 says that "everyone who calls on the name of Yahweh will be saved" (HCSB). Both Peter and Paul applied the passage to Jesus, thereby equating Jesus with the God of the Old Testament. After all, Paul said that the Son created the heavens and the earth (Colossians 1:16). After God rescued Israel from Egyptian bondage, after he brought them through the Red Sea and the wilderness, and after he shared a big meal on the mountain with them, God finally called Moses to Mount Sinai to get the Ten Commandments—along with all the other regulations that God had for his people. The law of God came as a consequence of God's relationship with his people, not as the cause of it.

The Father was merciful to his people. He let them see him in all his glory by letting them see his Son. Just as Moses and his family did, we now have direct access to God, without barriers or fear.

Only One God, or Else

The LORD spoke to Moses, saying,

"You shall also say to the sons of Israel:

'Any man from the sons of Israel or from the aliens sojourning in Israel who gives any of his offspring to Molech, shall surely be put to death; the people of the land shall stone him with stones.

'I will also set My face against that man and will cut him off from among his people, because he has given some of his offspring to Molech, so as to defile My sanctuary and to profane My holy name.

'If the people of the land, however, should ever disregard that man when he gives any of his offspring to Molech, so as not to put him to death, then I Myself will set My face against that man and against his family, and I will cut off from among their people both him and all those who play the harlot after him, by playing the harlot after Molech.

'As for the person who turns to mediums and to spiritists, to play the harlot after them, I will also set My face against that person and will cut him off from among his people.'"

Leviticus 20:1–6 NASB

※

*W*hat you put your faith in matters. Being spiritual or having faith is not necessarily a good thing. The Canaanites' faith led them to worship Molech by sacrificing children to him. The Israelites started worshipping him too. Sacrifices to Molech were made in the Hinnom Valley near Jerusalem. Child sacrifice happened regularly from the time the people of Israel entered the land until the Babylonian captivity. Even Solomon worshipped Molech.

God warned the Israelites against the practice in the very earliest Mosaic legislation, where the worship of other gods and seeking out mediums and spiritists were compared to prostitution. The image of adultery would later be used by the Hebrew prophets as a metaphor for Israel's unfaithfulness to God. Mediums and spiritists sought aid from those who had died. Like idolatry, seeking help from the dead was forbidden, but the Israelites freely ignored God's prohibitions. Even Saul, Israel's first king, wound up consulting a medium at the end of his life (1 Samuel 28:7).

God promised judgment against those who worshipped other gods or sought guidance that should come only from him. What motivated God's prohibition? It was a mercy: the other gods did not exist. Mediums and spiritists could not contact the dead. Putting faith and trust in that which does not exist is both a waste of time and dangerous. It is akin to trusting in sugar pills when you need an antibiotic. It's silly to consult the occult when you have the Bible.

Picking Up Sticks

"If it's just one person who sins by mistake, not realizing what he's doing, he is to bring a yearling she-goat as an Absolution-Offering. The priest then is to atone for the person who accidentally sinned, to make atonement before GOD so that it won't be held against him.

"The same standard holds for everyone who sins by mistake; the native-born Israelites and the foreigners go by the same rules.

"But the person, native or foreigner, who sins defiantly, deliberately blaspheming GOD, must be cut off from his people: He has despised GOD's word, he has violated GOD's command; that person must be kicked out of the community, ostracized, left alone in his wrongdoing."

Once, during those wilderness years of the People of Israel, a man was caught gathering wood on the Sabbath. The ones who caught him hauled him before Moses and Aaron and the entire congregation. They put him in custody until it became clear what to do with him. Then GOD spoke to Moses: "Give the man the death penalty. Yes, kill him, the whole community hurling stones at him outside the camp."

So the whole community took him outside the camp and threw stones at him, an execution commanded by GOD and given through Moses.

Numbers 15:27–36 MSG

※

*G*od's judgment sometimes seems like an overreaction. But it never is. God does only what is necessary.

In the time of Moses, an unnamed man gathered some wood on the Sabbath day. After Moses asked God about the man's behavior, God ordered the man's execution by throwing large rocks at him until he died. Nowhere else does there seem to be a death penalty associated with violations of the Sabbath.

God made a distinction between those who sinned deliberately and those who didn't. A deliberate choice to violate God's command was harshly punished, while the inadvertent sinner could find mercy. The sin of the unnamed individual in this passage was a conscious, willful action, a kind of rebellion against God. He was not someone who simply wasn't thinking or someone who decided his need for firewood justified his behavior.

In this case, the violation of the Sabbath by working was merely a symptom of a greater problem: the belief that human ways and choices are better than God's ways and decrees. The belief that God doesn't care or understand human needs is a trap. God loves us more than we could possibly love ourselves.

Punishment from God

Korah had convinced the rest of the Israelites to rebel against their two leaders.

When that happened, the LORD appeared in all his glory and said to Moses and Aaron, "Get away from the rest of the Israelites so I can kill them right now!"

But the two men bowed down and prayed, "Our God, you gave these people life. Why would you punish everyone here when only one man has sinned?"

The LORD answered Moses, "Tell the people to stay away from the tents of Korah, Dathan, and Abiram."

Moses walked over to Dathan and Abiram, and the other leaders of Israel followed. Then Moses warned the people, "Get away from the tents of these sinful men! Don't touch anything that belongs to them or you'll be wiped out." So everyone moved away from those tents, except Korah, Dathan, Abiram, and their families.

Numbers 16:19–27 CEV

*G*od's judgment is selective. He sorts things out before he strikes. He never just "kills them all," even in Sodom and Gomorrah. Korah was a Levite and a relative of Moses and Aaron. Dathan and Abiram were part of the tribe of Reuben. Korah, Dathan, Abiram, and about 250 other community leaders had decided that Moses and Aaron did not deserve their places of authority. They were convinced that Moses and Aaron had failed. They looked back to Egypt as a "land flowing with milk and honey" and pointed out that they had yet to reach the promised land. Instead, they were stuck in a desert where they believed they were just going to die.

The opponents of Moses and Aaron did not believe that God could or would take care of them. They did not believe that Moses and Aaron were God's representatives.

Moses and Aaron begged God to limit his judgment to just those who had sinned. God listened. Korah, Dathan, Abiram, and their families were swallowed up by the earth—and God sent fire that consumed the 250 community leaders who had joined the rebellion. If God is for you, no one can stand against you.

Fraternizing with the Enemy

An Israelite man came bringing a Midianite woman to his relatives in the sight of Moses and the whole Israelite community while they were weeping at the entrance to the tent of meeting. When Phinehas son of Eleazar, son of Aaron the priest, saw [this], he got up from the assembly, took a spear in his hand, followed the Israelite man into the tent, and drove it through both the Israelite man and the woman— through her belly. Then the plague on the Israelites was stopped, but those who died in the plague numbered 24,000.

The LORD spoke to Moses, "Phinehas son of Eleazar, son of Aaron the priest, has turned back My wrath from the Israelites because he was zealous among them with My zeal, so that I did not destroy the Israelites in My zeal. Therefore declare: I grant him My covenant of peace. It will be a covenant of perpetual priesthood for him and his descendants, because he was zealous for his God and made atonement for the Israelites."

The name of the slain Israelite man, who was struck dead with the Midianite woman, was Zimri son of Salu, the leader of a Simeonite ancestral house. The name of the slain Midianite woman was Cozbi, the daughter of Zur, a tribal head of an ancestral house in Midian.

Numbers 25:6–15 HCSB

Giving in to temptation doesn't lead to happiness. Balak, the king of Moab, had asked Balaam to curse the Israelites. Balaam could only offer Israel repeated blessings, but he told Balak that he could harm Israel—and get God to curse them—by sending women to seduce the Israelite men into idolatry.

When Phinehas, one of Aaron's grandsons, witnessed an Israelite man taking such a woman into his tent, he took direct action. God praised Phinehas for his zeal and rewarded him with a promise: his descendants would always be priests before God.

Phinehas's actions might seem disturbing to us, but as a priest, he was acting not as a vigilante but as a representative of the people. The Israelites had made a contract with God to worship him alone and obey his regulations. The consequence of disobedience was severe. Phinehas worked to try to keep that from happening, just as a police officer might use deadly force to keep a criminal from harming someone.

God is able and willing to protect you from temptation, just as Phinehas protected Israel by his actions. God will make it so that you don't even notice the temptations that are too much for you. For the rest of the temptations you face, God will give you a way resist.

Welcome to Your Execution

Moses came and recited all the words of this song in the hearing of the people, he and Joshua son of Nun. When Moses had finished saying all these words to all Israel, he said, "Take to heart all these words to which I give witness today and urgently command your children to put them into practice, every single word of this Revelation. Yes. This is no small matter for you; it's your life. In keeping this word you'll have a good and long life in this land that you're crossing the Jordan to possess."

That same day GOD spoke to Moses: "Climb the Abarim Mountains to Mount Nebo in the land of Moab, overlooking Jericho, and view the land of Canaan that I'm giving the People of Israel to have and hold. Die on the mountain that you climb and join your people in the ground, just as your brother Aaron died on Mount Hor and joined his people.

"This is because you broke faith with me in the company of the People of Israel at the Waters of Meribah Kadesh in the Wilderness of Zin—you didn't honor my Holy Presence in the company of the People of Israel. You'll look at the land spread out before you but you won't enter it, this land that I am giving to the People of Israel."

Deuteronomy 32:44–52 MSG

*M*oses would have to die before he could visit Israel. The Israelites ran out of water at a place called Meribah Kadesh. Previously, Moses had gotten water from a rock by hitting it with his staff. But this time, God told him just to talk to the rock. Instead, Moses angrily whacked at it while he yelled at the Israelites. The water still didn't come out. Getting water from the rock wasn't magic that required just the right incantation. The water came from God. But Moses did not obey God. He let his temper get the better of him.

Because of his disobedience, God decided to punish him by not allowing him to reach the promised land. God told Moses exactly where and when he would die, as if he were a prisoner on death row being led to the gallows. God would let Moses see the promised land, but not enter it alive. "To join his people" was a Hebrew idiom that simply meant to be buried. It came from ancient burial customs where all members of a family were interred together in a family tomb after death. Often, therefore, the idiom was quite literal.

Years later, on the Mount of Transfiguration, together with Elijah, Moses would finally visit the land he'd been barred from in life.

Priestly Misconduct

A man of God came to Eli and said to him, "This is what the LORD says: 'Didn't I reveal Myself to your ancestral house when it was in Egypt and belonged to Pharaoh's palace? I selected your house from the tribes of Israel to be priests, to offer sacrifices on My altar, to burn incense, and to wear an ephod in My presence. I also gave your house all the Israelite fire offerings. Why, then, do all of you despise My sacrifices and offerings that I require at the place of worship? You have honored your sons more than Me, by making yourselves fat with the best part of all of the offerings of My people Israel.'

"Therefore, the LORD, the God of Israel, says:

'Although I said your family and your ancestral house would walk before Me forever, the LORD now says, "No longer!"

I will honor those who honor Me, but those who despise Me will be disgraced.

"'Look, the days are coming when I will cut off your strength and the strength of your ancestral family, so that none in your family will reach old age.'"

1 Samuel 2:27–31 HCSB

⁂

There's more to love than hugs and kisses. Eli thought he loved his sons. But his choices showed he loved neither them nor God. Eli did nothing to change things. He criticized his sons and told them they should change their behavior, but he did nothing more than talk. Though he had the power to strip them of their position and to replace them with others, he abdicated his responsibility as a priest and as their father. He allowed them to continue serving.

God, therefore, told Eli that he would do what Eli wouldn't: he'd remove Eli's sons from their positions. This couldn't have come as a surprise to Eli. Two of Aaron's sons, Nadab and Abihu, had died simply for offering unauthorized fire. Eli's sons were guilty of far worse: greed and idolatry. Eli's sons had demanded extra meat from those who came to sacrifice in order to satisfy their gluttony. Worse, they were sleeping with the priestesses of Asherah in the tabernacle. Many Israelites had started worshipping other gods and goddesses, and the goddess Asherah was one of the most popular. Men worshipped her by doing what Eli's sons did, thereby engaging in a form of sympathetic magic: Asherah was a fertility goddess and by so worshipping her, she was supposed to grant fertility to crops, farm animals, and wives. Eli never did anything to stop his sons' wickedness.

If we love our children, we discipline them. We honor God when we refuse to tolerate their wrongdoing and instead encourage righteousness.

Kill Them All

Samuel also said to Saul, "The LORD sent me to anoint you king over His people, over Israel. Now therefore, heed the voice of the words of the LORD. Thus says the LORD of hosts: 'I will punish Amalek for what he did to Israel, how he ambushed him on the way when he came up from Egypt. Now go and attack Amalek, and utterly destroy all that they have, and do not spare them. But kill both man and woman, infant and nursing child, ox and sheep, camel and donkey.'"

So Saul gathered the people together and numbered them in Telaim, two hundred thousand foot soldiers and ten thousand men of Judah. And Saul came to a city of Amalek, and lay in wait in the valley . . .

And Saul attacked the Amalekites, from Havilah all the way to Shur, which is east of Egypt. He also took Agag king of the Amalekites alive, and utterly destroyed all the people with the edge of the sword. But Saul and the people spared Agag and the best of the sheep, the oxen, the fatlings, the lambs, and all that was good, and were unwilling to utterly destroy them.

1 Samuel 15:1–5, 7–9 NKJV

God's mercy for Israel meant judgment for the Amalekites. When Israel was on its way out of Egypt, the Amalekites attacked them at a place called Rephidim. Joshua led a fight against them. Moses stood with his staff raised. While he held it up, Israel would be winning. If he lowered his hands, however, the Amalekites would start to win. So Aaron and Hur held his hands up until Joshua and his men were finally victorious. God told Moses that he would one day blot out the name of the Amalekites (Exodus 17:14; Deuteronomy 25:17–19).

When Samuel told Saul to wipe out every last Amalekite, he was telling Saul to fulfill a promise that God had made to Moses.

Saul, however, did not completely carry out the will of God. He spared the Amalekite king, Agag, along with the best sheep and cattle. This violation of God's command would cost Saul his throne. Samuel told Saul that obedience was better than sacrifice and that rebellion and arrogance were like divination and idolatry. Saul was, for all practical purposes, rejecting God—just as that unnamed man in the time of Moses had rejected God by insisting on gathering wood on the Sabbath (Day 219). When our children do not finish their chores, leave the floor only half vacuumed, or fail to put the cleaning supplies away, we might become annoyed. Similarly, we don't deserve a pat on the back because we keep most of the Ten Commandments. God expects us to do what he asked, and to finish what we start. Halfway isn't good enough.

You're the Man!

Nathan then said to David, "You are the man! Thus says the LORD God of Israel, 'It is I who anointed you king over Israel and it is I who delivered you from the hand of Saul.

'I also gave you your master's house and your master's wives into your care, and I gave you the house of Israel and Judah; and if that had been too little, I would have added to you many more things like these!

'Why have you despised the word of the LORD by doing evil in His sight? You have struck down Uriah the Hittite with the sword, have taken his wife to be your wife, and have killed him with the sword of the sons of Ammon.

'Now therefore, the sword shall never depart from your house, because you have despised Me and have taken the wife of Uriah the Hittite to be your wife.'

"Thus says the LORD, 'Behold, I will raise up evil against you from your own household; I will even take your wives before your eyes and give them to your companion, and he will lie with your wives in broad daylight.

'Indeed you did it secretly, but I will do this thing before all Israel, and under the sun.' "

Then David said to Nathan, "I have sinned against the LORD." And Nathan said to David, "The LORD also has taken away your sin; you shall not die."

2 Samuel 12:7–13 NASB

❧

Just because God is merciful doesn't mean there's no punishment. David took Bathsheba to his bed and got her pregnant. Trying to hide what he had done, he had her husband put into the front lines of a battle so he would die.

David was guilty of two crimes that were punishable by death: adultery and murder (Leviticus 20:10; Numbers 35:31). There were no mitigating circumstances. There was no sacrifice to be offered or restitution to be paid. But the prophet Nathan told David that God had taken his sin away and that he wouldn't die.

But David still suffered. The infant born of the illicit relationship died. His firstborn son, Absalom, the heir to the throne, had his younger brother Amnon murdered after Amnon raped his sister Tamar. Later, Absalom led a rebellion against David and took David's concubines as his own. Absalom died in the resulting civil war, and David was restored to his throne. Bathsheba gave birth to another son, Solomon, who would take the throne after David. God was merciful, but David still suffered for his sins. God may not spare us from our sins' consequences, but he will give us the great gift of his forgiveness.

Justice Is Served

During David's reign there was a famine for three successive years, so David inquired of the LORD. The LORD answered, "It is because of the blood shed by Saul and his family when he killed the Gibeonites."

The Gibeonites were not Israelites but rather a remnant of the Amorites. The Israelites had taken an oath concerning them, but Saul had tried to kill them in his zeal for the Israelites and Judah. So David summoned the Gibeonites and spoke to them. He asked the Gibeonites, "What should I do for you? How can I wipe out this guilt so that you will bring a blessing on the LORD's inheritance?"

The Gibeonites said to him, "We are not asking for money from Saul or his family, and we cannot put anyone to death in Israel."

"Whatever you say, I will do for you," he said.

They replied to the king, "As for the man who annihilated us and plotted to exterminate us so we would not exist within the whole territory of Israel, let seven of his male descendants be handed over to us so we may hang them in the presence of the LORD at Gibeah of Saul, the LORD's chosen."

The king answered, "I will hand them over."

2 Samuel 21:1–6 HCSB

❀

*R*eneging on a promise will cost you, and the consequences can be unpredictable. During the time of Joshua, when the Israelites were conquering and wiping out the Canaanites, a group of Israelites from Gibea pretended to come from a long ways off. God had prohibited Israel from making treaties of peace with any Canaanites, but it was fine if the Israelites made them with other people. So the Israelites made a treaty with the Gibeonites. The Israelites soon learned of the subterfuge, but because of the treaty, the Canaanites came under Israel's protection. The Gibeonites, like Rahab in Jericho, had turned to God.

In his zeal to wipe out the remaining Canaanites, Saul had also attacked the people of Gibea. David had not known about this crime, but thanks to a famine, David learned what Saul had done. He asked the Gibeonites what penalty should be paid for their losses, and he agreed to go along with the Gibeonites' request for vengeance.

The Gibeonites had repented and come under the protection of the Israelites. Saul had violated that protection and attacked the innocent. Like Jonathan, his sons had served as soldiers in Saul's army. They had therefore participated in their father's crime. They were not innocent at all, and so they suffered justly. We can be sure that our sins will find us out.

A House Divided

One day as Jeroboam was leaving Jerusalem, the prophet Ahijah from Shiloh met him along the way. Ahijah was wearing a new cloak. The two of them were alone in a field, and Ahijah took hold of the new cloak he was wearing and tore it into twelve pieces. Then he said to Jeroboam, "Take ten of these pieces, for this is what the LORD, the God of Israel, says: 'I am about to tear the kingdom from the hand of Solomon, and I will give ten of the tribes to you! But I will leave him one tribe for the sake of my servant David and for the sake of Jerusalem, which I have chosen out of all the tribes of Israel. For Solomon has abandoned me and worshiped Ashtoreth, the goddess of the Sidonians;

Chemosh, the god of Moab; and Molech, the god of the Ammonites. He has not followed my ways and done what is pleasing in my sight. He has not obeyed my decrees and regulations as David his father did.

"'But I will not take the entire kingdom from Solomon at this time. For the sake of my servant David, the one whom I chose and who obeyed my commands and decrees, I will keep Solomon as leader for the rest of his life. But I will take the kingdom away from his son and give ten of the tribes to you.'"

1 Kings 11:29–35 NLT

God's judgment is precise. Because of his many women, Solomon turned from his devotion to God and began worshipping other deities (1 Kings 11:2–4). The worship of Molech often involved the sacrifice of one's children. As a consequence of Solomon's unfaithfulness, God decided to make Jeroboam king over all the tribes but Judah. God's judgment on Solomon was not as harsh as it might have been; he lost nothing during his lifetime. In fact, he died a rich and powerful ruler.

The division between the northern tribes and Jerusalem would last barely two hundred years. Hezekiah, a descendant of Solomon, did his best to obey God. During his time, the breakaway Northern Kingdom was destroyed by the Assyrians. Its royal family and the rich, fewer than thirty thousand people, were taken captive. Those who remained wound up under the control of Jerusalem—and Solomon's descendants—once again. People from the northern tribes celebrated Passover in Jerusalem (2 Chronicles 30:1–27). Later, during the reign of Josiah, people in what had been the Northern Kingdom paid money to the temple (2 Chronicles 34:10). Despite his sin, Solomon became one of the ancestors of the Messiah.

Mercy is a gift, and God always leaves us hope and a way back to him.

❈❈❈❈❈❈❈❈❈❈❈❈❈❈❈❈❈❈❈❈❈❈❈❈❈❈

Burning Human Bones

A man of God came from Judah to Bethel by a revelation from the LORD while Jeroboam was standing beside the altar to burn incense. The man of God cried out against the altar by a revelation from the LORD: "Altar, altar, this is what the LORD says, 'A son will be born to the house of David, named Josiah, and he will sacrifice on you the priests of the high places who are burning incense on you. Human bones will be burned on you.'" He gave a sign that day. He said, "This is the sign that the LORD has spoken: 'The altar will now be ripped apart, and the ashes that are on it will be spilled out.'"

When the king heard the word that the man of God had cried out against the altar at Bethel, Jeroboam stretched out his hand from the altar and said, "Arrest him!" But the hand he stretched out against him withered, and he could not pull it back to himself. The altar was ripped apart, and the ashes spilled off the altar, according to the sign that the man of God had given by the word of the LORD.

Then the king responded to the man of God, "Please plead for the favor of the LORD your God and pray for me so that my hand may be restored to me." So the man of God pleaded for the favor of the LORD, and the king's hand was restored to him and became as it had been at first.

1 Kings 13:1–6 HCSB

❈

*G*od's gift of a throne came with strings. Solomon's son lost the ten tribes of the north because of his idolatry. God gave those tribes to Jeroboam. But Jerusalem, still controlled by David's heir, remained the place where people went to worship God. Fearful that his new kingdom would be undermined by continued faithfulness to God in Jerusalem, Jeroboam built golden calves and set them up in Dan and Bethel as alternate worship sites. He even established a separate priesthood to officiate at the new shrines he had built (1 Kings 12:25–33).

Jeroboam simply didn't believe that God could keep him in power. Because he was unfaithful and led his people into sin, God eventually sent a prophet to proclaim judgment against him.

Jeroboam's reaction to the prophet's words was predictably unwelcoming. But God protected his spokesperson and even granted healing to Jeroboam in the midst of judgment. Jeroboam never repented of what he had done, however. For political purposes, he maintained the false religion he had created, and so the prophet's words came true. It didn't have to be that way. Jeroboam could have changed how things turned out, but he refused. Sadly, just because Jeroboam knew what to do didn't mean he would do it. We can strive to do otherwise.

Hit Me!

The LORD commanded a prophet to say to a friend, "Hit me!" But the friend refused, and the prophet told him, "You disobeyed the LORD, and as soon as you walk away, a lion will kill you." The friend left, and suddenly a lion killed him.

The prophet found someone else and said, "Hit me!" So this man beat him up.

The prophet left and put a bandage over his face to disguise himself. Then he went and stood beside the road, waiting for Ahab to pass by.

When Ahab went by, the prophet shouted, "Your Majesty, right in the heat of battle, someone brought a prisoner to me and told me to guard him. He said if the prisoner got away, I would either be killed or forced to pay seventy-five pounds of silver. But I got busy doing other things, and the prisoner escaped."

Ahab answered, "You will be punished just as you have said."

The man quickly tore the bandage off his face, and Ahab saw that he was one of the prophets. The prophet said, "The LORD told you to kill Benhadad, but you let him go. Now you will die in his place, and your people will die in place of his people."

Ahab went back to Samaria, angry and depressed.

1 Kings 20:35–43 CEV

*W*hat God asks people to do doesn't always make obvious sense. But who can be trusted more than God? Benhadad was the king of Aram, and he had led an army against Israel. Ahab's victory over the invader could have been utter and complete—not only was Ben-Hadad's army destroyed, but also the king was in Ahab's hand. Ahab freed the captured king and made a peace treaty with him.

God sent a prophet to bring a message of judgment against Ahab. And once again, the prophet's job was not an easy one. Rather than simply giving him words to say, God turned the prophet into a prop to illustrate the message. When his friend refused to injure him, he had to pronounce a death sentence against him. Sometimes God's judgments seem very harsh.

Most people would not want to hurt a friend; his reluctance is understandable. But God had demanded it, and the friend knew that it was a command from God. The law is quite clear: anyone who sins defiantly is blaspheming God and must be cut off from his people (Numbers 15:30–31). The friend knew better, and his refusal to abide by the word of God is what led to his death. No matter how odd it may seem, you're wise to do just what God asks.

Jezebel Is Dog Food

Ahab said to Elijah, "Have you found me, O my enemy?" He answered, "I have found you. Because you have sold yourself to do what is evil in the sight of the LORD, I will bring disaster on you; I will consume you, and will cut off from Ahab every male, bond or free, in Israel; and I will make your house like the house of Jeroboam son of Nebat, and like the house of Baasha son of Ahijah, because you have provoked me to anger and have caused Israel to sin. Also concerning Jezebel the LORD said, 'The dogs shall eat Jezebel within the bounds of Jezreel.' Anyone belonging to Ahab who dies in the city the dogs shall eat; and anyone of his who dies in the open country the birds of the air shall eat."

(Indeed, there was no one like Ahab, who sold himself to do what was evil in the sight of the LORD, urged on by his wife Jezebel. He acted most abominably in going after idols, as the Amorites had done, whom the LORD drove out before the Israelites.)

When Ahab heard those words, he tore his clothes and put sackcloth over his bare flesh; he fasted, lay in the sackcloth, and went about dejectedly. Then the word of the LORD came to Elijah the Tishbite: "Have you seen how Ahab has humbled himself before me? Because he has humbled himself before me, I will not bring the disaster in his days; but in his son's days I will bring the disaster on his house."

1 Kings 21:20–29 NRSV

❈

*S*ometimes it's the last person you expect who gets it right. Jezebel was the daughter of Ethbaal, king of the Sidonians, and the wife of Ahab. Together, Ahab and Jezebel led their people into worshipping other gods. Elijah prophesied against Ahab and predicted disaster for his family. Like the previous two royal dynasties (those of Jeroboam and Baasha), his, too, would be cut off and replaced by some other family. Worse, his wife would not just die; she would become food for dogs. For an Israelite, the most important thing was to have offspring and to have a proper burial. Ahab learned that he and his family would have neither.

Ahab's response to Elijah's words was not to breathe out threats, arrest him, or lock him away. Instead, he humbled himself. He took the prophet's words seriously and reacted appropriately.

The consequence was that God showed him mercy. Punishment would still fall on his family, but it wouldn't happen as long as Ahab lived. In the face of repentance, God is quick to show mercy and grace.

God's Lying Spirit

Micaiah told him, "In a vision I saw all Israel scattered on the mountains, like sheep without a shepherd. And the LORD said, 'Their master has been killed. Send them home in peace.' "

"Didn't I tell you?" the king of Israel exclaimed to Jehoshaphat. "He never prophesies anything but trouble for me."

Then Micaiah continued, "Listen to what the LORD says! I saw the LORD sitting on his throne with all the armies of heaven around him, on his right and on his left. And the LORD said, 'Who can entice Ahab to go into battle against Ramoth-gilead so he can be killed?'

"There were many suggestions, and finally a spirit approached the LORD and said, 'I can do it!'

"'How will you do this?' the LORD asked.

"And the spirit replied, 'I will go out and inspire all of Ahab's prophets to speak lies.'

"'You will succeed,' said the LORD. 'Go ahead and do it.'

"So you see, the LORD has put a lying spirit in the mouths of all your prophets. For the LORD has pronounced your doom."

1 Kings 22:17–23 NLT

Ahab was an evil king. He abused his power and led his people to worship false gods. The death of such a tyrant was a relief to his oppressed people. It was an answer to their prayers for mercy.

Naboth had a vineyard near Ahab's palace in Samaria. When Naboth refused to sell it, Jezebel, Ahab's wife, conspired to kill Naboth so that Ahab could seize the property (1 Kings 21). Through Elijah, God proclaimed judgment against Ahab: the place where Naboth's blood had been licked by dogs was the same spot where Ahab's blood would be licked.

Jehoshaphat, the king of Judah, visited Ahab. Ahab asked him to join in his plan to take Ramoth Gilead. Jehoshaphat suggested they ask God first, and all Ahab's prophets predicted success. Jehoshaphat was unimpressed, however, since none of Ahab's prophets were prophets of God. Reluctantly, Ahab called upon Micaiah, God's prophet, who predicted a disaster.

Ahab did not believe Micaiah; for that matter, neither did Jehoshaphat. So they went off to war against Aram. Micaiah's words came true, and Ahab was mortally wounded in battle. God's judgment against him happened just as God had predicted—and planned. Knowing without doing can lead to disaster. We need to actually do what God wants.

Burned to a Crisp

The king sent a captain with fifty men to Elijah . . . Out of the blue lightning struck and incinerated the captain and his fifty.

The king sent another captain with his fifty men, "O Holy Man! King's orders: Come down. And right now!"

Elijah answered, "If it's true that I'm a 'holy man,' lightning strike you and your fifty men!" Immediately a divine lightning bolt struck and incinerated the captain and his fifty.

The king then sent a third captain with his fifty men. For a third time, a captain with his fifty approached Elijah. This one fell on his knees in supplication: "O Holy Man, have respect for my life and the souls of these fifty men! Twice now lightning from out of the blue has struck and incinerated captains with their fifty men; please, I beg you, respect my life!"

The angel of GOD told Elijah, "Go ahead; and don't be afraid." Elijah got up and went down with him to the king.

Elijah told him, "GOD's word: Because you sent messengers to consult Baal-Zebub the God of Ekron, as if there were no God in Israel to whom you could pray, you'll never get out of that bed alive—already you're as good as dead."

2 Kings 1:9–16 MSG

❀

*B*ad things happen to those who oppose God and don't ask for mercy. Ahab, the king of Israel in Samaria, had died, and his son Ahaziah had become king in his place. Jezebel, his mother, was still alive. Ahaziah fell through a lattice and seriously injured himself. Instead of seeking God's help, he sent messengers to consult a false god. Elijah intercepted the messengers and told them that Ahaziah would die from his injuries.

Unlike his father, who repented at the prophet's words, Ahaziah sent soldiers to arrest Elijah. The first group died when Elijah called fire down on them. Ahaziah sent a second contingent to get Elijah, and the same thing happened to them. Ahaziah sent a third group. The leader of the third group begged for mercy, and Elijah granted it. Elijah went with them to face Ahaziah, and he simply said again what he had told the king's messengers: you're going to die. So Ahaziah died, and his brother, Joram, took the throne in his place. Unlike his father, Ahab, Ahaziah did not repent or humble himself before God. He remained defiant and suffered accordingly. The reason God punishes is to change behavior. When we have a humble and loving attitude toward God, he has mercy on us.

End of a Dynasty

The young man, the servant of the prophet, went to Ramoth-gilead.

When he came, behold, the captains of the army were sitting, and he said, "I have a word for you, O captain." And Jehu said, "For which one of us?" And he said, "For you, O captain."

He arose and went into the house, and he poured the oil on his head and said to him, "Thus says the LORD, the God of Israel, 'I have anointed you king over the people of the LORD, even over Israel.

'You shall strike the house of Ahab your master, that I may avenge the blood of My servants the prophets, and the blood of all the servants of the LORD, at the hand of Jezebel.

'For the whole house of Ahab shall perish, and I will cut off from Ahab every male person both bond and free in Israel.

'I will make the house of Ahab like the house of Jeroboam the son of Nebat, and like the house of Baasha the son of Ahijah.' "

2 Kings 9:4–9 NASB

*J*udgment sometimes falls without mercy—at least from the perspective of the judged. But the destruction of the wicked brings merciful relief to everyone else. Elisha became the chief prophet after Elijah was taken up to heaven in a chariot. One day he called one of the younger prophets and sent him to Ramoth-Gilead to anoint Jehu, one of Joram's generals, as the new king of Israel. Ramoth-Gilead was where the evil king Ahab had died in battle, after ignoring God's words from his prophet Micaiah. God had earlier issued a dire judgment through Elijah upon Ahab's family. God's words came true, thanks to Jehu.

Of all the kings that the Northern Kingdom of Israel would ever have, only Jehu would worship God. He reluctantly accepted his new position and killed the king of Israel, Joram. But then he enthusiastically destroyed the entire family of Ahab and had their severed heads stacked into two piles at the entrance to the capital city, Samaria. Next he had Ahab's widow, Jezebel, killed. Finally, he tricked all the prophets and priests of Baal into coming to one location for a supposed worship festival. Once assembled, he ordered them all slaughtered and burned their bodies on the altars of Baal. For all practical purposes, Jehu ended the worship of Baal in Israel, although he did nothing about the golden calves that Jeroboam had set up in Bethel and Dan. It isn't easy, but it is important, to work toward removing the things in life that keep us from being all we can be for God.

To the Fourth Generation

That's the story of Jehu's wasting of Baal in Israel.

But for all that, Jehu didn't turn back from the sins of Jeroboam son of Nebat, the sins that had dragged Israel into a life of sin—the golden calves in Bethel and Dan stayed.

GOD commended Jehu: "You did well to do what I saw was best. You did what I ordered against the family of Ahab. As reward, your sons will occupy the throne of Israel for four generations."

Even then, though, Jehu wasn't careful to walk in GOD's ways and honor the God of Israel from an undivided heart. He didn't turn back from the sins of Jeroboam son of Nebat, who led Israel into a life of sin.

It was about this time that GOD began to shrink Israel. Hazael hacked away at the borders of Israel from the Jordan to the east—all the territory of Gilead, Gad, Reuben, and Manasseh from Aroer near the Brook Arnon. In effect, all Gilead and Bashan.

2 Kings 10:28–33 MSG

❧

*I*dols are abhorrent to God, but like most Israelites, Jehu just didn't get it. He had led a rebellion, killed Joram, a son of Ahab, and killed every member of Joram's family, including Jezebel, Ahab's wife, and the queen mother. Then he wiped out all the prophets, servants, and priests of Baal, tore down Baal's temple, and desecrated his altars.

Despite all that, however, he did not undo the problem that Jeroboam, the first rebel king of the Northern Kingdom of Israel had created at the founding of the nation: the golden calf idols in Dan and Bethel. Jehu only got rid of Baal worship. Though that was a good thing and God blessed him for it, guaranteeing that his royal dynasty would endure for four generations, it wasn't enough.

Given the fact that they were meant to represent God, rather than false deities, why did God dislike the calf idols at Dan and Bethel? Human beings are the image and likeness of God, to be loved just as God is loved. Creating idols stands in the way of recognizing the full value of human beings as God's only image. We're supposed to catch a glimpse of God in one another and not get distracted by idols. Loving God is easy since he doesn't cut us off on the freeway or otherwise bug us. But if we claim to love God, whom we can't see, but hate the people whom we do, then we really don't love God. How we treat the real image of God—other human beings—reflects whether and how we really love God.

Tingle with Horror

The LORD said through his servants the prophets: "King Manasseh of Judah has done many detestable things. He is even more wicked than the Amorites, who lived in this land before Israel. He has caused the people of Judah to sin with his idols. So this is what the LORD, the God of Israel, says: I will bring such disaster on Jerusalem and Judah that the ears of those who hear about it will tingle with horror. I will judge Jerusalem by the same standard I used for Samaria and the same measure I used for the family of Ahab. I will wipe away the people of Jerusalem as one wipes a dish and turns it upside down. Then I will reject even the remnant of my own people who are left, and I will hand them over as plunder for their enemies. For they have done great evil in my sight and have angered me ever since their ancestors came out of Egypt."

2 Kings 21:10–15 NLT

❄

*G*od was patient with his people. Ever since they came out of Egypt, they worshipped other gods alongside their worship of Yahweh. Despite all the prophets—and despite all the judgments of God designed to get them to change their ways and do what they had promised in the centuries-old contract that they had signed—they continued worshipping false gods. The king and his family, the rich and the privileged, led the idolatry. Their lack of caring for their fellow Israelites paralleled their lack of caring for God. They oppressed the poor and disadvantaged. Manasseh, the son of the good king Hezekiah, took the throne when he was twelve and ruled in Jerusalem fifty-five years. In that time he restored Baal and Asherah worship and burned his son as a sacrifice. With Manasseh going over the top in his worship of false gods, God finally pronounced his judgment: the Israelites would lose their land and go into exile. Their slavery to their sins would become manifest in their return to physical slavery. Metaphorically, the people were back to Egypt again.

In captivity, however, many of the Israelites got the message and humbled themselves before God. Even Manasseh turned to God (2 Chronicles 33:11–17, 19). That's what God wanted. His purpose in judgment was not vengeance. His purpose in judgment was to get his people to change their minds, to reconsider. He wanted to restore the relationship they had broken. We, too, can restore our relationship with God when we humble ourselves before him.

Acute Intestinal Distress

A letter came to Jehoram from Elijah the prophet, saying:

This is what the LORD God of your ancestor David says: "Because you have not walked in the ways of your father Jehoshaphat or in the ways of Asa king of Judah but have walked in the way of the kings of Israel, have caused Judah and the inhabitants of Jerusalem to prostitute themselves like the house of Ahab prostituted itself, and also have killed your brothers, your father's family, who were better than you, the LORD is now about to strike your people, your sons, your wives, and all your possessions with a horrible affliction. You yourself [will be struck] with many illnesses, including a disease of the intestines, until your intestines come out day after day because of the disease."

The LORD put it into the mind of the Philistines and the Arabs who live near the Cushites to attack Jehoram. So they went to war against Judah and invaded it. They carried off all the possessions found in the king's palace and also his sons and wives; not a son was left to him except Jehoahaz, his youngest son.

After all these things, the LORD afflicted him in his intestines with an incurable disease. This continued day after day until two full years passed. Then his intestines came out because of his disease, and he died from severe illnesses. But his people did not hold a fire in his honor like the fire in honor of his fathers.

2 Chronicles 21:12–19 HCSB

Jehoram immediately murdered his six brothers when he became king of Judah at age thirty-two. He then married a daughter of King Ahab and adopted his religious practices—the worship of Baal and Asherah.

Because he led his people to worship idols rather than the God of Israel, God punished him. God had told the Israelites in the time of Moses that just as a father disciplined his children, so God would discipline them. Jehoram received a harsh punishment and died of a painful and embarrassing ailment. But as harsh as the punishment was, however, it still came with mercy. Because God had promised to preserve David's line, God did not kill off all Jehoram's children. He left behind one—his youngest, Ahaziah, who was no better than his father.

Had Jehoram heeded God and repented, his life would have been different. His children's lives would have been different. Perhaps the history of Judah would have turned out differently too. As Jeremiah pointed out, it is never too late to turn around and change your life. God will always respond to a changed heart, because repentance and restoration are God's goals whenever he brings judgment.

Among the "Gods"

God has taken his place in the
divine council;
   in the midst of the gods he
   holds judgment:
"How long will you judge unjustly
   and show partiality to the wicked?
   Selah
Give justice to the weak and
the orphan;
   maintain the right of the lowly
   and the destitute.
Rescue the weak and the needy;
   deliver them from the hand of
   the wicked."

They have neither knowledge nor
understanding,
   they walk around in darkness;
   all the foundations of the earth
   are shaken.
I say, "You are gods, children of the
   Most High, all of you;
   nevertheless, you shall die
   like mortals, and fall like any
   prince."
Rise up, O God, judge the earth;
   for all the nations belong to you!

Psalm 82 NRSV

*K*ings have no divine right to their thrones. The unjust ruler will eventually suffer God's certain wrath. The kings of all the nations around Israel were more than simply arrogant and self-absorbed. They actually believed—and the people of their nations believed with them—that they were in fact incarnations of their gods. The pharaoh of Egypt believed that he was Ra, the sun god, reincarnated. The king of Babylon believed himself to be the incarnation of Marduk.

There is no God but Yahweh. God knows that, and so does the author of this psalm. Who are these "gods" that Yahweh is taking his place among? The "divine council" and the "gods" over which God held court were not other deities. They were the arrogant kings of the earth who liked to imagine they were something more than human.

In this psalm, the one true God addressed them sarcastically, asking if they really were gods, then why didn't they act like it? Instead of being righteous, they were wicked. Instead of dispensing justice, they created most of the oppression and injustice that existed in their lands. God told them that he therefore was going to execute judgment against them. Despite what they thought about themselves, they were mere mortals. And they would die like everyone else. Though the divine kings might not offer justice to their suffering people, though they might lack mercy, God would be merciful to their people and give the divine oppressors what they deserved at last. Sooner or later God eliminates evil. Eventually, God gives relief from crushing burdens.

Let's Talk

I, the LORD, invite you
    to come and talk it over.
Your sins are scarlet red,
    but they will be whiter
    than snow or wool.
If you willingly obey me,
    the best crops in the land
    will be yours.
But if you turn against me,
    your enemies will kill you.
I, the LORD, have spoken.
Jerusalem, you are like
    an unfaithful wife.
Once your judges were honest
    and your people lived right;
    now you are a city
    full of murderers.

Your silver is fake,
    and your wine
    is watered down.
Your leaders have rejected me
    to become friends of crooks;
    your rulers are looking
    for gifts and bribes.
Widows and orphans
    never get a fair trial.
I am the LORD All-Powerful,
    the mighty ruler of Israel,
    and I make you a promise:
You are now my enemy,
    and I will show my anger
    by taking revenge on you.

Isaiah 1:18–24 CEV

God offers hope, even as the sword of his judgment is swinging. God called Isaiah to be a prophet not long before the Assyrians destroyed the Northern Kingdom of Israel and a couple of generations before Babylon invaded the Southern Kingdom of Judah.

Things did not have to turn out badly. God wanted the Israelites' lives to be good and happy. He wanted to bless his people. God wanted his people to turn back to him. They could do the right thing voluntarily, or God could force the issue. The choice was theirs. Through Isaiah, he warned them that they were forcing his hand. Just as Israel was bound by contract with God, so God was bound by contract to Israel. He had agreed to the contract's terms, and he would not violate them. But God's judgment wasn't simply about the legalities of the situation. God's judgment was about correcting wrongs and bringing justice to the oppressed. People were suffering because of the sins of the leadership classes. God couldn't let that suffering continue forever. A day of reckoning had to come. Those who were wronged deserved to have the wrong righted. Either the leadership could right the wrongs themselves or God would do it for them. But the wrongdoers could always repent. God wanted to save them as much as he wanted to save the wronged. Which means even when we're the ones who have done wrong, we can have hope.

Taking Credit Not Due

When the Lord has finished all his work on Mount Zion and on Jerusalem, he will punish the arrogant boasting of the king of Assyria and his haughty pride. For he says:

"By the strength of my hand I have
   done it, and by my wisdom, for I
   have understanding;
I have removed the boundaries
   of peoples, and have plundered their
   treasures; like a bull I have brought
   down those who sat on thrones.
My hand has found, like a nest,
   the wealth of the peoples;
   and as one gathers eggs that have
   been forsaken, so I have gathere
   all the earth;

and there was none that moved a wing, or opened its mouth, or chirped."
Shall the ax vaunt itself over the one who wields it, or the saw magnify itself against the one who handles it?
As if a rod should raise the one who lifts it up, or as if a staff should lift the one who is not wood!

Isaiah 10:12–15 NRSV

Whatever good you manage to accomplish, it is actually God who does it (1 Corinthians 15:10; Philippians 2:13). In 722 BC, the Assyrians would conquer the Northern Kingdom of Israel and carry a bit fewer than thirty thousand people away as captives, mostly just the rich and powerful. God decided to bring the Assyrians against them to punish the Israelites for their idolatry and for their mistreatment of the poor and weak. By punishing them, God could help them realize the error of their ways, repent, and turn back to God.

The Assyrians cared only about conquest. Oblivious to the hand of God, the Assyrians imagined themselves in charge of their own fates.

Although God judged his people, the old promise he had made to Abraham remained: "Whoever curses you I will curse" (Genesis 12:3 NIV). So even though the Assyrians were fulfilling God's purposes, they fell under his condemnation, both for being arrogant and for daring to harm Israel.

God's judgment on Assyria fell within two generations. The Assyrian army, together with their Egyptian allies, was defeated at a place called Carchemish in 605 BC by Nebuchadnezzar and his father. God judged the judgmental. God is always looking out for his people, even when he is in the middle of punishing them. You can never escape God's love or protection.

Day 240

The Day of the Lord

Behold, the day of the LORD comes,
    Cruel, with both wrath and
      fierce anger,
To lay the land desolate;
And He will destroy its sinners
    from it.
For the stars of heaven and their
    constellations
Will not give their light;
The sun will be darkened in its
    going forth,
And the moon will not cause its
    light to shine.
"I will punish the world for
    its evil,
And the wicked for their iniquity;
I will halt the arrogance of
    the proud,
And will lay low the haughtiness
    of the terrible.
I will make a mortal more rare
    than fine gold,

A man more than the golden
    wedge of Ophir.
Therefore I will shake the heavens,
And the earth will move out of
    her place,
In the wrath of the LORD of hosts
And in the day of His fierce anger.
It shall be as the hunted gazelle,
And as a sheep that no man
    takes up;
Every man will turn to his
    own people,
And everyone will flee to his
    own land.
Everyone who is found will be
    thrust through,
And everyone who is captured will
    fall by the sword.
Their children also will be dashed
    to pieces before their eyes;
Their houses will be plundered
And their wives ravished."

Isaiah 13:9–16 NKJV

God understands your righteous indignation. Prophecies were often given as poetry to increase their emotional impact. God's judgment against Babylon was rendered even more horrific through poetry.

Like the Assyrians before them, the Babylonians were guilty of harming God's chosen people, and God used the Persians to destroy them.

Most of the time the words translated *world* and *earth* refer not to the planet but to a land—in this case, the land of Babylon. The "day of the LORD" described any time of God's judgment. The darkening of the stars, moon, and sun that God described were fulfilled in the destruction of the city of Babylon: the flames that consumed it and the smoke that rose blackened the sky. God had witnessed a few cities burn and so described the experience vividly.

God brought comfort to his people Israel by promising them vengeance. No matter how dark it seems, no matter how strong your enemies might be, God can—and will—have the last word.

Without Money and Without Cost

Ho! Every one who thirsts, come to
the waters;
And you who have no money
come, buy and eat.
Come, buy wine and milk
Without money and without cost.
Why do you spend money for what is
not bread,
And your wages for what does
not satisfy?
Listen carefully to Me, and eat
what is good,
And delight yourself in
abundance.
Incline your ear and come to Me.
Listen, that you may live;
And I will make an everlasting
covenant with you,

According to the faithful mercies
shown to David.
Behold, I have made him a witness to
the peoples,
A leader and commander for
the peoples.
Behold, you will call a nation you do
not know,
And a nation which knows you
not will run to you,
Because of the LORD your God,
even the Holy One of Israel;
For He has glorified you.

Isaiah 55:1–5 NASB

❈

The Israelites knew the cost of everything and the value of nothing. They had trusted in fantasies that could not save. Although Isaiah began his prophetic message with warnings about the coming judgment, he later explained that God's judgment was not the end of the line for them. He told them that though they had forgotten God and no longer knew him, they could be reminded. Their ignorance could be corrected. And it wouldn't cost anything.

A parent might explain to his child that though certain privileges have been taken away, a change in behavior or attitude could lead to their restoration. The child is not left without hope or understanding of how to restore the relationship or get things back to the way they were. God, being the ideal Father, let his people know that the judgment they faced was not the end to their relationship with him. Instead, they had the means to make it even better than it was before. Because of God's punishment, a nation that had lost sight of God would find God. Following Israel's seventy-year captivity in Babylon, they never again felt a temptation to turn to other gods. From that time forward, the Israelites remained faithful to their belief in one, and only one, God. God's commitment to them remained unbroken. God had been merciful to David despite his sins. God would be merciful to Israel too. We needn't fear God's discipline. It is always for our own good.

Clapping Trees, Singing Mountains

The rain and snow come down from
   the heavens and stay on the ground
   to water the earth.
They cause the grain to grow, producing seed for the farmer and bread for
   the hungry.
It is the same with my word.
I send it out, and it always
   produces fruit.
It will accomplish all I want it to, and
   it will prosper everywhere I send it.
You will live in joy and peace.
The mountains and hills will burst
into song, and the trees of the field
   will clap their hands!
Where once there were thorns, cypress
   trees will grow.
Where nettles grew, myrtles will
   sprout up.
These events will bring great honor to
   the LORD's name; they will be an everlasting sign of his power and love.

Isaiah 55:10–13 NLT

Just as you wouldn't expect a car owner's manual to be a book of love poetry, so you shouldn't expect a book of love poetry to explain the finer points of car repair. Poetry is designed to appeal to the emotions and create an emotional response; it isn't designed to report facts. Isaiah's prophecy is a poem and needs to be understood that way. Feel God's unrestrained joy!

God compared the words he gave his people to rain falling on parched, barren ground. After a long winter in Israel, the landscape was brown and lifeless. Then suddenly, in the spring, thanks to all the winter storms, the grass sprouted and the flowers bloomed. The brown hills became lush, green, and beautiful, producing abundant crops. God's word worked the same way: it always produced a beautiful result.

God promised the Israelites future joy and happiness, a time of abundance in contrast to their self-inflicted hardship that had left the land parched, stripped of all its wealth and people. Neither Isaiah nor his listeners expected inanimate objects suddenly to become noisy and animated. Isaiah's point—God's point— was that the suffering of the moment, the punishment of the moment, was just that: for the moment. God's punishment was for their own good. Some day they would understand that. Someday, the winter storms would make sense to them. Good times would come again.

Our temporary suffering pales in importance alongside the future happiness God promises.

Serendipity

"I revealed myself to those who did
    not ask for me;
      I was found by those who did not
      seek me.
      To a nation that did not call on
      my name,
      I said, 'Here am I, here am I.'
All day long I have held out my hands
    to an obstinate people,
who walk in ways not good,
    pursuing their own
      imaginations—
a people who continually provoke me
    to my very face,
    offering sacrifices in gardens
    and burning incense on altars
    of brick;
who sit among the graves
    and spend their nights keeping
      secret vigil;
    who eat the flesh of pigs,
    and whose pots hold broth of
      unclean meat;

who say, 'Keep away; don't come
    near me, for I am too sacred
    for you!'
      Such people are smoke in
      my nostrils, a fire that keeps
      burning all day.
"See, it stands written before me:
    I will not keep silent but will pay
      back in full;
    I will pay it back into their laps—
both your sins and the sins of
    your fathers,"
      says the LORD.
      "Because they burned sacrifices on
      the mountains
    and defied me on the hills,
    I will measure into their laps
    the full payment for their
      former deeds."

Isaiah 65:1–7 NIV

God doesn't like self-righteousness, and human righteousness is never really righteous anyway (Isaiah 64:6). Nevertheless, God offered hope to those hopeless, deluded people. The Israelites had consistently been slow to accept God's message. God would not, and could not reject his people Israel.

Though God turned to the Gentiles, and though God judged the people of Israel and sent them into captivity, nevertheless, the Israelites would remain forever God's people.

The Israelites had involved themselves in various pagan practices, including how they offered sacrifices, what they sacrificed, and to whom they offered sacrifices, as well as their consumption of forbidden nonkosher food. God assured them they would be punished according to their misdeeds, but at the same time, God offered them mercy and the chance for restoration—and not only to them, but to all people. People the world over are looking for God, and he'll offer his mercy to all who seek it.

❀❀❀❀❀❀❀❀❀❀❀❀❀❀❀❀❀❀❀❀❀❀❀❀❀❀❀❀❀❀❀

Empty Suits

The LORD says:

Don't brag about your wisdom
   or strength or wealth.
If you feel you must brag,
   then have enough sense
   to brag about worshiping me,
   the LORD.
What I like best
   is showing kindness,
   justice, and mercy
   to everyone on earth.

Someday I will punish the nations of Egypt, Edom, Ammon, and Moab, and the tribes of the desert. The men of these nations are circumcised, but they don't worship me. And it's the same with you people of Judah. Your bodies are circumcised, but your hearts are unchanged.

Jeremiah 9:23–26 CEV

❀

*P*eople get full of themselves sometimes. Jeremiah began prophesying when the nation of Judah was doing just fine. They were wealthy and life was comfortable, at least for the ruling class. There were problems, however. The ruling class was not kind, they were not merciful, and justice was rare. They mistreated the poor and disadvantaged. They went through the motions of worshipping Yahweh, but their hearts weren't in it.

God pointed out that worshipping him was something more than just rituals, fine words, and circumcision. After all, the Jews weren't the only circumcised people in the Middle East. The Egyptians, the Edomites (descended from Jacob's brother Esau), the Moabites (descended from Lot, Abraham's nephew), and others were all just as circumcised as the Jews were. But that didn't mean they loved God. And that wouldn't stop God from punishing them.

The Israelites resembled the nations of Egypt, Edom, Amon, Moab, and the desert tribes, not just in their circumcision, but also in their worship. Like their neighbors, the Israelites worshipped many other gods besides Yahweh. Just because they told God they loved him didn't mean they really did.

Their neighbors, like Israel, used to boast about their kind treatment of widows and orphans, even as they stole their last loaf of bread and took the roofs over their heads. Every king in the world liked to boast that he was kind to the disadvantaged and gave his people justice, even as he lied and cheated and stole from them.

Pretty words on royal monuments and rituals like circumcision can be meaningless. What matters are hard things, like changed hearts leading to compassion, action, and true worship.

Sour Grapes

The LORD All-Powerful, the God of Israel, said:

I promise to set the people of Judah free and to lead them back to their hometowns. And when I do, they will once again say,

"We pray that the LORD
will bless his home,
the sacred hill in Jerusalem
where his temple stands."

The people will live in Jerusalem and in the towns of Judah. Some will be farmers, and others will be shepherds. Those who feel tired and worn out will find new life and energy, and when they sleep, they will wake up refreshed.

Someday, Israel and Judah will be my field where my people and their livestock will grow. In the past, I took care to uproot them, to tear them down, and to destroy them. But when that day comes, I will take care to plant them and help them grow. No longer will anyone go around saying,

"Sour grapes eaten by parents
leave a sour taste in the mouths
of their children."

When that day comes, only those who eat sour grapes will get the sour taste, and only those who sin will be put to death.

Jeremiah 31:23–30 CEV

God distinguishes between the guilty and the innocent. And God reassured his people that his punishments against the guilty were not forever. Someday life would be good again; the Israelites would go home and return to their former lives, like criminals released from prison. Once again, they would go about their business and do what they used to do. When that day came, they would stop imagining that God was just out to get them or that his punishments did not distinguish between those who deserved it and those who didn't.

It was part of Israel's legal code that "parents are not to be put to death for their children, nor children put to death for their parents; each of you will die for your own sin" (Deuteronomy 24:16). God never violated his own commandments, and yet a false proverb had become widely quoted in Israel. The proverb suggested that God punished children for what their parents did. God, through Jeremiah, reiterated reality: only those who did wrong would be punished for it. There's no such thing as collateral damage with God's punishments. He brings his judgment only upon those who deserve it. God pays attention to all the details, and we can trust him to do the right thing.

God Made Backup Copies

The word of the LORD came to Jeremiah after the king had burned the scroll and the words which Baruch had written at the dictation of Jeremiah, saying,

"Take again another scroll and write on it all the former words that were on the first scroll which Jehoiakim the king of Judah burned.

"And concerning Jehoiakim king of Judah you shall say, 'Thus says the LORD, "You have burned this scroll, saying, 'Why have you written on it that the king of Babylon will certainly come and destroy this land, and will make man and beast to cease from it?'"

'Therefore thus says the LORD concerning Jehoiakim king of Judah, "He shall have no one to sit on the throne of David, and his dead body shall be cast out to the heat of the day and the frost of the night.

"I will also punish him and his descendants and his servants for their iniquity, and I will bring on them and the inhabitants of Jerusalem and the men of Judah all the calamity that I have declared to them—but they did not listen." ' "

Then Jeremiah took another scroll and gave it to Baruch the son of Neriah, the scribe, and he wrote on it at the dictation of Jeremiah all the words of the book which Jehoiakim king of Judah had burned in the fire; and many similar words were added to them.

Jeremiah 36:27–32 NASB

Human judgment is often as ineffective as it is wrong. Jehoiakim, king of Judah, learned the hard way that censorship was an ineffective means of quieting God. Josiah, king of Judah, had restored the worship of God in Israel. Josiah then fought a battle against Pharaoh Neco, but he was killed. The pharaoh then put Josiah's son on the throne and changed his name to Jehoiakim. In his third year, Nebuchadnezzar of Babylon invaded and made him a vassal. Jehoiakim did not like the message that Jeremiah had pronounced. He decided to destroy the message, as if the word of God could be undone by burning it.

God's word is not dependent upon people's believing it for its effectiveness. Believed or not, what God says will have its way. God didn't forget what he had said, unlike a public speaker who might have problems if he lost his notes. Instead, God just spoke them again. Jeremiah had no trouble restoring what had been burned. And it didn't keep God from adding even more to what he had said originally. He was not intimidated or silenced.

Destroying the message is no more effective—or reasonable—than attacking the messenger. We can be confident that God's word is good for today and all time.

The Watchman

So you, mortal, I have made a sentinel for the house of Israel; whenever you hear a word from my mouth, you shall give them warning from me. If I say to the wicked, "O wicked ones, you shall surely die," and you do not speak to warn the wicked to turn from their ways, the wicked shall die in their iniquity, but their blood I will require at your hand. But if you warn the wicked to turn from their ways, and they do not turn from their ways, the wicked shall die in their iniquity, but you will have saved your life.

Now you, mortal, say to the house of Israel, Thus you have said: "Our transgressions and our sins weigh upon us, and we waste away because of them; how then can we live?" Say to them, As I live, says the Lord God, I have no pleasure in the death of the wicked, but that the wicked turn from their ways and live; turn back, turn back from your evil ways; for why will you die, O house of Israel?

Ezekiel 33:7–11 NRSV

When the world's idea of failure happens, it doesn't mean God doesn't love us anymore. Success is simply doing what God has asked, regardless of the consequences. God did not tell Ezekiel that anyone would necessarily repent or even believe his words. What mattered to God, what was "success" to God, was simply that Ezekiel would do what God had asked. Ezekiel's responsibility was to warn the Israelites. What the Israelites did with his warning was up to them. He might feel bad for what happened to the people, but he could never feel guilty. He would be a failure only if he kept silent. If a building lacks fire alarms and smoke detectors and people die, the building owner will be held accountable. But if the alarms are there and no one heeds them, then those who die in the flames have only themselves to blame.

A ringing fire alarm did not mean those in the building should just give up hope. It meant they should run to salvation. Likewise, guilt should not make Israel despair. Guilt's purpose was not to destroy, but to motivate change. God didn't want to destroy sinners, just their sin.

God hoped desperately that his people would heed the warnings delivered by Ezekiel. God's happiness comes when people repent and turn from their sins. God derives no pleasure when his warnings are ignored. God does not delight in bringing judgment to us. He delights in our rescue.

🌼🌼🌼🌼🌼🌼🌼🌼🌼🌼🌼🌼🌼🌼🌼🌼🌼🌼🌼🌼🌼🌼🌼🌼🌼🌼🌼🌼🌼🌼🌼

Just Not Paying Attention

Say thus to them, "Thus says the Lord GOD: 'As I live, surely those who are in the ruins shall fall by the sword, and the one who is in the open field I will give to the beasts to be devoured, and those who are in the strongholds and caves shall die of the pestilence. For I will make the land most desolate, her arrogant strength shall cease, and the mountains of Israel shall be so desolate that no one will pass through. Then they shall know that I am the Lord, when I have made the land most desolate because of all their abominations which they have committed.'

"'As for you, son of man, the children of your people are talking about you beside the walls and in the doors of the houses; and they speak to one another, everyone saying to his brother, "Please come and hear what the word is that comes from the LORD." So they come to you as people do, they sit before you as My people, and they hear your words, but they do not do them; for with their mouth they show much love, but their hearts pursue their own gain. Indeed you are to them as a very lovely song of one who has a pleasant voice and can play well on an instrument; for they hear your words, but they do not do them. And when this comes to pass—surely it will come—then they will know that a prophet has been among them."

Ezekiel 33:27–33 NKJV

🌼

*E*zekiel's first vision and call to the role of prophet occurred when he was about thirty years old (Ezekiel 1:1). He had been taken into captivity in Babylon, along with many of the upper classes of Jerusalem, during the reign of Jehoia-chin, king of Judah, who had also been taken into captivity as well. This happened about a decade before Nebuchadnezzar would destroy Jerusalem and burn down the temple.

Ezekiel's ministry was primarily to his fellow captives, warning them about what was going to happen to the people left behind in Jerusalem and Judah. But God explained that until his prophecies came true, the people would not believe him. For them, Ezekiel was merely a source of entertainment. Nothing more. No one took him seriously.

The people claimed they heard him; they mouthed all the right words. But in reality, they cared nothing about God or his prophet. Just because people hear the words of God doesn't mean they'll choose to change their lives. We can nevertheless be faithful in speaking God's truth.

Where Is God?

"Now, therefore," says the Lord,
"Turn to Me with all your heart,
With fasting, with weeping, and
with mourning."
So rend your heart, and not
your garments;
Return to the Lord your God,
For He is gracious and merciful,
Slow to anger, and of great kindness;
And He relents from doing harm.
Who knows if He will turn
and relent,
And leave a blessing behind Him—
A grain offering and a drink offering
For the Lord your God?
Blow the trumpet in Zion,
Consecrate a fast,
Call a sacred assembly;
Gather the people,
Sanctify the congregation,
Assemble the elders,

Gather the children and nursing babes;
Let the bridegroom go out from
his chamber,
And the bride from her dressing room.
Let the priests, who minister to
the Lord,
Weep between the porch and the altar;
Let them say, "Spare Your people,
O Lord,
And do not give Your heritage to
reproach,
That the nations should rule
over them.
Why should they say among
the peoples,
'Where is their God?' "
Then the Lord will be zealous for
His land,
And pity His people.

Joel 2:12–18 NKJV

"Where is God?" is a common question in the midst of a disaster. In the case of Israel, the question might have arisen in the minds of outsiders as they witnessed the destruction of God's chosen people, the Israelites, at the hands of the Babylonians or some other invader.

Through Joel, God called upon his people to repent wholeheartedly. If only they responded to the punishment, he could restore them and silence those who might imagine that the suffering of his chosen ones meant he wasn't there.

When God's people finally repented, the outsiders would witness their restoration and their return to glory. Instead of asking, "Where is God?" they would finally realize, "Oh, well there he is!"

People do not wonder where God is when times are good. Instead, they exclaim praises and thanks and shout, "God is good!" and "Behold the hand of God," and "See how God moves." No one facing happiness asks, "Why me?" or "Where is God?" God calls us to bring our attitudes into alignment with our actions.

Let Justice Roll Down

Alas, you who are longing for the day
of the LORD,
> For what purpose will the day of
> the LORD be to you?
> It will be darkness and not light;
As when a man flees from a lion
> And a bear meets him,
> Or goes home, leans his hand
> against the wall
> And a snake bites him.
Will not the day of the LORD be dark-
ness instead of light,
> Even gloom with no brightness
> in it?
"I hate, I reject your festivals,
> Nor do I delight in your solemn
> assemblies.
"Even though you offer up to Me burnt
offerings and your grain offerings,
> I will not accept them;
> And I will not even look at the
> peace offerings of your fatlings.

"Take away from Me the noise of
your songs;
> I will not even listen to the sound
> of your harps.
"But let justice roll down like waters
And righteousness like an ever-flowing
stream.
"Did you present Me with
sacrifices and grain offerings in the
wilderness for forty years, O house of
Israel?
"You also carried along Sikkuth
your king and Kiyyun, your images,
the star of your gods which you made
for yourselves.
"Therefore, I will make you go
into exile beyond Damascus," says
the LORD, whose name is the God
of hosts.

Amos 5:18–27 NASB

❋

*T*he day of the Lord was not a time of celebration. It was a time of judgment. Those who wanted justice might be among the first on the chopping block. The Israelites sacrificed to God and performed circumcisions just as they were supposed to. But unfortunately, they also sacrificed to other gods as well. Therefore, God decided to send them to Babylon.

Sikkuth and Kiyyun were linked with the gods Jupiter and Saturn. In Canaanite mythology, Saturn and Jupiter were identified with El and Baal. They were part of Israel's religious life even as far back as the wanderings in the wilderness. The worship of other gods is what motivated Joshua to famously stand before the people and ask them to "choose you this day" whom to worship.

God had been patient, gently working for a long time in an attempt to turn his people from their tendency to mix the false worship of mythical gods with the true worship of Yahweh. But mercy had to end. It became necessary to move on to something harsher: the day of the Lord. God can't let us get away with our bad behavior forever. He loves us too much.

Day 251

※※※※※※※※※※※※※※※※※※※※※※※※※※※※※※※※※※※※

But They Deserve to Die!

Jonah went out of the city and sat down east of the city, and made a booth for himself there. He sat under it in the shade, waiting to see what would become of the city.

The LORD God appointed a bush, and made it come up over Jonah, to give shade over his head, to save him from his discomfort; so Jonah was very happy about the bush. But when dawn came up the next day, God appointed a worm that attacked the bush, so that it withered. When the sun rose, God prepared a sultry east wind, and the sun beat down on the head of Jonah so that he was faint and asked that he might die. He said, "It is better for me to die than to live."

But God said to Jonah, "Is it right for you to be angry about the bush?" And he said, "Yes, angry enough to die." Then the LORD said, "You are concerned about the bush, for which you did not labor and which you did not grow; it came into being in a night and perished in a night. And should I not be concerned about Nineveh, that great city, in which there are more than a hundred and twenty thousand persons who do not know their right hand from their left, and also many animals?"

Jonah 4:5–11 NRSV

※

People like stories where the bad guy gets his just deserts. That's exactly what Jonah was hoping for Nineveh. Jonah hated it. The capital of an Assyrian Empire was cruel and threatened Israel. But God told Jonah to warn the Ninevites that judgment was imminent. Jonah refused and boarded a ship going the opposite direction. He expected God to kill him for his disobedience. Jonah was fine with that because, lacking his warning, Nineveh would be destroyed. Jonah thought he could get his way and thwart God. To Jonah's surprise, God put him in a fish's belly instead. He learned God was smarter than he was and that there were worse punishments than death. Three days later, God asked again, and Jonah obeyed. What Jonah feared most was what happened: Nineveh repented, and God forgave the Ninevites.

But God showed Jonah mercy as well. As Jonah sat outside Nineveh hoping that God would punish the city, Jonah's misery in the hot sun was relieved by a vine that gave him shade. When it shriveled and died, he wished he could die too. The story ends with a question from God: if Jonah can feel concern over a mere plant, then what should God feel for human beings? Jonah learned why God much prefers mercy to judgment.

God Does Not Change

"See, I will send my messenger, who will prepare the way before me. Then suddenly the Lord you are seeking will come to his temple; the messenger of the covenant, whom you desire, will come," says the LORD Almighty.

But who can endure the day of his coming? Who can stand when he appears? For he will be like a refiner's fire or a launderer's soap. He will sit as a refiner and purifier of silver; he will purify the Levites and refine them like gold and silver. Then the LORD will have men who will bring offerings in righteousness, and the offerings of Judah and Jerusalem will be acceptable to the LORD, as in days gone by, as in former years.

"So I will come near to you for judgment. I will be quick to testify against sorcerers, adulterers and perjurers, against those who defraud laborers of their wages, who oppress the widows and the fatherless, and deprive aliens of justice, but do not fear me," says the LORD Almighty.

"I the LORD do not change. So you, O descendants of Jacob, are not destroyed. Ever since the time of your forefathers you have turned away from my decrees and have not kept them. Return to me, and I will return to you," says the LORD Almighty.

"But you ask, 'How are we to return?'"

Malachi 3:1–7 NIV

G od has judged us completely, pouring out final judgment on every human being.

That sounds harsh, since no one can stand before God's judgment. But his judgment is designed to refine, not destroy. Metal is not heated in a furnace to get rid of it, but to remove its impurities and make it stronger. Clothing is not put through the laundry for the purpose of ruining it, but rather to clean it.

The list of sins that God gave, ranging from religious practices to the mistreatment of the weak, were the common impurities of the nation of Israel. They were the reason God sent them to Babylon for cleansing.

Although the words of God's prophecy are attributed to Malachi, they were most likely actually written by Isaiah. The phrase "my messenger" is the Hebrew word *Malachi*. In the first verse of the prophecy, it was simply not translated.

God's character never changes. Just as God rescued his people from Egyptian bondage and didn't destroy them, so he would rescue the Israelites from Babylon. God always acts the same way, and remembering how God helped us in the past is a comfort now and for the years to come.

Forgiveness and Anger

Forgiveness of wrongdoers can feel like betrayal to those who have been wronged. Anger in the face of injustice is a good thing; it serves as motivation to action and redress. But anger can turn into bitterness and depression. Forgiveness is the granting of mercy to one who deserves anger. Forgiveness is a decision against justice. Forgiveness gives a benefit to one who does not deserve it.

Ingratitude arises from failing to recognize the value of those who have done a service for us. Thankfulness comes from noticing the one who performed a service more than the service itself. Thankfulness comes when we truly love the one who loves us.

※

You, Lord, are kind and ready to forgive,
abundant in faithful love to all who call on You.

Psalm 86:5 HCSB

Never Again

God said to Noah, "Come out of the ark, you and your wife and your sons and their wives. Bring out every kind of living creature that is with you—the birds, the animals, and all the creatures that move along the ground—so they can multiply on the earth and be fruitful and increase in number upon it."

So Noah came out, together with his sons and his wife and his sons' wives All the animals and all the creatures that move along the ground and all the birds everything that moves on the earth—came out of the ark, one kind after another.

Then Noah built an altar to the Lord and, taking some of all the clean animals and clean birds, he sacrificed burnt offerings on it. The Lord smelled the pleasing aroma and said in his heart: "Never again will I curse the ground because of man, even though every inclination of his heart is evil from childhood. And never again will I destroy all living creatures, as I have done.

"As long as the earth endures,
seedtime and harvest,
cold and heat,
summer and winter,
day and night
will never cease."

Genesis 8:15–22 NIV

※

*A*fter God told Noah and those with him that it was safe to exit the ark, Noah's first reaction was to thank God for sparing him and protecting him. After God smelled Noah's sacrifice, he promised he would never again destroy all life. The ground would not be cursed again either.

God did not make the promise to Noah, his family, or the animals because the human race had suddenly become righteous. In fact, God pointed out that every thought of every human was always tinged with wrongness.

The Babylonian version of the Flood story describes the aftermath of the Flood differently from the Bible. When the Babylonian version of Noah made his sacrifice, the gods surrounded it "like flies." The Babylonians believed that sacrifices were how the gods were supplied with food. Having wiped out the human race, they'd gone weeks without a sacrifice, so they were starving. In contrast, after the biblical account of the Flood, God merely smelled the sacrifice of Noah. And having smelled it, he then decided not to destroy the world again.

Why did God decide not to destroy the world again after smelling the sacrifice? God knew that a sacrifice was a better solution for offenses than the destruction of the offenders, but he also knew that he would someday provide an ultimate sacrifice to solve the problem of our failings for good.

Idol Worshippers

God told Jacob, "Return to Bethel, where I appeared to you when you were running from your brother Esau. Make your home there and build an altar for me."

Jacob said to his family and to everyone else who was traveling with him:

Get rid of your foreign gods! Then make yourselves acceptable to worship God and put on clean clothes. Afterwards, we'll go to Bethel. I will build an altar there for God, who answered my prayers when I was in trouble and who has always been at my side.

So everyone gave Jacob their idols and their earrings, and he buried them under the oak tree near Shechem.

While Jacob and his family were traveling through Canaan, God terrified the people in the towns so much that no one dared bother them.

Genesis 35:1–5 CEV

*L*ove really does cover over a multitude of sins. God took care of his people even when they didn't believe the right things or do the right things. Jacob and his family left Jacob's uncle Laban. On the way back to Canaan, the night before he met his estranged brother Esau, Jacob wrestled with God. Later, he and his family settled down near Shechem, where he had purchased some land. Jacob had prospered. And yet, after all that time with his uncle Laban and after all his prosperity near Shechem, Jacob and his family remained less than fully devoted to God. His family—his wives and his children and his servants—were worshipping gods other than Yahweh, and Jacob had allowed them to do so for years. But when God told Jacob to visit Bethel and build an altar to him, Jacob got an idea. He finally decided that his family needed to get rid of their idols as part of a purification process for going to worship the God of his fathers. He had met God twenty years before at Bethel when he was fleeing from Esau. Jacob had always been grateful God had taken care of him through all the hard times in his life to that point. Apparently, though, until that moment, it hadn't occurred to him to worship God exclusively.

God was merciful to Jacob and took care of him, despite how little Jacob understood about God, how poorly he behaved, or how inadequately he had worshipped God. Despite Jacob's failings, God still had a relationship with him. God will likewise maintain a relationship with us, no matter our failings. Because of Jacob's relationship with God, his life was transformed and he became a new man, so new that God ultimately changed Jacob's name to Israel. Such change in our lives is inevitable when God intervenes.

When It Rained Bread

The whole congregation of the Israelites complained against Moses and Aaron in the wilderness. The Israelites said to them, "If only we had died by the hand of the LORD in the land of Egypt, when we sat by the fleshpots and ate our fill of bread; for you have brought us out into this wilderness to kill this whole assembly with hunger."

Then the LORD said to Moses, "I am going to rain bread from heaven for you, and each day the people shall go out and gather enough for that day. In that way I will test them, whether they will follow my instruction or not. On the sixth day, when they prepare what they bring in, it will be twice as much as they gather on other days." So Moses and Aaron said to all the Israelites, "In the evening you shall know that it was the LORD who brought you out of the land of Egypt, and in the morning you shall see the glory of the LORD, because he has heard your complaining against the LORD. For what are we, that you complain against us?" And Moses said, "When the LORD gives you meat to eat in the evening and your fill of bread in the morning, because the LORD has heard the complaining that you utter against him—what are we? Your complaining is not against us but against the LORD."

Exodus 16:2–8 NRSV

❈

*I*t's easy to have a bad attitude. After four hundred years of slavery in Egypt, after ten plagues, after passing through the Red Sea, and as soon as they felt the barest hint of hunger, the people of Israel told Moses and Aaron they wished they were back in Egypt. They were certain that the only thing left for them was a miserable death by starvation.

God didn't get mad. He simply took care of their needs; he had never intended for them to die in the wilderness by starvation. In fact, the food they worried about getting continued to show up day after day for the next forty years.

We worry so much about our circumstances that, like the Israelites, we doubt God will actually take care of us. It's easier for us to think that he intends to maximize our misery. Despite our irrational ingratitude and despite our poor attitudes, God will take care of us, just as he took care of the Israelites. God cares for us despite our ephemeral moods and emotions.

Cleanliness Next to God

The LORD spoke to Moses, saying: "You shall also make a laver of bronze, with its base also of bronze, for washing. You shall put it between the tabernacle of meeting and the altar. And you shall put water in it, for Aaron and his sons shall wash their hands and their feet in water from it. When they go into the tabernacle of meeting, or when they come near the altar to minister, to burn an offering made by fire to the LORD, they shall wash with water, lest they die. So they shall wash their hands and their feet, lest they die. And it shall be a statute forever to them—to him and his descendants throughout their generations."

Exodus 30:17–21 NKJV

God told Moses to make a basin of bronze and put it between the tent where God met with Moses and the altar where the priests would perform sacrifices so that the priests could wash their hands and feet. The ceremonial washing required of the priests before they went in to perform the sacrifices had nothing to do with personal hygiene. Instead, the purpose of the washing was entirely symbolic. They washed off the dirt from their hands and feet as they performed the sacrifices with their hands and walked in the holy places, signifying they were properly prepared to serve God. It was akin to the time when God told Moses at their first meeting by the burning bush to take off his sandals because he was on holy ground. If the priests did not wash their hands and feet before going to the altar, they would die. Why such a harsh penalty?

The priests were washing not only for themselves. They were representatives of the nation and were responsible not just for their own relationship with God but also for the relationships of all the people. If the priests, who stood as the link between God and the people, failed to perform their proper duties, they would fail to make atonement for the sins of the nation. The failure of the priests to abide by even the smallest details could lead to many deaths.

The washing was an external sign of what should have been true inwardly—a clean heart and a clean conscience. Even today, we need to make sure nothing stands in the way of our fellowship with God.

Going It Alone

The LORD spoke to Moses, "Depart, go up from here, you and the people whom you have brought up from the land of Egypt, to the land of which I swore to Abraham, Isaac, and Jacob, saying, 'To your descendants I will give it.'

"I will send an angel before you and I will drive out the Canaanite, the Amorite, the Hittite, the Perizzite, the Hivite and the Jebusite.

"Go up to a land flowing with milk and honey; for I will not go up in your midst, because you are an obstinate people, and I might destroy you on the way."

When the people heard this sad word, they went into mourning, and none of them put on his ornaments.

For the LORD had said to Moses, "Say to the sons of Israel, 'You are an obstinate people; should I go up in your midst for one moment, I would destroy you. Now therefore, put off your ornaments from you, that I may know what I shall do with you.' "

So the sons of Israel stripped themselves of their ornaments, from Mount Horeb onward.

Exodus 33:1–6 NASB

After Moses had gone to get the Ten Commandments the first time, he returned to discover that the people, with the help of Aaron his brother, had built for themselves golden calves to worship. God was angry, but he promised he'd fulfill the promises to the Israelites. He would send an angel to get rid of the troubling inhabitants of Canaan. The Canaanites were the descendants of Noah's grandson Canaan, whom he had cursed. They worshipped multiple gods and goddesses and regularly sacrificed children as burnt offerings. God was bringing the Israelites against them as a judgment for their wickedness. But with the golden calf incident, the Israelites had become guilty of many of the very things for which God needed to judge the Canaanites. God was so furious he didn't want to travel with them himself anymore. If he went with them, he might destroy them all. So God told them to mourn while he considered what he was going to do with them. God needed time alone to consider his options.

Mourning was an appropriate response to sin, because in sinning we harm ourselves—the people God loves. It made God unhappy and angry when his people hurt themselves. In mourning, we come together with God and agree with his feelings. God subsequently replaced the commandments he had given Moses and forgave the people, so he continued with them. It is wonderful to know that God will forgive us as well and continue with us.

How to Worship

The LORD called to Moses from the Tabernacle and said to him, "Give the following instructions to the people of Israel. When you present an animal as an offering to the LORD, you may take it from your herd of cattle or your flock of sheep and goats.

"If the animal you present as a burnt offering is from the herd, it must be a male with no defects. Bring it to the entrance of the Tabernacle so you may be accepted by the LORD. Lay your hand on the animal's head, and the LORD will accept its death in your place to purify you, making you right with him. Then slaughter the young bull in the LORD's presence, and Aaron's sons, the priests, will present the animal's blood by splattering it against all sides of the altar that stands at the entrance to the Tabernacle. Then skin the animal and cut it into pieces. The sons of Aaron the priest will build a wood fire on the altar. They will arrange the pieces of the offering, including the head and fat, on the wood burning on the altar. But the internal organs and the legs must first be washed with water. Then the priest will burn the entire sacrifice on the altar as a burnt offering. It is a special gift, a pleasing aroma to the LORD."

Leviticus 1:1–9 NLT

✳

*T*he book of Leviticus was an instruction manual on how to use the tabernacle for its intended purpose, the worship of God. God offered detailed instructions about how the Israelites were supposed to worship him. He explained what they could sacrifice and what they could not sacrifice. He told them when to sacrifice. He told them how the priests were to behave and how they were to dress. He told them everything they needed to know to worship him exactly the way he wanted them to.

The purpose of the sacrificial system, the purpose of all the many details, was to create a complete picture for his people. It gave them outward signs of what was supposed to be going on in their hearts. The symbols of worship were not the substance of true worship. The rituals served as symbols of the inner reality. Their worship of God was intended to reflect the relationship they had with him.

Every day we eat things that used to be alive, whether it is the meat from an animal or bread made from wheat. Something has to die in order for us to keep on living. The sacrificial system used that physical reality to portray spiritual truths. From these rituals and sacrifices, we learn more about our duty to God—reverence, submission, and commitment.

Giving God the Best Stuff

The LORD told Moses to tell Aaron and his sons and everyone else the rules for offering sacrifices. He said:

The animals that are to be completely burned on the altar must have nothing wrong with them, or else I won't accept them. Bulls or rams or goats are the animals to be used for these sacrifices. When you offer a sacrifice to ask my blessing, there must be nothing wrong with the animal. This is true, whether the sacrifice is part of a promise or something you do voluntarily. Don't offer an animal that is blind or injured or that has an infection or a skin disease. If one of your cattle or lambs has a leg that is longer or shorter than the others, you may offer it voluntarily, but not as part of a promise. As long as you live in this land, don't offer an animal with injured testicles. And don't bring me animals you bought from a foreigner. I won't accept them, because they are no better than one that has something wrong with it.

Leviticus 22:17–25 CEV

※

God does not run a thrift store. Those who give cast-off clothing and other used items to the church often do so because even though they no longer wish to use the discarded items themselves, they believe others will want to. God wanted his people to give up prized possessions when they gave him their stuff. In ancient Israel, practically everyone was a farmer. Their animals were their wealth. Imagine setting your money aflame on an altar, and you'll have a good sense of what the animal sacrifices meant to the Israelites. Giving God the lesser, broken, or damaged animals would have been a natural temptation. After all, God wasn't obviously visible or obviously there. Perhaps he was a long way off. What would it matter what sort of animal was burned on the altar? Wasn't it all symbolic anyway? But that was precisely it. What mattered to God was the intent of the individual, the depth of his sacrifice, the meaning behind the offering.

Giving the best animals, the perfect animals, the most valuable animals demonstrated a commitment to God. Why were the animals male? A single male could impregnate many females; the male represented future wealth. Farmers normally had many female animals, but only a handful of males: one bull, many cows; one ram, many sheep; one rooster, many hens. Likewise, an animal with damaged testicles could not produce offspring. Sacrificing such a beast would be no sacrifice at all.

God expects the best from us, and so our sacrifices should indeed be sacrifices.

Day 260

Until It Comes Out Your Nose

The LORD said to Moses, "Gather for me seventy of the elders of Israel, whom you know to be the elders of the people and officers over them; bring them to the tent of meeting, and have them take their place there with you. I will come down and talk with you there; and I will take some of the spirit that is on you and put it on them; and they shall bear the burden of the people along with you so that you will not bear it all by yourself. And say to the people: Consecrate yourselves for tomorrow, and you shall eat meat; for you have wailed in the hearing of the LORD, saying, 'If only we had meat to eat! Surely it was better for us in Egypt.' Therefore the LORD will give you meat, and you shall eat. You shall eat not only one day, or two days, or five days, or ten days, or twenty days, but for a whole month—until it comes out of your nostrils and becomes loathsome to you—because you have rejected the LORD who is among you, and have wailed before him, saying, 'Why did we ever leave Egypt?'"

Numbers 11:16–20 NRSV

⁂

*C*onsistency is a good thing—unless you're consistently wrong. The Israelites were consistent in how they responded to every crisis they faced: they blamed Moses, they blamed God, and they assumed the worst motives. When they faced a problem, the people of Israel believed there was no solution. They were certain that the only possible outcome was their miserable deaths.

God did not take kindly to their continuing ingratitude. He didn't like it that they always assumed his goal was to harm them. Pessimism was not the right attitude to have with God. But ever since the first two humans in the garden of Eden assumed God was holding out on them, human beings have had a hard time trusting God to take care of them. The Israelites, like all of us, became natural pessimists at the first sign of pain.

And what did God do in the face of the Israelites' bad attitude? They had blamed Moses all the time, so now seventy of the ringleaders would get the Spirit of God so they could share in Moses' burden. They were hungry for meat, so God gave them exactly what they asked for. In fact, he gave them too much of a good thing. He gave them so much of what they asked for that they would get sick of it. God will bless us more than we can imagine, and sometimes more than we want.

Drop Dead

The LORD spoke to Moses and Aaron, saying, "How long shall I bear with this evil congregation who complain against Me? I have heard the complaints which the children of Israel make against Me. Say to them, 'As I live,' says the LORD, 'just as you have spoken in My hearing, so I will do to you: The carcasses of you who have complained against Me shall fall in this wilderness, all of you who were numbered, according to your entire number, from twenty years old and above. Except for Caleb the son of Jephunneh and Joshua the son of Nun, you shall by no means enter the land which I swore I would make you dwell in. But your little ones, whom you said would be victims, I will bring in, and they shall know the land which you have despised. But as for you, your carcasses shall fall in this wilderness. And your sons shall be shepherds in the wilderness forty years, and bear the brunt of your infidelity, until your carcasses are consumed in the wilderness. According to the number of the days in which you spied out the land, forty days, for each day you shall bear your guilt one year, namely forty years, and you shall know My rejection. I the LORD have spoken this. I will surely do so to all this evil congregation who are gathered together against Me. In this wilderness they shall be consumed, and there they shall die.' "

Numbers 14:26–35 NKJV

Sometimes people just don't want to be happy. The Israelites never faced a crisis without panicking. Rather than thinking that God would take care of them as he had in all the previous crises, they assumed the worst. Rather than embracing the challenge, they rejected hope. As nice as the promised land might be, they decided it was simply impossible to get. God had surely brought them that far just to kill them.

Given that time after time they had responded with the same thought, that they were in the wilderness to die, God finally decided to grant them what so obviously was their fondest desire. They thought they were going to die? Then fine, they could die. They would stay in the wilderness until the last of their ungrateful generation had succumbed to old age. Only then would their children and their descendants after them get to enter the place God had promised to give them. God would fulfill his word—and he would fulfill their word too.

It is human to assume the worst when facing a crisis, but when we enthusiastically commit to follow God's will, he rewards our obedience.

❀❀❀❀❀❀❀❀❀❀❀❀❀❀❀❀❀❀❀❀❀❀❀❀❀❀❀❀❀❀❀

Complaint Department

The LORD spoke to Moses, saying,

"Speak to the sons of Israel, and get from them a rod for each father's household: twelve rods, from all their leaders according to their fathers' households. You shall write each name on his rod, and write Aaron's name on the rod of Levi; for there is one rod for the head of each of their fathers' households.

"You shall then deposit them in the tent of meeting in front of the testimony, where I meet with you.

"It will come about that the rod of the man whom I choose will sprout. Thus I will lessen from upon Myself the grumblings of the sons of Israel, who are grumbling against you."

Moses therefore spoke to the sons of Israel, and all their leaders gave him a rod apiece, for each leader according to their fathers' households, twelve rods, with the rod of Aaron among their rods. So Moses deposited the rods before the LORD in the tent of the testimony. Now on the next day Moses went into the tent of the testimony; and behold, the rod of Aaron for the house of Levi had sprouted and put forth buds and produced blossoms, and it bore ripe almonds.

Numbers 17:1–8 NASB

❀

 ome people just never learn. After the exodus from Egypt, after the manna, and after losing the promised land for a generation, a group of discontented people approached Moses and Aaron. Korah and about 250 men decided to challenge Moses and Aaron for leadership. In the end, God had the ground open up and swallow Korah and his followers. An additional 14,700 people died in the plague that followed.

But even after God had done all that, there were *still* those who wondered if Aaron was really the one who should be the high priest. Doubt seemed to be the default setting for the Israelites. They were always ready to follow self-appointed leaders and continuously question those appointed by God. After Aaron's staff alone had budded, clearly showing whom God had chosen to offer sacrifices, the response of the rest of the people was finally to be terrified. At long last, they wondered if God might strike them down, just as he'd killed Korah and the rest. Fear of the Lord was the beginning of wisdom.

God's will is rarely hard to discern. If God wants something done, if he has in mind who is to do it, he will make it abundantly clear. A person must be willfully obtuse to resist God. Often when we say we don't know God's will, it isn't so much that we don't know it, it's just that we don't like it.

You're Just Trying to Kill Us

There was no water for the people to drink at that place, so they rebelled against Moses and Aaron. The people blamed Moses and said, "If only we had died in the LORD's presence with our brothers! Why have you brought the congregation of the LORD's people into this wilderness to die, along with all our livestock? Why did you make us leave Egypt and bring us here to this terrible place? This land has no grain, no figs, no grapes, no pomegranates, and no water to drink!"

Moses and Aaron turned away from the people and went to the entrance of the Tabernacle, where they fell face down on the ground. Then the glorious presence of the LORD appeared to them, and the LORD said to Moses, "You and Aaron must take the staff and assemble the entire community. As the people watch, speak to the rock over there, and it will pour out its water. You will provide enough water from the rock to satisfy the whole community and their livestock."

So Moses did as he was told. He took the staff from the place where it was kept before the LORD. Then he and Aaron summoned the people to come and gather at the rock. "Listen, you rebels!" he shouted. "Must we bring you water from this rock?" Then Moses raised his hand and struck the rock twice with the staff, and water gushed out. So the entire community and their livestock drank their fill.

Numbers 20:2–11 NLT

✻

Once before, the people had found themselves short of water. And just as they had reacted to everything that had ever been the least bit hard, they accused God and Moses of seeking their ruin. Once again, they waxed nostalgic over their prosperity in Egypt—that place from which for generations they had begged God to rescue them.

God responded by satisfying their needs. Never once, when they were hungry or thirsty, did God leave them in that state. God always provided for them.

Moses, however, being human, had finally had enough. After all the crabbing and complaining, after all the negativity, he finally snapped. He let his temper get the better of him. God told Moses to speak to the rock. Instead, he yelled at the people and hit the rock. Despite his disobedience, God still brought water out of the rock, because that was what God had intended to do. God was not thwarted in fulfilling his will by the disobedience of a human being.

God will do what he wants to do for us whether we obey him or not. Problems that result from our obstinacy often stem from little faith on our part, and the solution for that can be fairly straightforward.

Contracts Have Consequences

The Lord raised up judges, who saved them from the power of their marauders, but they did not listen to their judges. Instead, they prostituted themselves with other gods, bowing down to them. They quickly turned from the way of their fathers, who had walked in obedience to the Lord's commands. They did not do as their fathers did. Whenever the Lord raised up a judge for the Israelites, the Lord was with him and saved the people from the power of their enemies while the judge was still alive. The Lord was moved to pity whenever they groaned because of those who were oppressing and afflicting them. Whenever the judge died, the Israelites would act even more corruptly than their fathers, going after other gods to worship and bow down to them. They did not turn from their [evil] practices or their obstinate ways.

The Lord's anger burned against Israel, and He declared, "Because this nation has violated My covenant that I made with their fathers and disobeyed Me, I will no longer drive out before them any of the nations Joshua left when he died. [I did this] to test Israel and to see whether they would keep the Lord's way by walking in it, as their fathers had." The Lord left these nations and did not drive them out immediately. He did not hand them over to Joshua.

Judges 2:16–23 HCSB

Joshua's conquest of the promised land was incomplete. Before he died, he told the people of Israel they needed to make a choice about whom they would worship. They responded by promising to worship Yahweh. They even ratified a treaty with God. According to that treaty, if the people were not faithful in worshipping Yahweh and treating one another with love, then God would no longer give them victory over their enemies.

When God stood before the Israelites after Joshua had died, he reminded them of the terms of their agreement with him. As the generations passed, however, they repeatedly forgot about the treaty, and so God repeatedly punished them with foreign conquerors. But whenever they repented, God raised up leaders—the judges—to rescue his people from those oppressors. As the book of Judges so sadly relates, every time they were rescued, they quickly reverted to their old behavior.

After seven hundred years of idolatry, God drove Israel into seventy years of exile. Following those seven hundred years of spiritual exile and seventy years of physical exile, the Israelites finally rejected idolatry. God's mysterious ways of working succeeded. They always do.

Trying to Get Our Attention

Every time the Israelites would plant crops, the Midianites invaded Israel together with the Amalekites and other eastern nations.

They rode in on their camels, set up their tents, and then let their livestock eat the crops as far as the town of Gaza. The Midianites stole food, sheep, cattle, and donkeys. Like a swarm of locusts, they could not be counted, and they ruined the land wherever they went.

The Midianites took almost everything that belonged to the Israelites, and the Israelites begged the LORD for help.

Then the LORD sent a prophet to them with this message:

I am the LORD God of Israel, so listen to what I say. You were slaves in Egypt, but I set you free and led you out of Egypt into this land. And when nations here made life miserable for you, I rescued you and helped you get rid of them and take their land.

I am your God, and I told you not to worship Amorite gods, even though you are living in the land of the Amorites. But you refused to listen.

Judges 6:3–10 CEV

❁

*G*od didn't just punish his people for breaking the terms of the agreement he had with them. He also lectured them, by means of the prophets. When they cried out to him because of the Midianite raiders—the same people who had taken Joseph into slavery into Egypt—God didn't immediately stop the raiders from taking their stuff. Instead, he talked to them about what they were doing. He reminded them of where they had come from, how he had taken care of them, and what he expected from them. Nothing very complicated. It was good that they finally decided to talk to him again after abandoning him for the other gods. But they needed to be reminded why they found themselves in the circumstances they were in, and what they needed to do to get out of them and to keep the same thing from happening again.

After his lecture, God raised up Gideon to deliver his people. Unfortunately, the people would soon revert to their old ways. But for a time—all the years that Gideon would live—the people would be faithful to God.

God is not one to bring judgment against people quickly. He knows how weak we are, and he gives us a long time to repent before he begins overt attempts to get our attention. When his people first cried to God for help, they recognized only their pain, not its cause. God's words from the prophet explained the reason for their pain. We can thank God for his words. They are the key to knowing what he wants and why.

God Sees Through Disguises

When she came, she pretended to be another woman. But when Ahijah heard the sound of her feet, as she came in at the door, he said, "Come in, wife of Jeroboam; why do you pretend to be another? For I am charged with heavy tidings for you. Go, tell Jeroboam, 'Thus says the Lord, the God of Israel: Because I exalted you from among the people, made you leader over my people Israel, and tore the kingdom away from the house of David to give it to you; yet you have not been like my servant David, who kept my commandments and followed me with all his heart, doing only that which was right in my sight, but you have done evil above all those who were before you and have gone and made for yourself other gods, and cast images, provoking me to anger, and have thrust me behind your back; therefore, I will bring evil upon the house of Jeroboam. I will cut off from Jeroboam every male, both bond and free in Israel, and will consume the house of Jeroboam, just as one burns up dung until it is all gone. Anyone belonging to Jeroboam who dies in the city, the dogs shall eat; and anyone who dies in the open country, the birds of the air shall eat; for the Lord has spoken.'"

1 Kings 14:5–11 NRSV

❋

*Y*ou can fool some of the people some of the time, but you can never fool God. The prophet Ahijah was old and blind. Years before, he had told Jeroboam that he would become king over the ten tribes of the north. But rather than following God, Jeroboam had made the Israelites worship two calf idols instead of Yahweh.

When Jeroboam's son became ill, he sent his wife to Ahijah to find out what would become of his son. Although she disguised herself, she couldn't hide the truth from Ahijah, given that he was a genuine prophet. So Ahijah gave her the bad news from God: not only would Jeroboam's sick son not survive, neither would any of Jeroboam's family. Two years into the reign of his surviving son Nadab, a leader from the tribe of Issachar named Baasha rebelled. Baasha killed Nadab, became king in his place, and then murdered Jeroboam's entire remaining family.

God later judged Baasha for having killed Jeroboam's family (1 Kings 16:7). Even though Jeroboam was evil, that did not make murdering him the right thing for Baasha to do just because God had predicted what would happen. Two wrongs never make a right. Justice isn't served by means of wrong actions, no matter how good the outcome.

Don't Know What You're Talking About

The LORD said to Job,
  "Will the faultfinder contend with
    the Almighty?
      Let him who reproves God
        answer it."
Then Job answered the LORD and said,
  "Behold, I am insignificant; what
    can I reply to You?
      I lay my hand on my mouth.
  "Once I have spoken, and I will
    not answer;
      Even twice, and I will add
        nothing more."
Then the LORD answered Job out of the
  storm and said,
  "Now gird up your loins like
    a man;
      I will ask you, and you in-
        struct Me.
  "Will you really annul My
    judgment?
      Will you condemn Me that
        you may be justified?

"Or do you have an arm like God,
    And can you thunder with a
      voice like His?
"Adorn yourself with eminence
    and dignity,
      And clothe yourself with
        honor and majesty.
"Pour out the overflowings of
    your anger,
      And look on everyone who is
        proud, and make him low.
"Look on everyone who is proud,
    and humble him,
      And tread down the wicked
        where they stand.
"Hide them in the dust together;
    Bind them in the
      hidden place.
"Then I will also confess to you,
    That your own right hand can
      save you."

Job 40:1–14 NASB

※

*I*gnorance isn't bliss. Job's problem was limited understanding. At the time that Job lived, the Bible consisted of only the books of Moses and Joshua.

Job and his friends still thought they knew what was going on. Job's friends were convinced he was guilty of a major sin, while Job was certain that God's attack on him was without cause. In fact, God himself said that his suffering was without cause, but only in the sense that he wasn't being punished for misbehavior. The explanation for Job's trials was Satan's belief that people served God only as a means to an end. Satan and Job's friends believed good behavior purchased God's blessing. God's purpose in what happened to Job was to demonstrate that Satan's position was mistaken. In fact, a human being could remain faithful to God even if he wasn't getting anything out of it.

God told Job that knowing his own limitations should have been enough to keep him from complaining about what had happened. We're wise if we, like Job, learn to be quiet rather than being quick to make snap judgments.

God Doesn't Need Your Stuff

O my people, listen as I speak.
    Here are my charges against you,
      O Israel:
    I am God, your God!
I have no complaint about your
    sacrifices or the burnt offerings you
    constantly offer.
But I do not need the bulls from
    your barns
      or the goats from your pens.
For all the animals of the forest
    are mine, and I own the cattle on a
    thousand hills.
I know every bird on the mountains,
    and all the animals of the field
      are mine.

If I were hungry, I would not tell you,
    for all the world is mine and
      everything in it.
Do I eat the meat of bulls?
    Do I drink the blood of goats?
Make thankfulness your sacrifice
    to God, and keep the vows you
    made to the Most High.
Then call on me when you are
    in trouble, and I will rescue you,
    and you will give me glory.

Psalm 50:7–15 NLT

God doesn't need us to take care of him. He is not a king dependent upon his subjects to pay their taxes. Nor is he like the gods of the other nations around Israel. The idolaters of the surrounding countries believed that their gods would starve if they stopped bringing them offerings. They thought the gods might grow restless if they were not praised. They believed they might become angry if they didn't get everything they needed to be comfortable.

But the God of Israel, Yahweh, was not like those gods—the gods that the Israelites kept worshipping. God had certainly told the people to offer sacrifices, and he didn't want them to stop. But he did want them to do it with understanding. They were not feeding God. God was not like some king who needed to be bribed or flattered. They had missed the whole point of worshipping God. Sacrifice was intended to reflect the relationship between God and the worshipper. What was important for the Israelites was not to perform rituals, but instead to live an upright life. It was important for them to love God and to love their brothers and sisters. True worship was not in the spilled blood of slaughtered animals, but in helping the poor and downtrodden and in giving thanks to God (Micah 6:6–8). It is all too easy to be caught up in the rituals and to forget what they're really all about.

God Will Fill Your Mouth

He established it as a statute for Joseph
  when he went out against Egypt,
    where we heard a language we did
    not understand.
He says, "I removed the burden from
  their shoulders;
    their hands were set free from
    the basket.
In your distress you called and I rescued you, I answered you out of a
thundercloud;
    I tested you at the waters
    of Meribah.
  Selah

"Hear, O my people, and I will warn
  you—
    if you would but listen to me,
    O Israel!
You shall have no foreign god
  among you;
    you shall not bow down to an
    alien god.
I am the LORD your God,
  who brought you up out of Egypt.
  Open wide your mouth and I will
  fill it."

Psalm 81:5–10 NIV

It's hard not to become cynical. Shortly after the Israelites had received manna from God, they ran short of water. Moses struck the rock of Horeb, and water came out to supply the needs of the people of Israel. The place was ever after called Massah and Meribah. *Massah* meant "testing," and *Meribah* meant "quarreling." The names signified the complaining and doubt of the Israelites. *Joseph* was used as a synonym for "Israel."

God reminded them how he had taken care of them in the past, how he had gone out against Egypt when he brought the plagues against them. He reminded them how there was nothing in their behavior that would motivate someone to take care of them. But when they had asked for his help, he had given it to them. In response, all he expected was ordinary gratitude. He asked only that they would listen to him and that they wouldn't worship any other gods.

The author of this psalm is Asaph. But was it the Asaph whom David picked to oversee music used in worship, or was it the Asaph who served as a recorder in the time of Hezekiah? Or was it some other Asaph for whom we have no record? There's no way of knowing. But what God expressed as his primary concern in the words of this psalm was his concern in the time of David as much as it was his concern in the time of Hezekiah. It was what all the prophets kept repeating. God wanted his people to worship him rather than to worship false, nonexistent deities that couldn't help them and never had. God's reliability and power, by contrast, were obvious. God had earned the trust of his people.

Forget the Vacation

The LORD is our God,
and we are his people,
the sheep he takes care of
in his own pasture.
Listen to God's voice today!
Don't be stubborn and rebel
as your ancestors did
at Meribah and Massah
out in the desert.
For forty years
they tested God and saw
the things he did.

Then God got tired of them
and said,
"You never show good sense,
and you don't understand
what I want you to do."
In his anger, God told them,
"You people will never enter
my place of rest."

Psalm 95:7–11 CEV

*G*od is eternal, but his patience is not. God ultimately disciplined his people. Time after time he had been there for them. God, through the words of this psalm, reminded the Jewish people how he had taken them out of Egypt, how he had seen to their every need, how he had satisfied their every complaint, and yet nothing was ever enough for them. On their long journey through the wilderness, it was the place where Moses had struck a rock in order to provide water. It was just one of many times they would question God's goodness. Finally, when he brought them at last to the promised land, they turned up their noses and told him no. They didn't believe they would be able to take the land. Instead, they believed God had merely brought them there in order to destroy them. They believed it would be better simply to return to Egypt (Numbers 14:1–4).

The ingratitude of his people, leading them to refuse God's gift, led God to postpone the gift. Instead of giving it to the people he had rescued from slavery, he would wait one generation. He would give it to their children instead. They repeatedly wished they could be back in Egypt, as if being a slave was such a good thing. Since they didn't really want to be rescued, he gave them what they kept saying they wanted.

Rather than rejoicing in the gift God had given them, they found only fault. Rather than trusting that God was good, they suspected he had something bad in mind for them. We can learn from this and be confident of God's goodness even in the midst of hard times.

In the Deep End

The LORD also spoke to me
  again, saying:
    "Inasmuch as these
      people refused
    The waters of Shiloah that
      flow softly,
    And rejoice in Rezin and in
      Remaliah's son;
    Now therefore, behold, the Lord
      brings up over them
    The waters of the River, strong
      and mighty—

The king of Assyria and all
    his glory;
He will go up over all his channels
And go over all his banks.
He will pass through Judah,
He will overflow and pass over,
He will reach up to the neck;
And the stretching out of
    his wings
Will fill the breadth of Your land,
    O Immanuel."

Isaiah 8:5–8 NKJV

Rezin was the king of Damascus who had been paying tribute to the king of Assyria for years. Tired of paying the annual fees, he finally organized a rebellion against Assyria. But the Assyrians crushed it and executed him. Remaliah was the father of Pekah, an official of Pekahiah, the king of the Northern Kingdom of Israel. Remaliah's son Pekah assassinated Pekahiah and became king in his place. Then he joined Rezin's ill-fated rebellion against Assyria. Later, Hoshea murdered Pekah and became king in his place, only to rebel in turn a few years later. Assyria then destroyed the Northern Kingdom of Israel just as it had destroyed Rezin's Damascus. About twenty-five thousand Israelites were then taken away as captives to Assyria. The kingdom of Israel, established by the rebellion of Jeroboam against Solomon's son Rehoboam, came to an end. Shiloah, also called Siloam, was a reservoir within Jerusalem fed from the spring of Gihon. The water of this reservoir was the city's principal source of water. King Hezekiah of Judah had built a tunnel connecting the spring with that reservoir.

God criticized the people of Israel for putting their faith in those rulers rather than putting their faith in God. God used Shiloah's waters metaphorically. The northern tribes had rejected Jerusalem. They had rejected Jerusalem's king, a descendant of David, and they had rejected Jerusalem's God, worshipping instead the calf idols that Jeroboam, Israel's first king, had established. In rejecting the peace that God could have brought them, the people of Israel instead embraced the destruction from Assyria.

We too easily cast away God's truth in exchange for the world's lies. Only in the end do we realize how empty those lies inevitably are.

Lip Service

The Lord said,
 "Because this people draw near
  with their words
 And honor Me with their
  lip service,
 But they remove their hearts far
  from Me,
 And their reverence for Me consists of tradition learned by rote,
 Therefore behold, I will once
  again deal marvelously with this
  people, wondrously marvelous;
 And the wisdom of their wise men
  will perish,
 And the discernment of their dis-
  cerning men will be concealed."

Woe to those who deeply hide their
 plans from the LORD,
  And whose deeds are done in a
   dark place,
  And they say, "Who sees us?" or
   "Who knows us?"
 You turn things around!
  Shall the potter be considered as
   equal with the clay,
  That what is made would say to its
   maker, "He did not make me";
  Or what is formed say to him who
   formed it, "He has no under-
   standing"?

Isaiah 29:13–16 NASB

In the ancient world of which Israel was a part, the worship of gods consisted of ceremonies and rituals. In order to get the gods to perform as they
wanted, the people believed that all they was needed were the right words,
said just the right way, accompanied by just the right sacrifices, incense, and
music. If everything was done just right by the priests, then the gods would be
mollified and would answer them favorably.

But Israel's God was not like that. He was not a force of nature to be manipulated as a man might manipulate an ax. In fact, God told the Israelites that he
didn't really care much about what they said. What mattered was what they did,
how they lived. It is easy to focus on the forms, ceremonies, and rituals. Like
lawyers, we become concerned that we say just the right words in just the right
order. We want our words to be exactly what has always been said so no one
is disturbed and no one can misunderstand. But words easily become empty.
They can be reduced to mere superstition, as if the right words are a substitute
for a right heart.

God is concerned with how we treat other people and how we are when no
one sees us but him. God cannot be manipulated with words any more than he
can be carved from wood.

Was It Really So Hard?

Yet you have not called upon me,
O Jacob, you have not wearied yourselves for me, O Israel.
You have not brought me sheep for
burnt offerings, nor honored me
with your sacrifices.
I have not burdened you with
grain offerings nor wearied you
with demands for incense.
You have not bought any fragrant
calamus for me, or lavished on me
the fat of your sacrifices.
But you have burdened me with
your sins and wearied me with
your offenses.

I, even I, am he who blots out your
transgressions, for my own sake, and
remembers your sins no more.
Review the past for me, let us argue
the matter together; state the case for
your innocence.
Your first father sinned; your
spokesmen rebelled against me.
So I will disgrace the dignitaries of
your temple, and I will consign
Jacob to destruction and Israel to
scorn.

Isaiah 43:22–28 NIV

*I*srael had ignored God, and they had worshipped other gods instead. There were no real sacrifices being offered to Yahweh. What they claimed as sacrifices were meaningless because their hearts were not in it.

When God spoke to the Israelites through the prophet Isaiah, he spoke in poetry, but not by rhyming sounds. The nature of the Hebrew language makes the rhyming of sounds too easy. Hebrew poetry rhymes by using synonymous concepts, repeating the same thought in parallel lines. Thus, *Jacob* is synonymous with *Israel*, *sin* with *offense*, and *burnt offering* with *sacrifices*.

From the beginning of God's relationship with the Jewish people, they had sinned by worshipping idols. Jacob's family had been idolatrous, and idols had been a part of the royal family of Israel from its inception. God had forgiven them nevertheless.

Because we like to be in control, we like to believe that our behavior determines whether we have a relationship with God. It doesn't. God has forgiven us and made us his people. In fact, it is because we are his people now that he disciplines us, just as he disciplined the ancient Israelites.

Disconnected from the Truth

People of Israel,
     you come from Jacob's family
     and the tribe of Judah.
You claim to worship me,
     the Lord God of Israel,
     but you are lying.
You call Jerusalem your home
     and say you depend on me,
     the Lord All-Powerful,
     the God of Israel.
Long ago I announced
     what was going to be,
then without warning,
     I made it happen.
I knew you were stubborn
     and hardheaded.
And I told you these things,
     so that when they happened
you would not say,
     "The idols we worship did this."

Isaiah 48:1–5 CEV

*I*f God did not speak, there would be no certainty regarding God's actions. When God performed his great miracles, rescuing Israel from Egypt, bringing them manna, conquering the promised land, or, finally, bringing judgment on his people and taking them away to captivity in Mesopotamia, the events alone were not enough to explain what was going on. If God had remained silent, if he had not given his words to his prophets, then his people would have been able to explain away everything that happened.

When God spoke to the Israelites, he always spoke to them through messengers. Isaiah was one in a long line of such spokespeople for God. Why did God take the approach of using intermediaries? Perhaps because in the time of Moses, the people had begged God not to talk to them aloud for fear that they might die (Exodus 20:18–19). But the indirect route that he used after that was no less clear than if he had knocked on each Israelite's door and chatted with him one-on-one. And it was no less personal.

God's prophets were like the gift card on a bunch of roses received by an unfaithful wife. She wanted to believe it was her lover who had been so thoughtful. But when she opened the card, she saw they had come from her husband.

Because God spoke, the people were not able to argue that some other gods were responsible. When their crops came in and they had plenty, they had to turn away from God's words if they wanted to ascribe their blessings to their idols.

We can be thankful that God is not silent. The Bible is a witness. We can read it to understand what God has done and is doing.

God Is Not Impressed

"We have fasted before you!" they say.
"Why aren't you impressed?
We have been very hard on ourselves,
and you don't even notice it!"
"I will tell you why!" I respond.
"It's because you are fasting to please
yourselves.
Even while you fast, you keep
oppressing your workers.
What good is fasting when you keep
on fighting and quarreling?
This kind of fasting will never get you
anywhere with me.
You humble yourselves by going
through the motions of penance,
bowing your heads like reeds
bending in the wind.
You dress in burlap and cover
yourselves with ashes.
Is this what you call fasting?
Do you really think this will
please the LORD?

No, this is the kind of fasting I want:
Free those who are wrongly
imprisoned; lighten the burden of
those who work for you.
Let the oppressed go free, and remove
the chains that bind people.
Share your food with the hungry,
and give shelter to the homeless.
Give clothes to those who need them,
and do not hide from relatives
who need your help.
Then your salvation will come like the
dawn, and your wounds will
quickly heal.
Your godliness will lead you forward,
and the glory of the LORD will protect you from behind."

Isaiah 58:3–8 NLT

❀

*I*t is human nature to imagine that depriving ourselves makes us better people. Office workers often one-up one another describing how hard they work, how many hours of sleep they miss, and how many weekends they spend in the office—as if those things prove that useful labor actually happened.

God was not impressed by his people wearing uncomfortable clothing or going without food, because all that did was build their egos. They could pat themselves on the back for their suffering, for how good they must be for what they had given up, for how much God must owe them. But God really cared only about how people treated one another, not what they imagined consti-tuted piety.

How many, if any, religious bumper stickers are on our cars or how expen-sive our Bibles might be doesn't matter. God doesn't care about the trappings of piety. He cares about our generous and charitable acts when we reach out to help others.

So What?

"Nevertheless, I will bring health and healing to it; I will heal my people and will let them enjoy abundant peace and security. I will bring Judah and Israel back from captivity and will rebuild them as they were before. I will cleanse them from all the sin they have committed against me and will forgive all their sins of rebellion against me. Then this city will bring me renown, joy, praise and honor before all nations on earth that hear of all the good things I do for it; and they will be in awe and will tremble at the abundant prosperity and peace I provide for it."

This is what the LORD says: "You say about this place, 'It is a desolate waste, without men or animals.' Yet in the towns of Judah and the streets of Jerusalem that are deserted, inhabited by neither men nor animals, there will be heard once more the sounds of joy and gladness, the voices of bride and bridegroom, and the voices of those who bring thank offerings to the house of the LORD, saying,

'Give thanks to the LORD Almighty,
for the LORD is good;
his love endures forever.'
For I will restore the fortunes of the
    land as they were before," says
    the LORD.

Jeremiah 33:6–11 NIV

The prophet Jeremiah hoped his people could understand the heart of God so they could understand what he was doing to them. Jeremiah warned Israel of the impending Babylonian invasion and captivity, the inevitable punishment for their disobedience. But God also gave them comfort. His punishment was designed to correct, not destroy. And the correction would achieve its goal of changing the hearts of God's people so they could one day be restored to their place. The torn-down cities of Israel would be rebuilt, and the land and people would once again prosper. Life would become normal once again, with the sounds of happy voices filling the streets and worshippers filling the rebuilt house of God in Jerusalem. No discipline seemed fun at the time it happened. Only afterward could anyone recognize its purpose. Only afterward could they see that the punishment was actually a gift. The Israelites would mourn until the suffering inflicted by Babylon ended.

When God restored the Israelites to their land, their joy came from the fact that they could finally see that God still loved them and that they were, indeed, still his people. Afterward, they could recognize the value of what God had given them by taking so much away. Some gifts won't be recognizable as gifts when we first receive them—but over time, we at last discern their worth.

Payback Time

What are you to me, O Tyre and Sidon, and all the regions of Philistia? Are you paying me back for something? If you are paying me back, I will turn your deeds back upon your own heads swiftly and speedily. For you have taken my silver and my gold, and have carried my rich treasures into your temples. You have sold the people of Judah and Jerusalem to the Greeks, removing them far from their own border. But now I will rouse them to leave the places to which you have sold them, and I will turn your deeds back upon your own heads. I will sell your sons and your daughters into the hand of the people of Judah, and they will sell them to the Sabeans, to a nation far away; for the LORD has spoken.

Proclaim this among the nations:

Prepare war, stir up the warriors.
Let all the soldiers draw near, let them
    come up.
Beat your plowshares into swords,
    and your pruning hooks
        into spears;
    let the weakling say, "I am
        a warrior."
Come quickly,
    all you nations all around,
    gather yourselves there.
Bring down your warriors, O LORD.
Let the nations rouse themselves,
    and come up to the valley of
        Jehoshaphat;
for there I will sit to judge
    all the neighboring nations.

Joel 3:4–12 NRSV

The call to arms preceded the call to peace. When Isaiah spoke of beating swords into plowshares and spears into pruning hooks, he was taking a common phrase and twisting it in a new way. Ordinarily, the farmers had to take their tools of life and turn them into instruments of death when enemies came.

God told Israel's neighbors who had profited from the destruction and captivity of his people that they would be paid back in kind. Just as the Jewish people had been sold to the Greeks in the northwest, so the people of Tyre and Sidon would be sold to the Sabeans living in the southeast, on the edge of the Arabian peninsula—as far from their homeland as they had sent the Israelites.

Jehoshaphat was a king of Judah who had faced an overwhelming Assyrian army. God had destroyed that army without Jehoshaphat having to fight. Tyre and Sidon's fate would be the same as the Assyrians of Jehoshaphat's day. Those assembled against them would only have to bend over to pick up the spoils.

God has ways of solving problems that are beyond us. The exciting thing about an insurmountable problem is seeing what God will do about it when we turn our eyes to him.

Sold for a Pair of Sandals

Because of the three great sins of Israel
    —make that four—I'm not putting
    up with them any longer.
They buy and sell upstanding people.
    People for them are only *things*—
    ways of making money.
They'd sell a poor man for a pair
    of shoes.
      They'd sell their own
      grandmother!
They grind the penniless into the dirt,
    shove the luckless into the ditch.
Everyone and his brother sleeps with
    the "sacred whore"—
    a sacrilege against my Holy Name.
Stuff they've extorted from the poor
    is piled up at the shrine of
    their god,
While they sit around drinking wine
    they've conned from their victims.
In contrast, I was always on your side.
    I destroyed the Amorites who
    confronted you,

Amorites with the stature of
    great cedars, tough as thick oaks.
I destroyed them from the top
    branches down.
      I destroyed them from the
      roots up.
And yes, I'm the One who delivered
    you from Egypt, led you safely
    through the wilderness for
    forty years
And then handed you the country of
    the Amorites like a piece of cake on
    a platter.
I raised up some of your young men
    to be prophets, set aside your best
    youth for training in holiness.
Isn't this so, Israel?

Amos 2:6–11 MSG

Hebrew poetry is created by rhyming ideas rather than sounds—that is, by writing parallel lines that use synonyms. Numbers, however, lack synonyms, and so the convention for poets when they chose to use numbers was to give two sequential numbers—as here three, then four. The poet intended all along to list four things, of course. So what four sins was Israel guilty of?

Judges took bribes to punish people for crimes they hadn't committed. They oppressed the poor and the suffering. They profaned the name of God when both a man and his father used the same prostitute. And finally, they got drunk in the temple from the wine they had taken unjustly.

God took this bad behavior as ingratitude.

The consequence, of course, would be God's discipline. God intended to help them learn to be thankful, to help them learn to be loving to one another and to him. We live our faith when we reach beyond ourselves and use our resources and talents to help those in need.

Merciful Judgment

The LORD said to Cain:

What's wrong with you? Why do you have such an angry look on your face? If you had done the right thing, you would be smiling. But you did the wrong thing, and now sin is waiting to attack you like a lion. Sin wants to destroy you, but don't let it! Cain said to his brother Abel, "Let's go for a walk." And when they were out in a field, Cain killed him. Afterwards the LORD asked Cain, "Where is Abel?"

"How should I know?" he answered. "Am I supposed to look after my brother?"

Then the LORD said:

Why have you done this terrible thing? You killed your own brother, and his blood flowed onto the ground. Now his blood is calling out for me to punish you. And so, I'll put you under a curse. Because you killed Abel and made his blood run out on the ground, you will never be able to farm the land again. If you try to farm the land, it won't produce anything for you. From now on, you'll be without a home, and you'll spend the rest of your life wandering from place to place.

"This punishment is too hard!" Cain said. "You're making me leave my home and live far from you. I will have to wander about without a home, and just anyone could kill me." "No!" the LORD answered. "Anyone who kills you will be punished seven times worse than I am punishing you." So the LORD put a mark on Cain to warn everyone not to kill him. But Cain had to go far from the LORD and live in the Land of Wandering, which is east of Eden.

Genesis 4:6–16 CEV

Eye for eye, tooth for tooth. Cain murdered his brother and deserved to die. All the ancient law codes, from Egypt to Mesopotamia, included death as the sole penalty for murder. After the great Flood, God ordered capital punishment for murder. The death penalty was part of the law of Moses. But some murderers were forgiven: Moses, David, and Cain.

God had rejected Cain's offering, but he accepted his brother's. Why? God didn't reject it because of the offering that Cain brought to God; he rejected it because of the heart Cain had brought to God. God warned Cain about his anger. Rather than repenting, Cain gave in to it and murdered his sibling.

God did not order Cain's execution. Cain's punishment was exile from his people and from his chosen profession as a farmer. But God protected Cain from human vengeance. Rather than allowing justice—eye for eye—God granted Cain mercy. God loves the unlovely and offers hope to the unworthy.

Stop or Else!

Abraham journeyed from there to the South, and dwelt between Kadesh and Shur, and stayed in Gerar. Now Abraham said of Sarah his wife, "She is my sister." And Abimelech king of Gerar sent and took Sarah.

But God came to Abimelech in a dream by night, and said to him, "Indeed you are a dead man because of the woman whom you have taken, for she is a man's wife."

But Abimelech had not come near her; and he said, "Lord, will You slay a righteous nation also? Did he not say to me, 'She is my sister'? And she, even she herself said, 'He is my brother.' In the integrity of my heart and innocence of my hands I have done this."

And God said to him in a dream, "Yes, I know that you did this in the integrity of your heart. For I also withheld you from sinning against Me; therefore I did not let you touch her. Now therefore, restore the man's wife; for he is a prophet, and he will pray for you and you shall live. But if you do not restore her, know that you shall surely die, you and all who are yours."

So Abimelech rose early in the morning, called all his servants, and told all these things in their hearing; and the men were very much afraid.

Genesis 20:1–8 NKJV

✳

*S*ometimes God protects his people even when they don't deserve it. Abraham lied to Abimelech. Oh, sure, Sarah was his half sister, but what mattered in their relationship was the fact that Sarah was his wife. But Abraham was afraid. He imagined the worst of Abimelech and the other people of his land. He assumed they were so wicked they would kill him and steal his beautiful wife.

Despite Abraham's lies, however, God protected Abimelech from doing something that Abimelech had never intended to do. Abimelech didn't want to take another man's wife, and he was appalled by Abraham's actions. But God showed Abraham mercy. God protected Sarah despite Abraham's poor choices. And he protected Abraham. Abimelech didn't kill Abraham or even curse him. Instead, Abimelech paid him a thousand shekels of silver—about twenty-five pounds worth—and gave him cattle, sheep, and slaves. Abraham lied, put a king and his people in jeopardy from God, and put his wife into the arms of another man—and wound up richer because of it.

Abraham was spared from what he deserved and got instead what he didn't deserve. Abimelech was spared as well. The story of Abraham and Abimelech is an odd illustration of mercy and grace. God really does work in mysterious ways.

But She Doesn't Deserve It!

The Lord said to Moses, "Go down, because your people, whom you brought up out of Egypt, have become corrupt. They have been quick to turn away from what I commanded them and have made themselves an idol cast in the shape of a calf. They have bowed down to it and sacrificed to it and have said, 'These are your gods, O Israel, who brought you up out of Egypt.'

"I have seen these people," the Lord said to Moses, "and they are a stiff-necked people. Now leave me alone so that my anger may burn against them and that I may destroy them. Then I will make you into a great nation."

But Moses sought the favor of the Lord his God. "O Lord," he said, "why should your anger burn against your people, whom you brought out of Egypt with great power and a mighty hand? Why should the Egyptians say, 'It was with evil intent that he brought them out, to kill them in the mountains and to wipe them off the face of the earth'? Turn from your fierce anger; relent and do not bring disaster on your people. Remember your servants Abraham, Isaac and Israel, to whom you swore by your own self: 'I will make your descendants as numerous as the stars in the sky and I will give your descendants all this land I promised them, and it will be their inheritance forever.'" Then the Lord relented and did not bring on his people the disaster he had threatened.

Exodus 32:7–14 NIV

❀

*L*ove covers a multitude of sins. Moses left the Israelites in his brother Aaron's hands when he went to get God's Ten Commandments on a mountain. He was gone a long time. The people grew restless, and so Aaron helped them build idols to worship in place of God. He even told them the idols represented the gods that had rescued them from Egypt. Then they had a wild party.

God was furious. He felt the same pain, the same anger that a spouse feels when the other spouse has an affair. In fact, later prophets would use adultery as a picture of idolatry. God's first response was to dump the Israelites and replace them with Moses. It's hard to forgive because forgiving means you have to give up on getting justice.

Moses didn't dispute that the people of Israel deserved punishment, but he begged God to forgive them. He reminded God how important the Israelites were to him. He pointed out that the Egyptians would misinterpret God's justice for malevolent intent, and so God forgave the Israelites. The relationship meant more to God than getting even. When we're willing to change, God is willing to forgive.

It's All About Attitude

If you are poor and cannot afford to bring an animal, you may bring two doves or two pigeons. One of these will be a sacrifice to ask my forgiveness, and the other will be a sacrifice to please me.

Give both birds to the priest, who will offer one as a sacrifice to ask my forgiveness. He will wring its neck without tearing off its head, splatter some of its blood on one side of the bronze altar, and drain out the rest at the foot of the altar. Then he will follow the proper rules for offering the other bird as a sacrifice to please me.

You will be forgiven when the priest offers these sacrifices as the price for your sin.

If you are so poor that you cannot afford doves or pigeons, you may bring two pounds of your finest flour. This is a sacrifice to ask my forgiveness, so don't sprinkle olive oil or sweet-smelling incense on it. Give the flour to a priest, who will scoop up a handful and send it up in smoke together with the other offerings. This is a reminder that all of the flour belongs to me. By offering this sacrifice, the priest pays the price for any of these sins you may have committed. The priest gets the rest of the flour, just as he does with grain sacrifices.

Leviticus 5:7–13 CEV

✺

*G*od did not want money to stand in the way of people coming to him. The poor were not to be excluded from forgiveness just because they were poor.

Sacrifices of animals in an agrarian society were sacrifices of wealth and were the equivalent of taking money out of the bank and setting it on fire. Sacrifice was not an easy thing for anyone to do, and God understood how hard it was. Therefore, how much a person sacrificed depended upon how much they could afford. The rich offered the most—large animals. The further down the economic scale, the smaller and less valuable the offerings became. At the lowest level, just a little flour would suffice. The poorest of the poor could still manage a handful of flour because God had made a law that fields could not be harvested completely. Enough grain had to be left for the poor to glean (Leviticus 23:22).

Attitude, not blood, was the key to a good sacrifice. For a person to stay alive, something had to die, whether it was the animal that provided the steak dinner or the wheat plant whose seeds were ground up to make bread. In either case, the picture of the sacrifice was preserved. Death gave life.

Two Angers

Balaam replied to the servants of Balak, "Although Balak were to give me his house full of silver and gold, I could not go beyond the command of the LORD my God, to do less or more. You remain here, as the others did, so that I may learn what more the LORD may say to me." That night God came to Balaam and said to him, "If the men have come to summon you, get up and go with them; but do only what I tell you to do." So Balaam got up in the morning, saddled his donkey, and went with the officials of Moab.

God's anger was kindled because he was going, and the angel of the LORD took his stand in the road as his adversary. Now he was riding on the donkey, and his two servants were with him. The donkey saw the angel of the LORD standing in the road, with a drawn sword in his hand; so the donkey turned off the road, and went into the field; and Balaam struck the donkey, to turn it back onto the road. Then the angel of the LORD stood in a narrow path between the vineyards, with a wall on either side. When the donkey saw the angel of the LORD, it scraped against the wall, and scraped Balaam's foot against the wall; so he struck it again.

Numbers 22:18–25 NRSV

Just because God lets you do it doesn't mean you should. God told Balaam not to do what Balak, king of the Moabites, had asked. But like a child who continues pleading with his parent long after the parent has said no, so Balaam, because money was being dangled before him, kept begging God.

Angry that Balaam insisted on going, God sent an angel to block his path. Balaam's donkey saw the angel and tried to avoid him. Balaam reacted by beating his donkey, but the donkey refused to go anywhere he wasn't supposed to go.

In contrast, Balaam insisted on going his own way, regardless. He pronounced a blessing rather than a curse upon Israel, but he figured out a way—or so he thought—to get around God's constraint. He told Balak to send women to seduce the Israelites into idolatry. Balaam might not be able to curse the Israelites, but he thought he could get God to curse them. That way, Balak would still pay him. But it didn't work out the way he and Balak hoped. Instead, it cost both of them their lives (Joshua 13:22). Going against God will always end badly, but doing things God's way will lead you to genuine satisfaction and joy.

A Kingdom Divided

The Lord was angry with Solomon because his heart was turned away from the Lord, the God of Israel, who had appeared to him twice, and had commanded him concerning this thing, that he should not go after other gods; but he did not observe what the Lord had commanded.

So the Lord said to Solomon, "Because you have done this, and you have not kept My covenant and My statutes, which I have commanded you, I will surely tear the kingdom from you, and will give it to your servant.

"Nevertheless I will not do it in your days for the sake of your father David, but I will tear it out of the hand of your son.

"However, I will not tear away all the kingdom, but I will give one tribe to your son for the sake of My servant David and for the sake of Jerusalem which I have chosen."

1 Kings 11:9–13 NASB

*E*ven smart people can do stupid things. Solomon was an idolater. He had built temples to the gods of his wives and offered sacrifices to them. And yet Solomon had known God, had worshipped God, and had been given the gift of wisdom by God. He was noted as the wisest man who ever lived.

In his covenant with Israel, God explained all the things a king must do and all the things he must not do (Deuteronomy 17:14–20). Solomon ignored it all. He married many wives, and just as God predicted, they encouraged him to worship other gods. He amassed great wealth, which also turned him away from his commitment to God. He went to Egypt to get horses, despite God's prohibition. He even married one of Pharaoh's daughters. As Solomon grew old, he became increasingly despondent. He lost sight of God's will for his life and turned into an idolater.

Despite his relationship with God, despite his wisdom, Solomon still went astray. His life serves as a grim reminder that even the wisest person can become foolish.

God's judgment on Solomon was not as harsh as we might imagine it should have been. God did not strike Solomon with illness or strip him of his position. Instead, he stripped Solomon's future from him. After his death, his son would oversee the loss of Solomon's wealthy kingdom. Ten of the twelve tribes would break away to form a new nation, with a king not descended from Solomon to rule over them. God's discipline, like his blessing, can come in ways that we least expect.

This Will Hurt Me More Than You

When the LORD saw it, He spurned
them,
    Because of the provocation of His
    sons and His daughters.
And He said: "I will hide My face
from them, I will see what their end
will be,
    For they are a perverse generation,
    Children in whom is no faith.
They have provoked Me to jealousy by
what is not God;
    They have moved Me to anger by
    their foolish idols.
    But I will provoke them to jeal-
    ousy by those who are not
    a nation;
    I will move them to anger by a
    foolish nation.
For a fire is kindled in My anger,
    And shall burn to the lowest hell;

It shall consume the earth with
    her increase,
And set on fire the foundations of
    the mountains.
I will heap disasters on them;
    I will spend My arrows on them.
They shall be wasted with hunger,
    Devoured by pestilence and bitter
    destruction;
    I will also send against them the
    teeth of beasts,
    With the poison of serpents of
    the dust.
The sword shall destroy outside;
    There shall be terror within
    For the young man and virgin,
    The nursing child with the man of
    gray hairs."

Deuteronomy 32:19–25 NKJV

God suffered just thinking about the need to bring punishment upon his people. God knew them, and he knew what they would do. Shortly before they entered the promised land, God had Moses teach the people a song. The song was a dirge that described the future of his people.

God knew they would be unfaithful to him, and so he composed the music to go with the punishment that was inevitably to come upon them. The later prophets, from Isaiah to Malachi, picked up God's lyrics and merely repeated them.

God described his anger as a fire that burned "to the lowest hell." Throughout the Bible, the image of fire would become a metaphor for God's wrath and judgment. The "lowest hell" is a translation of the Hebrew word *sheol*, which actually referred to the grave rather than to the place of eternal torment for the wicked.

Despite everything, God was still willing to make them his people. He knew they'd abandon him. But he also knew he could redeem them. He knew that in the end, he could fix them. All their pain and all his pain was still worth it because he loved them so much. God loves us more than we can fathom.

❀❀❀❀❀❀❀❀❀❀❀❀❀❀❀❀❀❀❀❀❀❀❀❀❀❀❀❀❀❀

A Woman's Prophetic Warning

Hilkiah the priest, Ahikam, Acbor, Shaphan and Asaiah went to speak to the prophetess Huldah, who was the wife of Shallum son of Tikvah, the son of Harhas, keeper of the wardrobe. She lived in Jerusalem, in the Second District.

She said to them, "This is what the LORD, the God of Israel, says: Tell the man who sent you to me, 'This is what the LORD says: I am going to bring disaster on this place and its people, according to everything written in the book the king of Judah has read. Because they have forsaken me and burned incense to other gods and provoked me to anger by all the idols their hands have made, my anger will burn against this place and will not be quenched.' Tell the king of Judah, who sent you to inquire of the LORD, 'This is what the LORD, the God of Israel, says concerning the words you heard: Because your heart was responsive and you humbled yourself before the LORD when you heard what I have spoken against this place and its people, that they would become accursed and laid waste, and because you tore your robes and wept in my presence, I have heard you, declares the LORD. Therefore I will gather you to your fathers, and you will be buried in peace. Your eyes will not see all the disaster I am going to bring on this place.'"

So they took her answer back to the king.

2 Kings 22:14–20 NIV

❀

During the reign of Josiah, the last good king, the priests discovered the Book of the Law while renovating the temple; probably it was the book of Deuteronomy. Besides being guilty of idolatry and mistreating the poor, the Israelites had misplaced their copy of God's Word, a metaphor for how they had misplaced God from their lives. When King Josiah read the book, he realized that God was angry with Israel. He sent Hilkiah, along with other religious and government officials, to the prophetess Huldah. We know nothing more about her than what is related in this passage.

Huldah confirmed that they were in serious trouble with God. Then Josiah went to the temple and read the words of the treaty to the people. Because of Huldah's words, he knew that God's judgment would not come in his day. But he hoped that if he could get the Jewish people to repent, God might put off the judgment for them.

Unfortunately, the people of Judah did not repent. Without repentance, discipline is inevitable. God wants to change our lives for the best, and he'll do whatever it takes to make that happen.

Putting Words into God's Mouth

The LORD said to Eliphaz:

What my servant Job has said about me is true, but I am angry at you and your two friends for not telling the truth. So I want you to go over to Job and offer seven bulls and seven goats on an altar as a sacrifice to please me. After this, Job will pray, and I will agree not to punish you for your foolishness.

Eliphaz, Bildad, and Zophar obeyed the LORD, and he answered Job's prayer.

After Job had prayed for his three friends, the LORD made Job twice as rich as he had been before. Then Job gave a feast for his brothers and sisters and for his old friends. They expressed their sorrow for the suffering the LORD had brought on him, and they each gave Job some silver and a gold ring.

The LORD now blessed Job more than ever; he gave him fourteen thousand sheep, six thousand camels, a thousand pair of oxen, and a thousand donkeys.

In addition to seven sons, Job had three daughters, whose names were Jemimah, Keziah, and Keren Happuch. They were the most beautiful women in that part of the world, and Job gave them shares of his property, along with their brothers.

Job lived for another one hundred forty years—long enough to see his great-grandchildren have children of their own—and when he finally died, he was very old.

Job 42:7–17 CEV

---

*Y*ou can't buy off God. For all his complaining to God, Job was right and his friends were wrong. After all, as God himself admitted to Satan, Job's suffering really was without cause (Job 2:3). Job's friends had falsely accused him of some gross and secret sin. Worse, they had insisted that the only reason for being good was to get God's blessing. Why had they argued that way? If Job had actually suffered without cause and if good things could happen to the evil and bad to the good, then that meant bad things might happen to Job's three friends. They couldn't control the outcome of their lives.

If we're good because we think God will then be obligated to bless us, we're not being good at all. Even worse, we're accusing God of not being good. We're telling him that the only reason he is nice to us is that we've earned his favor. That's why God so harshly criticized Job's friends.

Why are we kind to our loved ones? Is it only because we hope to get something out of them? The same sort of behavior, no matter how we might try to pretty it up with spiritual verbiage, is just not good behavior.

A Happy Place

This is what the Sovereign LORD says:
"My servants will eat,
but you will starve.
My servants will drink,
but you will be thirsty.
My servants will rejoice,
but you will be sad and ashamed.
My servants will sing for joy,
but you will cry in sorrow
and despair.
Your name will be a curse word among
my people, for the Sovereign LORD
will destroy you and will call his
true servants by another name.
All who invoke a blessing or take
an oath will do so by the God
of truth.
For I will put aside my anger and
forget the evil of earlier days.

"Look! I am creating new heavens and
a new earth, and no one will even
think about the old ones anymore.
Be glad; rejoice forever in my creation!
And look! I will create Jerusalem
as a place of happiness.
Her people will be a source of joy.
I will rejoice over Jerusalem and
delight in my people.
And the sound of weeping and crying
will be heard in it no more."

Isaiah 65:13–19 NLT

ollowing the Babylonian captivity, God intended to restore his people to their land. God contrasted those who had repented and those who had not, those who served God and those who rejected him. His people had fallen into disrepute by worshipping false gods, but now they would worship only him. Their name was one of the most important things they had because their name was their reputation. By a "new name" God meant that they would get a new start. They could get a new reputation.

The "new heavens and a new earth" also signified the fresh start, their renewed state after their captivity. Think of how you feel when you're finally well after an illness, or how the world seems when you are in love. That is the sense God was imparting to his people. Their hard service was over. They got to go home. Life would be good again.

The image of new heavens and a new earth reflected the promises God laid out in his original covenant or treaty with Israel during the time of Moses. Just as God had promised judgment and exile for their disobedience, so he also gave them lavish promises for obedience: long life, no miscarriages, and abundant crops. Discipline is never forever because the discipline of God always works. We're better off because of it.

Has God Got News for You!

You have heard; look at all this.
And you, will you not declare it?
I proclaim to you new things from
this time,
Even hidden things which you
have not known.
They are created now and not
long ago;
And before today you have not
heard them,
So that you will not say, 'Behold, I
knew them.'
You have not heard, you have
not known.
Even from long ago your ear has
not been open,
Because I knew that you would
deal very treacherously;
And you have been called a rebel
from birth.
For the sake of My name I delay
My wrath,
And for My praise I restrain it
for you,
In order not to cut you off.
Behold, I have refined you, but not
as silver;
I have tested you in the furnace
of affliction.
For My own sake, for My own sake,
I will act;
For how can My name
be profaned?
And My glory I will not give
to another.

Isaiah 48:6–11 NASB

❧

God didn't intervene just for other people somewhere else. God reassured his people that he was as actively involved with them then as he had ever been.

Solomon was two hundred years in the past when the prophet Isaiah brought his message to Israel. The Assyrians were threatening to destroy the nation. The Israelites wondered why God couldn't act for them as he had for their ancestors. But their attitude was a failure of perception and perspective.

The stories in the Bible are truncated summaries that show the highlights of God. Sometimes, though, they fail to show the day-to-day grind. Readers don't get to witness every day Joseph was in jail. They don't witness Joseph getting up, eating, and working hour after endless hour for eighteen long years before he finally got out. The real work of God in life is punctuated, unexpected, and often visible only in hindsight. In the living of life, God's intervention and miracles are often not seen. God's hand tends to remain hidden in the shadows and soft thumps of the ordinary.

God mostly works slowly and gradually through our days, which are strung together like pearls on a string with the annoyances and trials of ordinary existence. God does it for his own purposes, and for his own glory. It isn't because we are good that God works on our behalf; it is because he loves us.

God's Anger Is Not Forever

"Of whom were you worried
and fearful
When you lied, and did not
remember Me
Nor give Me a thought?
Was I not silent even for a
long time
So you do not fear Me?
"I will declare your righteousness and
your deeds,
But they will not profit you.
"When you cry out, let your collection
of idols deliver you.
But the wind will carry all of
them up,
And a breath will take them away.
But he who takes refuge in Me will
inherit the land
And will possess My holy
mountain."
And it will be said,

"Build up, build up, prepare the
way,
Remove every obstacle out of the
way of My people."
For thus says the high and exalted One
Who lives forever, whose name
is Holy,
"I dwell on a high and holy place,
And also with the contrite and
lowly of spirit
In order to revive the spirit of
the lowly
And to revive the heart of
the contrite.
"For I will not contend forever,
Nor will I always be angry;
For the spirit would grow faint
before Me,
And the breath of those whom I
have made."

Isaiah 57:11–16 NASB

✺

The long stretches of silence when God does nothing to the wicked can lull everyone into a false sense of security. Isaiah warned the people that God had been watching and that their judgment was coming soon for their idolatry. The Assyrians were about to destroy them. God would indeed make himself heard.

God never stopped caring when Joseph remained a slave or in prison for eighteen long years. He never stopped caring when the Israelites rotted in Egypt for four hundred years. And he never stopped caring when his people suffered captivity in Babylon for seventy years. God does not contend with people without end; he does not leave them to twist in the wind. God understands that human beings are limited, that there is only so much they can endure.

Like a good trainer with his athletes, God knows they can be pushed further than they imagine. Just one more push-up; just one more lap. Then do it again. But eventually it will be time to hit the showers. Eventually game time comes. Relief arrives only after hard work, after all. No one gets a vacation because he was sitting around all day. One gets a vacation for a reason: hard work.

✳✳✳✳✳✳✳✳✳✳✳✳✳✳✳✳✳✳✳✳✳✳✳✳✳✳✳✳✳✳✳

Step Away from the Cup

Wake up, wake up, O Jerusalem!
>You have drunk the cup of the
>LORD's fury.
You have drunk the cup of terror,
>tipping out its last drops.
Not one of your children is left alive
>to take your hand and guide you.
These two calamities have fallen
>on you:
>>desolation and destruction, fam-
>>ine and war.
And who is left to sympathize
>with you?
>Who is left to comfort you?
For your children have fainted and lie
>in the streets,
>>helpless as antelopes caught in
>>a net.
The LORD has poured out his fury;
>God has rebuked them.

But now listen to this, you
>afflicted ones who sit in a drunken
>stupor, though not from
>drinking wine.
This is what the Sovereign LORD,
>your God and Defender, says:
"See, I have taken the terrible cup from
>your hands.
>>You will drink no more of
>>my fury.
Instead, I will hand that cup to your
>tormentors,
>>those who said, 'We will trample
>>you into the dust and walk on
>>your backs.'"

Isaiah 51:17–23 NLT

✳

$\mathcal{P}$eople are not always quick to leave their misery, just as animals don't always run out of opened cages.

God painted the image of a drunk sitting in his own filth and misery, draining the last drops from his cup and looking for more. Israel was like an addict. The Israelites were so lost in their problem, they couldn't see the way out. All they knew was the place where they were, the condition they were in. They couldn't see the chance for something to change, for a way to escape, for sobriety. All they knew was their sin, their idolatry, and their suffering. They had endlessly worshipped the gods and goddesses for generations, and for generations it had gotten them nowhere.

People easily get locked into a cycle of self-destruction. For those on the outside, like God, the solution was obvious. But until God yanked the cup from their drunken, shaking hands and lifted them up, they couldn't comprehend that things could be any way other than the way they were. They knew only one life, and they thought that life was the only one possible. The captivity in Babylon at last broke the cycle for them. What will it take for God to break your destructive cycle? Let God help you sooner rather than later.

Like Unplowed Ground

Listen to the noise
    on the hilltops!
    It's the people of Israel,
    weeping and begging me
    to answer their prayers.
They forgot about me
    and chose the wrong path.
I will tell them, "Come back,
    and I will cure you
    of your unfaithfulness."
They will answer,
    "We will come back, because you
    are the LORD our God.
On hilltops, we worshiped idols
    and made loud noises,
    but it was all for nothing—
    only you can save us.
Since the days of our ancestors
    when our nation was young,
    that shameful god Baal has taken
    our crops and livestock,
    our sons and daughters.
We have rebelled against you

just like our ancestors,
    and we are ashamed of our sins."
The LORD said:
Israel, if you really want
    to come back to me, get rid
    of those disgusting idols.
Make promises only in my name,
    and do what you promise!
    Then all nations will praise me,
    and I will bless them.
People of Jerusalem and Judah,
    don't be so stubborn!
Your hearts have become hard,
    like unplowed ground
    where thornbushes grow.
With all your hearts,
    keep the agreement
    I made with you.
But if you are stubborn
    and keep on sinning,
    my anger will burn like a fire
    that cannot be put out.

Jeremiah 3:21–4:4 CEV

*R*epentance is more than simply saying "I'm sorry." It takes time and effort. Ever since the Israelites left Egypt, they worshipped other gods. After more than four hundred years of disobedience, the prophet Jeremiah warned them that they faced imminent destruction from the Babylonians.

God, through Jeremiah, told the Israelites that if they really wanted to come back to him, they needed to get rid of the idols that hadn't done anything for them but relieve them of money and time. The people were stubborn and hard-hearted. Freeing them from their unfaithfulness would not be easy. It would be like working in unplowed ground full of thorns. Getting a good crop out of that sort of land was hard. Unless they got to work immediately, God would have to judge them. Of course, if the unplowed ground is full of weeds, fire is one of the quickest ways to get rid of them. His listeners, mostly farmers, understood. Painful as it might be for the land in question, the result would be good. God intends to fix his people. He has the cure.

Windbags

How can I pardon you?
> Your children have forsaken me,
> and have sworn by those who are
> no gods.
When I fed them to the full,
> they committed adultery
> and trooped to the houses
> of prostitutes.
They were well-fed lusty stallions,
> each neighing for his
> neighbor's wife.
Shall I not punish them for
> these things?
> > says the LORD;
> and shall I not bring retribution
> on a nation such as this?
Go up through her vine-rows
> and destroy,
but do not make a full end;
strip away her branches,
> for they are not the LORD's.
For the house of Israel and the house
> of Judah have been utterly faithless
> to me, says the LORD.
They have spoken falsely of the LORD,
> and have said, "He will
> do nothing.
No evil will come upon us,
> and we shall not see sword
> or famine."
The prophets are nothing but wind,
> for the word is not in them.
Thus shall it be done to them!

Jeremiah 5:7–13 NRSV

❋

*D*enial is a common human choice. When a man falls from a high building, nothing bad happens during the first few seconds of his plunge, but that doesn't mean nothing bad will ever happen. In the case of Israel, the people deluded themselves into believing that God's mercy and forbearance meant that they could keep on behaving abominably. Moreover, so-called prophets encouraged them to keep going as they were. While Jeremiah prophesied that Judah was doomed to destruction by Babylon, other prophets were predicting just the opposite. False prophets outnumbered true prophets.

The delusion that God would do nothing to punish them went hand in hand with their worship of false gods, whom they continued to worship even though the false gods never did anything for them. Life went on as it always had. Every day, the sun came up and the sun went down. The years passed, the seasons came at their appointed times, and the rain fell on everyone just the same.

The people came to pay as little attention to Yahweh and his true prophets as they did to their other gods and their false prophets. Both were meaningless in their minds. But God, unlike the idols, was real. At the right moment, he acts. God does not ignore his people.

✳✳✳✳✳✳✳✳✳✳✳✳✳✳✳✳✳✳✳✳✳✳✳✳✳✳✳✳✳✳✳✳✳✳✳✳✳✳

Withheld Good

"Nevertheless in those days," says the LORD, "I will not make a complete end of you. And it will be when you say, 'Why does the LORD our God do all these things to us?' then you shall answer them, 'Just as you have forsaken Me and served foreign gods in your land, so you shall serve aliens in a land that is not yours.'

"Declare this in the house of Jacob
And proclaim it in Judah, saying,
'Hear this now, O foolish people,
Without understanding,
Who have eyes and see not,
And who have ears and hear not:
Do you not fear Me?' says the LORD.
'Will you not tremble at My presence,
Who have placed the sand as the
   bound of the sea,
By a perpetual decree, that it cannot

pass beyond it?
And though its waves toss to and fro,
Yet they cannot prevail;
Though they roar, yet they cannot pass
   over it.
But this people has a defiant and rebel-
   lious heart;
They have revolted and departed.
They do not say in their heart,
"Let us now fear the LORD our God,
Who gives rain, both the former and
   the latter, in its season.
He reserves for us the appointed weeks
   of the harvest."
Your iniquities have turned these
   things away,
And your sins have withheld good
   from you.'"

Jeremiah 5:18–25 NKJV

✳

People can say no to God, but no other of God's creation can. When God created the heavens and the earth, the physical objects had no choice in what they were to do. The earth rotates on its axis. It isn't given the option to cease rotating or to rotate in a different direction. Likewise, gravity can't just stop doing its job, and the sky can't suddenly turn green.

God contrasts his people with the waves of the sea. The waves are constrained. They have no choice but to obey God. But his people can do whatever they want. God's people have simply disappeared; they no longer go to him. They don't even consider the possibility of repenting because they don't understand the need. They have gone astray so far and have rebelled so much that they can't recognize the problem.

Jeremiah's job was to let the people know why they were suffering and what they could do to fix the situation. Unfortunately, the people just didn't get it—not then, anyway.

But God didn't give up on them. In fact, he promised that someday they would return to him.

Day 295

Why Does It Hurt?

You understand, O Lord;
  remember me and care for me.
  Avenge me on my persecutors.
  You are long-suffering—do not
    take me away;
  think of how I suffer reproach for
    your sake.
When your words came, I ate them;
  they were my joy and my heart's
    delight, for I bear your name,
  O Lord God Almighty.
I never sat in the company of revelers,
  never made merry with them;
  I sat alone because your hand was
    on me and you had filled me
    with indignation.
Why is my pain unending
  and my wound grievous and
    incurable?
  Will you be to me like a
    deceptive brook, like a spring
    that fails?

Therefore this is what the Lord says:
  "If you repent, I will restore you
    that you may serve me;
  if you utter worthy, not
    worthless, words,
  you will be my spokesman.
  Let this people turn to you,
    but you must not turn to them.
I will make you a wall to this people,
  a fortified wall of bronze;
  they will fight against you
  but will not overcome you,
  for I am with you to rescue and
    save you," declares the Lord.
"I will save you from the hands of
  the wicked and redeem you from the
  grasp of the cruel."

Jeremiah 15:15–21 NIV

❀

Sometimes, no matter how carefully instructions are followed, things still don't work. Jeremiah found joy in God, but not in how his life had gone. No one believed him. The political and religious establishment not only didn't pay attention to what he told them, but they also worked against him. They threatened him and sometimes followed through on their threats. He wondered if God was as fickle as the wadis, the streambeds of Israel. The wadis had water sometimes after a rain, but all too often they offered nothing but sand.

Jeremiah felt as if no one cared and that even God had abandoned him. God reassured him, though perhaps not in a way Jeremiah was looking for. God told Jeremiah that the people would continue to oppose him but that their opposition would be ineffective. When Jeremiah thought about being delivered from his problems, he had hoped his problems would simply go away. He hadn't expected to be told he would simply have to bear up under them. God takes care of his servants, but not always in ways they might imagine or want.

Weren't You Listening?

The LORD has sent prophets to you time after time, but you refused to listen. They told you that the LORD had said:

Change your ways! If you stop doing evil, I will let you stay forever in this land that I gave your ancestors. I don't want to harm you. So don't make me angry by worshiping idols and other gods.

But you refused to listen to my prophets. So I, the LORD, say that you have made me angry by worshiping idols, and you are the ones who were hurt by what you did. You refused to listen to me, and now I will let you be attacked by nations from the north, and especially by my servant, King Nebuchadnezzar of Babylonia. You and other nearby nations will be destroyed and left in ruins forever. Everyone who sees what has happened will be shocked, but they will still make fun of you. I will put an end to your parties and wedding celebrations; no one will grind grain or be here to light the lamps at night. This country will be as empty as a desert, because I will make all of you the slaves of the king of Babylonia for seventy years.

When that time is up, I will punish the king of Babylonia and his people for everything they have done wrong, and I will turn that country into a wasteland forever.

Jeremiah 25:4–12 CEV

✸

*S*ometimes bad things happen to people just because the world is a hard place. Bad people do bad things, and sometimes they do bad things to good people. Sometimes tornadoes strike, earthquakes come, illnesses devastate.

When children are punished by their parents, they're usually not surprised by the punishment. They know they have disobeyed, and the parents have made clear why and for how long the punishment will last. The grounding lasts for a specified number of days or weeks; the phone is confiscated for a set time. Then all is well.

When God punished Israel, there was no surprise involved. God had sent prophets to explain what was going to happen and why it was going to happen. He explained how long it was going to last. Israel went into captivity starting in 605 BC, and Cyrus issued the decree allowing the captives to return home seventy years later in 535 BC.

When bad things happen, it doesn't automatically mean that God is punishing you. God's discipline is not something that comes upon you unexpectedly and without warning. If something bad happens to you, it might simply be because you're still living on the wrong side of eternity.

❋❋❋❋❋❋❋❋❋❋❋❋❋❋❋❋❋❋❋❋❋❋❋❋❋❋❋❋

The Signpost Ahead

Is Ephraim My dear son?
  Is he a pleasant child?
  For though I spoke against him,
  I earnestly remember him still;
  Therefore My heart yearns for him;
  I will surely have mercy on him,
    says the LORD.
  "Set up signposts,
  Make landmarks;
  Set your heart toward
    the highway,

The way in which you went.
Turn back, O virgin of Israel,
Turn back to these your cities.
How long will you gad about,
O you backsliding daughter?
For the LORD has created a new
    thing in the earth—
A woman shall encompass
  a man."

Jeremiah 31:20–22 NKJV

❋

*I*t's easy to lose the way. Sometimes we think we can't go home again, or that we can't get there from where we are. When Jeremiah began prophesying to the people of Judah and Jerusalem, more than a hundred years had passed since the Northern Kingdom of Israel had been taken into captivity. It may have seemed to the people of Judah that God had abandoned the people taken by the Assyrians, that he didn't care about them anymore, and that they wouldn't ever go back home.

The Assyrians had exiled those most likely to lead a rebellion—the royal family and the wealthy. According to the Assyrian records, they took away about twenty-five thousand people from a population numbering perhaps a million. Those Jewish exiles were not put in refugee camps. Rather, they were resettled in villages and cities throughout Assyria.

God promised the people of Judah that those who had been taken away would someday come back. In fact, both the exiles in Assyria and the exiles in Babylon would be allowed to return. God would give them careful directions.

God's intent was to offer comfort to his people. God didn't disappear when the bad times came. The Israelites couldn't go anywhere to get away from God. His question for them was simple: How long are you going to stay away? Come on home, he told them. He waited for them to come. God created something new and different—something unexpected for that culture: the woman—that is, Israel—would take the initiative. She would make the first move. Like the prodigal son who left his wrongdoing and ran back to his father, so Israel would come to God rather than God having to search for Israel and drag them back. God helps lost people find their way.

God's Abundance

The LORD became jealous for his land,
 and had pity on his people.
In response to his people the
 LORD said:
I am sending you grain, wine, and oil,
 and you will be satisfied;
and I will no more make you
 a mockery among the nations.
I will remove the northern army far
 from you, and drive it into a parched
 and desolate land,
its front into the eastern sea, and its
 rear into the western sea;
 its stench and foul smell will rise up.
 Surely he has done great things!
Do not fear, O soil;
 be glad and rejoice,
 for the LORD has done great things!

Do not fear, you animals of the field,
 for the pastures of the wilderness
 are green;
the tree bears its fruit, the fig tree and
 vine give their full yield.
O children of Zion, be glad and rejoice
 in the LORD your God;
for he has given the early rain for your
 vindication, he has poured down for
 you abundant rain, the early and the
 later rain, as before.
The threshing floors shall be full
 of grain, the vats shall overflow with
 wine and oil.

Joel 2:18–24 NRSV

*N*o problem lasts forever. Joel likely prophesied after the Israelites had returned from exile in Babylon. Through Joel, God promised deliverance from the plague of locusts attacking the Israelites: the "northern army." Locusts consumed every green thing in their path, leaving nothing behind except the expectation of famine. Locusts meant that the food the recently returned exiles thought they were going to have was suddenly gone. The future was stripped from the exiles just as the locusts stripped the leaves from the plants. The harvest was doomed.

But God promised his people, who had responded to him in prayer, that he had heard their requests and their repentance. He would keep them alive; they would not starve. The rains would come at the right time, the crops would be abundant, and they would have overflowing food instead of the feared starvation. They would have more than they needed: grain for bread, oil for cooking, and wine from the grapes. The necessities of their continued life would remain. The northern army—that is, the locusts—would be driven away, sent out to sea. God does not let his people's problems destroy them. We always come out on the other side.

Day 299

Snake Bites

Because you impose heavy rent on
the poor
And exact a tribute of grain
from them,
Though you have built houses of
well-hewn stone,
Yet you will not live in them;
You have planted pleasant vine-
yards, yet you will not drink
their wine.
For I know your transgressions are
many and your sins are great,
You who distress the righteous
and accept bribes
And turn aside the poor in
the gate.
Therefore at such a time the prudent
person keeps silent, for it is an
evil time.
Seek good and not evil, that you
may live;
And thus may the LORD God of
hosts be with you,
Just as you have said!
Hate evil, love good,
And establish justice in the gate!
Perhaps the LORD God of hosts
May be gracious to the remnant
of Joseph.
Therefore thus says the LORD God of
hosts, the Lord,
"There is wailing in all the plazas,
And in all the streets they say,
'Alas! Alas!'
They also call the farmer
to mourning
And professional mourners to
lamentation.
"And in all the vineyards there
is wailing,
Because I will pass through the
midst of you," says the LORD.
Alas, you who are longing for the day
of the LORD,
For what purpose will the day of
the LORD be to you?
It will be darkness and not light.

Amos 5:11–18 NASB

Be careful what you wish for. There may be unexpected consequences. Amos was not a professional prophet (Amos 7:14). Unlike most of the prophets in the Bible, Amos had not been called to a permanent ministry as Jeremiah or Isaiah had. Instead, he was a simple layman whose primary focus in life was growing figs and overseeing shepherds. But one day, while he was tending sheep, he heard the voice of God and had no choice but to relate his message to the people of Israel.

Amos began his ministry by proclaiming God's judgment against all the nations around Israel before suddenly unleashing the primary focus of God's message: Israel, too, must face judgment. The day of the Lord was not just a day for judging the enemies of Israel; it was also a day for judging Israel. The destruction of Israel's enemies did not mean the end of their problems. Sometimes people have enemies and problems because they deserve them.

Judgment and Rescue

Thus says the Lord:
"Though they are safe, and like-
wise many,
Yet in this manner they will be
cut down
When he passes through.
Though I have afflicted you,
I will afflict you no more;
For now I will break off his yoke
from you,
And burst your bonds apart."
The Lord has given a command
concerning you:
"Your name shall be perpetuated
no longer.
Out of the house of your gods

I will cut off the carved image and
the molded image.
I will dig your grave,
For you are vile."
Behold, on the mountains
The feet of him who brings
good tidings,
Who proclaims peace!
O Judah, keep your
appointed feasts,
Perform your vows.
For the wicked one shall no more
pass through you;
He is utterly cut off."

Nahum 1:12–15 NKJV

✿

*P*eace is good news. Loved ones return home, fear eases, and normal life resumes. Though the messenger is not responsible for the quality of the news, he often is blamed when the news isn't so good. The bearer of good news, however, is praised, thanked, and hugged. He is thought handsome and smart; even his feet look good. The prophet Isaiah used similar wording in Isaiah 52:7. More than a century before Nahum, the prophet Jonah was sent to warn Nineveh, the capital of Assyria, of God's judgment. By Nahum's time, Israel, consisting of the northern ten tribes, had been in Assyrian captivity for nearly a century. Repeatedly over the years, Assyria threatened Judah too. Nahum predicted the downfall of Nineveh. When it happened, the people of Judah rejoiced. But Nahum warned that soon Judah would face its own judgment by the Babylonians who had just conquered Nineveh.

God's intention toward his people was designed to correct their faults, not to destroy the people. Their penchant for other gods would be removed. Both the idols and the idolaters would vanish, and they would be at peace with God. Humanity, like Judah, stood condemned by its sins. But God proclaimed peace. Their crimes were forgiven. Their debt was paid. Evil was vanquished and rendered powerless.

God's judgment leads to blessings and happiness.

Restored

"Therefore wait for Me," says the LORD,
"Until the day I rise up for plunder;
My determination is to gather
  the nations
To My assembly of kingdoms,
To pour on them My indignation,
All My fierce anger;
All the earth shall be devoured
With the fire of My jealousy.
"For then I will restore to the peoples a
  pure language,
That they all may call on the name of
  the LORD,
To serve Him with one accord.
From beyond the rivers
  of Ethiopia
My worshipers,
The daughter of My dispersed ones,
Shall bring My offering.
In that day you shall not be shamed
  for any of your deeds
In which you transgress against Me;
For then I will take away from
  your midst
Those who rejoice in your pride,
And you shall no longer be haughty
In My holy mountain.
  I will leave in your midst
A meek and humble people,
And they shall trust in the name of
  the LORD.
The remnant of Israel shall do no
  unrighteousness
And speak no lies,
Nor shall a deceitful tongue be found
  in their mouth;
For they shall feed their flocks and
  lie down,
And no one shall make them afraid."

Zephaniah 3:8–13 NKJV

Waiting is hard to do. But waiting is just what God asked for. Zephaniah prophesied during the reign of Josiah at the same time Jeremiah was prophesying. Josiah tried to eliminate the worship of false gods. During the restoration of the temple in Jerusalem, the high priest discovered the Book of the Law, most likely Deuteronomy. The Northern Kingdom of Israel had been in captivity for decades. Judah was on the brink of facing the same disaster as their northern neighbors, and for the same reasons. He told them what it would be like in exile.

In the midst of their punishment, Judah would beg for instant relief. God knew that his people wanted things to get better immediately. But he would make them spend the full time in captivity. The years assigned for their punishment were not arbitrary.

God knew that in order to fix the idolatry problem, his people would have to endure precisely the sorts of ordeals they ultimately went through. Anything else, any shortcuts, would fail to achieve the necessary goal. People want their cake now. But it is better to wait until it has fully baked.

God Won't Forget to Forgive

The Angel of the LORD answered and said, "O LORD of hosts, how long will You not have mercy on Jerusalem and on the cities of Judah, against which You were angry these seventy years?"

And the LORD answered the angel who talked to me, with good and comforting words. So the angel who spoke with me said to me, "Proclaim, saying, 'Thus says the LORD of hosts:

"I am zealous for Jerusalem
And for Zion with great zeal.
I am exceedingly angry with the
   nations at ease;
For I was a little angry,

And they helped—but with
   evil intent."
'Therefore thus says the LORD:
   "I am returning to Jerusalem
   with mercy;
My house shall be built in it," says
   the LORD of hosts,
"And a surveyor's line shall be
   stretched out over Jerusalem." '
"Again proclaim, saying, 'Thus says the
LORD of hosts:
   "My cities shall again spread out
   through prosperity;
The LORD will again comfort Zion,
And will again choose Jerusalem." ' "

Zechariah 1:12–17 NKJV

*N*eglecting God means neglecting what really matters in life. After the Jewish people returned from their seventy-year captivity in Babylon to a Jerusalem that was nothing but rubble, Zechariah prophesied. Zechariah had a vision of a man riding a red horse standing among the myrtle trees in a ravine. Behind him were red, brown, and white horses. An angel explained to Zechariah that they were the ones God had sent through the whole earth. The earth was at rest and in peace. Then the angel asked God about Jerusalem and Judah. He wondered how much longer Israel would have to suffer, given that everywhere else seemed to be in good shape.

God proclaimed to Zechariah through his angel that Jerusalem and the temple were going to be rebuilt. In fact, Zechariah's primary ministry to the people who had come back to the land was that the time for rebuilding the temple was right then and they should not allow themselves to become distracted by anything else. Following their exile, idolatry was no longer a concern.

The issues for the Israelites after captivity were entirely different. God warned them that they were more concerned with themselves than with God. They believed that if they didn't get their houses built and their farms reestablished first, they were doomed. They failed to trust God to provide for their daily needs. Those who love God and make him their priority can be confident that they will be his priority.

Take Off Those Filthy Clothes!

The angel showed me Jeshua the high priest standing before the angel of the LORD. The Accuser, Satan, was there at the angel's right hand, making accusations against Jeshua. And the LORD said to Satan, "I, the LORD, reject your accusations, Satan. Yes, the LORD, who has chosen Jerusalem, rebukes you. This man is like a burning stick that has been snatched from the fire."

Jeshua's clothing was filthy as he stood there before the angel. So the angel said to the others standing there, "Take off his filthy clothes." And turning to Jeshua he said, "See, I have taken away your sins, and now I am giving you these fine new clothes."

Then I said, "They should also place a clean turban on his head." So they put a clean priestly turban on his head and dressed him in new clothes while the angel of the LORD stood by.

Then the angel of the LORD spoke very solemnly to Jeshua and said, "This is what the LORD of Heaven's Armies says: If you follow my ways and carefully serve me, then you will be given authority over my Temple and its courtyards. I will let you walk among these others standing here.

"Listen to me, O Jeshua the high priest, and all you other priests. You are symbols of things to come. Soon I am going to bring my servant, the Branch."

Zechariah 3:1–8 NLT

*S*atan doesn't make stuff up when he accuses people. There's no need. Who is Satan? He is an evil supernatural being about whom very little is ever revealed. We don't even know his real name. Satan is not his name; the word *Satan* simply means "accuser." It is only a description of who he was.

Jeshua was a priest in the time of Zechariah. Satan was a tattletale, gleefully trying to point out his mistakes because he thought he was getting away with stuff. God's response to Satan was to rebuke him. Then God worked at making Jeshua a better person, cleaning him up, giving him new clothes, and encouraging him to make better choices in the future. Jeshua hadn't gotten away with anything.

Jeshua, like all the priests, was a symbol of what was going to come—the one who offered the sacrifice as well as the sacrifice himself. Interestingly, Jeshua's name was the same as that which would be given to the Messiah many years later. Like Jeshua, our wrongdoings are covered. When Satan accuses us, God simply rebukes him.

His Own Parents Will Stab Him

"On that day a fountain will be opened to the house of David and the inhabitants of Jerusalem, to cleanse them from sin and impurity.

"On that day, I will banish the names of the idols from the land, and they will be remembered no more," declares the LORD Almighty. "I will remove both the prophets and the spirit of impurity from the land. And if anyone still prophesies, his father and mother, to whom he was born, will say to him, 'You must die, because you have told lies in the LORD's name.'

When he prophesies, his own parents will stab him.

"On that day every prophet will be ashamed of his prophetic vision. He will not put on a prophet's garment of hair in order to deceive. He will say, 'I am not a prophet. I am a farmer; the land has been my livelihood since my youth.' If someone asks him, 'What are these wounds on your body?' he will answer, 'The wounds I was given at the house of my friends.'"

Zechariah 13:1–6 NIV

Not everyone claiming to be a prophet is actually from God. Moses warned the people to pay attention to two things regarding those who claimed to be prophets. First, did what they say come true? Second, whether it came true or not, were they advocating turning from God to other gods? If what they said happened, and if they were insisting on worship of only Yahweh, then they were prophets of God. Otherwise, they were not to be feared or paid attention to.

Prior to the Babylonian captivity, many people claimed to be prophets. Kings wanted prophets and would hire them. Much like modern astrologers, the words of the hired prophets were just as useful and accurate as the horoscopes that people read in their morning papers or on Web sites. Nevertheless, a king would give such prophets good wages for periodically standing before him to announce that the king's plans were good and blessed by God. The purpose of this was mostly ceremonial, like the prayers offered before public events today, with little meaning beyond offering a patina of religiosity. Such royal prophets never proclaimed a genuine message from God or offered up any uncomfortable truths.

Zechariah warned that such prophets were going to have to find a different way to make a living. No one, not even their closest family members, would support their delusional ministry. In fact, the prophets would be ashamed of ever having done such a thing and would find excuses to explain away the evidence of their past lying and the reason for their punishments. We can't use God as a tool for getting rich.

Joy and Sadness

Sadness is a heavy weight, the consequence of loss and disappointment. It is an emotion familiar to God. He is not separated from the people he made and loves. When people hurt, God hurts with them. When people are happy, God feels their joy. That's the nature of loving others: their hearts become your heart, and whatever they feel, you feel.

※

I will rejoice and be glad in Your lovingkindness,
because You have seen my affliction;
You have known the troubles of my soul.
Psalm 31:7 NASB

God Was Sorry

It came about, when men began to multiply on the face of the land, and daughters were born to them, that the sons of God saw that the daughters of men were beautiful; and they took wives for themselves, whomever they chose.

Then the LORD said, "My Spirit shall not strive with man forever, because he also is flesh; nevertheless his days shall be one hundred and twenty years."

The Nephilim were on the earth in those days, and also afterward, when the sons of God came in to the daughters of men, and they bore children to them. Those were the mighty men who were of old, men of renown.

Then the LORD saw that the wickedness of man was great on the earth, and that every intent of the thoughts of his heart was only evil continually.

The LORD was sorry that He had made man on the earth, and He was grieved in His heart.

The LORD said, "I will blot out man whom I have created from the face of the land, from man to animals to creeping things and to birds of the sky; for I am sorry that I have made them."

But Noah found favor in the eyes of the LORD.

Genesis 6:1–8 NASB

By the time of Noah, God regretted but wasn't surprised by what man did, and he provided a way back to himself. So he resolved to destroy the people for their wickedness. They did not love God, and they did not love other people. But then God noticed Noah, and he discovered that he really liked Noah. So instead of wiping out all of humanity—he just wiped out most of it.

Questions regarding the identity of the "daughters of men" and the "sons of God" have resulted in a lot of discussion. Some people have imagined angels marrying women and having children. The "daughters of men" are just human women, and the "sons of God" are just human men. Luke's genealogy, after all, pointed out that Adam was the son of God (Luke 3:38). The offspring of these marriages were described as *Nephelim*, a word elsewhere translated as "giants." It's the same Hebrew word used later in the Bible to describe Goliath, the Philistine warrior slain by David. Here in Genesis, it referred not to physical stature but to the stature of their reputations.

God was sorrowed by how the human race had turned out, and he would soon do something about it with Noah's help. Noah loved and obeyed God, and he found favor with God. We can resolve to emulate Noah's love and obedience to God so that we, too, can find favor with God and make him happy.

Celebrate Good Times

Celebrate this Festival of Unleavened Bread, for it will remind you that I brought your forces out of the land of Egypt on this very day. This festival will be a permanent law for you; celebrate this day from generation to generation. The bread you eat must be made without yeast from the evening of the fourteenth day of the first month until the evening of the twenty-first day of that month. During those seven days, there must be no trace of yeast in your homes. Anyone who eats anything made with yeast during this week will be cut off from the community of Israel. These regulations apply both to the foreigners living among you and to the native-born Israelites. During those days you must not eat anything made with yeast. Wherever you live, eat only bread made without yeast.

Exodus 12:17–20 NLT

❀

*G*od isn't a killjoy. He isn't afraid that somewhere, somehow, someone is having a good time and he needs to stop it. God is all about joy. He wanted his people to remember with joy what God had done for them by rescuing them from Egyptian bondage. Their rescue from Egypt was a good reason to celebrate, much as Americans celebrate Independence Day or enjoy Thanksgiving. God wanted the Israelites to set aside time to party not just for an hour or a day, but for a whole week. Their fun was not to be cut short.

Why did God say no yeast at this annual party? Unlike the modern world where we can make or get food quickly, in ancient times, making food was a slow process. There were no fast-food restaurants just around the corner. There wasn't even any quick-rising yeast for their bread machines. And so they didn't have time to make bread the right way since they had only a few hours' warning that they would be leaving Egypt for good. Rushed to cook plain dough into bread for their journey, they ended up with crackers—*matzo*—instead. To remind them of that rushed night before their deliverance, during their seven-day festival they were not allowed to have normal bread, only matzo. And the annual celebration was for anyone who happened to be living among the Jewish people, even foreigners, so long as they obeyed the rules of the festivity.

Given that the Israelites enjoyed their celebrations, we should never imagine that we are somehow less godly, less connected to God, or less holy because we happen to be having a good time with our friends and family. Being spiritual includes having fun.

You Need a Break

The LORD said to Moses, "Say to the Israelites, 'You must observe my Sabbaths. This will be a sign between me and you for the generations to come, so you may know that I am the LORD, who makes you holy.

"'Observe the Sabbath, because it is holy to you. Anyone who desecrates it must be put to death; whoever does any work on that day must be cut off from his people. For six days work is to be done, but the seventh day is a Sabbath of rest, holy to the LORD. Whoever does any work on the Sabbath day must be put to death. The Israelites are to observe the Sabbath, celebrating it for the generations to come as a lasting covenant. It will be a sign between me and the Israelites forever, for in six days the LORD made the heavens and the earth, and on the seventh day he abstained from work and rested.' "

When the LORD finished speaking to Moses on Mount Sinai, he gave him the two tablets of the Testimony, the tablets of stone inscribed by the finger of God.

Exodus 31:12–18 NIV

✻

All work and no play doesn't just make Jack a dull boy, it can make him sick and unproductive. In college, we might brag about how we pulled all-nighters. But God isn't so impressed. He thinks we should take some time off on a regular basis, one day a week, every week. Even God took a day off after he created the world. Do we need rest less than God?

We need time off just for our own health and happiness. Working all the time isn't good for us. Frankly, it ultimately reduces our productivity, and taking an hour off here and there doesn't cut it. The ancient Israelites were expected to take a whole day just to do nothing with it. They didn't spend their day off mowing the grass, cleaning the garage, or building a shed. Instead, they were required just to do nothing—goof off, be lazy, sleep and eat and play. Not only did the Israelites not get to work, they couldn't make anyone else work for them. No slaves could work; not even the animals could work. No cooking was allowed either. No one was allowed to start a fire. The people had to eat whatever they already had on hand. God was serious about the resting thing. It was designed, just like all the laws God made, for our good. So take some time off. The world won't end because you took the pressure off and relaxed one day this week.

Opening Day for Worship

The LORD said to Moses:

Set up my tent on the first day of the year and put the chest with the Ten Commandments behind the inside curtain of the tent. Bring in the table and set on it those things that are made for it. Also bring in the lampstand and attach the lamps to it. Then place the gold altar of incense in front of the sacred chest and hang a curtain at the entrance to the tent. Set the altar for burning sacrifices in front of the entrance to my tent. Put the large bronze bowl between the tent and the altar and fill the bowl with water. Surround the tent and the altar with the wall of curtains and hang the curtain that was made for the entrance.

Use the sacred olive oil to dedicate the tent and everything in it to me. Do the same thing with the altar for offering sacrifices and its equipment and with the bowl and its stand. Bring Aaron and his sons to the entrance of the tent and have them wash themselves. Dress Aaron in the priestly clothes, then use the sacred olive oil to ordain him and dedicate him to me as my priest. Put the priestly robes on Aaron's sons and ordain them in the same way, so they and their descendants will always be my priests.

Moses followed the LORD's instructions.

Exodus 40:1–16 CEV

*W*orship is more than ritual. Until the tabernacle was built, until the clothing had been made for Aaron and his sons, until the altar, ark, and lampstands had been made, and until the oil had been pressed and mixed with just the right spices, the Israelites had not performed sacrifices or conducted formalized rituals associated with worshipping God. Centuries later, Jesus would tell a Samaritan woman that one day people would no longer worship God in a temple at all, but rather in spirit and in truth.

The tabernacle and its rituals were not the essence of worshipping God. They were simply an outward expression of what had been, would be, and would continue to be the inner reality in people's relationship with God. Worshipping God was always performed in spirit and in truth, not by means of the outward rituals. Those rituals were supposed to portray the attitudes in people's minds. Robes, spices, and sacrifice were designed to serve as illustrations of a relationship that already existed.

The outward show can never take the place of a life lived with God. Real worship happens when people love God and love the people around them. Real worship is shown by acts of kindness.

Let's Go Camping

The fifteenth day of the seventh month, when you have gathered in the produce of the land, you shall keep the festival of the LORD, lasting seven days; a complete rest on the first day, and a complete rest on the eighth day. On the first day you shall take the fruit of majestic trees, branches of palm trees, boughs of leafy trees, and willows of the brook; and you shall rejoice before the LORD your God for seven days. You shall keep it as a festival to the LORD seven days in the year; you shall keep it in the seventh month as a statute forever throughout your generations. You shall live in booths for seven days; all that are citizens in Israel shall live in booths, so that your generations may know that I made the people of Israel live in booths when I brought them out of the land of Egypt: I am the LORD your God.

Leviticus 23:39–43 NRSV

Religion can be fun. The festivals, feasts, and worship ceremonies God gave the Israelites were supposed to be enjoyable for them. Once a year, for a whole week, the entire nation of Israel was supposed to go on a nationwide campout. Its purpose was to remind them of their forty years spent wandering in the wilderness when they had all lived in booths—temporary shelters like tents. And they were supposed to have fun doing this. It was a time off, a holiday. On the first and last day of the festival, they weren't supposed to do anything at all. The rest of the time, they were simply supposed to have a good time. Consider the implications. This was another whole week that God set aside every year for joy. It also meant a break from the daily routine. It gave the people a fresh outlook on life, reminding them of all the good that God had done for them, both past and present.

What kind of God insists that his people enjoy themselves? A God who really does love his people. What has gotten into our heads that somehow the best way to get close to God is to isolate ourselves and to deny ourselves the pleasures of life? Instead, God called his people to come together, to go on a big campout, to sit around campfires, cook food, and spend time with one another. God called his people to celebrate how much he loved them by rescuing them from Egyptian bondage and protecting and caring for them over forty years of wandering in the desert. God did not intend that it be difficult to know that he loves us. Worshipping God is a good time for all.

May God Make You Joyful

The LORD spoke to Moses, saying: "Speak to Aaron and his sons, saying, 'This is the way you shall bless the children of Israel. Say to them:

"The LORD bless you and keep you;
The LORD make His face shine
    upon you,
        And be gracious to you;

The LORD lift up His countenance
    upon you,
        And give you peace." '
"So they shall put My name on the
    children of Israel, and I will
    bless them."

Numbers 6:22–27 NKJV

❈

I'm just blessed all over." The elderly man in our congregation always responded in the same way whenever anyone asked him how he was doing: whether times were good for him or not so good. How could he do that? He could do it because he knew he was with God and would be with God forever. *Bless* has become a religious word, all too easily spiritualized into an abstract unreality. It's not as complicated as we'd like to make it. The word translated *bless* means simply "to make happy." God told Moses that the priests should tell the people regularly that God was watching over them with the intent of making them happy. A blessing is simply the opposite of a curse—it is the opposite of misery and unhappiness.

The priests would offer those words of blessing to the Israelites when they came to Jerusalem to worship at the temple—on annual holidays and whenever someone offered a sacrifice. Sacrifices were offered for giving thanks, for the birth of a child, and especially for sin. God offered the light of his shining face to all who came before his priests, no matter the reason they came. Whether the worshipper came joyfully, or in tears of grief over guilt, after the sacrifice, God had the priests send him away with the same blessing. God offered mercy to the sinner who repented so that he could leave cleansed, as if he'd never sinned at all.

God's will for people is that they should be joyful. When God made the world, he saw that it was good, not evil. God did not set out to make us miserable. But it is easy to lose sight of God when a crisis leaps in our faces. The old man who, in whatever circumstances, could recognize that he was "blessed all over" knew the simple truth that allowed him to weather the storms of life. He knew that he belonged to God, that God was with him, and that God would remain with him forever. He didn't let his circumstances hide God.

Death Was No Surprise

When they set out from Kadesh, the sons of Israel, the whole congregation, came to Mount Hor.

Then the LORD spoke to Moses and Aaron at Mount Hor by the border of the land of Edom, saying,

"Aaron will be gathered to his people; for he shall not enter the land which I have given to the sons of Israel, because you rebelled against My command at the waters of Meribah.

"Take Aaron and his son Eleazar and bring them up to Mount Hor; and strip Aaron of his garments and put them on his son Eleazar. So Aaron will be gathered to his people, and will die there."

So Moses did just as the LORD had commanded, and they went up to Mount Hor in the sight of all the congregation.

After Moses had stripped Aaron of his garments and put them on his son Eleazar, Aaron died there on the mountain top. Then Moses and Eleazar came down from the mountain.

When all the congregation saw that Aaron had died, all the house of Israel wept for Aaron thirty days.

Numbers 20:22–29 NASB

*D*eath comes to us all. One day, the world will go on without us. It won't even give us a moment's thought, any more than we spare a moment's thought for our great-grandparents, whom most of us wouldn't recognize and whose names we probably don't even know.

God told Aaron the precise moment and place when he would die. Like a prisoner on death row, God led him to Mount Hor and, while everyone watched, his life ended. It was a sad time for Aaron, a sad time for Moses, and a sad time for the people of Israel who set aside the traditional month for mourning.

God prefers that we be joyful, but there are times when sadness is not only appropriate but also inevitable. Jesus wept at Lazarus's tomb, even though he knew that within minutes Lazarus would walk out very much alive. God knew that Aaron would not stay dead forever since there is a time coming when all will be raised from the dead back to life. But the promise of such a resurrection does not make the current moment of pain go away. Face the pain, acknowledge it, and mourn.

Aaron's death was no surprise, but the Israelites were still sad for a long time. Likewise, don't think you can't or shouldn't be sad when facing a similar tragedy. And don't think you have to get over your loss immediately. Take however long you need. But also know that eventually the time of mourning will end, whether in thirty days or longer, and you'll go back to living your life.

Water in a Thirsty Land

From there the Israelites traveled to Beer, which is the well where the LORD said to Moses, "Assemble the people, and I will give them water." There the Israelites sang this song:

"Spring up, O well!
     Yes, sing its praises!
Sing of this well,
     which princes dug,
which great leaders hollowed out
     with their scepters and staffs."

Then the Israelites left the wilderness and proceeded on through Mattanah, Nahaliel, and Bamoth. After that they went to the valley in Moab where Pisgah Peak overlooks the wasteland.

Numbers 21:16–20 NLT

❊

*W*hen people do something nice for you, thank them. Shortly after the incident with the poisonous snakes, the Israelites moved on in their travels. Along the way, God told the people that he would give them water. And so at a place called Beer, they received something to drink. *Beer* in this case is not a brewed beverage. It is a Hebrew word that means "spring" or "well." When they got to that spring of water, they sang a song about it, praising the water and giving thanks to those who had dug the well. They didn't sing a song praising God. They didn't praise God for providing it at all, even though God told Moses that he was the one giving them the water.

Did they do something wrong? Did they make God angry or hurt God's feelings? Had Moses failed to tell the people that the water was from God? Were the people once again forgetting who it was that took care of them? That wasn't the case. What's remarkable is that this was one of the first times the people were complaint-free. They didn't complain that God wanted them to die in the wilderness, and they didn't wish they could return to Egypt.

Certainly, it is appropriate to thank God for the food we eat, for the jobs we have, for the good things that come to us in life. But it is just as appropriate to praise those who grew and harvested the food, who cooked the food, who provided the jobs, and who manufactured the joys we experience in life. It is people who bring us our food, who sign our paychecks, who keep the water flowing to our showers, who get the electricity into our homes so we can watch the game on a Saturday afternoon on our televisions. It's okay to praise those things that make our lives better and to give thanks to those who make it possible. Loving people is the best way to show our love for God. Being happy with the people God loves and praising them for jobs they do well make God happy. Simply knowing we are happy about good things makes God happy too.

A Place for Everyone

The LORD said to Moses, "Command the Israelites and say to them: 'When you enter Canaan, the land that will be allotted to you as an inheritance will have these boundaries:

"'Your southern side will include some of the Desert of Zin along the border of Edom. On the east, your southern boundary will start from the end of the Salt Sea, cross south of Scorpion Pass, continue on to Zin and go south of Kadesh Barnea. Then it will go to Hazar Addar and over to Azmon, where it will turn, join the Wadi of Egypt and end at the Sea.

"'Your western boundary will be the coast of the Great Sea. This will be your boundary on the west.

"'For your northern boundary, run a line from the Great Sea to Mount Hor and from Mount Hor to Lebo Hamath. Then the boundary will go to Zedad, continue to Ziphron and end at Hazar Enan. This will be your boundary on the north.

"'For your eastern boundary, run a line from Hazar Enan to Shepham. The boundary will go down from Shepham to Riblah on the east side of Ain and continue along the slopes east of the Sea of Kinnereth. Then the boundary will go down along the Jordan and end at the Salt Sea.

"'This will be your land, with its boundaries on every side.'"

Numbers 34:1–12 NIV

A place for everything and everything in its place. God is a God of order. God had promised Abraham that the Israelites would have a land to call their own. At last, the day came that God gave them the details. He set up the borders and announced that the place was theirs. The place-names setting the boundaries of their land were familiar to the ancient Hebrews.

Whatever it is that God has asked of you, he has given you your place. He has given you your job, and he has given you a place to live. He has established the boundaries of your life.

The Desert of Zin was part of the modern Negev, the desert south of Jerusalem. The Salt Sea is today more commonly called the Dead Sea. We know the Great Sea now as the Mediterranean, while Israel's northern boundary was about where the modern border divides Israel from Lebanon.

God did not give the Israelites the entire world as their home. He gave them just a small plot of land. The total size of the land God gave Israel is about the same as the state of New Jersey. But that was all they needed. We need to be satisfied with whatever it is God has given us. He has given us enough for our current needs.

An Unhappy God

The LORD told Samuel, "Saul has stopped obeying me, and I'm sorry that I made him king."

Samuel was angry, and he cried out in prayer to the LORD all night. Early the next morning he went to talk with Saul. Someone told him, "Saul went to Carmel, where he had a monument built so everyone would remember his victory. Then he left for Gilgal."

Samuel finally caught up with Saul, and Saul told him, "I hope the LORD will bless you! I have done what the LORD told me."

"Then why," Samuel asked, "do I hear sheep and cattle?"

"The army took them from the Amalekites," Saul explained. "They kept the best sheep and cattle, so they could sacrifice them to the LORD your God. But we destroyed everything else."

"Stop!" Samuel said. "Let me tell you what the LORD told me last night."

"All right," Saul answered.

Samuel continued, "You may not think you're very important, but the LORD chose you to be king, and you are in charge of the tribes of Israel. When the LORD sent you on this mission, he told you to wipe out those worthless Amalekites. Why didn't you listen to the LORD? Why did you keep the animals and make him angry?"

1 Samuel 15:10–19 CEV

✳

*J*ust as God became sorry in the time of Noah that he had made the human race, so the day came when he became sorry he had made Saul Israel's first king. God told Samuel about his disappointment and sent Samuel to confront Saul.

Rather than acknowledging that he had disobeyed the commandment of God, Saul offered excuses and justifications. In essence, Saul told God, "You just don't understand my special circumstances." Neither Samuel nor God would have any of it.

God had needed Saul to wipe out the Amalekites. He hadn't asked for a sacrifice of some of the animals; he hadn't asked that certain individuals among the Amalekites be spared. Besides, it wasn't about sacrifice in the first place. It was, instead, all about lining Saul's pockets and the pockets of his favorites. He had succumbed to political expediency and greed. Saul's behavior exemplified the whole reason God hadn't wanted the Israelites to have a king in the first place.

If you love God, just do what God has asked. Don't try to find ways out of it to satisfy what you think is best for you, as if God doesn't really have your best interests in mind. Either you love God or you don't. Saul didn't.

Stop Your Caterwauling

The LORD said to Samuel, "How long will you grieve over Saul? I have rejected him from being king over Israel. Fill your horn with oil and set out; I will send you to Jesse the Bethlehemite, for I have provided for myself a king among his sons." Samuel said, "How can I go? If Saul hears of it, he will kill me." And the LORD said, "Take a heifer with you, and say, 'I have come to sacrifice to the LORD.' Invite Jesse to the sacrifice, and I will show you what you shall do; and you shall anoint for me the one whom I name to you." Samuel did what the LORD commanded, and came to Bethlehem. The elders of the city came to meet him trembling, and said, "Do you come peaceably?" He said, "Peaceably; I have come to sacrifice to the LORD; sanctify yourselves and come with me to the sacrifice." And he sanctified Jesse and his sons and invited them to the sacrifice.

1 Samuel 16:1–5 NRSV

Sometimes you just have to let go of an issue. Samuel liked Saul and didn't like what had happened with him. He hoped there was some way to fix the situation, restore the relationship, and get God and Saul back together. But it was too late for that. God had given Saul his job as a king, and, just as easily, God would take it away from him. God had never promised Saul a permanent position. Saul had served on a trial basis and had failed his performance review. So God told Samuel to let it go. It was time to find Saul's replacement.

That, of course, raised a new concern for Samuel: Saul was still the king, regardless of God's pronouncements against him. Samuel knew that Saul would kill him as a traitor if he anointed someone else to take his place. God reassured Samuel, however, and told him how to keep the plan hidden from Saul. God did not tell Samuel to lie, unless you want to argue that an undercover police officer or a spy is lying by not blowing their cover. Like a general misleading the enemy or a quarterback misleading the opposing team, God told Samuel how to mislead Saul and get the job done that he needed to do.

If God has given us something to do, then it isn't impossible for us to do it. If God wants it to get done, then it will get done. No one can thwart God—or us, if we're doing what God wants from us.

But I Don't Want to Die

In those days Hezekiah was sick and near death. And Isaiah the prophet, the son of Amoz, went to him and said to him, "Thus says the LORD: 'Set your house in order, for you shall die, and not live.' "

Then he turned his face toward the wall, and prayed to the LORD, saying, "Remember now, O LORD, I pray, how I have walked before You in truth and with a loyal heart, and have done what was good in Your sight." And Hezekiah wept bitterly.

And it happened, before Isaiah had gone out into the middle court, that the word of the LORD came to him, saying, "Return and tell Hezekiah the leader of My people, 'Thus says the LORD, the God of David your father: "I have heard your prayer, I have seen your tears; surely I will heal you. On the third day you shall go up to the house of the LORD. And I will add to your days fifteen years. I will deliver you and this city from the hand of the king of Assyria; and I will defend this city for My own sake, and for the sake of My servant David." ' "

Then Isaiah said, "Take a lump of figs." So they took and laid it on the boil, and he recovered.

2 Kings 20:1–7 NKJV

God is open to hearing you out. Hezekiah was considered one of the righteous kings of Judah. That didn't keep him from becoming deathly ill. When Isaiah visited him, he gave the king bad news from God: "You're going to die."

That was not what Hezekiah wanted to hear, so he prayed. God answered his prayer favorably, granting him fifteen more years of life.

The lump of figs placed on the boil was a symbol for Hezekiah that God would act. The figs were an illustration; lumps of figs do not inherently have healing properties that somehow Hezekiah's physicians had missed until then.

Had God lied to Hezekiah when he first told him he would die? Had Hezekiah's eloquence in his prayer changed God's mind? Neither. Hezekiah had mistakenly assumed God meant he would die from his illness. In response to Hezekiah's prayer, God told him he would still die. But God added a new detail: not just yet.

His son Manasseh was twelve when Hezekiah finally died fifteen years later. Hezekiah could have trained him well in the years he had with him. Instead, Manasseh was the most evil king Judah would ever have. Hezekiah failed to take the opportunity God gave him. It's easy to miss the opportunities that could have been ours.

No Forgiveness for Now

You assessed your defenses that Day,
   inspected your arsenal of weapons
   in the Forest Armory. You found
the weak places in the city walls
that needed repair. You secured the
water supply at the Lower Pool. You
took an inventory of the houses in
Jerusalem and tore down some to
get bricks to fortify the city wall. You
built a large cistern to ensure plenty
of water.
You looked and looked and looked,
   but you never looked to him who
gave you this city, never once consulted the One who has long had
plans for this city.
The Master, GOD-of-the-Angel-Armies,
called out on that Day,

Called for a day of repentant tears,
   called you to dress in somber
   clothes of mourning.
But what do *you* do? You throw a
   party!
   Eating and drinking and dancing
   in the streets!
You barbecue bulls and sheep, and
   throw a huge feast—
   slabs of meat, kegs of beer.
"Seize the day! Eat and drink!
   Tomorrow we die!"
GOD-of-the-Angel-Armies whispered
   to me his verdict on this frivolity:
   "You'll pay for this outrage until the
   day you die." The Master, GOD-of-
the-Angel-Armies, says so.

Isaiah 22:8–14 MSG

❀

When God gave this message to the prophet Isaiah, a hundred years would pass before the Babylonians would burn down Jerusalem and destroy the sacred temple. God outlined the preparations that had been made for the sieges: the rebuilding of the walls and the water tunnel by King Hezekiah. Despite those physical preparations, however, no spiritual preparations had been made at all. Instead of feeling regret for how they had turned to idols and oppressed the widows, the orphans, and the poor, the Israelites kept living their lives as if nothing was wrong. They worshipped false gods. They partied instead of repenting. They did not fix their real problems, which had nothing to do with walls or water systems.

They never asked God to help them, even though God pointed out that the consequences for their behavior and their attitudes were dire. The people chose instead to "Seize the day! Eat and drink!" Rather than the forgiveness they might have enjoyed, they would suffer in the years of siege against Jerusalem and would ultimately die. Our first response in similar circumstances needs to be to trust God and to ask for his guidance.

Closed-Minded Stupidity

Such stupidity and ignorance!
> Their eyes are closed, and they
> cannot see.
> Their minds are shut, and they
> cannot think.
The person who made the idol never
stops to reflect,
> "Why, it's just a block of wood!
I burned half of it for heat
> and used it to bake my bread and
> roast my meat.
How can the rest of it be a god?
> Should I bow down to worship a
> piece of wood?"
The poor, deluded fool feeds on ashes.
> He trusts something that can't
> help him at all.
Yet he cannot bring himself to ask,
> "Is this idol that I'm holding in
> my hand a lie?"
"Pay attention, O Jacob,

for you are my servant, O Israel.
I, the LORD, made you, and I will not
forget you.
I have swept away your sins like
a cloud.
> I have scattered your offenses like
> the morning mist.
Oh, return to me, for I have paid the
price to set you free."
Sing, O heavens, for the LORD has done
this wondrous thing.
> Shout for joy, O depths of
> the earth!
Break into song,
> O mountains and forests and
> every tree!
For the LORD has redeemed Jacob
and is glorified in Israel.

Isaiah 44:18–23 NLT

✻

*T*he problem with worshipping false gods is that they are false. It is like believing a chain letter. You'll not only fail to see the promised millions, but you'll also lose what little you have. The Israelites had put their faith in stuff that didn't exist. They had been conned. Trusting in charms, horoscopes, crystals, and the like was foolish. They were going to get hurt, and God didn't want his people to get hurt.

Rather than trusting God, who was reliable, people looked to things that would fade away. Despite the Israelites' stupidity, God had forgiven them. He stood ready and willing to rescue them from all their problems. He had taken care of all the details. All the Israelites had to do was take God's hand. All that was left to do was rejoice over God's salvation. Everything had been fixed; there was nothing left to worry about.

God knows just how stupid we can be when it comes to sin. He knows how easily we let it con us. There's nothing left to do now but to rejoice that God has provided the way out of our mess.

Can a Mother Forget Her Baby?

Shout for joy, O heavens;
    rejoice, O earth;
        burst into song, O mountains!
For the LORD comforts his people
    and will have compassion on his
        afflicted ones.
But Zion said, "The LORD has
    forsaken me, the Lord has
    forgotten me."
"Can a mother forget the baby at
    her breast and have no compassion
    on the child she has borne?
        Though she may forget,
        I will not forget you!
See, I have engraved you on the palms
    of my hands;
        your walls are ever before me.

Your sons hasten back,
    and those who laid you waste
        depart from you.
Lift up your eyes and look around;
    all your sons gather and come
        to you.
As surely as I live," declares
    the LORD,
"you will wear them all
    as ornaments;
you will put them on, like
    a bride."

Isaiah 49:13–18 NIV

*I*n the midst of our problems, it is impossible to see anything bright. We feel nothing but our pain; we see nothing but the oppressive darkness; we feel nothing but the walls closing in on us. The heavens are brass; we're alone and nothing is getting better. There is no warmth, only the bitter cold of the moment.

In that impossible instant of Israel's pending destruction, God reassured his people that he had not forgotten them. He compared his suffering people to an infant in his mother's arms. The infant might be crying, wailing, hungry, or fearful. In his small, undeveloped mind, all he knows is the pain of his empty belly and the dark night surrounding it. But his mother can hardly forget her child, can hardly not feel compassion for his suffering. Likewise, God was there, offering comfort and hope as they left for exile in Assyria or Babylonia.

God had not gone away. His people were no further away from him in a foreign land than they had ever been. God wasn't insensitive to their pain, and he had not forgotten them. All they had to do was calm down, look around, and realize that everything was going to be okay. What was lost was being restored. The broken places were being repaired. It really would all be okay.

When we are in the dark places and can't see God because we're absorbed in our momentary pain, God will take care of us.

Everything Will Be Okay

Lift up your eyes and look around;
   they all gather together, they come
      to you;
your sons shall come from far away,
   and your daughters shall be car-
      ried on their nurses' arms.
Then you shall see and be radiant;
   your heart shall thrill and rejoice,
because the abundance of the sea shall
   be brought to you, the wealth of the
   nations shall come to you.
A multitude of camels shall cover you,
   the young camels of Midian
      and Ephah;
   all those from Sheba shall come.
They shall bring gold and
   frankincense, and shall proclaim the
   praise of the LORD.
All the flocks of Kedar shall be
   gathered to you, the rams of

Nebaioth shall minister to you;
they shall be acceptable on my altar,
   and I will glorify my
      glorious house.
Who are these that fly like a cloud,
   and like doves to their windows?
For the coastlands shall wait for me,
   the ships of Tarshish first,
to bring your children from far away,
   their silver and gold with them,
for the name of the LORD your God,
   and for the Holy One of Israel,
   because he has glorified you.

Isaiah 60:4–9 NRSV

❈

*O*ur memories are colored by our assumptions and incomplete information. We see tomorrow only in terms of what little we know today. Today seems long, while the past is fleeting and tomorrow never comes.

But through Isaiah, God reassured his people that after their coming captivity in Babylon, all would be well. God promised to revive normal commerce with their neighbors, and gave them a list. Ephah was one of the five sons of Midian, a grandson of Abraham and his wife Keturah. Midian became a nation to the east of the Dead Sea, while Ephah was one of the cities in that nation. There were many places around the Mediterranean called Tarshish. They were where ore was refined into metal. The "ships of Tarshish" were refinery ships carrying that metal. Both Kedar and Nabaioth were sons of Ishmael, Isaac's half brother. Keder referred to a confederation of Arab tribes in the northern part of the Arabian Peninsula that traded mostly sheep. The same was so with Nabaioth.

God promised to bring them back, not just to their land, but to him. A human lifetime is a very tiny speck on the face of eternity. But it's all we can see just now. We need to seek God's perspective on it all. If we had that, we'd relax more and worry less, or not at all.

An Everlasting Covenant

"I, the LORD, love justice;
I hate robbery for burnt offering;
I will direct their work in truth,
And will make with them an everlast-
    ing covenant.
Their descendants shall be known
    among the Gentiles,
And their offspring among the people.
All who see them shall
    acknowledge them,
That they are the posterity whom the
    LORD has blessed."
I will greatly rejoice in the LORD,
My soul shall be joyful in my God;
For He has clothed me with the gar-
    ments of salvation,

He has covered me with the robe of
    righteousness,
As a bridegroom decks himself
    with ornaments,
And as a bride adorns herself with
    her jewels.
For as the earth brings forth
    its bud,
As the garden causes the things that are
    sown in it to spring forth,
So the Lord GOD will cause righteous-
    ness and praise to spring forth
    before all the nations.

Isaiah 61:8–11 NKJV

❈

*G*od loves justice. But how does that work with the fact that he keeps offering—and giving—mercy to those who are evil? Justice means punishing the guilty, giving them what they deserve, and not letting them off the hook. But God often forgives, often spares, and often offers hope to those who most deserve—in our estimation—to suffer his anger. So how can God say he loves justice? Because he loves it when the good get what they deserve. But wait, God said there are no good people, only evil people. So how does that work? God transforms the evil into the good. He destroys the wicked when he makes them righteous. Justice comes to the bad guys in their transformation into good guys. Rather than explosions and body parts sent flying, God blows up their sins and destroys the wickedness in their hearts. He delivers justice to the wicked heart when he replaces it with his own heart of righteousness.

God's justice against the wicked happened with the sacrifice. Just as something dies to provide our food to keep us alive, so a sacrifice for sin was a life given in exchange for the justice deserved. Justice was served more thoroughly in sacrifice than any explosion sending bad guys to oblivion at the end of a movie. Human justice, the justice we think of, results in the destruction of sinners. God's justice results in the destruction of evil and the rescue of wrongdoers.

No Pain in Childbearing

Before she travailed, she brought forth;
Before her pain came, she gave birth
  to a boy.
Who has heard such a thing? Who has
  seen such things?
    Can a land be born in one day?
    Can a nation be brought forth all
    at once?
    As soon as Zion travailed, she also
    brought forth her sons.
"Shall I bring to the point of birth and
  not give delivery?" says the LORD.
"Or shall I who gives delivery shut the
  womb?" says your God.

Be joyful with Jerusalem and rejoice
  for her, all you who love her;
    Be exceedingly glad with her, all
    you who mourn over her,
That you may nurse and be satisfied
  with her comforting breasts,
That you may suck and be
  delighted with her
  bountiful bosom.

Isaiah 66:7–11 NASB

❈

God can fix problems in unexpected ways. A common human failing is to imagine we know how any given problem is going to be fixed. Israel had gone into Babylonian exile. Israel had been destroyed as a nation, and it had ceased to exist. Then God promised that the nation would be restored all at once. That was precisely what happened when Cyrus issued his decree around 536 BC that the people of Israel were to return and rebuild their shattered homeland—only seventy years after the first deportation in the time of Nebuchadnezzar. With that decree, on a single day, the nation was restored. All at once, upon the arrival of thousands of refugees sent back home, the depopulated capital was suddenly crowded.

Just as the people of Israel had mourned the destruction of their capital, their temple, and their homeland, so they would rejoice when they were at last able to return and restore their fortunes. Though the decree of Cyrus had made them a nation in only a day, they'd have a hundred years of work ahead of them to rebuild first the temple and then the wall around the city. Ezra, Nehemiah, and many prophets would remind the people where they had come from and what they still needed to do.

God does not punish endlessly. Suffering does not endure without end. Someday, too, the current crisis, the current moment of pain will end, and we will once again be happy. If nothing else—and it is far more than nothing—we have an eternity with God to look forward to.

Triumph over the Enemy

This is what the LORD says:
"I will give Jerusalem a river of peace
    and prosperity.
        The wealth of the nations will
            flow to her.
Her children will be nursed at
    her breasts, carried in her arms, and
    held on her lap.
I will comfort you there in Jerusalem
        as a mother comforts her child."
When you see these things, your heart
    will rejoice.
        You will flourish like the grass!
Everyone will see the LORD's hand of
    blessing on his servants—
and his anger against his enemies.
See, the LORD is coming with fire,
    and his swift chariots roar like a
        whirlwind.
He will bring punishment with the
    fury of his anger and the flaming fire
    of his hot rebuke.
The LORD will punish the world by fire
    and by his sword.
He will judge the earth,
    and many will be killed by him.

Isaiah 66:12–16 NLT

*W*hy can't we be happy today the way we'll be tomorrow when God makes everything okay? As human beings, we can only respond to what we can see, whether it is the pain of the moment or the anticipation of whatever we think is likely to happen tomorrow. Pain overwhelms us more than joy ever can; the suffering we experience goes deeper than our pleasures and affects us more strongly. No one goes into counseling to uncover repressed memories of happiness. No one endures flashbacks of good times or finds their current circumstances circumscribed by memories of ecstasy gone by.

God promised the Israelites that they would find comfort in Jerusalem once again, like a baby in its mother's arms. He also promised them vengeance.

The words translated *earth* and *world* in context refer to the lands of Mesopotamia, the "world" of the Assyrians and the Babylonians. God promised the Israelites that he would avenge their pain against those who had destroyed their homeland and taken them away into captivity. God's promises of tomorrow were intended to bring joy in the midst of their exile far from their home. The thought that the enemies of the Jewish people would suffer just as they were was emotionally satisfying. Only with God can we come to a place of optimism, of recognizing that the future memories we will have of eternal bliss can deeply constrain our experiences of today. Likewise, the satisfaction of God's yet-to-be certain judgment on our enemies should be able to render aid to us as we endure their blows today.

My People Are Fools

"Your own conduct and actions
     have brought this upon you.
This is your punishment.
     How bitter it is!
     How it pierces to the heart!"
Oh, my anguish, my anguish!
     I writhe in pain.
Oh, the agony of my heart!
     My heart pounds within me,
     I cannot keep silent.
For I have heard the sound of
     the trumpet;
     I have heard the battle cry.
Disaster follows disaster;
     the whole land lies in ruins.

In an instant my tents are
     destroyed, my shelter in a moment.
How long must I see the battle
     standard and hear the sound of
     the trumpet?
"My people are fools;
     they do not know me.
They are senseless children;
     they have no understanding.
They are skilled in doing evil;
     they know not how to do good."

Jeremiah 4:18–22 NIV

God thinks we're foolish. In fact, he knows we are, and it disappoints him. Jeremiah described God's dismay. Some people might think the expressions of anguish and the writhing in pain in this passage are the prophet Jeremiah's reactions to God's words. In fact, God is actually describing his own emotional state. God was anguished over the fate of his people. He was extremely upset over what the Babylonians were doing, knowing that the pain of his people was entirely unnecessary. If only they had listened to him! If only they had turned from their wickedness and embraced him instead of all their idols. If only they had loved the people around them instead of loving only themselves. God thought his people were foolish—as indeed they were.

They were foolish because they didn't know God. *Knowing* in Hebrew thought was always practical and gained by experience. In certain contexts, it was used as a euphemism for sexual intercourse. Because the Israelites had turned from God to worship idols, they had no experience any longer with God. They had come to believe that Yahweh was just like the idols they worshipped— weak and ineffectual. They had forgotten everything God had done for them, and they resisted his efforts to relieve their ignorance. Their resistance to God's will was peculiarly irrational. They didn't know how foolish their actions were, how senseless and self-destructive. As we get to know God, we understand there is reason for obedience that only a fool would pass up.

Our Pain Is God's Pain

"The harvest is past, the summer is
  ended, and we are not saved."
For the hurt of my poor people I
  am hurt, I mourn, and dismay has
  taken hold of me.
Is there no balm in Gilead?
    Is there no physician there?
Why then has the health of my
  poor people not been restored?
O that my head were a spring of water,
    and my eyes a fountain of tears,
so that I might weep day and night
    for the slain of my poor people!
O that I had in the desert a traveler's
  lodging place, that I might leave my
  people and go away from them!

For they are all adulterers,
    a band of traitors.
They bend their tongues like bows;
    they have grown strong in the
    land for falsehood, and not
    for truth;
for they proceed from evil to evil,
    and they do not know me, says
    the LORD.

Jeremiah 8:20–9:3 NRSV

God expressed his suffering over the suffering of his people. Their wounds were self-inflicted. They turned their backs on God and went their own way. They believed lies rather than the truth, and, consequently, they no longer knew God. They believed lies about him, had false notions about his intentions, and believed the worst about him in order to justify for themselves the poor choices they made. Like a husband watching his wife spiral down into addiction, leave him for abusive relationships, and suffer privation and misery, so God was miserable. He was miserable not just because of the loss of affection, but because he still loved his estranged wife, Israel, and hoped to rescue her from herself. God regularly used the image of adultery, as he did here, for the idolatry of his people.

God knew that his people would eventually repent and turn to him. But in the meantime, God cried over their condition. Gilead, the hill of testimony and the region around it, was noted for its spices, oils, and aromatic gums. The question regarding balm in Gilead was rhetorical, akin to asking people in a swimming pool if they're wet enough yet. The solution for Israel's suffering was obvious to God. Their pain was unnecessary. They already knew what God expected. We call Jeremiah the Weeping Prophet because he so often expressed God's deep sorrow. Our pain truly is God's as well.

Don't Waste Your Time

"A voice of wailing is heard from Zion:
  'How we are plundered!
  We are greatly ashamed,
  Because we have forsaken
    the land,
  Because we have been cast out of
    our dwellings.' "
Yet hear the word of the LORD,
  O women,
  And let your ear receive the word
    of His mouth;
  Teach your daughters wailing,
  And everyone her neighbor a
    lamentation.
For death has come through our
  windows,
  Has entered our palaces,
  To kill off the children—no longer
    to be outside! . . .

Thus says the LORD:
  "Let not the wise man glory in
    his wisdom,
  Let not the mighty man glory in
    his might,
  Nor let the rich man glory in
    his riches;
  But let him who glories glory in
    this,
  That he understands and
    knows Me,
  That I am the LORD, exercising
    lovingkindness, judgment, and
    righteousness in the earth.
  For in these I delight," says
    the LORD.

Jeremiah 9:19–21, 23–24 NKJV

*L*ife is more than our stuff. It is more than whom we know, how talented we are, or how strong we are. Life consists in knowing God, in knowing he is strong and talented, knows everything, and owns the cattle on a thousand hills.

The Israelites had focused their attention on themselves and their needs. They forgot that God knew their needs better than they did. They stressed over their circumstances and tried to fix them on their own. They abandoned God and turned to the lies they thought would protect them. They lost everything because they misplaced life's source.

God warned them they would need the services of professional mourners because what they would soon face from Babylon was so horrific. In ancient Israel, as in many ancient cultures, it wasn't uncommon to hire people to cry over a dead loved one at a funeral.

The people of Israel had reason to mourn. They mourned for the loss of their loved ones and homes. But what they should have mourned more was their lost relationship with God. They should have mourned over the reason they had lost everything they cared for, which was because they had forgotten to care for God. God is the source of all we have.

Do Not Seek Great Things

The word that Jeremiah the prophet spoke to Baruch the son of Neriah, when he had written these words in a book at the instruction of Jeremiah, in the fourth year of Jehoiakim the son of Josiah, king of Judah, saying, "Thus says the LORD, the God of Israel, to you, O Baruch: 'You said, "Woe is me now! For the LORD has added grief to my sorrow. I fainted in my sighing, and I find no rest." '

"Thus you shall say to him, 'Thus says the LORD: "Behold, what I have built I will break down, and what I have planted I will pluck up, that is, this whole land. And do you seek great things for yourself? Do not seek them; for behold, I will bring adversity on all flesh," says the LORD. "But I will give your life to you as a prize in all places, wherever you go." ' "

Jeremiah 45:1–5 NKJV

🌼

*L*osing perspective is easy. Baruch—the man who had served as Jeremiah's secretary for years, writing down the words that he received from God—was overcome by his own suffering and fell into despair. God told him to get over it. In the first place, it wasn't all about him. In the second place, God promised to protect him and keep him alive, no matter where he went, no matter what he had to face.

Jehoiakim became king of Judah after Pharaoh Neco killed Jehoiakim's father, Josiah, in battle, while Neco was on his way to fight the Babylonians. Neco lost that battle against Babylon in Jehoiakim's fourth year. Jehoiakim then became subject to Babylon. But three years after God's word came to Baruch, Jehoiakim rebelled, triggering the Babylonian invasion of Jerusalem that would ultimately lead to its destruction.

When everything goes wrong, it is hard to avoid Baruch's attitude. All we want then is for the pain to go away. When we face financial ruin, when someone close to us dies, or when we become seriously ill, the only thing that can make us feel good is to hear that we have money, our loved one is not dead, or a miracle cure will make us all better.

God told Baruch not to seek great things for himself. Instead, he should be satisfied simply to be alive. Bad things happen in life, and if you're going to be alive, you're going to experience some bad things. That's how it works. The question Baruch had to answer for himself, and that we need to answer for ourselves, is simply this: Isn't a life with God enough?

Keeping It All Inside

The word of the LORD came to me: "Son of man, with one blow I am about to take away from you the delight of your eyes. Yet do not lament or weep or shed any tears. Groan quietly; do not mourn for the dead. Keep your turban fastened and your sandals on your feet; do not cover the lower part of your face or eat the customary food of mourners."

So I spoke to the people in the morning, and in the evening my wife died. The next morning I did as I had been commanded.

Then the people asked me, "Won't you tell us what these things have to do with us?"

So I said to them, "The word of the LORD came to me: Say to the house of Israel, 'This is what the Sovereign LORD says: I am about to desecrate my sanctuary—the stronghold in which you take pride, the delight of your eyes, the object of your affection. The sons and daughters you left behind will fall by the sword. And you will do as I have done. You will not cover the lower part of your face or eat the customary food of mourners.'"

Ezekiel 24:15–22 NIV

*W*hat if you weren't allowed to cry? Ezekiel was taken into Babylonian captivity a few years before the Babylonians had burned Jerusalem and destroyed the temple. Ezekiel prophesied to Israelites who had been carried off around the same time. God often had him act out his prophetic messages. For instance, Ezekiel once went outside, put a brick down in the dirt, and laid siege to it as a child might play with toy soldiers. It illustrated what Babylon was going to do to Jerusalem. This time, God's message was personally devastating. God told him his beloved wife would die. Worse, he wouldn't even be permitted the normal Jewish mourning rituals—no torn garments, no outward weeping.

What Ezekiel was asked to do was something strange. But it served to illustrate the nature of the coming disaster: not only would Jerusalem fall to the Babylonian invaders, but they would also march into the temple, including the Most Holy Place reserved for the high priest, and the invaders would steal everything of value. The sacred objects used for sacrifice would wind up in Nebuchadnezzar's palace. Then, after the temple had been stripped of valuables, the Babylonians would burn it to the ground. When the temple was destroyed, the people of Israel would not have the opportunity to express sorrow. God wanted them to recognize the sheer horror of what was to come.

Keeping his sorrow bottled up inside was a nearly unbearable burden for Ezekiel. Yet he did what God asked, and we have his example to follow.

Ashes upon the Earth

The word of the LORD came to me, saying, "Son of man, take up a lamentation for the king of Tyre, and say to him, 'Thus says the Lord GOD:

"You were the seal of perfection,
Full of wisdom and perfect in beauty.
  You were in Eden, the garden
    of God;
Every precious stone was your
  covering:
The sardius, topaz, and diamond,
Beryl, onyx, and jasper,
Sapphire, turquoise, and emerald
  with gold.
The workmanship of your timbrels
  and pipes
Was prepared for you on the day you
  were created.
"You were the anointed cherub who
  covers;
I established you;
You were on the holy mountain
  of God;
You walked back and forth in the
  midst of fiery stones.
    You were perfect in your ways
      from the day you were created,

Till iniquity was found in you.
"By the abundance of your trading
You became filled with violence
  within,
And you sinned;
Therefore I cast you as a profane thing
Out of the mountain of God;
And I destroyed you,
  O covering cherub,
From the midst of the fiery stones.
"Your heart was lifted up because of
  your beauty;
You corrupted your wisdom for the
  sake of your splendor;
I cast you to the ground,
I laid you before kings,
That they might gaze at you.
"You defiled your sanctuaries
By the multitude of your iniquities,
By the iniquity of your trading;
Therefore I brought fire from
  your midst;
It devoured you,
And I turned you to ashes upon
  the earth
In the sight of all who saw you.'"'

Ezekiel 28:11–18 NKJV

*W*e are neither the masters of our fates nor the captains of our souls. Sometimes, like the king of Tyre, we forget that. Tyre was a prosperous city thanks to its extensive trade. God compared its king to the first human in Paradise. Like Adam, the king of Tyre would be expelled from the city. First, the Babylonians would repeatedly sack Tyre, and then Alexander the Great would destroy it.

The king of Tyre was called a cherub because, as the city's anointed king, he guarded it. The king of Tyre believed himself to be a god. But even arrogant kings are mortal, and God easily put him in his place.

No matter how much control we may think we have, no matter how well off we may be, our lives and our fortunes are in God's hands.

God's Churning Heart

"How can I give you up, Ephraim?
How can I hand you over, Israel?
How can I make you like Admah?
How can I set you like Zeboiim?
My heart churns within Me;
My sympathy is stirred.
I will not execute the fierceness of My
anger;
I will not again destroy Ephraim.
For I am God, and not man,
The Holy One in your midst;
And I will not come with terror.
"They shall walk after the LORD.
He will roar like a lion.
When He roars,
Then His sons shall come trem-
bling from the west;

They shall come trembling like a bird
from Egypt,
Like a dove from the land
of Assyria.
And I will let them dwell in
their houses,"
Says the LORD.
"Ephraim has encircled Me with lies,
And the house of Israel
with deceit;
But Judah still walks with God,
Even with the Holy One who
is faithful."

Hosea 11:8–12 NKJV

❀

*I*t is hard to punish those we love. God knew that he had to punish the Israelites for cheating on him with other gods, but it caused him inner turmoil. God describes his heart churning within him. What does that mean? On the one hand, God was angry. On the other hand, God loved his people and wanted only to bless them. He wanted them to be happy and at ease. But he also wanted them to be the best that they could be. He knew what they really needed, and to his great sorrow, he knew they needed to be disciplined. God rose above his emotions and did what needed to be done: he disciplined his people for their sins. But he disciplined them only as much as they needed, and no more. As he said, he wasn't "man" and didn't get carried away with his anger.

How could God rise above his churning heart? He could see beyond his immediate pain and the immediate pain of his people. He knew what was broken in his people. More important, he knew they needed to be transformed, and he knew how to make that transformation happen. He knew how to convince them there were no other gods. He knew how to get them to turn back to him with love. He didn't let his churning heart keep him from the painful solution. Don't let your churning heart keep you from doing what you need to do either.

Future Tense

"Up, up! Flee from the land of the north," says the LORD; "for I have spread you abroad like the four winds of heaven," says the LORD. "Up, Zion! Escape, you who dwell with the daughter of Babylon."

For thus says the LORD of hosts: "He sent Me after glory, to the nations which plunder you; for he who touches you touches the apple of His eye. For surely I will shake My hand against them, and they shall become spoil for their servants. Then you will know that the LORD of hosts has sent Me.

"Sing and rejoice, O daughter of Zion! For behold, I am coming and I will dwell in your midst," says the LORD. "Many nations shall be joined to the LORD in that day, and they shall become My people. And I will dwell in your midst. Then you will know that the LORD of hosts has sent Me to you. And the LORD will take possession of Judah as His inheritance in the Holy Land, and will again choose Jerusalem. Be silent, all flesh, before the LORD, for He is aroused from His holy habitation!"

Zechariah 2:6–13 NKJV

God loved the world, not just the nice people. Zechariah prophesied to the newly returned former captives from Babylon about seventy years after Jeremiah. While they were rebuilding Jerusalem and the temple, God told his people to rejoice because he was bringing non-Israelites to join them.

The Jewish people thought Yahweh was only for them, but this thinking was normal for the ancient world. The gods of Egypt were just that, the gods of Egypt. The same was true with the gods of Babylon, Greece, and Rome. It was culturally unnatural to think of one's gods in universal terms. But that is precisely the message that God was trying to get across to his people. Now that they had returned from Babylon, they understood at last that they were to worship none but Yahweh. At that point, the prophets began working on the people to broaden their comprehension of what God had maintained as far back as the first chapter of Genesis: not only was Yahweh the only God they could worship, and not only was he the only God who existed, but he was also not the exclusive property of the Israelites.

Not until persecution in the first century forced the early Jewish disciples of Jesus to share the gospel did the universality of Israel's God finally make sense to them. God is for everybody, even those we don't care about.

The King Is Coming!

"Rejoice greatly, O daughter of Zion!
Shout, O daughter of Jerusalem!
Behold, your King is coming to you;
He is just and having salvation,
Lowly and riding on a donkey,
A colt, the foal of a donkey.
I will cut off the chariot
   from Ephraim
And the horse from Jerusalem;
The battle bow shall be cut off.
He shall speak peace to the nations;
His dominion shall be 'from sea
   to sea,
And from the River to the ends of
   the earth.'

"As for you also,
Because of the blood of your covenant,
I will set your prisoners free from the
   waterless pit.
Return to the stronghold,
You prisoners of hope.
Even today I declare
That I will restore double to you.
For I have bent Judah, My bow,
Fitted the bow with Ephraim,
And raised up your sons, O Zion,
Against your sons, O Greece,
And made you like the sword of a
   mighty man."

Zechariah 9:9–13 NKJV

❦

The kingdom of God is unlike any earthly kingdom. The King who would come to Israel following its captivity in Babylon would not arrive by means of earthly power. He would not be exalted as an earthly king might be exalted. And his kingdom would not be established by power or force. God would remove the weapons of war that the kingdoms of the world used from Ephraim, what had been the Northern Kingdom of Israel, and Jerusalem, the capital of the Southern Kingdom of Judah. Rather than becoming an earthly power, the restored and unified Israel and Judah would become a spiritual power. The promised king would come in humility. He would establish a kingdom of peace that would extend to all the world.

The "prisoners" set free from a "waterless pit" refers to the Israelites held captive by Babylon. God predicted that Babylon would be replaced by Persia and that the Persians would send the people of God back to their promised land. The reference to Greece indicated that when the Persians fell to Greece—specifically to Alexander the Great—Israel was going to be spared and protected by God. God's methods for establishing his coming kingdom were different from the world's methods. God intended to conquer the human heart.

Whom They Have Pierced

I will pour out on the house of David and on the inhabitants of Jerusalem, the Spirit of grace and of supplication, so that they will look on Me whom they have pierced; and they will mourn for Him, as one mourns for an only son, and they will weep bitterly over Him like the bitter weeping over a firstborn.

In that day there will be great mourning in Jerusalem, like the mourning of Hadadrimmon in the plain of Megiddo.

The land will mourn, every family by itself; the family of the house of David by itself and their wives by themselves; the family of the house of Nathan by itself and their wives by themselves; the family of the house of Levi by itself and their wives by themselves; the family of the Shimeites by itself and their wives by themselves; all the families that remain, every family by itself and their wives by themselves.

In that day a fountain will be opened for the house of David and for the inhabitants of Jerusalem, for sin and for impurity.

Zechariah 12:10–13:1 NASB

*L*ove means saying you're sorry. And saying you're sorry is only the beginning. God promised his people that a day would come when they would recognize how much they had hurt him with their idolatry. Their recognition would be the result of a divine gift—the gift of repentance. Such repentance would come because of God's action—the outpouring of his Spirit—in the lives of his people.

The mourning of "Hadadrimmon in the plain of Megiddo" refers to what happened at that spot, a village on the plain of Megiddo. King Josiah, who was considered a good and righteous king and one of the best that Israel ever had, was killed there by Pharaoh Neco (2 Chronicles 35:22–25). His death was mourned bitterly by the people of Israel. Jeremiah composed a lament on his behalf. God compared that national mourning over Josiah to the mourning that would come over the death of the Messiah some five hundred years later. On the day of this mourning, God promised that he would cleanse all people of their sins and not just the people of Israel.

Sorrow over sin, over what we've done to God, comes because God works in our hearts. Repentance is not just saying we're sorry; repentance is a full recognition of the wrong we've done and a determination to change and not do it again. Even more, there is a desire to try to fix whatever we've done wrong, to make amends. The truly repentant person offers no excuses and willingly accepts any punishment. True repentance can come only from God.

Peace and Conflict

Conflict is inevitable in human affairs. Sometimes it's what God wants. God led Israel in countless wars. We are in conflict with the world, the flesh, and the devil. We are not at peace with our sins. Only in overcoming our enemies can peace come. God does not promise a stress-free life. Instead, he promises to fight alongside us, to lead us to a peace that comes from victory over our foes.

❋

A time to love, and a time to hate;
a time for war, and a time for peace.
Ecclesiastes 3:8 NRSV

Sibling Rivalry

Isaac pleaded with the LORD for his wife, because she was barren; and the LORD granted his plea, and Rebekah his wife conceived. But the children struggled together within her; and she said, "If all is well, why am I like this?" So she went to inquire of the LORD.

And the LORD said to her:

"Two nations are in your womb,
Two peoples shall be separated from
     your body;
One people shall be stronger than
     the other,
And the older shall serve the younger."

So when her days were fulfilled for her to give birth, indeed there were twins in her womb. And the first came out red. He was like a hairy garment all over; so they called his name Esau. Afterward his brother came out, and his hand took hold of Esau's heel; so his name was called Jacob. Isaac was sixty years old when she bore them.

So the boys grew. And Esau was a skillful hunter, a man of the field; but Jacob was a mild man, dwelling in tents. And Isaac loved Esau because he ate of his game, but Rebekah loved Jacob.

Genesis 25:21–28 NKJV

*Y*ou needn't be careful what you pray for, because God's answers are always for the best. Isaac was past forty when he married Rebekah. When she was unable to get pregnant, Isaac prayed that she would. God answered Isaac's prayer by giving her twins. The pregnancy was a difficult one, so she asked God what was going on. He told her that the two children she was about to have would become two nations at odds with each other. God also told her that the older son would serve the younger. In that culture, the older always was the one in charge. He received the largest share of the inheritance, along with the blessing of the first-born. Rebekah took God's words to heart and sought to make them come true.

The firstborn was Esau, whose name meant "hairy." He was covered with red fur. The second born was Jacob, whose name meant "heel grabber," since he was holding his brother's heel when he was born. His name was also an idiom that meant "cheater" or "con man."

Jacob was the child of promise, the child through whom all the blessings first given to Abraham and then to Isaac would pass. God would later change Jacob's name to Israel. From Israel, the Messiah would come. God's answer to Isaac's concern for his wife, that she could get pregnant, not only blessed him but also changed the course of history and blessed the entire world. God's answer to our prayers may have repercussions far greater than we can imagine.

Why Did You Steal My Gods?

When it was told Laban on the third day that Jacob had fled, then he took his kinsmen with him and pursued him a distance of seven days' journey, and he overtook him in the hill country of Gilead. God came to Laban the Aramean in a dream of the night and said to him, "Be careful that you do not speak to Jacob either good or bad."

Laban caught up with Jacob. Now Jacob had pitched his tent in the hill country, and Laban with his kinsmen camped in the hill country of Gilead. Then Laban said to Jacob, "What have you done by deceiving me and carrying away my daughters like captives of the sword?

"Why did you flee secretly and deceive me, and did not tell me so that I might have sent you away with joy and with songs, with timbrel and with lyre; and did not allow me to kiss my sons and my daughters? Now you have done foolishly.

"It is in my power to do you harm, but the God of your father spoke to me last night, saying, 'Be careful not to speak either good or bad to Jacob.'

"Now you have indeed gone away because you longed greatly for your father's house; but why did you steal my gods?"

Genesis 31:22–30 NASB

God talks to everyone, wrongdoer or righteous. If he didn't, he'd be talking only to himself. Laban was Jacob's uncle, and he was an idolater. He was also a scoundrel who had taken advantage of Jacob, cheating him repeatedly. His daughters knew what he was capable of, so his daughter Rachel, Jacob's wife, had stolen the household idols when they ran away. She did that because whoever held those idols was guaranteed to receive the inheritance. It was the equivalent of running off with Laban's safe-deposit box and his debit card. But, of course, it also meant that Laban, his daughters, and even Jacob, being part of a polytheistic culture, still thought in terms of multiple gods, even as Jacob worshipped the God of his fathers, Abraham and Isaac.

The night before Laban caught up with the fleeing Jacob, God issued a warning: Laban could say nothing "good or bad" to him. That is, God prevented Laban from being able to pronounce either a curse or a blessing on his son-in-law. Such blessings and cursings were taken quite seriously by all involved. God protected Jacob by preventing anything bad from happening to him. God also prevented Jacob from thinking that the good that would follow in his life came from his idolatrous uncle rather than from its true source, the God of Abraham and Isaac.

It is God who takes care of us. Nobody else.

Obedience to God

Before Moses left Midian, the LORD said to him, "Return to Egypt, for all those who wanted to kill you have died."

So Moses took his wife and sons, put them on a donkey, and headed back to the land of Egypt. In his hand he carried the staff of God.

And the LORD told Moses, "When you arrive back in Egypt, go to Pharaoh and perform all the miracles I have empowered you to do. But I will harden his heart so he will refuse to let the people go. Then you will tell him, 'This is what the LORD says: Israel is my firstborn son. I commanded you, "Let my son go, so he can worship me." But since you have refused, I will now kill your firstborn son!' "

On the way to Egypt, at a place where Moses and his family had stopped for the night, the LORD confronted him and was about to kill him. But Moses' wife, Zipporah, took a flint knife and circumcised her son. She touched his feet with the foreskin and said, "Now you are a bridegroom of blood to me." (When she said "a bridegroom of blood," she was referring to the circumcision.) After that, the LORD left him alone.

Exodus 4:19–26 NLT

There is only one way—God's way. God told Moses it was safe to go back to Egypt.

Apparently Moses' wife, Zipporah, a Midianite, had resisted circumcising their son. So, on the way back to Egypt, God threatened to kill him. Why? Centuries earlier, God had told Abraham that those who were not circumcised had broken God's covenant and would be cut off from their people (Genesis 17:14).

Moses was about to become the leader of the people of Israel. In returning to Egypt, Moses and his family were making the choice to be part of Israel rather than part of Midian. Circumcising their son was a rite of conversion for Zipporah. It was also a choice for their son, doubtless a grown man when Zipporah circumcised him. Moses had been forty years old when he left Egypt. He was eighty years old at the time he was returning. He and Zipporah had been married for a very long time. But Zipporah was not happy about having to circumcise her son. She felt that she was paying a new dowry—this time in blood—just to remain Moses' wife and to keep her already old son. She didn't like having to start all over again, as if she were a new bride. She was old. Moses was old. But God asked them to begin brand-new lives. It's never too late to do things right.

His Banner over Me

The Amalekites came and attacked the Israelites at Rephidim. Moses said to Joshua, "Choose some of our men and go out to fight the Amalekites. Tomorrow I will stand on top of the hill with the staff of God in my hands."

So Joshua fought the Amalekites as Moses had ordered, and Moses, Aaron and Hur went to the top of the hill. As long as Moses held up his hands, the Israelites were winning, but whenever he lowered his hands, the Amalekites were winning. When Moses' hands grew tired, they took a stone and put it under him and he sat on it. Aaron and Hur held his hands up— one on one side, one on the other—so that his hands remained steady till sunset. So Joshua overcame the Amalekite army with the sword.

Then the LORD said to Moses, "Write this on a scroll as something to be remembered and make sure that Joshua hears it, because I will completely blot out the memory of Amalek from under heaven."

Moses built an altar and called it The LORD is my Banner. He said, "For hands were lifted up to the throne of the LORD. The LORD will be at war against the Amalekites from generation to generation."

Exodus 17:8–16 NIV

*S*ymbols matter. Our lives are full of them. Stop signs. Traffic lights. The letters that spell out words. Moses' staff had been his tool as a shepherd. He had just struck it against a rock to give the Israelites water. It had become a sign of God's work in his life. So he lifted it over his head while the Israelite's fought. That uplifted staff served as a symbol of God's watchful care over his people during their first battle. Aaron and Hur joined with Moses to demonstrate unity of purpose with God in the fight against their enemies, the Amalekites.

Neither the staff nor Moses' hands were magic. God was at war against the Amalekites. Moses didn't credit Joshua, the staff, Aaron, Hur, or himself for the victory. God had saved the people that day in answer to the prayers symbolized by their upraised hands holding Moses' staff.

God told Moses that the job was not yet done. The day was to be commemorated and remembered, because a time would come in the future when the last of the Amalekites would be relegated to history. The fulfillment of God's promise came during the reign of Israel's first king, Saul.

Symbols and commemorations help us remember what God has done in our lives. They prepare us by giving us the strength to face what our futures hold.

Big Sister, Little Brother

Although Moses was the most humble person in all the world, Miriam and Aaron started complaining, "Moses had no right to marry that woman from Ethiopia! Who does he think he is? The LORD has spoken to us, not just to him." The LORD heard their complaint and told Moses, Aaron, and Miriam to come to the entrance of the sacred tent. There the LORD appeared in a cloud and told Aaron and Miriam to come closer. Then after commanding them to listen carefully, he said:

"I, the LORD, speak to prophets
in visions and dreams.
But my servant Moses
is the leader of my people.
He sees me face to face,
and everything I say to him
is perfectly clear.
You have no right to criticize
my servant Moses."

The LORD became angry at Aaron and Miriam. And after the LORD left and the cloud disappeared from over the sacred tent, Miriam's skin turned white with leprosy. When Aaron saw what had happened to her, he said to Moses, "Sir, please don't punish us for doing such a foolish thing. Don't let Miriam's flesh rot away like a child born dead!"

Moses prayed, "LORD God, please heal her."

But the LORD replied, "Miriam would be disgraced for seven days if her father had punished her by spitting in her face. So make her stay outside the camp for seven days, before coming back."

Numbers 12:1–14 CEV

Just who did Moses think he was? Zipporah had been Moses' wife when he returned to Egypt. Whether she had died, whether Moses had divorced her, or whether Moses was adding a second wife to his household is unknown. For some reason, Miriam and Aaron thought Moses had no right to marry the Ethiopian woman. By claiming that God spoke to them, too, they meant to imply that God agreed with them.

God told Moses' siblings that they had no business claiming to be speaking for God when they weren't. God spoke to Moses face-to-face, but not with them.

Moses' sister Miriam was singled out for punishment. Perhaps she was the ringleader. In any case, God gave her leprosy, which turned her as white as snow. But her punishment was only temporary. God healed her within a week.

God will protect his own. If God is for us, who can be against us? Even our closest family members can't stand in God's way.

Burning Down a City

The LORD said to Joshua, "Stretch out the sword that is in your hand toward Ai; for I will give it into your hand." And Joshua stretched out the sword that was in his hand toward the city. As soon as he stretched out his hand, the troops in ambush rose quickly out of their place and rushed forward. They entered the city, took it, and at once set the city on fire. So when the men of Ai looked back, the smoke of the city was rising to the sky. They had no power to flee this way or that, for the people who fled to the wilderness turned back against the pursuers. When Joshua and all Israel saw that the ambush had taken the city and that the smoke of the city was rising, then they turned back and struck down the men of Ai. And the others came out from the city against them; so they were surrounded by Israelites, some on one side, and some on the other; and Israel struck them down until no one was left who survived or escaped. But the king of Ai was taken alive and brought to Joshua.

Joshua 8:18–23 NRSV

❦

*V*ictory is sweet. The first battle against Ai had been a disaster because one man had stolen some plunder from God at Jericho. Ai was a small city compared to Jericho. *Ai* means "ruin," because the village that Joshua faced was just that, the barely inhabited rubble of an earlier city, long destroyed. The second battle, with God's instructions, went much better. Joshua's early career repeated incidents similar to those faced by Moses in order that the Israelites could recognize that God was with him just as he had been with Moses.

Just as Moses, with the help of Aaron and Hur, had held his staff up symbolically while Joshua led Israel to battle against the Amalekites, so God told Joshua to raise his sword over the city of Ai. Joshua's troops that had been in hiding in ambush entered the city and set it afire. The enemy troops of Ai that had been pursuing Jacob and the soldiers with him saw their city in flames and lost heart, making it easy then for the Israelites to conquer them. When the king of Ai came before Joshua, Joshua himself executed him by impaling him on a pole. Afterward, he had the king's body thrown down at the entrance of the city. They raised a large pile of stones over the body as a memorial to Israel's victory.

God will grant us victory over our troubles, whether they be external or internal.

God's Tactics

The men of Gibeon sent word to Joshua camped at Gilgal, "Don't let us down now! Come up here quickly! Save us! Help us! All the Amorite kings who live up in the hills have ganged up on us."

So Joshua set out from Gilgal, his whole army with him—all those tough soldiers! GOD told him, "Don't give them a second thought. I've put them under your thumb—not one of them will stand up to you."

Joshua marched all night from Gilgal and took them by total surprise. GOD threw them into total confusion before Israel, a major victory at Gibeon. Israel chased them along the ridge to Beth Horon and fought them all the way down to Azekah and Makkedah. As they ran from the People of Israel, down from the Beth Horon ridge and all the way to Azekah, GOD pitched huge stones on them out of the sky and many died. More died from the hailstones than the People of Israel killed with the sword.

The day GOD gave the Amorites up to Israel, Joshua spoke to GOD, with all Israel listening:

"Stop, Sun, over Gibeon;
Halt, Moon, over Aijalon Valley."
And Sun stopped,
Moon stood stock still
Until he defeated his enemies.

Joshua 10:6–13 MSG

God takes care of those on his side even if they aren't exactly nice people. God had told the Israelites not to make alliances with the Canaanites. But the Gibeonites of Canaan tricked the Israelites into believing they'd come from a distant land, so the Israelites made a treaty with the Gibeonites. When the other Canaanites in the land learned that Gibeon had gone over to the Israelite invaders, they were furious and attacked them. Because of the treaty the Israelites had with the Gibeonites, Israel had no choice but to come to their aid.

God told Joshua not to worry. God promised that he would take care of things for them. God threw rocks from out of the sky, slaughtering the Canaanite armies arrayed against Gibea and the Israelites. Then God spoke, stopping the moon and the sun in the sky. Since it was not possible to fight in the dark, it gave the Israelites extra time and Joshua achieved a great victory.

Just as God had spoken to create the sun and the moon, so his power over the universe was undiminished. Joshua's—and Israel's—confidence in God's power grew immensely after this.

Just because we don't see how to fix a problem doesn't mean that God is similarly blind.

Brother Against Brother

In the morning, the Israelites set out and camped near Gibeah. The men of Israel went out to fight against Benjamin and took their battle positions against Gibeah. The Benjaminites came out of Gibeah and slaughtered 22,000 men of Israel on the field that day. But the Israelite army rallied and again took their battle positions in the same place where they positioned themselves on the first day. They went up, wept before the LORD until evening, and inquired of Him: "Should we again fight against our brothers the Benjaminites?"

And the LORD answered: "Fight against them."

On the second day the Israelites advanced against the Benjaminites. That same day the Benjaminites came out from Gibeah to meet them and slaughtered an additional 18,000 Israelites on the field; all were armed men.

The whole Israelite army went to Bethel where they wept and sat before the LORD. They fasted that day until evening and offered burnt offerings and fellowship offerings to the LORD. Then the Israelites inquired of the Lord. In those days, the ark of the covenant of God was there, and Phinehas son of Eleazar, son of Aaron, was serving before it. The Israelites asked: "Should we again fight against our brothers the Benjaminites or should we stop?"

The LORD answered: "Fight, because I will hand them over to you tomorrow."

Judges 20:19–28 HCSB

꙰

*S*ome things are worth fighting for. An unnamed Levite had traveled far to get his estranged concubine back from her father. On the journey home, he had stopped for the night in the tribal lands of the Benjaminites at Gibeah. There his concubine was raped and murdered by a group of men from that village. But the people of Benjamin refused to bring those guilty men to justice. So the other tribes of Israel went to war against the Benjaminites in order to rectify the injustice.

The first attack against Benjamin failed disastrously, despite the fact that God had told the Israelites to go up and fight them. After a second defeat, the Israelites prayed, and again God told them to fight. At last, on the third attempt, Israel routed the armies of Benjamin, nearly exterminating the tribe.

It was God's will for Israel to seek justice against Benjamin. Just because things didn't go well—in fact went very badly—for a while did not mean that Israel wasn't hearing from God or wasn't doing what God wanted. Just because you have problems doesn't mean you aren't doing precisely what God wants you to be doing. In fact, it is rare for God's will to go smoothly. Narrow is the road and hard is the way that leads to righteousness.

God Strikes the Enemies

The Philistines also went and deployed themselves in the Valley of Rephaim. So David inquired of the LORD, saying, "Shall I go up against the Philistines? Will You deliver them into my hand?"

And the LORD said to David, "Go up, for I will doubtless deliver the Philistines into your hand."

So David went to Baal Perazim, and David defeated them there; and he said, "The LORD has broken through my enemies before me, like a breakthrough of water." Therefore he called the name of that place Baal Perazim. And they left their images there, and David and his men carried them away.

Then the Philistines went up once again and deployed themselves in the Valley of Rephaim. Therefore David inquired of the LORD, and He said, "You shall not go up; circle around behind them, and come upon them in front of the mulberry trees. And it shall be, when you hear the sound of marching in the tops of the mulberry trees, then you shall advance quickly. For then the LORD will go out before you to strike the camp of the Philistines." And David did so, as the LORD commanded him; and he drove back the Philistines from Geba as far as Gezer.

2 Samuel 5:18–25 NKJV

*S*ometimes war is the answer. It just depends on what the question is. Shortly after David became king over a united twelve tribes of Israel, the Philistines set out to crush his new kingdom. The Philistines had long been a problem for Israel. Samson had fought them during the era of the judges. In the time of Samuel, they had captured the ark. Saul had fought them. David had killed their champion, the giant Goliath. They had but a few years before they destroyed the nation of Israel—or so they had thought—when they killed Saul and the crown prince, Jonathan. But David had come to power and reunified what had been the scattered tribes of the Jewish people. So the Philistines deployed themselves in the Valley of Rephaim, the broad plain southwest of Jerusalem, the city that David had just taken from the Jebusites and was establishing as his new capital. David asked God if he should respond to the Philistine provocation. God told him to attack them. So at Baal Perazim, located just northwest of Jerusalem, David defeated the Philistines and captured their idols. The capture of the idols demonstrated to both Israel and the Philistines that the God of Israel was the stronger God. *Baal Perazim* means "lord of breakthroughs." Yahweh had "broken through" his enemies like water punching through a dam.

God can break through whatever stands in our way.

Stop the War

As for the sons of Israel who lived in the cities of Judah, Rehoboam reigned over them. Then King Rehoboam sent Adoram, who was over the forced labor, and all Israel stoned him to death. And King Rehoboam made haste to mount his chariot to flee to Jerusalem.

So Israel has been in rebellion against the house of David to this day.

It came about when all Israel heard that Jeroboam had returned, that they sent and called him to the assembly and made him king over all Israel. None but the tribe of Judah followed the house of David.

Now when Rehoboam had come to Jerusalem, he assembled all the house of Judah and the tribe of Benjamin, 180,000 chosen men who were warriors, to fight against the house of Israel to restore the kingdom to Rehoboam the son of Solomon.

But the word of God came to Shemaiah the man of God, saying,

"Speak to Rehoboam the son of Solomon, king of Judah, and to all the house of Judah and Benjamin and to the rest of the people, saying,

'Thus says the LORD, "You must not go up and fight against your relatives the sons of Israel; return every man to his house, for this thing has come from Me." ' " So they listened to the word of the LORD, and returned and went their way according to the word of the LORD.

1 Kings 12:17–24 NASB

*D*oing God's will sometimes means not doing our will. When Solomon died, his son Rehoboam took the throne and ignored wise counsel. The tribes to his north rebelled against him and chose Jeroboam as their king instead of him. Only the Levites, the people of Benjamin, and the tribe of Simeon remained loyal to him. Rehoboam's first instinct was to crush the rebellion.

Although Rehoboam was something of a fool when it came to politics, he was not willing to resist God. When God told him to stand down because the rebellion and the division of the nation were God's will, Rehoboam listened.

The rupture of the kingdom, though precipitated by Rehoboam's folly, was in fact God's punishment against Solomon for his idolatry. That idolatrous tendency grew. Jeroboam, the rebel king in the north, set up false temples with idols in place of the temple in Jerusalem. What began with Solomon infected the divided people of Israel. It ultimately led to the Assyrian and Babylonian captivities, when God judged not just the house of David but his whole people.

Doing what God wants is always the wisest course of action.

God Doesn't Have Limits

The man of God went to the king of Israel and said, "This is what the LORD says: The Arameans have said, 'The LORD is a god of the hills and not of the plains.' So I will defeat this vast army for you. Then you will know that I am the LORD."

The two armies camped opposite each other for seven days, and on the seventh day the battle began. The Israelites killed 100,000 Aramean foot soldiers in one day. The rest fled into the town of Aphek, but the wall fell on them and killed another 27,000. Ben-hadad fled into the town and hid in a secret room.

Ben-hadad's officers said to him, "Sir, we have heard that the kings of Israel are merciful. So let's humble ourselves by wearing burlap around our waists and putting ropes on our heads, and surrender to the king of Israel. Then perhaps he will let you live."

So they put on burlap and ropes, and they went to the king of Israel and begged, "Your servant Ben-hadad says, 'Please let me live!'"

The king of Israel responded, "Is he still alive? He is my brother!"

The men took this as a good sign and quickly picked up on his words. "Yes," they said, "your brother Ben-hadad!"

"Go and get him," the king of Israel told them. And when Ben-hadad arrived, Ahab invited him up into his chariot.

1 Kings 20:28–33 NLT

※

*R*eality has a way of getting in the way of delusion. The Arameans, like most people of the ancient world, believed that gods worked only in certain places. They had a god for each city. They had a god for sickness, a god for death, and a god for health. They had a god for blacksmiths and a god for farmers. The god of farmers could not help a blacksmith or vice versa. The god of Babylon had no power in Nineveh. So when the Arameans lost in a fight against Israel, the reason for their defeat seemed obvious: they had chosen to fight against Israel in the wrong place. Yahweh was a hill god. The equally obvious solution was to fight Israel in a valley. Surely Yahweh would be powerless there.

Unfortunately for the Arameans, their comprehension of reality was seriously flawed. They had lost because Yahweh was against them, and since he was the only God who actually existed, and since he had no limits at all, they were simply and fundamentally doomed.

The Arameans lost because God wanted them to lose. When God is for us, no one can be against us. No one can stand successfully against God's will.

Pride Goes Before a Fall

Isaiah son of Amoz sent a message to Hezekiah: "This is what the LORD, the God of Israel, says: I have heard your prayer concerning Sennacherib king of Assyria. This is the word that the LORD has spoken against him:

"'The Virgin Daughter of Zion
    despises you and mocks you.
    The Daughter of Jerusalem
    tosses her head as you flee.
Who is it you have insulted and blasphemed?
    Against whom have you raised
        your voice and lifted your eyes
        in pride?
Against the Holy One of Israel!
    By your messengers you have
        heaped insults on the Lord.
And you have said,
    "With my many chariots
    I have ascended the heights of the
        mountains, the utmost heights
        of Lebanon.
    I have cut down its tallest cedars,
        the choicest of its pines.
    I have reached its remotest parts,
        the finest of its forests.
I have dug wells in foreign lands
    and drunk the water there.
    With the soles of my feet
    I have dried up all the streams
        of Egypt."

2 Kings 19:20–24 NIV

*H*ezekiah was trapped in his city, besieged by a superior force. Hezekiah could see no hope; defeat seemed inevitable. He could count the number of forces against him, and he knew what Sennacherib had already done. In his march south, the Assyrian army had defeated every city and every nation he had gone to war against. When Sennacherib had sent his message demanding surrender and boasting of his might, his boast was not an empty one. It was based on firm, empirical evidence. He had a stellar résumé, an impeccable and flawless record of accomplishment. Hezekiah had no reason, humanly speaking, to hope.

But Hezekiah prayed to God anyway, spreading the insulting letter he had received from Sennacherib out on the altar to show it to God. God looked and told him not to worry. In fact, God's response to Sennacherib's arrogant letter was arrogance doubled, laughing and mocking at the enemy. Sennacherib's conquest of the north, against the cities of Tyre and Sidon in Lebanon, and his success in Egypt would mean nothing in the end. He had made a serious error in judgment when he chose to attack God's people. Israel was not like her neighbors. God is never afraid; so it's a wonder that we ever are.

God Has the Last Word

I promise that the king of Assyria won't get into Jerusalem, or shoot an arrow into the city, or even surround it and prepare to attack. As surely as I am the LORD, he will return by the way he came and will never enter Jerusalem. I will protect it for myself and for my servant David.

That same night the LORD sent an angel to the camp of the Assyrians, and he killed one hundred eighty-five thousand of them. And so the next morning, the camp was full of dead bodies. After this King Sennacherib went back to Assyria and lived in the city of Nineveh. One day he was worshiping in the temple of his god Nisroch, when his sons, Adrammelech and Sharezer, killed him with their swords. They escaped to the land of Ararat, and his son Esarhaddon became king.

2 Kings 19:32–37 CEV

🌼

*Y*our arm is too short to box with God. Sennacherib learned that lesson the hard way. His attack against Jerusalem and his arrogant words against the God of Israel all came to naught. In one night, nearly all Sennacherib's army died of a plague, forcing him to withdraw and head back home. Without Hezekiah having to do a thing, God had fixed his problem completely. He'd even given him the spoils of war without the war.

The ancient Assyrians kept a detailed history of the events that transpired every year. During that year, the records describe how Sennacherib laid siege to and conquered city after city as he marched south. But when the records speak of his attack on Jerusalem, the language shifts just slightly. Once again, the records describe the siege on Jerusalem, how he locked Hezekiah up inside the city like a bird in a cage. But strikingly missing from the record is any account of conquest or despoiling of the city. Totalitarian dictatorships, of which Assyria was definitely one, may not outright lie. But they like to hide embarrassing truths. Thus, the defeat was left unmentioned though victory was never claimed.

Sennacherib's humiliating loss was still known within the government, and such an egregious failure could not be tolerated. Sennacherib was removed from office in the most common way that kings were removed from office back then: he was assassinated not by strangers but by his family, two of his sons. Another son, Esarhaddon, took the throne after driving the assassins into exile.

Not only did God defeat the army of Sennacherib, but he also saw to it that Sennacherib personally paid for his arrogance against God. If we leave no place for God in our calculations, God might leave no place for us in his.

Peace in Our Time

At that time Merodach-baladan son of Baladan, king of Babylon, sent letters and a gift to Hezekiah since he heard that Hezekiah had been sick. Hezekiah gave them a hearing and showed them his whole treasure house—the silver, the gold, the spices, and the precious oil—and his armory, and everything that was found in his treasuries. There was nothing in his palace and in all his realm that Hezekiah did not show them.

Then the prophet Isaiah came to King Hezekiah and asked him, "What did these men say, and where did they come to you from?"

Hezekiah replied, "They came from a distant country, from Babylon."

Isaiah asked, "What have they seen in your palace?"

Hezekiah answered, "They have seen everything in my palace. There isn't anything in my treasuries that I didn't show them."

Then Isaiah said to Hezekiah, "Hear the word of the LORD: 'The time will certainly come when everything in your palace and all that your fathers have stored up until this day will be carried off to Babylon; nothing will be left,' says the LORD. 'Some of your descendants who come from you will be taken away, and they will become eunuchs in the palace of the king of Babylon.'"

Then Hezekiah said to Isaiah, "The word of the LORD that you have spoken is good," for he thought: Why not, if there will be peace and security during my lifetime?

2 Kings 20:12–19 HCSB

✳

God's words to Hezekiah—that the Babylonians who had just visited him as guests would return in the future as conquerors—came as good news to him. He recognized that the predication of future doom was just that, something for another day. He knew that in his time everything would be well, so that's all that fundamentally mattered.

Was he self-absorbed? Was he uncaring of his descendants? Not at all. The future was beyond his control. Each day had enough trouble of its own. All he could do was seek God and his righteousness. God was already in the future, and so it was God's concern only. The reality was, God was in the present, too, and the present was God's concern only as well. God had rescued Hezekiah from Sennacherib. He had rescued him from a serious illness. Why should Hezekiah worry about anything? Whatever God spoke was good, and he would rejoice in the fact that God was speaking to him and would take care of him.

We don't need to borrow trouble, and we don't need to worry about the future. God will take care of our needs, and he knows what tomorrow holds.

God Violently Stops Violence

There is a river whose streams make
glad the city of God,
the holy habitation of the
Most High.
God is in the midst of the city; it shall
not be moved;
God will help it when the
morning dawns.
The nations are in an uproar, the
kingdoms totter;
he utters his voice, the earth melts.
The LORD of hosts is with us;
the God of Jacob is our refuge.
Selah
Come, behold the works of the LORD;
see what desolations he has
brought on the earth.

He makes wars cease to the end of
the earth;
he breaks the bow, and shatters
the spear;
he burns the shields with fire.
"Be still, and know that I am God!
I am exalted among the nations,
I am exalted in the earth."
The LORD of hosts is with us;
the God of Jacob is our refuge.

Psalm 46:4–11 NRSV

It is easy to let the whirling storms distract us, get the better of us, and send us into a tizzy. But despite how everything seems to be whirling around, despite how everything seems chaotic, God is calmly in charge. The "river" that made God's city (Jerusalem) glad was a metaphor for God's favor on his people.

Israel was located at the crossroads of the world. All trade, all travel between the centers of world power in Mesopotamia in the north and Egypt in the south had to pass through the tiny nation of Israel. The only clear highways went straight through Israel's heart, and it was a choke point. Whoever controlled the land of Israel controlled world trade and could make a fortune.

The nations around Israel longed to secure that thoroughfare. Seeking dominance, armies from the north and south passed through and met in battle on the hills of Israel. Israel suffered in the cross fire.

But the nations were not in charge. God was overseeing it all, and he would, some day, end the conflict. The weapons of war and the men of battle would all be destroyed by the hand of God.

God can take the stormy heart, the heart raging with conflict, and give it peace. The strife, the disquiet, the confusion and pain of life can all be pacified by the God of the universe.

Enemies Make Good Footstools

The Lord said to my Lord,
"Sit at My right hand,
Till I make Your enemies
Your footstool."
The Lord shall send the rod of Your
strength out of Zion.
Rule in the midst of
Your enemies!
Your people shall be volunteers
In the day of Your power;
In the beauties of holiness, from
the womb of the morning,
You have the dew of Your youth.
The Lord has sworn
And will not relent,
"You are a priest forever
According to the order of
Melchizedek."
The Lord is at Your right hand;
He shall execute kings in the day
of His wrath.
He shall judge among the nations,
He shall fill the places with
dead bodies,
He shall execute the heads of
many countries.
He shall drink of the brook by
the wayside;
Therefore He shall lift up
the head.

Psalm 110:1–7 NKJV

God destroyed his enemies by making them his friends. God said that the enemies of his Son would be turned into his footstool and that he was a priest forever, in the order of Melchizedek. Melchizedek was the king of Jerusalem in the time of the patriarch Abraham. He was also described as a priest of God Most High (Genesis 14:18). Abraham had led an army against those who had attacked the city of Sodom and taken his nephew Lot captive. Following his victory and the rescue of his nephew and the other captives, Melchizedek had come to Abraham and blessed him. Abraham then gave Melchizedek a tenth of the spoils he had taken from the battle.

Nothing else is known about Melchizedek. He never showed up again in the story of Abraham. There was no genealogy given for him, and no descendants were listed. He simply appeared, played his brief role on the stage of scripture, and then vanished.

The job of priest and king had been united in Melchizedek. Melchizedek consequently served as a symbol or type of the Messiah, who someday would once again combine the kingly and priestly duties in one individual.

God promised victory to the kings and priests of Jerusalem, a victory that would ultimately be fulfilled in the coming of that Messiah, a man like Melchizedek whose name meant "king of righteousness." Such a man can judge us rightly, and forgive us mercifully.

Speedy Is the Prey

The LORD said to me, "Take for yourself a large tablet and write on it in ordinary letters: Swift is the booty, speedy is the prey.

"And I will take to Myself faithful witnesses for testimony, Uriah the priest and the son of Jeberechiah."

So I approached the prophetess, and she conceived and gave birth to a son. Then the LORD said to me, "Name him Maher-shalal-hash-baz; for before the boy knows how to cry out 'My father' or 'My mother,' the wealth of Damascus and the spoil of Samaria will be carried away before the king of Assyria."

Isaiah 8:1–4 NASB

*W*hen God solves a problem, it stays solved. Ahaz, the king of Judah in Jerusalem, was facing serious problems. The combined armies of Damascus and Samaria were marching against him. Although he feared for his life and the life of his nation, he resisted God's offers for help, preferring to scramble on his own. But God insisted on helping him anyway.

The very odd name of Isaiah's son, *Maher-shalal-hash-baz*, means "Swift is the booty, speedy is the prey." All names in Hebrew had obvious meanings to Hebrew speakers. But names usually were only one word, maybe two. The name for Isaiah's son was a full sentence. It was not an ordinary sort of name at all. God used the prophet's life as an illustration within the book of his prophecy. Just as God had Isaiah run around naked for three years and just as he'd had Isaiah bury and thus ruin a belt, so now the birth of his son also served God's purposes.

God predicted that Damascus and Samaria would be defeated by Assyria before Isaiah's son was old enough to say "My father" or "My mother." Thus within three years of God's words, they had both been crushed by Tiglath-Pileser, the king of Assyria. Ahaz—and Jerusalem—were safe.

Ahaz was never a good king. He was, in fact, an evil king. He once had the priest Uriah rebuild the altar in the temple and even gave him instructions on performing the sacrifices there. But although Ahaz worshipped Yahweh, he also worshipped the many gods of the Canaanites, including Baal and Asherah. He frequented all the hilltop shrines, where he offered incense and sacrifice. Worse, he was guilty of sacrificing several of his children as burnt offerings (2 Chronicles 28:1–4). But one son of Ahaz, a man named Hezekiah, became one of Judah's best kings ever, rejecting all that his father, Ahaz, had done. He attempted to bring a revival to the Jewish nation. Ahaz's life demonstrated that God's blessings fall on both the just and the unjust.

God Will Destroy Their Children

This is what the LORD of Heaven's
Armies says:
"I, myself, have risen against
Babylon!
I will destroy its children and its
children's children,"
says the LORD.
"I will make Babylon a desolate place
of owls, filled with swamps and
marshes.
I will sweep the land with the broom
of destruction.
I, the LORD of Heaven's Armies,
have spoken!"
The LORD of Heaven's Armies has
sworn this oath:
"It will all happen as I have planned.
It will be as I have decided.

I will break the Assyrians when they
are in Israel;
I will trample them on
my mountains.
My people will no longer be
their slaves nor bow down under
their heavy loads.
I have a plan for the whole earth,
a hand of judgment upon all
the nations.
The LORD of Heaven's Armies
has spoken—
who can change his plans?
When his hand is raised,
who can stop him?"

Isaiah 14:22–27 NLT

❋

*Y*ou can't spoil God's plans. Whatever God has decided to do is what will happen. Babylon and Assyria imagined themselves invincible. They thought they were in control. Reality was something else all together, and God's plans for them were a bit different from their plans for themselves. From God's perspective, the Assyrians and Babylonians were merely tools in his hands that he used for his purposes. When God was done with them, he set them aside.

For the Babylonians and Assyrians, the end of their power was a disappointment and a surprise. From the standpoint of the Jewish people, however, it was a moment of great pleasure, a time of intense thanksgiving. No more would the Jewish people be enslaved; no longer would they be barred from their homes. At long last, the great suffering they had endured as punishment for their sins would be lifted. Assyria would fall to Babylon. Babylon would fall to Persia. Persia would then send the Israelites home and even pay for the rebuilding of Jerusalem's temple. Hundreds of years before it came to pass, God let his people know everything would turn out well. He granted them his divine perspective.

We know how the story of the universe ends: God wins. Since we belong to God, we will win too. We have an eternity to spend with him. So things couldn't be better for us.

Trust Only God

This is a message about Egypt:
The LORD comes to Egypt,
   riding swiftly on a cloud.
The people are weak from fear.
Their idols tremble as he approaches
  and says,
"I will punish Egypt
   with civil war—
   neighbors, cities, and kingdoms
   will fight each other.
"Egypt will be discouraged
   when I confuse their plans.

They will try to get advice
   from their idols,
   from the spirits of the dead,
   and from fortunetellers.
I will put the Egyptians
   under the power of a cruel,
   heartless king.
I, the LORD All-Powerful,
   have promised this."

Isaiah 19:1–4 CEV

*L*ies can live for a long time. For thousands of years Egypt had endured as a major world power. Egyptians had worshipped their gods and performed their rituals with little change for those same thousands of years. They never felt the need for change and never knew the foundation of their civilization was like the sand beyond the Nile. The plagues from the time of Moses, when God had come upon them like a cloud, had passed from their memories and had no long-term effect on their history.

But God told them the time would come when their civilization would come crashing down. A few hundred years after Isaiah, Alexander the Great, the Macedonian general, conquered Egypt. He took its wealth for his own and crowned himself pharaoh. When he died, one of his generals, Ptolemy, took the Egyptian throne in his place. That general's descendants, known as the Ptolemies, ruled Egypt thereafter. The last of Ptolemy's descendants was a woman named Cleopatra. When she killed herself with an asp's bite, the Egyptian nation was absorbed by the Roman Empire. The cruel, heartless king who ruled them at last was the first emperor of Rome, Augustus Caesar, the adopted son of Cleopatra's love, Julius Caesar. Augustus would be followed by many other emperors.

The idols, the fortune-tellers, the mediums—those the Egyptians had depended upon for thousands of years—ultimately failed them. In the end, the Egyptians came to realize they had put their trust in empty lies. They abandoned their gods at last, turning first to those of the Romans who had conquered them, but then at last to the worship of the one true God.

We need to be careful about who and what we put our trust in. We can count only on God.

❀❀❀❀❀❀❀❀❀❀❀❀❀❀❀❀❀❀❀❀❀❀❀❀❀❀❀❀❀❀❀❀

A Precious Cornerstone

Thus says the Lord GOD:
> "Behold, I lay in Zion a stone for a
>   foundation,
> A tried stone, a precious corner-
>   stone, a sure foundation;
> Whoever believes will not
>   act hastily.
> Also I will make justice the mea-
>   suring line,
> And righteousness the plummet;
> The hail will sweep away the ref-
>   uge of lies,
> And the waters will overflow the
>   hiding place.
> Your covenant with death will be
>   annulled,
> And your agreement with Sheol
>   will not stand;
> When the overflowing scourge
>   passes through,
> Then you will be trampled down
>   by it . . .
> For the bed is too short to stretch
>   out on,
> And the covering so narrow that
>   one cannot wrap himself in
>   it.
> For the LORD will rise up as at
>   Mount Perazim.
> He will be angry as in the Valley
>   of Gibeon—
> That He may do His work, His
>   awesome work.
> And bring to pass His act, His
>   unusual act.
> For I have heard from the Lord
>   GOD of hosts,
> A destruction determined even
>   upon the whole earth.

Isaiah 28:16–19, 21–22 NKJV

❀

God overflows on his people, whether in blessing or chastisement. The "waters will overflow" and the reference to Mount Perazim echo David's words when he had his victory against the Philistines at Perazim right after he had became king of a unified Israel (2 Samuel 5:20). The Valley of Gibeon refers to the time David chased the Philistines from Gibeon to Gezer (1 Chronicles 14:16). God told the Israelites that just as Israel had defeated the Philistines, so the Assyrians would defeat the Israelites. As God had once fought against Israel's enemies, so God would now fight against Israel.

Sheol is merely the Hebrew word for "grave," and the covenant with it and death refer to the Israelite's mistaken notion that somehow their treaty with God precluded the possibility of anything bad ever happening to them. They forgot that God's treaty promised them not just prosperity but also great disaster if they failed to keep it.

Nevertheless, God promised that his people would be his people no matter what. He was responsible for them, and he had no choice but to discipline them. Disciplined or pampered, God's people remain his.

Like Dust with His Sword

"Coastlands, listen to Me in silence,
And let the peoples gain
new strength;
Let them come forward, then let
them speak;
Let us come together for
judgment.
"Who has aroused one from the east
Whom He calls in righteousness
to His feet?
He delivers up nations before him
And subdues kings.
He makes them like dust with
his sword,
As the wind-driven chaff with
his bow.
"He pursues them, passing on
in safety,
By a way he had not been
traversing with his feet.
"Who has performed and accom-
plished it,
Calling forth the generations
from the beginning?
'I, the LORD, am the first, and
with the last. I am He.' "
The coastlands have seen and
are afraid;
The ends of the earth tremble;
They have drawn near and
have come.
Each one helps his neighbor
And says to his brother,
"Be strong!"
So the craftsman encourages
the smelter,
And he who smooths metal with
the hammer encourages him
who beats the anvil,
Saying of the soldering,
"It is good";
And he fastens it with nails,
So that it will not totter.

Isaiah 41:1–7 NASB

✻

*S*ometimes God has to chase us. To the east of Israel lay the Persian Empire. God intended to use its king, Cyrus, to pursue the nations. When God pursues
people, it can be for good or ill. The word translated *pursues* in this passage is most
commonly used—as it is here—when someone is being chased, as an animal might
be chased by hunters. But it can also be used more positively, as in the final verse of
the famous Psalm 23, which explains that "goodness and lovingkindness" will "follow" us all the days of our life (NASB). That word translated as *follow* is the very word
here that appears as *pursues*. Goodness and love *pursue* us all the days of our lives.
God has to chase us. We resist his will for us. Too often, we fear what God wants to
do, imagining it is something he intends to do *to* us rather than *for* us.

The discipline that God was bringing against the Israelites for their unfaithfulness was going to be unpleasant. God didn't pretend otherwise. But like
bad-tasting medicine that makes people shudder, in the end it's for their good.
So it is with whatever God does. It may frighten us, but in the end, we'll recognize that it's all for the best.

God's Messiah

The LORD said to Cyrus, his chosen
    one:
    I have taken hold
    of your right hand
    to help you capture nations
    and remove kings from power.
City gates will open for you;
    not one will stay closed.
As I lead you,
    I will level mountains
    and break the iron bars
    on bronze gates of cities.
I will give you treasures
    hidden in dark
    and secret places.
Then you will know that I,
    the LORD God of Israel,
    have called you by name.

Cyrus, you don't even know me!
    But I have called you by name
    and highly honored you
    because of Israel,
    my chosen servant.
Only I am the LORD!
    There are no other gods.
    I have made you strong,
    though you don't know me.
Now everyone from east to west
    will learn that I am the LORD.
No other gods are real.
I create light and darkness,
    happiness and sorrow.
I, the LORD, do all of this.

Isaiah 45:1–7 CEV

*G*od can use anyone. The word translated *chosen servant* is the Hebrew word that comes into English as *Messiah* or by way of its Greek equivalent, *Christ*. The word more literally means "anointed one" and refers to how priests and kings had oil poured on their heads when they took their positions of authority.

Cyrus, the pagan king of Persia, the man who conquered Babylon and issued a decree that the captives of Israel could go home and rebuild God's temple in Jerusalem, was chosen by God for just that task. God had "anointed" him to perform a valuable service—defeat the enemies of his people Israel, rescue them, and set them free.

Even though Cyrus didn't know God, God knew him and used him for his own purposes. Thanks to Cyrus, a pagan, many people would come to know the one true God. God pointed out that there were no other gods. Yahweh alone existed. From Yahweh alone came all there was, whether light or dark, good or bad, happiness or sorrow. The universe as it exists in its many states was a consequence of God's creative effort.

We must never imagine that simply because God used us that it means everything is okay between God and us. How useful we are to God doesn't prove our righteousness. God used a pagan idolater and called him his messiah, after all.

Criticizing God

You heavens above, rain down
  righteousness;
    let the clouds shower it down.
    Let the earth open wide,
    let salvation spring up,
    let righteousness grow with it;
    I, the LORD, have created it.
Woe to him who quarrels with
  his Maker, to him who is but a
  potsherd among the potsherds on
  the ground.
    Does the clay say to the potter,
    "What are you making?"
    Does your work say,
    "He has no hands"?
Woe to him who says to his father,
    "What have you begotten?"
    or to his mother,
    "What have you brought to birth?"
This is what the LORD says—the Holy
  One of Israel, and its Maker:

Concerning things to come,
  do you question me about
    my children,
  or give me orders about the work
    of my hands?
It is I who made the earth
  and created mankind upon it.
  My own hands stretched out
    the heavens;
  I marshaled their starry hosts.
I will raise up Cyrus in my
  righteousness:
    I will make all his ways straight.
    He will rebuild my city
    and set my exiles free,
    but not for a price or reward,
    says the LORD Almighty.

Isaiah 45:8–13 NIV

*J*ust because you got mad at God doesn't mean you should have. God is God, and we aren't. Israel suffered because the people deserved to suffer for their idolatry. The Jewish people had no right to criticize God for how things turned out or for the pain and inconvenience they experienced any more than a broken bit of pottery on the ground had any cause to be speaking ill of the artist who made the pots.

God made the universe and everything in it. And when he made it, he announced that it was all good, from beginning to end. How could it be otherwise with God as its maker? The whole creation declared the glory of God. Is there suffering? Is there evil? God is still in control and going about the business of building his universe. The unfinished pot has no cause for criticism or concern. In the end, it will look just fine.

Even a king like Cyrus, who didn't know God, would perform God's will in a wonderful way. We can see only a tiny portion of eternity, the smallest fraction that exists during the course of our single life span, just as we don't see enough of the finished pot to criticize the artist putting it all together.

Judgment Is Coming

The word of the Lord came to me, saying, "Jeremiah, what do you see?" And I said, "I see a branch of an almond tree." Then the Lord said to me, "You have seen well, for I am watching over my word to perform it." The word of the Lord came to me a second time, saying, "What do you see?" And I said, "I see a boiling pot, tilted away from the north."

Then the Lord said to me: Out of the north disaster shall break out on all the inhabitants of the land. For now I am calling all the tribes of the kingdoms of the north, says the Lord; and they shall come and all of them shall set their thrones at the entrance of the gates of Jerusalem, against all its surrounding walls and against all the cities of Judah. And I will utter my judgments against them, for all their wickedness in forsaking me; they have made offerings to other gods, and worshiped the works of their own hands. But you, gird up your loins; stand up and tell them everything that I command you. Do not break down before them, or I will break you before them.

Jeremiah 1:11–17 NRSV

God communicated to Jeremiah on several levels: he told him things, he showed him images, and he asked him questions. God made certain that Jeremiah knew what he was saying so he could communicate God's message clearly to his people. God's people understood Jeremiah so well that they got angry with him. The government repeatedly incarcerated him and came close to executing him. The Israelites understood precisely the message God had for them; they knew that God was promising them disaster at the hands of the invading Babylonians. They simply chose not to believe it.

Right after God asked Jeremiah to be his prophet, God began training him to become his prophet, asking him questions about what he saw. Jeremiah's first vision was of an almond tree branch. The word for *almond* tree in Hebrew means "wakeful" or "vigilant" tree. Almond trees blossomed as early as January, long before any other tree put out buds for leaves. The "wakeful" branch signified God's intention to fulfill his word. He would be vigilant about it and bring it to pass soon. In fact, the prophecy was fulfilled within Jeremiah's lifetime. The second vision Jeremiah had was of a tilted, boiling pot. The pot signified the approaching disaster from Babylon.

Finally, God encouraged Jeremiah not to give up in the face of the difficult task that God had set for him to perform. He could count on God to take care of him.

Trusting the Wrong Thing

They have lied about the LORD,
And said, "It is not He.
Neither will evil come upon us,
Nor shall we see sword or famine.
And the prophets become wind,
For the word is not in them.
Thus shall it be done to them."
Therefore thus says the LORD God
of hosts:
"Because you speak this word,
Behold, I will make My words in
your mouth fire,
And this people wood,
And it shall devour them.
Behold, I will bring a nation
against you from afar,
O house of Israel," says the LORD.
"It is a mighty nation,
It is an ancient nation,
A nation whose language you do
not know,
Nor can you understand what
they say.
Their quiver is like an open tomb;
They are all mighty men.
And they shall eat up your harvest
and your bread,
Which your sons and daughters
should eat.
They shall eat up your flocks and
your herds;
They shall eat up your vines and
your fig trees;
They shall destroy your
fortified cities,
In which you trust, with
the sword."

Jeremiah 5:12–17 NKJV

✻

*E*ven smart people can be conned. The people of Israel were ordinary people and no less intelligent than anyone else. Nevertheless, the words of the prophets were not the sorts of words they wanted to hear, and so instead of heeding God, they listened to words that matched what they wanted God to be saying. Speaking a hard truth to power is usually a waste of time. But God told Jeremiah that he was with him, even though the Israelites dismissed the prophet's words as nothing but wind. But just as Jeremiah had once complained that God's words were a fire burning inside him (Jeremiah 20:9), so his words at last would burn those who heard them.

God's words could not help but have their effect simply because they were true. When the Babylonians set fire to Jerusalem, the truth of God's prophecy was obvious. Of course, believing at that moment of destruction was too late. They had not believed Jeremiah, whose words they could easily understand. But when the Babylonians attacked, they couldn't help but believe, even though they couldn't understand a word the Babylonians said.

The truth hurts, because reality can be sharp and prickly. But reality is all we have. Building our hopes on the pretty lies we prefer is ultimately disastrous.

But There Is No Peace

Thus says the LORD of hosts,
"They will thoroughly glean as the
vine the remnant of Israel;
Pass your hand again like a
grape gatherer
Over the branches."
To whom shall I speak and give
warning
That they may hear?
Behold, their ears are closed
And they cannot listen.
Behold, the word of the LORD has
become a reproach to them;
They have no delight in it.
But I am full of the wrath of the LORD;
I am weary with holding it in.
"Pour it out on the children in
the street
And on the gathering of young
men together;
For both husband and wife shall
be taken,
The aged and the very old." . . .
"Everyone is greedy for gain,
And from the prophet even to
the priest
Everyone deals falsely.
"They have healed the brokenness of
My people superficially,
Saying, 'Peace, peace,'
But there is no peace.
"Were they ashamed because of the
abomination they have done?
They were not even ashamed
at all;
They did not even know how
to blush.
Therefore they shall fall among
those who fall;
At the time that I punish them,
They shall be cast down," says
the LORD.

Jeremiah 6:9–11, 13–15 NASB

❋

The fortune-teller makes a fortune for himself by predicting just what his customers want to hear. A message of peace, prosperity, and health will always find a gullible audience.

As God's people in Jeremiah's day stood on the obvious brink of destruction, they were willing to suspend disbelief and cling to the words of those more concerned with lining their own pockets than with the truth of God.

They had become couch potatoes fattened on empty gods. The personal trainer—Babylon—had come to kick their lazy bodies off their beds of ease. But they only wanted a simple, quick, and painless fix from the disaster they had created.

God's Babylonian diet was the only solution to their polytheistic overindulgence. One way or another, they were going to get on that treadmill and lose it all. God will take us through what we need to go through, and we can know that he'll get the truth to us one way or another.

Incurable Sickness

Pack your bags and prepare to leave;
  the siege is about to begin.
For this is what the LORD says:
"Suddenly, I will fling out
  all you who live in this land.
I will pour great troubles upon you,
  and at last you will feel my anger."
My wound is severe,
  and my grief is great.
My sickness is incurable,
  but I must bear it.
My home is gone,
  and no one is left to help me
    rebuild it.
My children have been taken away,
  and I will never see them again.

The shepherds of my people have lost
  their senses.
  They no longer seek wisdom from
    the LORD.
Therefore, they fail completely,
  and their flocks are scattered.
Listen! Hear the terrifying roar of
  great armies
    as they roll down from the north.
The towns of Judah will be destroyed
  and become a haunt for jackals.

Jeremiah 10:17–22 NLT

According to Mark Twain, a lie can travel halfway around the world while the truth is putting on its shoes. Jeremiah was the prophet of the end, standing against such lies. He stood on the precipice and pointed at the pit with outstretched hand warning everyone to turn back. He warned them even as they closed their eyes, plugged their ears, and rushed headlong into it.

God felt agony as he watched his people plunge off the cliff to suffer the horrible consequences of their long disobedience. God was angry at his people's unfaithfulness, their insistence on chasing nonexistent gods every night instead of staying home with him. His heart was broken in anguish. He loved them so much that even as they turned away from him, betrayed him, and hated him, he took no pleasure in the discipline they forced him to give. As they lost their homes, their families, their loved ones, and as they were dragged into foreign bondage, God's heart was cut. God mourned the destruction of his beloved Jerusalem and temple more than his people did. Their suffering was his suffering; their burdens became his. God had warned them through Jeremiah right up to the very end, even as the Babylonians lay siege the gates of the city.

But his people had lost their senses: they threw away the truth and scrambled after lies. They exchanged hope for despair. They replaced stone and iron with sand and straw. Forbidden fruit tastes sweet, but in the end, it's just a lie that will make us sick.

Some of You Are Going to Die

The LORD said to me:

Even if Moses and Samuel were here, praying with you, I wouldn't change my mind. So send the people of Judah away. And when they ask where they are going, tell them that I, the LORD, have said:

Some of you are going to die
  of horrible diseases.
Others are going to die in war
  or from starvation.
The rest will be led away
  to a foreign country.
I will punish you
  in four different ways:
You will be killed in war

and your bodies dragged off
  by dogs, your flesh will be eaten
  by birds, and your bones will be
  chewed on by wild animals.
This punishment will happen
  because of the horrible things
  your King Manasseh did.
And you will be disgusting to
  all nations on earth.
People of Jerusalem,
  who will feel sorry for you?
Will anyone bother
  to ask if you are well?

Jeremiah 15:1–5 CEV

※

*H*ezekiah was described as one of the best kings of Judah. In contrast, his son, Manasseh, was considered one of the worst ever to sit on the throne of David. Despite that, he reigned fifty-five years, longer than any other Jewish king. He rejected the reforms that his father had made and reverted to the worship of Baal and Asherah, building multiple altars and high places for them. He burned his son as an offering, practiced soothsaying, and consulted with mediums and wizards. He led the people of Judah far away from Yahweh. God blamed him for the destruction that was coming from the Babylonians.

Josiah's subsequent reforms were inadequate. The judgment upon the nation had become inevitable. Moses had prayed for the Israelites after they had made the golden calves while he was getting the Ten Commandments. God had wanted to destroy the Israelites and raise up a new nation to replace them, but Moses' prayer had convinced God to spare them. Samuel had led Israel and gotten them not one but two kings, including David, who had established Israel as a powerful kingdom. But even Moses and Samuel would not be able to help Israel now.

God's point, of course, was simply that nothing but the coming discipline would be able to fix his people. God knew what his people really needed. They didn't need Moses and Samuel. They needed Jeremiah and the Babylonians. Whatever God does is what we need to happen.

You Deserved It

As for you, have no fear, my servant
  Jacob, says the LORD, and do not be
  dismayed, O Israel;
for I am going to save you from
  far away, and your offspring from
  the land of their captivity.
Jacob shall return and have quiet
  and ease, and no one shall make
  him afraid.
For I am with you, says the LORD, to
  save you;
I will make an end of all the nations
  among which I scattered you,
  but of you I will not make an end.
I will chastise you in just measure,
  and I will by no means leave
    you unpunished.
For thus says the LORD:
Your hurt is incurable, your wound
  is grievous.

There is no one to uphold your cause,
  no medicine for your wound,
  no healing for you.
All your lovers have forgotten you;
  they care nothing for you;
for I have dealt you the blow of
  an enemy, the punishment of a
  merciless foe . . .
Because your guilt is great, because
  your sins are so numerous,
  I have done these things to you.
Therefore all who devour you shall be
  devoured, and all your foes, everyone of them, shall go into captivity;
those who plunder you shall be
  plundered, and all who prey on you
  I will make a prey.

Jeremiah 30:10–16 NRSV

*God's people suffered for a reason. They were guilty. So why cry over the pain? God had made it abundantly clear why awful things were happening to Judah. There could be no surprise.

But just after God himself had told them that their pain couldn't be cured, God told them not to be dismayed. Even though no human could cure them, God could do anything. God promised that their destruction was not permanent. They would get to come home some day. They wouldn't have to stay in Babylon.

And as if that weren't enough, the Babylonians would suffer the same pain that the Jewish people were experiencing. Those who had plundered Israel would themselves be plundered. Those who had hurt them would themselves be hurt. God's promise came true seventy years later when the Persians conquered Babylon and sent the people of Israel back to their homeland.

Suffering, for whatever reason, is never an end unto itself. Life is not absurd or meaningless. God has a purpose even when we don't see it.

Day 363

※※※※※※※※※※※※※※※※※※※※※※※※※※※※※※※

You Will Die Peacefully

While Nebuchadnezzar king of Babylon and all his army and all the kingdoms and peoples in the empire he ruled were fighting against Jerusalem and all its surrounding towns, this word came to Jeremiah from the LORD: "This is what the LORD, the God of Israel, says: Go to Zedekiah king of Judah and tell him, 'This is what the LORD says: I am about to hand this city over to the king of Babylon, and he will burn it down. You will not escape from his grasp but will surely be captured and handed over to him. You will see the king of Babylon with your own eyes, and he will speak with you face to face. And you will go to Babylon.

"'Yet hear the promise of the LORD, O Zedekiah king of Judah. This is what the LORD says concerning you: You will not die by the sword; you will die peacefully. As people made a funeral fire in honor of your fathers, the former kings who preceded you, so they will make a fire in your honor and lament, "Alas, O master!" I myself make this promise, declares the LORD.'"

Then Jeremiah the prophet told all this to Zedekiah king of Judah, in Jerusalem, while the army of the king of Babylon was fighting against Jerusalem and the other cities of Judah that were still holding out—Lachish and Azekah. These were the only fortified cities left in Judah.

Jeremiah 34:1–7 NIV

※

There's good news and bad news. Which would you rather hear first? Zedekiah's sons would be executed in front of him. Immediately afterward, Zedekiah was blinded and then hauled away to Babylon in chains. Meanwhile, the city of Jerusalem, along with God's temple, was torched and burned to the ground. All this God had told Zedekiah before it happened, warning him that unless he changed his ways, this was how it would turn out. Instead of heeding God's words, given to him by the prophet Jeremiah, Zedekiah resisted God's will and attempted to achieve his own will by rebelling against Nebuchadnezzar.

But despite his poor choices, despite resisting God's will, and despite the terrible suffering he endured, the promise God gave him was fulfilled. God did not let Zedekiah die by the sword. Instead, he died peacefully—but far from home. And as the last king of Judah ever to sit on David's throne, he was mourned by the people of God when he died.

The outcome of Zedekiah's life was predicated on the choices he made. God is in control of the universe, but he exercises that control through the choices we make.

God's Battle-Ax

"You are My battle-ax and weapons
of war:
  For with you I will break the nation in pieces;
  With you I will destroy kingdoms;
  With you I will break in pieces the
  horse and its rider;
  With you I will break in pieces the
  chariot and its rider;
  With you also I will break in
  pieces man and woman;
  With you I will break in pieces old
  and young;
  With you I will break in pieces the
  young man and the maiden;
  With you also I will break in
  pieces the shepherd and
  his flock;
  With you I will break in pieces the
  farmer and his yoke of oxen;

And with you I will break in
  pieces governors and rulers.
"And I will repay Babylon
  And all the inhabitants of Chaldea
  For all the evil they have done
  In Zion in your sight," says
  the LORD.
"Behold, I am against you,
  O destroying mountain,
  Who destroys all the earth," says
  the LORD.
"And I will stretch out My hand
  against you,
  Roll you down from the rocks,
  And make you a burnt mountain.
    They shall not take from you
    a stone for a corner
  Nor a stone for a foundation,
  But you shall be desolate forever,"
  says the LORD.

Jeremiah 51:20–26 NKJV

✳

*B*abylon had served its purpose in bringing God's punishment against his people for their idolatry. The Babylonians had destroyed Jerusalem, taken away the entire nation's wealth, and hauled off its leading citizens into captivity.

Once the discipline had been successful, however, it was time to return things to the way they had been. The Israelites remained God's people; God's treaty with them was still operative. And the tool God had used against his people now needed to be punished. For this purpose, he chose the Persians, who would act as his battle-ax against the Babylonians. He would repay the Babylonians for their excesses, for going beyond what was necessary to achieve God's goals with his people. Despite their usefulness, the Babylonians were guilty of mistreating God's people, and they had to pay. That was also part of God's contract with Israel: those who cursed him God would curse, just as those who blessed Israel God would bless.

God is not unbiased when it comes to how he treats those who belong to him. Family gets special privileges, and no matter how mad God gets at his family, woe to those who dare to harm it.

❀❀❀❀❀❀❀❀❀❀❀❀❀❀❀❀❀❀❀❀❀❀❀❀❀❀❀❀❀❀❀

Your Enemy Is Gone

You will know that I, the LORD
   your God, live in Zion, my holy
   mountain.
Jerusalem will be holy forever,
     and foreign armies will never con-
     quer her again.
In that day the mountains will drip
   with sweet wine, and the hills will
   flow with milk.
Water will fill the streambeds of Judah,
   and a fountain will burst forth
     from the LORD's Temple,
   watering the arid valley of acacias.
But Egypt will become a wasteland
   and Edom will become a
   wilderness,

because they attacked the people
   of Judah and killed innocent people
   in their land.
But Judah will be filled with people
   forever, and Jerusalem will endure
   through all generations.
I will pardon my people's crimes,
     which I have not yet pardoned;
and I, the LORD, will make my home
   in Jerusalem with my people.

Joel 3:17–21 NLT

❀

At the beginning of his prophecy, Joel predicted that the land of Israel would be devastated by a locust plague. It arrived like an invading army. Perhaps the locusts served as a picture of the Babylonians, God's punishment for Israel's disobedience.

Though the Babylonians and their allies, Egypt and Edom, served as God's instruments of judgment, they slaughtered the innocent, not just the guilty. So God promised he would punish them for that. This happened within seventy years, when the Persians conquered Babylon and much of the rest of the Middle East. The Persians then issued a decree ordering that both Jerusalem and the temple be rebuilt and that the Jewish captives should go home.

The mountains of Judah were the least productive lands in Palestine. Judah's streams were wadis that had water in them but rarely. In contrast, both Egypt and Edom were noted for their lush fertility and abundant crops. So God was emphasizing the contrast between the blessings for God's people and the curse about to befall their enemies. The tables were about to be turned.

God then promised that he would live with his people forever. God fulfilled this promise with his new covenant—a covenant that would be written on the hearts of his people. God intended to make his people his temple, the place where he really could live with them forever. As Paul the apostle would later write, his people are now God's temple, and God's Spirit lives in their midst.